Serfdom in medieval England

Manchester University Press

MANCHESTER MEDIEVAL STUDIES

Series editor Professor S. H. Rigby

The study of medieval Europe is being transformed as old orthodoxies are challenged, new methods embraced and fresh fields of enquiry opened up. The adoption of interdisciplinary perspectives and the challenge of economic, social and cultural theory are forcing medievalists to ask new questions and to see familiar topics in a fresh light.

The aim of this series is to combine the scholarship traditionally associated with medieval studies with an awareness of more recent issues and approaches in a form accessible to the non-specialist reader.

To buy or to find out more about the books currently available in this series, please go to: https://manchesteruniversitypress.co.uk/series/manchester-medieval-studies/

Serfdom in medieval England

Theory and practice 1200 to 1500

Mark Bailey

MANCHESTER UNIVERSITY PRESS

Published by Manchester University Press
Oxford Road, Manchester, M13 9PL
www.manchesteruniversitypress.co.uk

British Library Cataloguing-in-Publication Data
A catalogue record for this book is available from the British Library

ISBN 978 1 5261 7297 6 hardback

First published 2025

EU authorised representative for GPSR:
Easy Access System Europe, Mustamäe tee 50, 10621 Tallinn, Estonia
gpsr.requests@easproject.com

Typeset by Newgen Publishing UK

Contents

Tables

Acknowledgements

This book emanated from a monograph on the decline of serfdom published in 2014, which generated several questions in my mind about some of the conventional interpretations of the medieval economy and society of England. I was able to explore some of these issues in 2019 through the medium of the Ford Lectures at the University of Oxford, subsequently published as another monograph in 2021. Both books focus on the consequences of the Black Death, but their evidence and lines of argument demanded a re-examination of the conditions prevailing in the immediate pre-plague era. The initial result of this process was the publication (in 2023) of an article on the pre-plague labour market, and this monograph comprises the next phase.

Academic research and writing is an odd process. On the one hand, the researcher needs – nay, demands – to be left well alone for long periods to pitch into the archives, to read, to think and to write. On the other hand, in order to carve such precious time and space the researcher is utterly dependent, for financial, operational and emotional support, as well as resourcing, on other people and institutions, each of whom – of course – should have an intuitive understanding of when to be present and when to be absent. In that broad spirit, I remain grateful to the electors to the James Ford Lectureship in British History, to the Mercers' Company and to the Governors of St Paul's School for their support in the early stages of this research. The Department of History at the University of East Anglia (UEA) is responsible for access to the library resources and research facilities essential to the completion of this work. For the company of medieval colleagues with a sense of perspective and humour, my thanks to Stephen Church, Hugh Doherty, Rob Liddiard, Tom Licence, Nicholas Vincent and Tom Williamson. Teaching a new first-year module on 'The Catastrophic Fourteenth Century' helped to clarify my thinking on the 'crisis' of the fourteenth century, sharpened further by discussions with those students at UEA. When a combination of the COVID-19 pandemic and UEA's wider difficulties forced a significantly reduced contract with the university and the perilous prospect of a greatly diminished livelihood, Aatif Hassan at Dukes Education offered the chance to fill the gap and join a rewarding educational environment. Throughout all this, Maureen, Ron, Julie, Katie and Harry Bailey have provided invaluable domestic support and understanding … and a canny sense of when to be absent.

Two anonymous referees for Manchester University Press (MUP) made perceptive comments on the original proposal and sample chapters, and the reader of the final manuscript was very supportive. Meredith Carroll, Siobhan Poole and Chia-Chieh Liu at MUP have been persistently supportive. I was very fortunate to acquire the services of Robert Whitelock, who proved to be a formidably good and eagle-eyed copy-editor, and of Heather Falvey, who compiled the index. Margaret Woods provided some useful references and David Addy drew one of the maps. James Davis shaped my thinking on serfs and mercantile law, and Deborah Boucoyannis and Chris Briggs each offered valuable comments on a mature draft of Chapter 4. I enjoyed exploring some of the issues in Chapter 6 with Bruce Campbell, whose own work has been influential in ways that will be evident throughout the book. At various times John Hatcher has discussed the ideas in Chapters 2–4 and 6: his early article on serfdom revitalised the subject, and ever since he has stimulated and challenged my approach to it. The greatest debt is to Steve Rigby, the series editor of Manchester Medieval Textbooks. He suggested serfdom initially as a suitable topic for the series, and subsequently has debated, via email and Zoom as well as face-to-face, the broad arguments and detailed points covered in this book. He has willingly and expeditiously dissected a succession of drafts with an inexorable critical precision and directness. There has been no compromise in his quest to expose shoddy arguments, clumsy phrases, loose ends, non sequiturs and inadequate notes, nor any limit to his admiration for Karl Popper and Manchester City.

The book is dedicated to the memory of two outstanding historians who passed away during its composition. Paul Hyams, native of Leeds but thereafter Professor of History at Cornell University and Fellow of Pembroke College, Oxford, argued, provoked, stimulated and challenged. His monograph on the common law set a standard to which I might aspire but which I will never reach. Duncan Bythell, from humble Lancastrian stock, became Vice Master of University College and Dean of the Faculty of Arts at the University of Durham, and is solely responsible for convincing a doubtful undergraduate that he might one day become a professional historian.

Maps

Introduction

Serfdom and historians

From the eighteenth century to the present day, the nature and effects of serfdom have been a central issue in interpretations of the medieval English society and economy.[1] Adam Smith believed that serfdom severely constrained the growth of commercial relations and the generation of sizeable agricultural surpluses for sale, because serfs were not 'capable of acquiring property. Whatever they acquired was acquired to their master, and he could take it from them at pleasure.'[2] In this way, it acted as a bulwark against the emergence of markets in medieval England and, by implication, as an impediment to the emergence of modern society. In a similar vein, nineteenth-century historians regarded the end of serfdom as an event of central importance in the genesis of modern social relations.[3] In the 1940s Maurice Dobb, a prominent Marxist historian, focused on the inequalities of serfdom, asserting that thirteenth-century lords taxed the serf 'beyond human endurance or else reduced his subsistence below the level of mere animal existence', severely depressing the productive capacity of medieval society and propelling it into crisis and decay.[4] In 2022 Sandro Carocci, an eminent Italian scholar, characterised the power of medieval English lordship over serfs as highly 'pervasive' by contemporary European standards: he claimed that the typical English lord intruded routinely 'in the sales, purchases and inheritances among peasants … [and] regulated to his own advantage the trade of cereals and access to pasture[;] he could forbid peasants to cut down trees, and he could regulate the upkeep of their houses, the availability of manure, and the way they hunted'. An English lord exercised 'an effective domination over his subjects[, influencing] in depth their social relationships and economic activities'.[5]

The intrusive and onerous character of English serfdom – arguably at its peak in the late thirteenth and early fourteenth centuries – coupled with its denial of peasant agency, its relegation of a sizeable proportion of the population to an excluded and exploited caste, and its role in stunting social and economic development, are also themes in the work of a pantheon of social scientists and historians, from Karl Marx and Thorold Rogers to Michael Postan, Rodney Hilton and Robert Brenner. In various ways, these scholars have explored how the highly inequitable social relations between lord and serf generated tensions that sowed the seeds of medieval society's eventual dissolution and paved the way for the emergence of new, ultimately capitalist, structures. This general approach remains influential to the present day, as Carocci's characterisation illustrates. Likewise, in 2016 Shami Ghosh contrasted the heavy burdens and restrictions faced by English serfs around 1300 with the less onerous system of southern Germany:

> during the thirteenth century, the manorial system reached its apogee in England; at this point, tenants were still burdened, at least in theory, by significant labour dues, as well as numerous restrictions on their activities and a variety of arbitrary exactions. In much of Germany, in contrast, the process of dissolution of the manorial system was already quite advanced.[6]

Two recent articles in leading economics journals that seek to assess the impact of the Black Death on European serfdom share this view of the English system as being restrictive and burdensome. Thus Remi Jedwab et al. state that 'in 1300, around 50 per cent of the English population lived under serfdom. Lords were able to extract the entire surplus beyond that required for subsistence in the form of labor dues or fines.'[7] Similarly, Margaret Peters categorises England as one of the most restrictive systems operating in Europe around 1300.[8]

Thus, from the eighteenth century to the present day, generations of historians – many of them Marxists, some of them not – have depicted English serfdom as socially restrictive and economically highly extractive. Indeed, the weight of opinion is so heavy that this traditional view might appear irrefutable. Yet even in the late nineteenth and early twentieth centuries, some historians – such as Frederic Seebohm and Sir Paul Vinogradoff – had observed from their sampling of local manorial sources that the burden of serfdom was lighter and more variable than these monolithic representations would indicate, although from the mid-twentieth century their ideas became unfashionable.[9] Since the 1980s, however, a mass of detailed and careful empirical research into the rich archival base surviving from scores of manors has supported many of their original observations and revealed a weaker and less pervasive form of serfdom than traditionally portrayed. For example, Christopher Dyer has concluded 'that many lords could not extract a great deal from their tenants', whose 'possessions were respected by lords'.[10] Sheilagh Ogilvie similarly portrays English serfdom as relatively weak and loosely organised by European standards, thereby providing 'interstices within which peasants could make their own choices'.[11] According to John Hatcher the consistency of the findings of detailed recent research has forged the 'emergence of a consensus [in the scholarship] on the reduced scale and significance of villeinage and a pronounced softening of the character of lordship'.[12] This research has exposed some shortcomings in the work of those scholars who have continued to assert the traditional view about the strength of serfdom.[13] For example, neither Jedwab et al.'s statement about the highly extractive powers of serfdom, nor Peters's assertion about the severe restrictions on the mobility of English serfs, engages with the raft of recent research showing that, in fact, few such restrictions existed.[14]

The simultaneous existence of two such contrasting and incompatible interpretations of the nature of English serfdom in the academic literature is confusing and contradictory to students and non-specialists alike. An understanding of how this has occurred, and why it persists, reveals much about the presumptions historians sometimes make and the methods they adopt. For example, some commentators have presumed that the existence of a wide-ranging and state-backed legal framework for villeinage in England, as set out by medieval lawyers, provided lords with extensive theoretical powers, drawing parallels with the highly restrictive systems of serfdom operating in eastern Europe, and especially Russia, in the early modern period.[15] In contrast, other historians have emphasised the considerable gap that existed in medieval England between the legal theory of villeinage and its actual practice.[16] The potential for confusion is illustrated by Carocci's statement about the 'pervasive' nature of English manorial lordship, which is based exclusively on single passage in a monograph by Dyer, an eminent British medievalist, sketching the *potential* range of seigniorial rights over English peasants. But Carocci overlooked a later passage in which Dyer pointed out that, in fact, many peasants were free and therefore were 'not liable to the bulk of the exactions and controls' to which serfs were theoretically subject. Dyer also cautioned that 'a gap is evident between the claims that lords made for their domination' of serfs and 'the reality of serfs' lives ... the examples of restriction and interference were not imposed universally ... other impositions were enforced inconsistently or scarcely at all ... there was a complex interaction between tenant and lord'.[17]

Another reason for the persistence of two very different depictions of English serfdom in the academic literature is the manner in which medieval historians who *are* undoubtedly familiar with the empirical evidence have sometimes represented the subject.[18] For example, in the 1960s Postan wrote of the 'very great' weight of obligations 'raking-off' more than half the output of thirteenth-century serfs and, similarly, in the 1980s J. L. Bolton portrayed the thirteenth century as 'the bad days' of serf exploitation.[19] Yet neither of these outstanding scholars drew upon a large corpus of evidence to support their bold generalisations, and subsequent research based on larger samples reveals a different picture. Even medieval scholars who are better acquainted with the reality on the ground are prone to contradictory judgements as to its weight and significance.[20] For example, in one essay published in 2007 Dyer estimated the average charge for merchet – the fine that the unfree were liable to pay their lord for permission to marry – at 'perhaps 2s., which was not a crippling charge for many peasants', whereas in another essay published around the same time he concluded that the sums paid for merchet 'were a burden, and peasants had to adjust their budgets to afford them, and in bad years they would cause real hardship'.[21] Thus the same evidence can sometimes be interpreted in different ways.

Another obstacle to obtaining a clear understanding of the nature of serfdom is a tendency to evaluate and disparage it in moral terms. Bush argues that such moral judgements involve the retrospective imposition of modern values, which regard legal bondage as abhorrent, onto medieval society, which in turn inhibits attempts to view serfdom objectively in its historical context.[22] Yet, despite this warning, Bush himself is unable to resist a value judgement of his own, describing some systems of serfdom as 'exploitative in the extreme', whereas others are 'surprisingly benign'.[23] There are plentiful examples of this approach, such as when J. W. Walker characterised merchet and leyrwite (a fine payable when a female serf gave birth outside wedlock) as 'the most odious of all manorial exactions'.[24] Likewise, in 2016 Jennifer Hole sought to establish whether the behaviour of English lords towards serfs was 'reasonable' or 'rapacious' in terms of how they imposed tallage (the ability of a lord to tax serfs) and entry fines (payable when a serf entered a landholding), whose levels could theoretically be adjusted according to 'the will of the lord'. Hole concluded that ecclesiastical lords were most likely to manipulate these dues 'rapaciously' to the disadvantage of their serfs.[25]

Such value judgements about the nature of medieval serfdom are invariably offered without any clarification or definition of what actually constitutes 'odious', 'rapacious', 'exploitative', 'reasonable' or 'benign' behaviour or, indeed, of whose judgements are being applied: are they those of medieval serfs, medieval lords or historians of medieval society?[26] Furthermore, such approaches also tend to be rather selective in their use of evidence. For example, Walker's heavy emphasis on the 'odious' nature of servile incidents overlooked their infrequency: in 193 Wakefield court sessions held between 1322 and 1333, comprising thousands of individual entries and involving hundreds of people, there are just eleven merchets (one per annum) and six leyrwites (one every two years).[27] Similarly, Hole's conclusions are based on a tiny sample of entry fines from a single manor and a fleeting survey of the operation of tallage.[28] Indeed, in Chapter 3 I provide a number of examples of how even detailed studies making use of empirical evidence can sometimes be guilty of cherry-picking a colourful example or two, or of relying on very small samples, to support a major and wide-ranging generalisation about serfdom: yet such evidence must be carefully contextualised if we are to understand its wider significance. Too often, the context is not carefully established, the typicality of the evidence is seldom clear and insufficient effort is made to generate large samples.[29] Thus, whilst individual examples are undoubtedly worthy of close attention, they need to be placed within their wider context in order to understand how representative they are of the reality of lord–peasant relations.

Thus, the simultaneous existence of two contradictory viewpoints about the nature of English serfdom 'reveals as much about the predilections of historians and the practice of history as it does about the nature of this classic medieval institution'.[30] They are the product of two different methodological approaches to the study of history, one focused more on ideological or moral assumptions and the other focused more on deductive analysis of large samples of evidence. One aim of this book is to elucidate these different approaches, while another is to establish decisively how serfdom did in fact operate on the eve of the Black Death. The latter can only be achieved through a direct comparison between theory and practice, through aggregating and contextualising data in a consistent fashion, and through distinguishing the norms of actual practice from eye-catching exceptions.

Definitions and varieties of serfdom

Serfdom is a deceptively simple shorthand term for any institutional system in which 'a landlord was legitimately entitled to restrict the choices of people living on his lands, including binding them to his territory, compelling them to work for him and limiting many of their other economic and demographic decisions', and, as such, it covered a wide range of different social arrangements across Europe and Asia during the last two millennia.[31] Yet, despite the wide variety of systems of serfdom, certain common traits can be identified.[32] Serfs were peasants tied legally to a lord in a variety of ways, typically through restrictions on migration, on marriage, and on their participation in factor and commodity markets. Serfs held land from their lord, in return for which they were required to pay him rent in some form, whether as money, as rent in kind or as labour services on the lord's home farm (the 'demesne'). Serfs possessed limited property rights over this land and the rent they rendered was, at least in legal theory, 'uncertain' in the sense of being liable to arbitrary rent hikes.[33] According to T. K. Dennison and Ogilvie:

> serfdom was a coercive relationship between a landowner (the lord) and peasants. Lords granted peasants rights over a piece of land to farm (individually or collectively) and provided security of these property rights. In return, peasants worked on the landlords' lands for a certain number of days per year (or paid an equivalent fee), paid additional fees and taxes, served in the military and/or bought specific goods from the lord.[34]

The serf differed from an enslaved person in a household or plantation in that they possessed the land, tools and livestock needed to provide their own subsistence, rather than being dependent on rations provided by the enslavers or landowners.[35]

Serfdom comprised two main components. In personal serfdom (or 'bondage by blood'), the legal status of the serf was inherited by all his or her progeny. Alternatively, in tenurial serfdom, 'bondage by tenancy', the tenant's obligations to the lord were the result of holding unfree land, which meant that someone who was legally free could acquire unfree land and so for the duration of the tenancy became subject to similar obligations as someone who was personally unfree. In societies where serfdom was inherited by all of the serf's offspring, a far higher proportion of the population were serfs than was the case where tenurial serfdom prevailed.[36] Furthermore, serfs – no less than free peasants – might also be subject to other restrictions imposed by their communities or by the state, such as agricultural by-laws or paying taxes.[37]

In recent years, older assumptions about medieval and early modern European serfdom as a generalised institution, in which lordship exercised a powerful grip over the labour, land and movement of serfs in broadly similar ways across the continent, have been replaced by a recognition of the wide variety of experiences in peasant property rights and legal status with which serfdom was compatible.[38] Furthermore, serfdom was widely diffused across medieval Europe, but it was not found everywhere and varying proportions of free peasants existed alongside those who were servile.[39] Paul Freedman and Monique Bourin thus warn against the danger of 'universalising the impress of servitude as if it has a stable and consistent definition over borders and centuries'.[40] Put another way, the relationship between lords and peasants was a 'fundamentally plural phenomenon, visible in infinite variation in different local contexts, with strong differences between chronological and geographical periods'.[41] In addition, as we have already stressed, the ideological or legal theory of a system of serfdom could differ from its practice.[42] When all of these variables are taken into account, the extent of the obligations and restrictions on the serf could differ markedly by both time and place.[43] The institutional context of serfdom varied over time and place, and those variations affected the behaviour of serfs and lords differently.[44]

Historians tend to categorise these differences into 'strong' or 'weak' systems of serfdom, depending on the proportion of the personally unfree within the population, the balance between servile and free tenures, the size of individual lordships, the extent to which the reality of serfdom corresponded to its legal theory, the range of restrictions to which serfs were subject, and the weight of the rents and the other dues owed to their lord. Hence, in regions where a high proportion of the population comprised serfs by blood – where free tenancies formed only a minority of holdings, seigniorial demesnes were large and exerted a high demand for servile labour, rents were uncertain, and servile restrictions were wide and effectively enforced – lords exercised considerable powers and this system of serfdom would be categorised as 'strong' or 'pervasive' or, in value-judgement terms, as 'oppressive' or 'exploitative'.[45] Conversely, where serfs by blood made up only a small minority – where free tenancies proliferated, seigniorial demesnes were small, and servile incidents were limited and relatively ineffective – seigniorial power was diluted and serfs enjoyed greater agency: such systems would be classed by historians as 'weak'; 'loose'; 'non-pervasive'; or, in value-judgement terms, as 'benign'.

Serfdom and its importance

Why is the study of serfdom important to historians? One reason is that a system shaping the social relations between a small elite of landlords and a sizeable minority or even a majority of the population was manifestly significant in defining the institutional framework of that society, influencing its laws, its social habits and attitudes, and its economic productivity and paths of development. It dictated personal status, inhibited choices, and created obstacles to wealth acquisition and social mobility for those cast as serfs.[46] Hilton described English serfs as 'victims' of seigniorial oppression, because of the restrictions on their movement and their exclusion from the common law and certain professions.[47] Reconstructing and understanding the significance of forms of legal and socio-economic exclusion is central to our understanding of diversity and its significance in the human past.

A second reason why historians have focused on serfdom is that it is often assigned a central role in precipitating a pan-European social and economic 'crisis' in the late thirteenth and early fourteenth centuries. The socio-economic stresses of this period are widely documented and little contested: in essence, a long and relatively uninterrupted phase of demographic, commercial, cultural and climatic 'efflorescence' first slowed in the late thirteenth century and then reversed around 1300, leading to a period characterised by widespread immiseration, repeated famines, increased warfare and taxation, disruption to international trade, and falling living standards. In this scenario the arrival of the Black Death in the 1340s merely accelerated a crisis and prolonged a downturn already in motion.[48] However, the root causes of this crisis *are* contested. One major approach has been to explain it in Malthusian terms, in which the demographic expansion eventually outstripped the capacity of the resource base to support it, triggering a decline in output per head, a fall in living standards and crises of subsistence.[49]

A second approach allocates pride of place to the social tensions and inequalities inherent in society in general and serfdom in particular for generating long-term socio-economic change. In this scenario, the inequitable allocation of land enabled lords, backed by their extensive jurisdictional powers, to extract much of the labour and produce of serfs as rent, tallage and other dues. When such 'surplus extraction' was combined with the tendency of lords to spend their revenues on conspicuous consumption and warfare rather than on investment in agriculture, it triggered a general crisis of productivity that was exacerbated by the prevailing conditions of high population pressure, shortages of land and an increasingly unstable climate.[50] Thus, according to Harry Kitsikopoulos, the crisis that changed the course of European history was rooted in the 'heavy reliance on seigniorial extractions ... [that] drained capital resources' away from the peasantry.[51]

These two explanations of the crisis of the early fourteenth century are closely associated with the traditional view of a highly extractive system of serfdom, in which the subordinate legal status of the serf translated into a depressed economic condition. Yet this assumption is hard to reconcile with detailed research revealing that in the early fourteenth century serfs were usually among the wealthiest taxpayers in rural communities. Consequently, other historians have downplayed the role of serfdom in causing the crisis, pointing instead to other causal factors, such as climate, warfare and disease.[52] As Chris Briggs states, 'scope remains for pointing the way towards a more detailed investigation of the mechanics of English serfdom ... and reconsidering the possible link between serfdom and arrested economic growth in the thirteenth and early fourteenth centuries'.[53]

A third reason why serfdom has attracted so much attention from historians is its potential role in explaining the divergent social and economic experiences of Europe following the arrival of the Black Death in Europe in the 1340s and the continuing high mortality of subsequent epidemics. The sudden then sustained reduction in the labour force and the relative abundance of land created new tensions between lords and peasants. Lords could respond to the shortages of tenants and labourers by maintaining or even intensifying the restrictions and impositions on serfs, and by binding peasants to the land to ensure a ready supply of tenants and of manual labour for their demesnes. Alternatively, peasants could take advantage of the shortages of tenants by seeking the removal of restrictive and demeaning servile ties and obtaining better terms and conditions as workers and tenants. As Brenner emphasised in a famous article in 1976, broadly similar demographic conditions across Europe resulted in very different social and economic outcomes: where market forces prevailed, and peasants and labourers took advantage of their improved bargaining position, as in many areas of north-west Europe, then serfdom dissolved. Where seigniorial will prevailed, as in many areas of eastern Europe, serfdom was either maintained or newly imposed.[54]

The fact that serfdom disappeared in some regions of Europe, but not in others, in the later Middle Ages is not disputed, and it underlines both the different institutional responses to pandemics and their differential impact on labour markets.[55] Once again, however, the key area of debate is what *caused* these differential outcomes. For Brenner, Hilton and many other historians, the pre-existing strength of English serfdom encouraged lords to increase their exploitation of serfs in the generation after the Black Death by means of a 'seignorial reaction', but this in turn triggered a backlash of resistance and revolt on the part of the peasants who, from the 1380s onwards, forced lords to relent and gradually bargain serfdom away.[56] In contrast, the restructuring of social relations in central and eastern Europe in the century after the Black Death had the general effect of suppressing peasant resistance and the imposition of harsher forms of serfdom (see Chapter 5).[57] However, this cogent and wide-ranging explanatory model has attracted substantial criticism from scholars in England and in eastern Europe: for example, a seigniorial reaction failed to materialise in much of England and the experience of serfdom in eastern Europe was more varied and nuanced. The direction, chronology and causes of serfdom's varied trajectory after 1350 are complex and, as yet, imperfectly understood.

The final reason why studying serfdom is important is the effect that its presence or absence had on regional trajectories of economic development between the sixteenth and nineteenth centuries. Its existence imposed, to varying degrees, obstacles and constraints on the ability of ordinary people to migrate, to marry, to acquire land, and to choose when and where to work. Historians have therefore linked serfdom to restrictions in the flows of capital and people into towns, impeding investment in agricultural technology, limiting levels of human capital formation and dampening economic incentives.[58] Indeed, Ogilvie has generated long-run estimates showing that between 1300 and 1900 serf-societies in Europe witnessed lower levels of per capita wealth and of rates of economic development than their non-serf counterparts.[59] Nor has serfdom only been seen as having economic consequences. Daniel Gingerich and Jan Vogler argue that the persistence of serfdom across many parts of eastern Germany inhibited the development of participatory political institutions, so providing an explanation for the tradition of conservative politics in nineteenth-century Germany, and Peters has argued that serfdom restricted the emergence of representative institutions in parts of central and eastern Europe.[60] Economic growth through peasant agency was certainly possible under less pervasive forms of serfdom, although, even there, peasants were forced 'to operate within institutional constraints that prevent land and labour from being allocated productively'.[61] The disappearance of serfdom created room for factor markets to expand, thereby removing a barrier to economic growth. If these arguments are correct, then the presence or absence of serfdom during the early modern period reverberated into the modern world: Peters argues that eastern Europe in the twentieth century was poorer and more autocratic as a consequence of the persistence of serfdom there throughout the early modern period.[62] Conversely, the decline of serfdom in countries such as England is linked to the growth of land, labour, capital and factor markets; increases in income per head; and the routeway to modernity.[63]

The purpose of this book is to review and reappraise the existing scholarship on medieval English serfdom by means of a detailed investigation of its nature in a wide range of locations on the eve of the Black Death, when it is widely regarded as being at its peak.[64] Drawing together the multiple strands of research and evidence into a single monograph will provide a comprehensive guide to how medieval serfdom really operated. It will also illuminate different methodological approaches to the practice of history, and how these inform contrasting and contradictory interpretations of the past. England occupies a prime position in the debates over serfdom, partly because of its emergence as the first industrial nation and partly because of the seminal work of Brenner in deploying the English example in his comparative approach. Yet the sources available to English historians for the study of serfdom in the late thirteenth and early fourteenth centuries are without parallel anywhere in the world: whether England is typical or not, whether it is exceptional or not (and this monograph does not express a view on such issues), nowhere in the globe is better equipped for a reconstruction of how its system of serfdom operated at this time.

The book begins with a reconstruction of the legal theory of serfdom – or common law villeinage, as it was known – and shows how that theory has influenced the ways in which some historians have represented its actual operation (Chapter 1). The next three chapters evaluate the detailed evidence for how serfdom operated between 1280 and 1350. The relative importance of personal and tenurial serfdom across England is discussed (Chapter 2), including the significance of labour services, which early historians regarded as the system's *raison d'être*; and the practical difficulties of segregating unfreedom from freedom are explored through the operation of heriot and mill suit. The uncertainty of servile incidents, meaning their unpredictable variability and precariousness, is often held to be a key feature of medieval systems of serfdom, so Chapter 3 assesses this issue in detail, focusing primarily on villeins' rights in property, their ability to marry and migrate, and their capacity for engaging in labour and land markets. Chapter 4 explores how far the exclusion of serfs from the royal courts, and their theoretical dependence on the manorial court of their own lord, diminished their access to and experience of justice. These core chapters reveal the size of the gap between the legal theory and the widespread practice of serfdom by examining large samples of data rather than relying on broad generalisations backed by individual or anecdotal examples. They show beyond any doubt that traditional views of serfdom as highly restrictive are based on theoretical presuppositions and moral judgements, which find little empirical support. In doing so, they affirm a new orthodoxy that English serfdom was a good deal weaker than its legal theory would indicate.

Part II shifts the focus of our study to explore the implications of this new orthodoxy for our wider understanding of the role of serfdom in processes of social and economic change in medieval England. Chapter 5 explains why the English system was weak on the eve of the Black Death, drawing some high-level comparisons between its underlying structure and that of those regions of early modern Europe where serfdom endured. The comparative approach reveals the relative strengths of the two systems, while also illuminating key structural differences. Chapter 6 considers what English serfdom contributed to the arrested economic growth and mounting stress that characterised the late thirteenth and early fourteenth centuries. Does its weakness mean that serfdom was irrelevant to economic and social development? If so, how then do we explain the slow-down and downturn of the pre-plague economy? These questions have not been adequately addressed before.

The confirmation that serfdom was relatively weak when plague struck England in 1348 also raises questions about how and when serfdom dissolved after the Black Death (Chapter 7). The traditional view is that lords attempted to reimpose many of their legal powers under serfdom in the third quarter of the fourteenth century, and that the ensuing peasant resistance caused serfdom to dissolve from the 1380s. However, this narrative has been recently challenged on the grounds that the 'seigniorial reaction' is a myth, and the irreversible and seismic shock of the Black Death caused the rapid retreat of personal and especially tenurial serfdom as early as the 1360s.[65] This revisionist view is consistent with the argument that serfdom was weak in the 1340s, but it requires a broader evidence base if it is to become the new orthodoxy for the post-plague period.[66] Hence Part III comprises case studies of three manors on the same estate to illustrate how serfdom operated there on the eve of the Black Death and how this changed following successive outbreaks of epidemic disease in the fourteenth century, and to examine first the chronology then the causes of its post-plague decline. The case studies are drawn from the estate of the abbey of St Albans (Hertfordshire), chosen because of its reputation among historians as one of the harshest enforcers of serfdom and therefore precisely the type of lord most likely to impose its full force and to maintain it for as long as possible. Chapter 8 comprises a case study of the management of serfdom on its manor of Codicote (Hertfordshire) between the 1320s and the 1370s. Chapters 9 and 10 continue with case studies of the manors of Winslow (Buckinghamshire) and Norton (Hertfordshire). The discussions include a close analysis of the mechanics and causes of the decline. The Conclusion draws these themes together to assess the forces shaping the institutional context of English serfdom, the persistence of highly contradictory views about its operation, the implications for processes of economic development, and the chronology of and reasons for its decline.

Notes

1 Throughout this book, the terms serfdom, villeinage, bondage and unfreedom are used interchangeably. It refers to seigneurs as lords, and to serfs as he/him, because the overwhelming majority of lords were male and adult male serfs had legal responsibility for their households.

2 A. Smith, *An Inquiry into the Nature and Causes of the Wealth of Nations* (New York: The Modern Library, 1937), pp. 364–5.

3 N. Hybel, *Crisis or Change: The Concept of Crisis in the Light of Agrarian Structural Reorganisation in Late Medieval England* (Aarhus: Aarhus University Press, 1989), pp. 49–50.

4 M. Dobb, *Studies in the Development of Capitalism*, 2nd edn (London: Routledge, 1976), pp. 42–3.

5 S. Carocci, 'The pervasiveness of lordship (Italy, 1050–1500)', *Past & Present*, 296 (2022): 3–47 (pp. 45–6).

6 S. Ghosh, 'Rural economies and transitions to capitalism: Germany and England compared (c. 1200–c. 1800)', *Journal of Agrarian Change*, 16:2 (2016): 255–90 (p. 258). The image of pervasive English manorialism is also portrayed in B. J. P. van Bavel, *Manors and Markets* (Oxford: Oxford University Press, 2010), p. 87.

7 R. Jedwab, N. D. Johnson and M. Koyama, 'The economic impact of the Black Death', *Journal of Economic Literature*, 60:1 (2022): 132–78 (p. 163).

8 M. E. Peters, 'Government finance and imposition of serfdom after the Black Death', *European Review of Economic History*, 27 (2023): 149–73.

9 F. Seebohm, *The English Village Community*, 4th edn (Cambridge: Cambridge University Press, 1890), pp. 29–31; P. Vinogradoff, *Villeinage in England: Essays in English Medieval History* (Oxford: Clarendon Press, 1892), p. 134; J. Hatcher, 'Lordship and villeinage before the Black Death: From Karl Marx to the Marxists and back again', in M. Kowaleski, J. Langdon and P. R. Schofield, eds, *Peasants and Lords in the Medieval English Economy: Essays in Honour of B. M. S. Campbell* (Turnhout: Brepols, 2015), pp. 113–46 (pp. 117–24).

10 C. Dyer, 'The ineffectiveness of lordship in England, 1200–1400', in C. Dyer, P. Coss and C. Whickham, eds, *Rodney Hilton's Middle Ages: An Exploration of Historical Themes*, *Past & Present* Supplements, 195, suppl. 2 (Oxford: Oxford University Press, 2007), pp. 69–86 (pp. 77–8).

11 S. Ogilvie, 'Choices and constraints in the pre-industrial countryside', in C. Briggs, P. M. Kitson and S. J. Thompson, eds, *Population, Welfare and Economic Change in Britain 1290–1834* (Woodbridge: Economic History Society, 2014), pp. 269–305 (pp. 303–4).

12 Hatcher, 'Lordship', p. 136.

13 M. L. Bush, 'Serfdom in medieval and modern Europe', in M. L. Bush, ed., *Serfdom and Slavery: Studies in Legal Bondage* (London: Routledge, 1996), pp. 199–224 (p. 212).

14 See below, Chapters 2–4. The evidence for limited mobility restrictions is summarised in M. Bailey, 'Servile and gender migration in late medieval England: The evidence of manorial court rolls', *Past & Present*, 261 (2023): 47–85 (pp. 55–60, Table 1).

15 P. Gatrell, 'Historians and peasants: Studies of medieval English society in a Russian context', *Past & Present*, 96 (1982): 22–50; P. Freedman, *The Origins of Peasant Servitude in Medieval Catalonia* (Cambridge: Cambridge University Press, 1991), pp. 11–12.
16 Hatcher, 'Lordship', pp. 124, 129–32.
17 Carocci, 'The pervasiveness of lordship', 45–6; C. Dyer, *An Age of Transition? Economy and Society in England in the Later Middle Ages* (Oxford: Oxford University Press, 2005), pp. 86, 90.
18 Hatcher, 'Lordship', p. 113.
19 M. M. Postan, 'Medieval agrarian society in its prime: England', in M. M. Postan, ed., *The Cambridge Economic History of Europe*, Vol. I, *The Agrarian Life of the Middle Ages*, 2nd edn (Cambridge: Cambridge University Press, 1966), pp. 549–659 (pp. 603–4); J. L. Bolton, *The Medieval English Economy, 1150–1500* (London: Dent, 1980), p. 213.
20 Hatcher, 'Lordship', pp. 126–7, 133–8.
21 C. Dyer, 'The language of oppression: The vocabulary of rents and services in England, 1000–1300', in M. Bourin and P. Martínez Sopena, eds, *Pour une anthropologie du prélèvement seigneurial dans les campagnes médiévales (XIe–XIVe siècles)*: Vol. II, *Les mots, les temps, les lieux* (Paris: Publications de Sorbonne, 2004), pp. 71–86 (p. 83); Dyer, 'The ineffectiveness of lordship', p. 74.
22 M. L. Bush, 'Introduction', in Bush, *Serfdom and Slavery*, pp. 1–17 (p. 17).
23 Bush, 'Serfdom', p. 199.
24 J. W. Walker, ed., *Court Rolls of the Manor of Wakefield*, Vol. V, *1322–31*, Yorkshire Archaeological Society, 109 (Leeds: Yorkshire Archaeological Society, 1944), pp. vi–vii.
25 J. Hole, *Economic Ethics in Late Medieval England, 1300–1500* (Basingstoke: Palgrave Macmillan, 2016), pp. 193, 195.
26 S. H. Rigby, *English Society in the Later Middle Ages: Class, Status and Gender* (Palgrave: London, 1995), pp. 52–7.
27 Calculated from Walker, *Court Rolls 1322–31*, pp. 11, 41, 112, 136, 179, 184; and also S. S. Walker, ed., *The Court Rolls of the Manor of Wakefield from October 1331 to September 1333*, Yorkshire Archaeological Society, Wakefield Court Roll Series, 3 (Leeds: Yorkshire Archaeological Society, 1983), pp. 46, 61–2, 96, 169, 183.
28 Hole, *Economic Ethics*, pp. 190–1, discussed in more detail below in Chapter 3. Hole's discussion of tallage did not reference the two fullest treatments then in print: N. Neilson, 'Customary rents', in P. Vinogradoff, ed., *Oxford Studies in Social and Legal History*, Vol. II (Oxford: Clarendon Press, 1910), pp. 90–5; and M. Bailey, *The Decline of Serfdom in Late Medieval England: From Bondage to*

Freedom (Woodbridge: Boydell Press, 2014), pp. 47–8, 57, 93, 96, 262–4, 278–9, 285–8.

29 Hatcher, 'Lordship', pp. 124, 129–32.

30 Ibid., 'Lordship', 113.

31 S. H. Rigby, 'Serfdom', in J. Mokyr, ed., *The Oxford Encyclopaedia of Economic History*, Vol. IV (Oxford: Oxford University Press, 2003), pp. 463–7; S. Ogilvie, 'Economics and history: Analyzing serfdom', in R. Bourke and Q. Skinner, eds, *History in the Humanities and Social Sciences* (Cambridge: Cambridge University Press, 2022), pp. 329–53 (p. 330).

32 Bush, 'Introduction', pp. 1–2.

33 M. Cerman, *Villagers and Lords in Eastern Europe, 1300–1800* (London: Bloomsbury, 2012), p. 13; S. Ogilvie and A. W. Carus, 'Institutions and economic growth in historical perspective', in P. Aghion and S. Durlauf, eds, *Handbook of Economic Growth* (Amsterdam: Elsevier, 2014), pp. 403–514 (p. 474).

34 T. K. Dennison and S. Ogilvie, 'Serfdom and social capital in Bohemia and Russia', *Economic History Review*, 60:3 (2007): 513–44.

35 Rigby, 'Serfdom', p. 463; Bush, 'Introduction'.

36 Rigby, 'Serfdom', p. 463.

37 Bush, 'Introduction', pp. 2, 14; Bush, 'Serfdom', pp. 201, 210.

38 Rigby, 'Serfdom', pp. 463–7; M. Cerman, 'Demesne lordship and rural society in early modern East Central and Eastern Europe: Comparative perspectives', *Agricultural History Review*, 59:2 (2011): 239–58 (pp. 239–43); Cerman, *Villagers and Lords*, pp. 2–6, 13–22, 132; S. Ogilvie, 'Serfdom and the institutional system in early modern Germany', in S. Cavaciocchi, ed., *Serfdom and Slavery in the European Economy, 11th–18th Centuries* (Florence: Firenze University Press, 2014), pp. 33–58 (pp. 35–6); Bailey, *The Decline of Serfdom*, pp. 1–61; Ogilvie, 'Choices and constraints', pp. 269, 274–6.

39 P. Freedman and M. Bourin, 'Introduction', in P. Freedman and M. Bourin, eds, *Forms of Servitude in Northern and Central Europe: Decline, Resistance and Expansion* (Turnhout: Brepols, 2005), pp. 1–18 (p. 5).

40 Ibid., p. 15.

41 Carocci, 'The pervasiveness of lordship', p. 8.

42 Bush, 'Introduction', pp. 15–16.

43 Bush, 'Serfdom', p. 199.

44 T. K. Dennison, 'The institutional context of serfdom in England and Russia', in Briggs et al., *Population, Welfare*, pp. 249–68 (pp. 250–2); Ogilvie, 'Choices and constraints'.

45 Bush, 'Serfdom', pp. 213, 216; Carocci, 'The pervasiveness of lordship', pp. 5–7, 32–4.

46 S. Dimmock, *The Origin of Capitalism in England, 1400–1600* (London: Brill, 2014), p. 72.

47 R. H. Hilton, *A Medieval Society: The West Midlands at the End of the Thirteenth Century* (Cambridge: Cambridge University Press, 1983), p. 166.

48 The vast literature is brilliantly synthesised in B. M. S. Campbell, *The Great Transition: Climate, Disease and Society in the Late Medieval World* (Cambridge: Cambridge University Press, 2016), pp. 134–331.

49 An argument summarised and critiqued in J. Hatcher and M. Bailey, *Modelling the Middle Ages: The Theory and Practice of England's Economic Development* (Oxford: Oxford University Press, 2000), pp. 21–65.

50 Ibid., pp. 66–120; R. H. Britnell, *Britain and Ireland 1050–1530* (Oxford: Oxford University Press, 2004), pp. 86–8.

51 H. Kitsikopoulos, 'England', in H. Kitsikopoulos, ed., *Agrarian Change and Crisis in Europe, 1200–1500* (Abingdon: Routledge, 2012), pp. 45–7, 335 (quotation pp. 45–6).

52 See, for example, Campbell, *The Great Transition*, pp. 134–331; P. R. Schofield, 'Peasants and food security in England and Wales c. 1300', *Journal of Medieval History*, 49:5 (2023): 588–606.

53 C. Briggs, 'English serfdom, c. 1200–c. 1350: Towards an institutionalist analysis', in S. Cavaciocchi, *Serfdom and Slavery*, pp. 13–32 (p. 14). See also S. Gibbs, *Lordship, State Formation and Local Authority in Late Medieval and Early Modern England* (Cambridge: Cambridge University Press, 2023), pp. 117–20.

54 R. Brenner, 'Agrarian class structure and economic development in pre-industrial Europe', in T. H. Aston and C. H. E. Philpin, eds, *The Brenner Debate: Agrarian Class Structure and Economic Development in Pre-Industrial Europe* (Cambridge: Cambridge University Press, 1985), pp. 10–63.

55 Jedwab et al., 'The economic impact', pp. 162–4; Peters, 'Government finance'.

56 For example, R. H. Hilton, *The Decline of Serfdom in Late Medieval England*, 2nd edn (London: Macmillan, 1969), 28–43. For a summary of these traditional arguments, see M. Bailey, *After the Black Death: Economy, Society and the Law in Fourteenth Century England* (Oxford: Oxford University Press, 2021), pp. 10–12, 83–4, 186–96.

57 R. Brenner, 'Property and progress: Where Adam Smith went wrong', in C. Wickham, ed., *Marxist History-writing for the Twenty-first Century* (Oxford: Oxford University Press, 2007), pp. 49–111 (pp. 81–92).

58 E. Melton, 'The agrarian East', in H. Scott, ed., *The Oxford Handbook of Early Modern European History, 1350–1750*, Vol. I, *Peoples and Place* (Oxford: Oxford University Press, 2015), pp. 428–54 (pp. 430–1); A. Klein and S. Ogilvie, 'Occupational structure in the Czech lands under the second serfdom', *Economic History Review*, 69 (2016): 493 (pp. 495–9); Peters, 'Government finance', pp. 149–50, 170.
59 Ogilvie, 'Economics and history', pp. 333–48, Figs 14.1 and 14.2.
60 D. W. Gingerich and J. P. Vogler, 'Pandemics and political development: The electoral legacy of the Black Death in Germany', *World Politics*, 73:3 (2021): 393–440; Jedwab et al., 'The economic impact', p. 164; Peters, 'Government finance', pp. 150, 170.
61 Ogilvie, 'Serfdom and the institutional system', p. 43.
62 Peters, 'Government finance', p. 170.
63 B. van Bavel, *The Invisible Hand* (Oxford: Oxford University Press, 2016), pp. 146–64.
64 See, for example, H. Kitsikopoulos, 'Standards of living and capital formation in pre-plague England: A peasant budget model', *Economic History Review*, 53 (2000): 237–61 (p. 254).
65 M. Bailey, 'The myth of the seigniorial reaction in England after the Black Death', in Kowaleski et al., *Peasants and Lords*, pp. 147–72; Bailey, *The Decline of Serfdom*, pp. 307–16; Bailey, *After the Black Death*, pp. 12–14, 83–112, 218–20, 297–316.
66 P. R. Schofield, *Peasants and Historians: Debating the Medieval English Peasantry* (Manchester: Manchester University Press), p. 104.

Part I

Serfdom in theory and practice

1

Serfdom in legal theory

The common law of villeinage

One of the main reasons why medieval English serfdom has been depicted as restrictive and burdensome is that it was defined this way in the common law of villeinage. Common law is a body of law built up through the decisions of royal courts rather than on set codes or statutes. It evolved broadly and organically between c. 1175 and c. 1225 with the expansion of royal justice: during this period new legal tribunals were established, a body of professional justices and lawyers emerged, and legal treatises were written and distributed. The king's judges constructed a corpus of case law as they heard a growing volume of disputes in royal courts, and through their decisions established precedents for the resolution of similar disputes, mainly relating to property, contracts and tort.

Common law lawyers were not particularly interested in the nature of serfdom per se, but nonetheless they were forced to consider it because of their concern to determine who could or could not access the royal courts. By the early thirteenth century there had emerged a set of 'rules and procedures by which the royal justices decided which of the king's subjects were entitled to the tenurial protection and other legal benefits of his courts'.[1] In essence, these directed that pleas relating to servile land (also known as 'villein', 'native', 'customary' and 'unfree' land) and to servile people (also described as serfs (*servi*), villeins (*villani*) and neifs (*nativi*)) were to be denied access to the royal courts. Consequently, neither tenants of villein land nor serfs had any defence in the common law against any action of their lord relating to servility.[2] The rules were not enshrined definitively in a single set of laws, and so have to be reconstructed through contemporary legal treatises, plea rolls, the judgments of royal courts and legal year books.[3] This new juridical concept, known as villeinage, was effectively a by-product of the emergence of the common law.[4] As the role of the state in the provision of justice expanded, and as the influence of professional lawyers grew, so the concept of unfree status was reorientated and standardised, and in strict legal terms it became more homogeneous, formal, narrow and specialised.

Under the common law land was designated either free or unfree. Legally, ownership ('seisin') of servile land belonged to the lord of the manor in which it lay, so that the tenant who occupied and cultivated it did so entirely at the lord's will and for no certain term, rent or services. For example, one legal opinion from an early fourteenth-century treatise – the *Mirror of Justices* – asserted that villeins 'hold only from day to day at the will of the lord by no certain services' and 'do not know in the evening what service they will do in the morning'.[5] Since the villein-holding belonged to the lord, the tenant was not to damage or waste it, for example by cutting down valuable timber or allowing buildings to dilapidate, because this eroded the capital assets of the lord. If there was a dispute between a lord and a villein over the land, or if the lord ejected the tenant, then the latter had no remedy in the common law. As villeins did not own their land, the common law prohibited them from selling or alienating it, and, if they did so, the lord was entitled to reclaim the land and eject the villein.[6] By extension, the lord could demand that any transfer of villein land – even to an heir – could only by made under his supervision and with his permission. Hence royal courts would not hear disputes relating to villein land, and the common law adopted the position that the tenant's occupation of villein land was insecure.[7]

The status of land was technically distinguished from the status of the people who held it. People were designated as either free or servile. The various nouns used to describe the latter – serf, neif, villein – were used indiscriminately and sometimes interchangeably to denote people who were hereditary serfs by birth through the male line.[8] The serf by blood belonged to the lord personally.[9] As the serf was the chattel of the lord, so the lord was the true owner of anything he possessed. According to the *Mirror of Justices* hereditary serfs 'cannot acquire anything save to the use of their lord', and likewise the legal authority known as Glanville, dating from the 1180s, stated 'a villein is adjudged without remedy to his lord together with his chattels'.[10] From this principle, it follows that 'the lord could take anything his villein held, and the villein had no redress in the common law'.[11] It followed that villeins could neither be nor have an heir (except their lord), that they could not devise their possessions or property by will, and that they were theoretically outside the jurisdiction of Christian courts where wills were determined.[12]

As land tenure and personal status were technically separate, it was possible for a free person to hold villein land and remain personally free.[13] In these circumstances, the free person was responsible as the tenant for all the rents and services attached to the unfree holding for so long as he held this tenure.[14] Conversely, if a serf managed to acquire free land then he remained the hereditary serf of his lord, although such occasions were unusual and the lord invariably charged his serf a fee for such an acquisition (see below, pp. 107–8). Yet the general presumption was that most tenants of villein land were also personally unfree. Indeed, legal theory conceived serfs as part of the holding and tenement they occupied. The *Dialogus de Scaccario* (1180s) regarded lords as owners of the land, the chattels and the bodies of their serfs, and could 'sell or otherwise alienate them if they like', and similarly the late-thirteenth-century treatise known as Britton regarded the villein as 'merely the chattel of his lord, to give and sell at his pleasure'.[15] Accordingly, as one legal opinion of the 1240s put it, 'earls, barons and free tenants may lawfully … sell their serfs like oxen or cows'.[16] There is certainly evidence of the sale of serfs, especially in the twelfth and early thirteenth centuries, although these were not sales of people in the open market but rather sales of servile land with their servile tenants attached.[17] The connection between serf and land is also reflected in the requirement that serfs should not leave their holding, or be educated to join holy orders, without the lord's permission.[18] The *Mirror of Justices* opined that serfs 'cannot escape, flee or withdraw themselves from their lands … and no one may receive them without the will of their lord'.[19] The prohibition on fleeing the holding was a key element of villeinage, and constituted an important distinguishing feature of serfs from freemen, who could leave their freeholding at will (and even a villein-holding if they held one). One thirteenth-century estate manual informed its readers that the villein was prohibited from departing the manor without seigniorial permission.[20] If serfs did flee the manor, the lord could seek the help of the king and his officials in returning them.[21]

Thus, the theoretical position of tenants of villein land and hereditary serfs under the common law was highly constrained. They did not possess any goods or rights relating to tenure or personal status as against their lord. The title to villein land could only be pleaded in the landlord's own manorial court, which meant that the villein's output was liable to increased impositions and to seizure on a seigniorial whim.[22] Thirteenth-century lawyers and judges stressed that 'the very essence of villeinage is uncertainty … serfs hold only from day to day at the will of their lords and for no certain services'.[23] Hyams succinctly summarised the theory of the common law of villeinage in the thirteenth century in the following way:

> the lord owns his villein as chattel and may sell him like one. Consequently, the villein himself owns nothing; all his land and goods belong to the lord. He cannot leave his land or alienate it without the lord's permission, and he is unprotected by the royal courts against the lord raising his rent or ejecting him. Having no property of his own, he has nothing to transmit to an heir, and thus has no legal heir except – for certain purposes – the lord.[24]

Common law villeinage: Some legal complexities

The strict legal theory of common law villeinage presents a cogent picture of the powers vested in landlords to subjugate their serfs. Furthermore, during the thirteenth century many landlords moved from a preference for renting out their manors to exploiting them and their jurisdictional rights directly using their own officials. This swing from the 'indirect' to 'direct' management of estates necessitated an overhaul and expansion of their administrative systems, based on a larger and more active estate bureaucracy. Hence lords greatly enhanced their administrative capability to enforce their extended legal powers under common law villeinage. These advantages were further strengthened by rising population, which created growing shortages of land and a surfeit of labour, and therefore tipped the balance of economic power in favour of lords.

The combination of these powerful forces meant that, according to many historians, the weight of English villeinage was greatest around 1300.[25] The key is whether legal theory did in fact match practice on the manor and whether lords really did exercise an arbitrary and capricious will over villeinage if they chose to do so.[26] In the following chapters I emphasise how the practice of villeinage differed from the rigours of its theory, but here I explore how the common law itself contained various complexities and ambiguities whose effect was to soften the harsh theory of villeinage in practice and even to offer various forms of protection to villeins.

One point to stress from the outset is that, even in terms of legal theory, serfdom in medieval England was not a form of slavery. The scope of the English medieval lord for action was never unfettered and uncontrolled, and 'English villeins were never submitted to extremes of seignorial constraint of the kind we label slavery'.[27] The serf's lack of rights against his lord under the common law did not mean that lords could do as they wished with the serf.[28] Sir Frederick Pollock and Frederic Maitland represented this distinction by describing the serf's legal position as 'unprotected' rather than 'rightless'.[29] For example, the lord could imprison and place villeins in stocks for misdemeanours, but could not beat or whip them.[30] Villeins could appeal their lord in the common law for sedition and serious assault.[31] Villeins were answerable for themselves as defendants in the common law and in statute law (such as for offences when selling bread and ale), were subject to criminal law, and could be summoned to royal courts to act as witnesses.[32] Hence, 'in criminal and police law, villeins were treated substantially as free persons'.[33]

Another significant aspect of villeins' standing in the common law was their freedom as against all parties other than their lord. The villein could not own and possess chattels of his own against his lord, but the medieval doctrine of possession limited the power of this rule so that the villein was 'as good as the owner in respect of third persons'.[34] In other words, the villein was only the villein of his lord, or, in the words of Henry de Bracton, 'as regards mankind at large the serf, so far from being a mere thing, is a freeman'.[35] Therefore a person could be the serf of one lord and the freeman of another, because 'the villein was free against the whole world except his lord'.[36] The clear implication is that the serf was free to plead in common law and other courts (see Chapter 4) in cases that did not involve his lord and did not infringe his lord's jurisdictional rights. Indeed, James Masschaele has called for more research into such participation of villeins in the machinery of royal justice.[37] In 1285 the Statute of Exeter formally permitted villeins to serve on juries investigating the conduct of royal coroners, which seems to imply that villeins were already a regular fixture in such work.[38] Villeins also served as local assessors for royal taxation: in 1341 all six of those appointed at Winslow (Buckinghamshire) were villein landholders.[39] Criminal law did not distinguish free from unfree, and applied equally to both.[40]

Finally, the common law offered little support and provided few effective remedies to lords whose villeins disobeyed them by, for example, refusing to perform their services or running away from the manor. Bracton suggests that if a runaway serf had not been retrieved within four days, then a legal writ should be issued for his return.[41] In the early thirteenth century royal officials had indeed provided some help to lords seeking to retrieve flown serfs following the issue of a writ, but thereafter such cases are very rare.[42] Hyams observes that any lord attempting to use the royal courts to retrieve a flown serf was likely to find the process expensive, long-winded and often unsuccessful.[43] Furthermore, and crucially, the principle in the *Mirror of Justices* that no lord might receive (as a tenant or as a labourer) the serf of another without the latter's permission was widely ignored, and lords routinely accepted the migrant serfs of others.[44] Consequently, lords were thrown back on their own initiative when dealing with emigrant serfs: they might send a posse to retrieve them physically, they might track and charge a serf for absence, or they might do nothing at all (see pp. 331–7).[45] In reality, even a powerful landlord such as Ramsey abbey seldom used either writs or coercion to recover flown serfs.[46]

The migrant serf who had settled as a landholder or a resident on the manor of another lord without interference from his own lord had obtained de facto freedom. The incomer could not become the serf of the lord of this new manor, because a serf could only be a serf of the lord of their home manor. Hence the serf who had flown his home manor A to settle permanently as a tenant of villein land on manor B remained the serf of lord A, and also the villein tenant – but not hereditary serf – of lord B. For example, when Austin

Crembell moved from his home manor of Aldham (Suffolk) to a manor 20 miles away, he continued to be described as a serf in the court rolls of the former but was never once described as a such in those of the latter.[47] Furthermore, the common law presented the migrant serf with the opportunity to obtain legal freedom if he remained resident in certain boroughs for a year and a day, then claimed borough privilege.[48] According to Ranulf de Glanville (1180s), 'if any serf shall have remained quietly in a privileged town for a year and a day, so that he shall have been received like a citizen into their common guild, he will be liberated from villeinage by that very fact'.[49] Not every town extended this privilege to immigrant serfs, however, which generated some peculiar intertwining of status, such as when one serf of the manor of Wakefield was also described as a merchant and burgess of the town of Wakefield itself.[50] Royal courts and officials offered few effective mechanisms for lords attempting to enforce their rights under villeinage, and the common law could confer legal freedom on serfs who had settled in certain towns.

Thus, the serf enjoyed some protection in the common law against the extremes of lordly behaviour, was answerable as an individual under both criminal law and certain aspects of common and statute law, could not be claimed as a serf by another lord, and was regarded as a free person against all but his lord. Collectively, these provisions created contradictions, anomalies and complexities around the legal position of the serf. For example, when the same person was the serf of lord A, but now resided on another manor some miles away as the de facto freeman of lord B, which of his chattels belonged to lord A and which were his own? Contemporary lawyers were aware of the existence of such knotty legal tangles. Indeed, some gladiatorial legal minds even tried to argue, somewhat tendentiously, that a villein could be freed in the common law if his lord took any actions inconsistent with villeinage, such as entering into a lease or a contract with him. The reasoning was that lords who entered into any kind of formal agreement with their own villeins were thereby implying that the latter possessed their own chattels and, by extension, must have acquired legal rights to protect those chattels.[51] Lords and royal officials routinely turned a pragmatic blind eye to an even more prominent and glaring anomaly: namely, that villeins were liable to royal taxation and to the requisitioning of their grain and livestock through royal purveyance, and could bear arms for the king, when in theory this was impossible since, as chattels of their lord, they had no possessions of their own to render to the Crown.[52] The fact that villeins did contribute routinely to royal taxation and purveyance created another legal conundrum: as villeins were taxed by the king and contributed to his military supplies routinely, why could they not access the king's courts of common law?[53]

Another major legal complication was the absence of any definitive proof of personal servility in the common law.[54] The most secure means of proof were the sworn testimonies on oath of an alleged serf's relatives confirming his status (known as 'suit of kin'), with the outcome preferably being documented in the court proceedings.[55] While this covered most eventualities, it was not sufficiently watertight to prevent some leakage of servile stock. Putting aside the practical difficulties of herding family members to court to provide testimony in the first place, once inside the court some intractable legal complications surrounded personal status. While the theory was simple and clear enough – personal status was heritable through the male line – the reality was rather more complicated, because lords could free serfs (through the process of manumission), men and women of servile and free status routinely intermarried, and paternity was not always certain.[56] The onus of proof was on the lord to prove servile status, not on the defendant to prove his freedom, because the basic stance in the common law was a presumption of liberty.[57] Doubts about the status of bastards, conceived out of wedlock, initially resulted in them following their mother's status, but by the early fourteenth century case law determined that all bastards were free.[58] Proving servile status in the common law was therefore beset with complications: or, as Hyams puts it, 'archaic and full of legal pitfalls'.[59] The difficulties that 'could be thrown in the way of the lord claiming the villein were almost innumerable … the serf received the benefit of any doubt'.[60] The corollary of this legal position must also be emphasised: the common law provided protection against the enserfment of the free. Contemporaries regarded the protection of freedom as the basic principle of English common law.[61]

The difficulties in proving servile status in the royal courts forced landlords to sue instead on the basis of tenure.[62] Proving the status of villein land was more straightforward, and worked very effectively when a lord was seeking to establish his rights of ownership over it.[63] As a consequence, practice in the common law tended to divorce villein status from tenure and to focus on proof of the latter: 'tenure was always a central factor in villeinage cases' in the royal courts.[64] This approach was not only more secure from a legal perspective, but also reflected the contemporaneous priorities of lords who, at least by the late thirteenth century, were more interested in tenurial than personal status, given the chronic scarcity of land and the abundance of labour. In this prevailing economic reality, the primary focus of lords was to protect the legal status of land rather than to unravel the potential tangles of personal status, especially when the common law was much better suited to proving the former than the latter.

Seigniorial confidence in the ability to prove the status of villein land in a court of common law became sufficiently high for them to tolerate freemen holding villein land, and even to license serfs to hold free land.[65] By the end of the thirteenth century freemen holding villein land were common throughout England.[66] In 1289, for instance, forty-four tenants of Redgrave and Hinderclay (Suffolk) held both villein and free land, whilst in 1306 Osbert de Aldham held 43 acres of free tenure and 25 acres of villein in Hadleigh (Suffolk).[67] One serf held a free burgage tenement in the borough of Wakefield.[68] Lords tolerated such crossover activity as long as it was recorded and licensed in their manorial court. For example, in 1316 a bastard – and therefore a freeman – became the tenant of villein land through his marriage to a female serf of Horbury (Yorkshire), and his entry into the land, and the additional payment of a 6s. 8d. fine were recorded in the manorial court rolls.[69] Serfs holding free land in East Anglia had to pay a notional sum to have the acquisition recorded as 'soiled' land.[70] It is worth repeating a point made at the beginning of this chapter: the freeman who held villein land did not become a hereditary serf, but he was required to discharge the tenurial obligations attached to the land. The hereditary serf who held a freeholding remained liable for the personal dues of servility, and had to register the tenure in the manorial court. Of course, freemen holding servile land and serfs holding free land contributed further to the complexities of tenurial and personal status, adding more shades of grey in the shadowy border between freedom and servility.[71]

What, then, were the main tests of servility in the common law? The basic premise was that personal and tenurial servility was strongly associated with a liability for particular renders or incidents, which were usually specified as those of merchet, weekly labour services and tallage.[72] Yet, as we shall see, none of these incidents applied exclusively to the servile and so, for most of the thirteenth century, no conclusive tests of villeinage existed in the common law.[73] As case law developed, however, and as definitions were tightened, a liability to either merchet or tallage emerged as the most reliable test of villeinage.

Merchet was a fine payable to obtain seigniorial permission for the serf to marry. Some historians have deemed it 'odious' and 'humiliatingly servile', because it was a render that enabled lords to interfere in a highly personal and defining moment of a peasant's life.[74] It existed by the mid-eleventh century, but was not widespread until a century later.[75] By 1300 merchet was payable by both the tenant of villein land (*ratione tenementi*) and hereditary serfs, especially females, regardless of whether they held land (*ratione personae*), and by this date it was firmly established as the most reliable test of servility.[76] Theoretically villeins on the vast majority of English manors were liable to pay merchet, although the exact criteria varied and, as we shall see, enforcement was another matter entirely. It was not, however, infallible.[77] Thus, on the one hand, a few free tenures were liable for merchet, and in places it carried no connotation of servility. For example, freemen on some of the Cambridgeshire manors of the bishopric of Ely (Doddington, Stretham, Wilburton and Willingham) owed merchet.[78] On the other hand, even villeins did not render merchet on some manors, such as those held on the Ancient Demesne of the Crown (see below, pp. 54–6) and on Netley abbey's manor of Totton (Hampshire).[79] There was not, in fact, a formal and inviolable requirement of serfs to obtain seigniorial permission to marry. Nor would the marriage of a serf who failed to pay merchet be invalidated, because marriage was seen first and foremost as a Christian covenant before God.[80]

The second main test of villeinage was liability to tallage (*tallagium*), also known as aid (*auxilium*). It existed in a variety of different forms across medieval English society, but it was essentially a prerogative tax levied by lords upon their dependants above and beyond the regular rents and services received for land. From the

1220s lawyers and administrators became more careful to create a distinction between the tallage of the freeman, which had to be justified and taken for the common good, and the tallage of the villein, which did not need to be justified and could be taken for the lord's use.[81] This distinction followed the logic of the common law, in which lords were notionally required to obtain their freemen's consent to be tallaged, whereas no prior consent was required from the villein whose chattels belonged to the lord.[82] Hence from the mid-thirteenth century manorial documents were often at pains to record that villein land was liable for tallage 'at the will of the lord' (*ad voluntatem domini*) to remove any doubt about its status.[83] Once again, however, it was not an infallible test, primarily because 'at no specific moment was the line between servile tallage at will and free consensual aid precise enough to constitute a clear test for the courts'.[84] The neat theoretical differences between the freeman's gracious aid and the villein's compulsory tallage often broke down in practice. On certain estates, both free and unfree paid the same tallage.[85] For example, in 1316 recognition fines – a variant of tallage payable at the accession of a new lord of a manor – totalling 23s. 7d. were paid to the new lord of the manor of Wakefield from each of the graveships within the manor, which included freeholders, and this sum also included contributions from 'the free burgesses of Wakefield' borough.[86] So, in many ways a serf liable for tallage 'did not differ from the townsman, the burgess, of whose freedom there was no question'.[87] The distinction between the voluntary 'aid' of the freeman and the involuntary tallage of the serf was a legal fiction.[88]

Interpreting common law villeinage

For all these many legal complexities and loose ends, some scholars of English serfdom have continued to emphasise the extensive, pervasive and invasive theoretical powers of lords over their serfs and to assume or to contend that these powers were also strongly characteristic of serfdom's operation in practice. For historians in this tradition, denying serfs access to the royal courts not only created an excluded social group, but had also placed them entirely at the beck, call and whim of the lord. According to Adam Lucas, the process of defining more carefully who had access to the royal courts in the early thirteenth century resulted in the imposition of unfree status 'on a much larger number of peasants than ever before'.[89] Brenner argued that the combination of a unified system of law and justice reinforced the capacity of lords to extract surpluses from servile peasants: the period from the 1180s to the 1220s saw 'a sudden and profound strengthening of lordly control over much of the peasantry', which he attributed to 'the dramatic extension of the scope of royal justice and of the common law'.[90] Spencer Dimmock adopts a similar stance, arguing that these processes resulted in 'further servile impositions ... the withdrawal of royal justice exposed them to the private law courts of their lords'.[91] Leon Slota has described the exclusion of serfs from the royal courts as a 'crippling' disability.[92] To be unfree was thus to possess a debased social standing, as was reflected in the changing meaning of the word 'villein' from a neutral noun for a peasant in the late eleventh century to one denoting an unfree peasant who was denied access to the royal courts by the mid-thirteenth century.[93]

In this interpretation, the common law made villeinage more 'oppressive', because the Crown not only strengthened the legal authority of landlords, but also provided them with unrestricted control over their unfree land and serfs through their own manorial courts, perhaps in compensation for opening up the royal courts to their free peasants.[94] Two early influential figures in this field were Postan and E. A. Kosminsky, both of whom independently depicted English villeinage as reaching the peak of its powers at the end of the thirteenth century. For Postan, the combination of high demographic pressure and the seigniorial ability to increase the weight of servile rents and services contributed materially to the impoverishment of the peasantry, exacerbating the problem of acute land shortage and increasing their vulnerability to Malthusian positive checks.[95] For Kosminsky, the development of the common law in the late twelfth century 'meant a further stage in the worsening of the position of the villeins ... a new step on the road towards ... the oppression of the servile peasants', and he repeatedly drew parallels between the English serf and the enslaved Roman.[96] He asserted that 'the desire of feudal lords [was] to extract the greatest possible revenues from their manors', and that this was achieved because the villein was subjected to the lord's will: during the course of the thirteenth century labour services were increased arbitrarily, coupled with extortionate hikes in monetary tallages and entry fines above and beyond the usual rents and services.[97]

Some modern scholars continue to promote these views. Brenner depicted the law as a tool used by elites to increase their powers of appropriation over the labour and land of the servile population, especially as population rose to a peak in the early fourteenth century, culminating in a crisis of productivity.[98] Hence, common law villeinage created 'an indispensable lever to raise dues arbitrarily on customary lands and tenants', and strengthened the extra-economic powers available to landlords to extract the surpluses of peasants through rent, labour and various monopolies.[99] Dimmock stated that the 'legal revolution' of common law villeinage exposed serfs 'to relatively high rents and arbitrary exploitation', and similarly Miriam Müller argued that 'the exploitation of the peasantry was an integral feature of the feudal system ... the framework of the manor therefore ensured the concentration of wealth in the hands of the rulers and the subjection of the peasantry to its jurisdiction'.[100] For Kitsikopoulos, the emergence of the common law presented lords with an 'exploitative extractive mechanism'.[101]

This particular view of English serfdom has been fortified by graphic examples of the ways in which serfs were demeaned and subjugated whenever powerful lords brought cases against them in the royal courts. In 1336, for instance, the abbot of Vale Royal put some of the serfs of his manor of Darnhall (Cheshire) in fetters and forced them to stand bareheaded and barefoot in the choir of the abbey church for daring (and failing) to argue their freedom in the royal courts.[102] In the 1270s Leicester abbey celebrated its legal victory over its villeins' attempt to claim freedom in verse.[103] In 1280 the abbot of Burton asserted in a royal court that his serfs on the manor of Mickleover (Derbyshire) 'have nothing except what they have in their bellies'.[104] Tension over the requirement to perform mill suit caused frequent conflict between the abbeys of St Albans and Cirencester and their villeins.[105]

These cases generate powerful images of subjection and subordination, although historians are divided as to their significance. For D. A. Carpenter, the Leicester abbey case confirms that 'the lord's coercive power was ultimately guaranteed by the state, and in particular by its law which denied the unfree peasant any remedy against many types of abuse … peasants should know their place and not seek to transform it'.[106] For Dyer, the cases provide windows into the mindset and attitudes of serfs to reveal an abhorrence of their status and a desire for freedom, and Hilton suspected they represent the tip of an iceberg.[107] In contrast, J. Z. Titow regarded them as highly unrepresentative, arguing that focusing on actions in the royal courts to understand lord–serf relations is as unhelpful as 'looking at hospital records to find out the state of the nation's health: one would hardly find a healthy person anywhere'.[108] Likewise, Hatcher has emphasised the rarity of such high-profile legal disputes: for him, they reflected either the extremes of lordly behaviour or the pursuit of arcane technical points of the law, rather than bearing much resemblance to reality.[109] Such starkly divergent interpretations of these legal cases are typical of both the diversity of opinion on English serfdom and the tendency for historians to interpret the same evidence in very different ways.

A graphic illustration of the tendency for key features of English serfdom to be interpreted in contradictory ways in the scholarship is the treatment of the common law itself. Most historians portray its emergence as detrimental to serfs, albeit with shades of opinion on just how detrimental.[110] Yet, in direct contrast, Robert Palmer has argued that the evolution and the spread of the common law had beneficial side-effects for villeins, because it introduced decision-making based on precedent and consistently applied rules. These undermined the personal and discretionary power of lords over peasants and, especially, peasant-held land, which in turn increased the peasant's security of tenure and ability to alienate it without lordly interference. As a result, the relationship between lord and tenant became more contractual and less personal, and land could be more easily traded as an economic resource. These developments were already apparent by c. 1200 in the transfer of freehold land and, during the course of the thirteenth century, spread to villein land.[111] Thus, Palmer argues that the introduction of new legal guidelines and modes of behaviour had the general effects of reducing lordly discretion, changing cultural perceptions of justice, and acting as a substantial socio-economic force within the whole of society. The common law, and the culture it promoted, seeped into English society in ways that were beneficial to peasants in general and villeins in particular, although this was a juristic accident, not an *intended* consequence. Historians have tended to overlook such indirect benefits, because the notion that villeins might have benefited from a legal system that directly excluded them is counterintuitive.

An even more radical interpretation of the influence of the common law on serfdom is evident within the work of the Toronto School of historians, which effectively implies its irrelevance to the day-to-day lives of villeins.[112] Instead of focusing on issues of exclusion and sources of conflict, this approach explores how the selective granting of some rights to the unfree under villeinage encouraged collaboration between villeins and their lords.[113] Historians such as James Raftis, Edward Britton and Sherri Olson emphasise cooperation rather than conflict in relations between lords and peasants, pointing to the role of serfs as seigniorial officials, and their capacity for independent leadership and economic decision making, and for self-government.[114] Hence, one prominent and detailed case study in the Toronto tradition hardly mentions the exclusion of villeins from the common law, and argues that the village community was more important to peasants than the constraints imposed by manorial lordship.[115] This line of argument helps to explain how, despite the supposed burdens of villeinage, tens of thousands of villeins had managed to construct sizeable holdings, accumulate economic and social capital, establish themselves among the peasant elite, and participate in a range of factor and commodity markets. In other words, English landlords proved unable to control or exploit villeins effectively, so instead adopted a pragmatic approach that recognised their mutual dependency and the villeins' commercial dynamism, and so sought simply to obtain some profit through servile incidents from their economic successes.[116] The argument that villeins were able to thrive without direct access to the common law appears to support the view of some development economists – such as Gregory Clark and Jürgen Schlumbohm – who see legal institutions as being largely irrelevant to peasants.[117]

The existence of three such contrasting and contradictory interpretations is explicable by the particular perspectives and the very different starting points from which each proceeds. Each focuses their attention on specific aspects of serfdom while placing much less emphasis on others. Hence Marxist-inspired interpretations focus on areas of conflict, exclusion and uncertainty – both theoretical and empirical – whereas Palmer focuses on the wider framework and the practical workings of the common law, and, finally, the Toronto School targets evidence of collaboration and cooperation between lords and villeins. Each interpretation has its value, and offers important insights into the nature of serfdom, yet their co-existence adds to the confusion and contradictions that swirl around the subject. In order to evaluate them, we must explore and understand both the complexities of the common law and the realities of the day-to-day relations between lords and villeins in pre-plague England.

Conclusion

By the thirteenth century the legal theory of common law villeinage excluded serfs from the royal courts and confirmed their subjection to the uncertain will of their lord. Yet tangles in the legal theory created complexities, anomalies, conflicts and contradictions in matters of the personal status of serfs and of villein tenure. As a result, serfs could pay taxes, they were answerable under criminal and statute law, and they could even defend themselves in the common law under certain circumstances. They were free against the whole world except their lord. Lords could not enserf new populations. Serfs who resided in a privileged borough for over a year could become legally free.

These complexities and loopholes were a function of the ways in which common law villeinage had emerged during the late twelfth and early thirteenth centuries. It was a by-product of the evolution of the common law, driven by a pragmatic need to establish which of the king's subjects were eligible to access his expanding system of courts, and which were not.[118] Such a need to establish who enjoyed such access required the creation of tests, but this was beset by difficulties. The problem was the blurred line between freedom and unfreedom in practice, exemplified by the fact that none of the services or incidents of tenure or personal status could be definitively distinguished as belonging exclusively to the unfree. The intertwining of incidents of freedom and villeinage, and the heterogeneity of villeinage from place to place, made it very difficult for the common law to segregate serfdom clearly and definitively from freedom. Intermarriage of the free and the unfree, potential uncertainties over patrimony, and the presumption to liberty in the common law created further difficulties in finding a watertight test for personal servility. This shifted the legal onus towards proving villein status through tenure, based on the tests of tallage and merchet, which were more secure but still not entirely watertight.[119] As a consequence, the common law never provided an incontrovertible definition of servility.[120] Furthermore, lords developed additional mechanisms for establishing the status of villein land, such as the written record of transfers of villein land framed in carefully chosen language in their manorial courts (see Chapter 3), and for establishing personal servility, such as the testimonies of jurors under oath (see Chapter 4).

Historians have devoted a good deal of time and effort to assessing how this narrower, more homogeneous and legalistic form of serfdom changed both the daily lives of the unfree and their social relations with their lords. Those who believe that practice followed the basic principles of the legal theory portray serfdom as restrictive and burdensome. Others argue that the legal theory was largely irrelevant to the daily lives of serfs. These contradictory interpretations are characteristic of scholarship on serfdom, which as a result can appear confusing and misleading. Resolving these issues requires a much deeper understanding of both the ways in which serfdom actually operated and the complex interplay between the common law and the lives of the unfree: what Hyams once described as the 'ebb and flow of influence from the common law to agrarian society'.[121] In particular, to what extent did a legal culture develop more widely as a consequence of the development of the common law, what were the procedural crossovers into other courts, and how far did these effect villeins?[122] It is to these issues that we now turn.

Notes

1 P. R. Hyams, *King, Lords and Peasants in Medieval England* (Oxford: Clarendon Press, 1980), p. xix.

2 C. Dyer, 'Memories of freedom: Attitudes towards serfdom in England 1200 to 1350', in Bush, *Serfdom and Slavery*, pp. 277–95 (p. 278).

3 See Hyams, *King, Lords*, pp. 221–65, for the chronology and development of the common law between the late twelfth and late thirteenth centuries.
4 A. Rio, *Slavery after Rome 500–1100* (Oxford: Oxford University Press, 2017), pp. 243–8; Hyams, *King, Lords*, p. 222.
5 Quoted in J. Hatcher, 'English serfdom and villeinage: Towards a reassessment', *Past & Present*, 90 (1981): 3–39 (p. 8); see also E. A. Kosminsky, *Studies in the Agrarian History of England in the Thirteenth Century* (Oxford: Basil Blackwell, 1956), p. 336.
6 Vinogradoff, *Villeinage*, pp. 45–7, 165–6; Hatcher, 'English serfdom', p. 8.
7 Vinogradoff, *Villeinage*, pp. 45–7; Hyams, *King, Lords*, pp. 38–44, 49–55.
8 Vinogradoff, *Villeinage*, p. 59, although some contemporary authorities did argue that there were differences between these terms, without being very clear on what they were (Hatcher, 'English serfdom', p. 8 n. 10).
9 Vinogradoff, *Villeinage*, pp. 44–5, 59–63, 77–8.
10 Quoted in Hatcher, 'English serfdom', p. 8; H. G. Richardson and G. O. Sayles, *Law and Legislation: From Aethelberht to Magna Carta* (Edinburgh: Edinburgh University Press, 1966), p. 139; Hyams, *King, Lords*, pp. 66–7.
11 Hyams, *King, Lords*, pp. 17–20 (quote p. 20).
12 Vinogradoff, *Villeinage*, p. 76.
13 Ibid., pp. 79–81; Hyams, *King, Lords*, pp. 25–7.
14 Vinogradoff, *Villeinage*, pp. 44–7, 77–81; Rigby, *English Society*, p. 33.
15 Vinogradoff, *Villeinage*, p. 44; F. Pollock and F. W. Maitland, *The History of English Law before the Time of Edward I*, Vol. I (Cambridge: Cambridge University Press, 1895), p. 414; L. Eldridge, *Law and the Medieval Village Community: Reinvigorating Historical Jurisprudence* (Abingdon: Routledge, 2023), p. 109.
16 Hyams, *King, Lords*, p. 3.
17 Ibid., pp. 4–5; Eldridge, *Law and the Medieval Village Community*, pp. 109–10.
18 E. P. Cheyney, 'The disappearance of English serfdom', *English Historical Review*, 15 (1900): 20–37 (pp. 21, 25).
19 Hatcher, 'English serfdom', p. 8; see also Richardson and Sayles, *Law and Legislation*, pp. 141–2.
20 Vinogradoff, *Villeinage*, p. 157.
21 Hyams, *King, Lords*, 28–37, 223–5; C. Dyer, 'Villeins, bondsmen, neifs, and serfs: New serfdom in England c. 1200–1600', in Freedman and Bourin, *Forms of Servitude*, pp. 419–36 (pp. 422–3).

22 Vinogradoff, *Villeinage*, pp. 44–58, 165–6; Hyams, *King, Lords*, pp. 2–37, 51–2, 66–7; Hatcher, 'English serfdom', p. 8.
23 T. W. Page, *The End of Villeinage in England* (New York: Macmillan, 1900), pp. 19–20; Hatcher, 'English serfdom', pp. 7–8; Hatcher, 'Lordship', p. 115.
24 Hyams, *King, Lords*, p. 2.
25 Ghosh, 'Rural economies', p. 258; J. R. Maddicott, *The English Peasantry and the Demands of the Crown 1294–1341*, *Past & Present* Supplements, 1 (Oxford: Past & Present Society, 1975), pp. 73–4.
26 Hyams, *King, Lords*, p. 2; R. Evans, 'Whose was the manorial court?', in R. Evans, ed., *Lordship and Learning: Studies in Memory of Trevor Aston* (Woodbridge: Boydell Press, 2004), pp. 154–68 (pp. 155–6); Hatcher, 'Lordship', pp. 113–15.
27 Hyams, *King, Lords*, p. xix; Eldridge, *Law and the Medieval Village Community*, p. 111; C. Dyer, *From Slavery to Freedom: How Worcestershire People Gained Their Liberty 1000 to 1600*, Worcestershire Historical Society, Occasional Publications, 15 (Worcester: Worcestershire Historical Society, 2024), pp. 6–11.
28 Hyams, *King, Lords*, p. 126.
29 Pollock and Maitland, *The History of English Law*, Vol. I, p. 417; see also Hyams, *King, Lords*, p. xx.
30 Hyams, *King, Lords*, pp. 137–9.
31 Although the extent to which they actually did so, and their likelihood of success, were low: Vinogradoff, *Villeinage*, pp. 67–73; Hyams, *King, Lords*, pp. 135–8, 150–1.
32 Pollock and Maitland, *The History of English Law*, Vol. I, p. 415, 419, 420–1; Vinogradoff, *Villeinage*, pp. 64–6; Hyams, *King, Lords*, 130–2.
33 Vinogradoff, *Villeinage*, p. 129.
34 Ibid., pp. 67–8, 128; Pollock and Maitland, *The History of English Law*, Vol. I, p. 419.
35 Pollock and Maitland, *The History of English Law*, Vol. I, p. 415; Eldridge, *Law and the Medieval Village Community*, p. 110.
36 Hyams, *King, Lords*, pp. 91–2.
37 J. Masschaele, *Jury, State and Society in Medieval England* (Basingstoke: Macmillan, 2008), p. 140.
38 Ibid., pp. 132–9.
39 D. Noy, 'Winslow in 1341: The *Nonarum Inquisitiones* and the reliability of medieval tax self-assessment', *Records of Buckinghamshire*, 55 (2015): 137–45 (pp. 138–9).
40 D. A. Carpenter, 'English peasants in politics 1258–1267', *Past & Present*, 126 (1992): 3–42 (p. 38).

41 Pollock and Maitland, *The History of English Law*, Vol. I, p. 418. See also R. Faith, *The Moral Economy of the Countryside* (Cambridge: Cambridge University Press, 2020), pp. 153–5.
42 Briggs, 'English serfdom', pp. 30–1.
43 Hyams, *King, Lords*, p. 31.
44 Bailey, 'Servile and gender migration', pp. 67–8.
45 Bailey, *The Decline of Serfdom*, 42–6.
46 J. A. Raftis, *Tenure and Mobility: Studies in the Social History of the Mediaeval English Village* (Toronto: Institute of Pontifical Studies, 1964), p. 141. Likewise, lords showed little interest in controlling pre-plague servile migration in Essex (L. R. Poos, *A Rural Society after the Black Death: Essex 1350–1525* (Cambridge: Cambridge University Press, 1990), p. 160), or indeed elsewhere (Bailey, 'Servile and gender migration', pp. 58–60, Tables 1 and 2).
47 M. Bailey, 'Austin Crembell: A medieval Suffolk commuter', *Proceedings of the Suffolk Institute of Archaeology and History*, 45:2 (2022): 284–8.
48 Cheyney, 'The disappearance', pp. 27–8; Hyams, *King, Lords*, pp. 167–9.
49 Cited in Cheyney, 'The disappearance', p. 28.
50 W. P. Baildon, ed., *Court Rolls of the Manor of Wakefield*, Vol. I, *1274 to 1297*, Yorkshire Archaeological Society Record Series, 29 ([Leeds]: Yorkshire Archaeological Society, 1901), p. 131.
51 Vinogradoff, *Villeinage*, p. 87.
52 Carpenter, 'English peasants', pp. 37–8; J. Masschaele, *Peasants, Merchants and Markets: Inland Trade in Medieval England, 1150–1350* (Basingstoke: Palgrave Macmillan, 1997), pp. 36–41.
53 P. R. Hyams, 'What did Edwardian villagers mean by law?, in Z. Razi and R. M. Smith, eds, *Medieval Society and the Manor Court* (Oxford: Clarendon Press, 1996), pp. 69–102 (p. 86).
54 Vinogradoff, *Villeinage*, pp. 81–8.
55 P. R. Hyams, 'The proof of villein status in the common law', *English Historical Review*, 89 (1974): 721–49; Hyams, *King, Lords*, pp. 171–4.
56 Pollock and Maitland, *The History of English Law*, Vol. I, p. 423; J. Hatcher, *Rural Economy and Society in the Duchy of Cornwall 1300–1500* (Cambridge: Cambridge University Press, 1970), p. 77; Hyams, *King, Lords*, pp. 175–6; Eldridge, *Law and the Medieval Village Community*, p. 112.
57 Vinogradoff, *Villeinage*, pp. 83–5.
58 Hyams, *King, Lords*, pp. 180–2.
59 Ibid., p. 118; see also Vinogradoff, *Villeinage*, p. 129.

60 Cheyney, 'The disappearance', pp. 29–30.
61 Hyams, *King, Lords*, pp. 203–8.
62 Ibid., p. 182.
63 Ibid., p. 118.
64 Ibid., p. 184; A. W. B. Simpson, *A History of the Land Law*, 2nd edn (Oxford: Oxford University Press, 1986), p. 158.
65 Vinogradoff, *Villeinage*, pp. 78–80; E. B. DeWindt, *Land and People in Holywell-cum-Needingworth: Structures of Tenure and Patterns of Social Organization in an East Midlands Village, 1252–1457* (Toronto: Institute of Pontifical Studies), p. 68; Hyams, *King, Lords*, pp. 67–8, 110–13; E. King, *Peterborough Abbey 1086–1310: A Study in the Land Market* (Cambridge: Cambridge University Press, 1973), pp. 99–125; E. McGibbon Smith, 'Reflections of reality in the manor court: Sutton-in-the-Isle, 1308–1391' (PhD thesis, University of Cambridge, 2005), p. 79; P. Larson, *Conflict and Compromise in the Late Medieval Countryside: Lords and Peasants in Durham 1349–1400* (London: Routledge, 2006), pp. 62–3.
66 A. E. Levett, *Studies in Manorial History* (Oxford: Oxford University Press, 1938), pp. 191–2; Baildon, *Court Rolls 1274 to 1297*, pp. 116, 120, 125, 242. J. Lister, ed., *Court Rolls of the Manor of Wakefield*, Vol. IV, *1315–1317*, Yorkshire Archaeological Society, 78 (Leeds: Yorkshire Archaeological Society, 1930), pp. 113, 201; Walker, *Court Rolls 1331–3*, p. 98.
67 J. Phillips, 'Collaboration and litigation in two Suffolk manor courts 1289 to 1364' (PhD thesis, University of Cambridge, 2005), p. 98; M. Woods, *Medieval Hadleigh: The Chief Manor and the Town* (Hadleigh: published privately, 2018), pp. 108–9.
68 Walker, *Court Rolls 1322–31*, p. 16; K. M. Troup, ed., *The Court Rolls of the Manor of Wakefield, October 1338 to September 1340*, Wakefield Court Rolls Series, 12 (Leeds: Yorkshire Archaeological Society, 1999), pp. 148, 170.
69 Lister, *Wakefield Court Rolls 1315–1317*, p. 114.
70 M. Bailey, 'Villeinage in England: A regional case study c. 1250–1349', *Economic History Review*, 62 (2009): 430–47 (441); Bailey, *The Decline of Serfdom*, pp. 113, 213, 225.
71 Levett, *Studies*, pp. 193–4; E. Miller, *The Abbey and Bishopric of Ely* (Cambridge: Cambridge University Press, 1951), p. 112; Eldridge, *Law and the Medieval Village Community*, 108.
72 C. Dyer, *Standards of Living in the Later Middle Ages: Social Change in England c. 1200–1520* (Cambridge: Cambridge University Press, 1989), p. 137; Dyer, 'Villeins, bondsmen', p. 423; Dyer, 'The ineffectiveness of lordship', pp. 73–4.

73 Vinogradoff, *Villeinage*, pp. 81–2, 153–5; Hyams, *King, Lords*, pp. 186–7.
74 Vinogradoff, *Villeinage*, p. 153; Hyams, *King, Lords*, p. 187.
75 J. Scammell, 'Freedom and marriage in medieval England', *Economic History Review*, 27 (1974): 523–37; R. Faith, *The English Peasantry and the Growth of Lordship* (Leicester: Leicester University Press, 1997), p. 257. For a summary of the literature on merchet, see Bailey, *The Decline of Serfdom*, 37–9.
76 Hyams, *King, Lords*, pp. 187–91; R. Faith, 'Seigneurial control of women's marriage', *Past & Present*, 99 (1983): 123–33 (p. 134); see also A. J. Horwood, ed., *Yearbooks of the Reign of Edward III*, Vol. VI (London: Longman, 1883–1911), p. xxiii.
77 Vinogradoff, *Villeinage*, pp. 203–4.
78 Ibid., pp. 155, 201–2; Levett, *Studies*, pp. 238–9; Kosminsky, *Studies*, pp. 198–200; Larson, *Conflict and Compromise*, p. 93; L. F. Salzman, ed., *Victoria County History, Cambridgeshire and Isle of Ely*, Vol. II (London: Institute of Historical Research, 1948), p. 64; H. M. Cam, ed., *Selected Historical Essays of F. W. Maitland* (Cambridge: Cambridge University Press, 1957), p. 17.
79 The National Archives, Kew (TNA), SC6/201/50–63.
80 L. R. Poos and L. Bonfield, eds, *Select Cases in Manorial Courts 1250–1550: Property and Family Law* (London: Selden Society, 1998), p. clxviii.
81 Vinogradoff, *Villeinage*, pp. 162–3; Hyams, *King, Lords*, pp. 191–2; M. Bailey, 'Tallage-at-will in later medieval England', *English Historical Review*, 134:566 (2019): 25–58 (pp. 26–30).
82 Hyams, *King, Lords*, pp. 191–3, 241, 267. See also Levett, *Studies*, p. 193; F. M. Page, *The Estates of Crowland Abbey* (Cambridge: Cambridge University Press, 1934) pp. 131–2; Dyer, 'The ineffectiveness of lordship', pp. 73–4; and E. B. Fryde, *Peasants and Landlords in Later Medieval England* (Stroud: Alan Sutton, 1996), pp. 23–4.
83 See, for example, the fixed communal tallage paid by the bondmen of Walcot in 1296–7 *pro voluntate domini*, in S. Raban, ed., *The White Book of Peterborough*, Northamptonshire Record Society (Peterborough: Dean and Chapter of Peterborough, 2001), p. 91; Levett, *Studies*, p. 193; A. E. Wilson, ed., *Custumals of the Manors of Laughton, Willingdon and Goring*, Sussex Record Society, 60 (Lewes: Sussex Record Society, 1961), pp. 50–1, 62, 65; and A. H. Denney, ed., *The Sibton Abbey Estates: Select Documents 1325–1509*, Suffolk Records Society, 1 (Ipswich: Suffolk Records Society, 1960), pp. 49–50.
84 Hyams, *King, Lords*, pp. 191; Bailey, 'Tallage-at-will', pp. 52–3.

85 Hatcher, *Rural Economy*, p. 69; Bailey, 'Villeinage', p. 450; Bailey, 'Tallage-at-will', pp. 53–4.
86 Lister, *Court Rolls 1315–1317*, p. 134.
87 Richardson and Sayles, *Law and Legislation*, p. 143.
88 Bailey, 'Tallage-at-will', pp. 52–7.
89 A. Lucas, *Ecclesiastical Lordship, Seigneurial Power and the Commercialization of Milling in Medieval England* (London: Routledge, 2014), p. 308. See also Hilton, *A Medieval Society*, p. 159; Faith, *The English Peasantry*, pp. 248, 263–6; and Kitsikopoulos, 'England', p. 46. For a contrasting interpretation, see Hyams, *King, lords*, pp. 249–57; and Hatcher, 'English serfdom', pp. 26–33.
90 R. Brenner, 'The rises and declines of serfdom in medieval and early modern Europe', in Bush, *Serfdom and Slavery*, pp. 247–76 (pp. 258–62, quotation p. 262).
91 Dimmock, *The Origin of Capitalism*, p. 70.
92 L. A. Slota, 'Law, land transfer, and lordship on the estates of St Albans abbey in the thirteenth and fourteenth centuries', *Law and History Review*, 6 (1988): 119–38 (p. 131).
93 W. Scase, *Literature and Complaint in England 1272–1553* (Oxford: Oxford University Press, 2007), pp. 8–9.
94 Z. Razi and R. M. Smith, 'The origins of the English manor courts as a written record', in Razi and Smith, *Medieval Society*, pp. 36–68 (pp. 40–3); Hilton, *A Medieval Society*, pp. 140, 166. Dyer, 'Memories of freedom', p. 277.
95 Postan, 'Medieval agrarian society', pp. 603–4. For a survey of this line of argument, see Hatcher and Bailey, *Modelling the Middle Ages*, pp. 21–65.
96 Kosminsky, *Studies*, pp. 328–9 (quotations), 330–1, 335; see also Eldridge, *Law and the Medieval Village Community*, pp. 111–12.
97 Kosminsky, *Studies*, pp. 330, 335, 346–50.
98 Brenner, 'Property and progress', pp. 81–6.
99 R. Brenner, 'The agrarian roots of European capitalism', in Aston and Philpin, *The Brenner Debate*, pp. 213–320 (pp. 258, 261); and refrained in R. Brenner, 'Property relations and the growth of agrarian productivity in late medieval and early modern Europe', in A. Bhaduri and R. Skarstein, eds, *Economic Development and Agricultural Productivity* (Cheltenham: Edward Elgar, 1997), pp. 9–42 (p. 34), where English lords achieved 'an unusually high level of cooperation with one another in operating their ... system of surplus extraction by economic extra-coercion', and enjoyed a 'golden age' between the late twelfth and early fourteenth century by the imposition of 'a tighter form of serfdom, of feudal domination, upon their tenants'. See also

Kosminsky, *Studies*, pp. 328–54; and the summary in Rigby, *English Society*, pp. 25–30.

100 Dimmock, *The Origin of Capitalism*, pp. 65, 73; M. Müller, 'Conflict and revolt: The Bishop of Ely and his peasants at the manor of Brandon in Suffolk c. 1300–81', *Rural History*, 23 (2012): 1–23 (p. 1).

101 Kitsikopoulos, 'England', pp. 46–7. See also H. S. Bennett, *Life on the English Manor: A Study of Peasant Conditions 1150–1400* (Cambridge: Cambridge University Press, 1937), p. 137, on the deleterious effects of seigniorial monopolies, such as mill suit, under serfdom.

102 G. C. Coulton, *The Medieval Village* (Cambridge: Cambridge University Press, 1925), pp. 131–5.

103 G. C. Homans, *English Villagers of the Thirteenth Century* (Cambridge, MA: Harvard University Press, 1941), pp. 276–83; Carpenter, 'English peasants', p. 36.

104 Coulton, *The Medieval Village*, p. 131; D. Crook, 'Freedom, villeinage and legal process: The dispute between the abbot of Burton and his tenants of Mickleover, 1280', *Nottingham Medieval Studies*, 44 (2000): 123–40; Dyer, 'The ineffectiveness of lordship', 73–4.

105 R. Holt, *The Mills of Medieval England* (Oxford: Basil Blackwell, 1988), pp. 40–5.

106 Carpenter, 'English peasants', p. 36.

107 Dyer, 'Memories of freedom', 280–6; R. H. Hilton, *Class Conflict and the Crisis of Feudalism*, 2nd edn (London: Verso, 1990), pp. 54–7.

108 J. Z. Titow, *English Rural Society 1200–1350* (London: George Allen and Unwin, 1969), p. 58.

109 Hatcher, 'English serfdom', pp. 4–5.

110 As discussed in Freedman, *The Origins*, pp. 221–3.

111 R. C. Palmer, 'The origins of property in England', *Law and History Review*, 3:1 (1985): 1–50; R. C. Palmer, 'The economic and cultural impact of the origins of property: 1180–1220', *Law and History Review*, 3 (1985): 375–96; R. C. Palmer, 'England: Law, society and the state', in S. H. Rigby, ed., *A Companion to Britain in the Late Middle Ages* (Oxford: Basil Blackwell, 2003), pp. 242–60 (pp. 242–4).

112 For example, neither Coulton, *The Medieval Village*, nor Homans, *English Villagers*, offers much direct discussion of the impact of the common law on villeins.

113 Rio, *Slavery*, p. 239; Rigby, *English Society*, pp. 25–34, 46–9; Schofield, *Peasants and Historians*, pp. 209–16.

114 J. A. Raftis, *Peasant Economic Development within the English Manorial System* (Stroud: Alan Sutton, 1996); E. Britton, *The Community of the Vill: A Study in the History of the Family and*

Village Life in Fourteenth-Century England (Toronto: Macmillan, 1977); S. Olson, *A Chronicle of All that Happens: Voices from the Village Court in Medieval England* (Toronto: Pontifical Institute of Medieval Studies, 1996), pp. 10–27; S. Olson, *A Mute Gospel: The People and Culture of the Medieval English Common Fields* (Toronto: Pontifical Institute of Medieval Studies, 2009), pp. 125–42; Eldridge, *Law and the Medieval Village Community*, pp. 138–40.

115 Britton, *The Community of the Vill*, pp. 175–8: neither villeinage nor serfdom features in the index to this book.

116 Raftis, *Peasant Economic Development*, pp. 8–27, 130–1; Olson, *A Mute Gospel*, 129; Olson, *A Chronicle*, p. 230.

117 G. Clark, *A Farewell to Alms: A Brief Economic History of the World* (Princeton: Princeton University Press, 2007), pp. 147, 173, 212–23; Dennison, 'The institutional context', pp. 249–50; Ogilvie, 'Choices and constraints', p. 295; Hyams, *King, Lords*, pp. 201–2.

118 Hyams, *King, Lords*, pp. xxi–xxii.

119 Ibid., pp. 67–8, 100.

120 Ibid., pp. 192, 240.

121 Ibid., p. 268.

122 Hyams, 'What did Edwardian villagers mean?', p. 84.

2

Serfdom in practice: Freedom and unfreedom

Having considered the legal theory of common law villeinage, and explored some of its complexities and loopholes, we need next to examine how villeinage operated in practice in the three generations before the Black Death.[1] As we have seen, a number of historians regard the reality of English serfdom as being closely aligned with its legal theory, and so portray it as economically burdensome, pervasive and exacting, with arbitrary seigniorial power wielding a primary influence over lord–peasant relations. Those who hold such views have often expressed their moral disapproval at the way in which villeinage intruded into the personal lives of serfs, notably through controls over their marriages, their sexual activities and the disposition of their estate after death. This view is often corroborated by means of colourful and anecdotal examples cherry-picked from legal and manorial records, or is simply asserted with hardly any reference to the detailed scholarship on the subject.[2] If we wish to understand the reality of lord–peasant relations in medieval England, as opposed to their legal representation, it is upon the large corpus of sources produced by estate administrators that our analysis must ultimately depend. Only a thorough examination of large samples of evidence and a wide range of case studies of lord–villein relations will reveal the extent and the size of the gap between theory and practice.

Early pioneers of this approach, such as William Ashley and Vinogradoff, pointed out that when the evidence from manorial documents is considered, 'villeinage assumes an entirely different aspect from that which legal theory tries to give it'.[3] More recently, historians such as Rigby, Hatcher and Bruce Campbell have drawn similar conclusions.[4] According to Campbell, 'the demise of serfdom and the relative weakening of seigniorial power were already in progress during the expansive years of the thirteenth century'.[5] Yet such studies stand in direct contrast to the views of those scholars who continue to argue that the theory and practice of serfdom were much more closely aligned. The existence of such contradictory views in the scholarship of the subject is a source of confusion and misunderstanding, especially for students and non-medievalists. These conflicting views spring from differences of opinion over four key aspects of serfdom: the extent to which lords altered villein rents or utilised the labour of serfs 'at their will'; the effectiveness with which lords enforced their economic monopolies – notably mill suit – relating to villeinage; the degree to which the legal 'uncertainty' of other servile incidents enabled lords to charge large fees when it suited them; and whether lords used their manorial courts to enforce their theoretical powers. We will address each of these issues in turn over the course of the next three chapters.

In this chapter, we begin by assessing the proportions of free and unfree people across rural England and the nature of lordship in the pre-plague era, before going on to explore the distinction between unfreedom and freedom. We have seen how the theory of common law villeinage was beset by legal complexities. Foremost among these was the intermingling of the free and the unfree. Serfs intermarried with freemen and -women; free people held unfree land, and vice versa; and the key incidents of villeinage – tallage-at-will and merchet – were sometimes paid by freemen. As we shall see, many of the other incidents and monopolies that are often seen as characterising servility – heriots; labour service; and, especially, mill suit – were also rendered by free peasants, creating further complications whose effect was to diminish the cogency of legal villeinage. As a result, it is not possible to disentangle the operation of serfdom cleanly from other elements of medieval social relations.

Serfdom and manorial lordship

The term 'manorial lordship' is being increasingly used to describe the nature of rural social relations within medieval society in preference to the word 'feudalism', because it is less problematic in its depiction of the system's social ties. Manorial lordship encompasses the status of lords, their landed resources, the proportion of free tenures and people on their manors as against those of the unfree, the relative and varied distribution of these elements over time and place, and the assorted linkages between these groups. Hence, a proper understanding of the influence of unfreedom in pre-plague England must begin with a brief survey of how it fitted within the system of manorial lordship: what was the relative importance of serfdom as a form of tenure and of personal status within medieval rural society, and what was its geographical distribution?

Answering this question is greatly aided by the recent computerised analysis of the surviving Hundred Rolls from 1274 and 1279, listing free and unfree tenants and their holdings in each vill, and of thousands of Inquisitions Post Mortem from 1300 to 1349, detailing the resources of the landed estates of lay lords holding directly from the Crown, manor by manor. Royal officials generated these documents, which contain considerable quantities of data about the composition of thousands of manors, including the proportions of free and unfree tenures.[6] From such sources, historians have estimated that in the early fourteenth century around 30 per cent of arable land in England was demesne, i.e. held directly by the lord; 35 per cent was held on free tenures; and the remaining 35 per cent on unfree tenures.[7] Around the same time, perhaps 40 per cent of the total population could be categorised as serfs and 60 per cent as free, the latter including around 20 per cent who lived in towns. The prevalence of personal status declined over time, so that by the end of the fourteenth century somewhere between 10 and 20 per cent of the population were serfs.[8]

There were an estimated 20,000 secular and ecclesiastical lords in pre-plague England.[9] The archetypal lord was male: less than one-fifth of 'lords' were female. Around 1,000 lords – whether lay or ecclesiastical – were fabulously wealthy, with incomes in excess of £200 per annum, although the overwhelming majority (perhaps 18,500 of the 20,000, known collectively as the gentry) had much lower incomes, closer to £15 per annum. The mean income from a single manor held by one of these lesser lords was £8 per annum, whereas the most valuable manors – yielding over £100 per annum – belonged to aristocratic lords (earls, barons and the wealthiest knights) and major ecclesiastical institutions, especially bishoprics and Benedictine monasteries).[10] In the Hundred Rolls, for example, 65 per cent of manors were small, often less than 200 acres, and just 13 per cent were large in the south Midland counties of Cambridgeshire, Bedfordshire, Buckinghamshire and Oxfordshire.[11] Furthermore, small manors tended to possess a distinctive structure dominated by free rents and free tenures, with a low proportion of villein tenures and few labour services.[12] In the Hundred Rolls 71 per cent of the 29,625 recorded peasant-holdings were free, and in the early fourteenth century around 85 per cent of the tenantry of the Berkeley estate (Gloucestershire) were free.[13] Villein tenure and status tended to increase in importance with the size of the manor: hence, the largest manors had a higher proportion of customary land and greater resources of servile labour. Serfdom was most strongly associated with large manors and higher-status lordship, especially anciently established monastic and aristocratic estates.

Whereas small and large manors, and free and unfree tenures, could be found throughout England, some very broad generalisations are possible thanks to Campbell and Ken Bartley's computerised analysis of the value of rents on lay manors documented in the Inquisitions Post Mortem, which is reproduced as Map 2.1.[14] These reveal how servile land was most prevalent in the far north and south-west of England, and in areas of the Midlands, where concentrations of large manors could be found. By contrast, free land was dominant in Kent and Essex, Lincolnshire, the Marcher counties on the border with Wales, and western Lancashire, and was also relatively important in East Anglia, the east Midlands and the area around London, where manors tended to be smaller. In much of the Midlands the relative importance of free and unfree tenures was balanced. Anomalies existed even within these broad patterns: for example, within the north hereditary serfs made up merely one-fifth of the population of County Durham, where freemen held large areas of unfree land, and serfs also represented a small minority of the population in the middle Tyne Valley (Northumberland).[15]

Generalising about the structure of seigniorial estates is more straightforward. First, they did not comprise large, contiguous

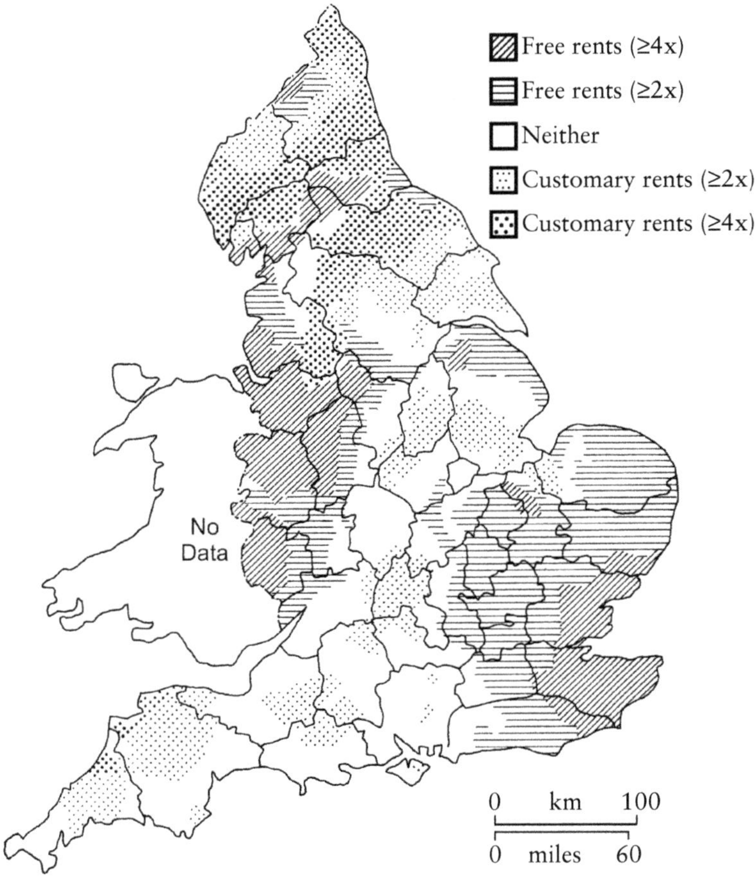

Map 2.1 Proportion of free and customary rents on lay manors in England 1300–48, from Inquisitions Post Mortem. Courtesy of B. M. S. Campbell, 'The agrarian problem in the early fourteenth century', *Past & Present*, 188 (2005): 3–70 (Map 1).

blocks of land. The vast majority of lords held no more than a couple of small, detached manors located in relatively close proximity to each other. Even the estates of the greatest lords comprised manors that were widely dispersed and intermingled with those of countless other lords. For example, the demesne manors of the estate of the bishop of Ely were spread across six counties and, while some of these were concentrated in localised clusters (such as nine manors in the northern silt fens), most were widely distributed over 100 miles from the south (Totteridge, Hertfordshire) to the north (East Dereham, Norfolk), and over 60 miles from west (Pidley, Huntingdonshire) to east (Bramford, Suffolk).[16] The existence of tighter geographical clusters of demesne manors within the same estate certainly enhanced the power and influence of that lord within a locality, but even these were interspersed with numerous manors held by other lords. Second, the manors themselves seldom constituted an unbroken expanse of real estate, because most villages were split between at least two manors. This tendency for fission and dispersal was most pronounced in East Anglia and south-east England: in east Suffolk, for example, there were usually at least five manors in each vill, whose lands lay intermingled with one another and could even be scattered into the bounds of neighbouring vills.[17] The fragmentation of seigniorial landholdings was likely to weaken the effectiveness of their powers over serfs by increasing the availability of land and work off the home manor, thereby increasing the outside options of serfs and making serfdom more difficult to enforce (Chapter 5).

Servile land made up around 35 per cent of all arable land in England, and hereditary serfs around half of the rural population. Servile tenures and personal status were found everywhere, although they were especially apparent in a crescent stretching from the far north of England through the Midlands to the extreme south-west of England, and were most common on the largest manors held by high-status landlords. Servile tenures were least prominent in the east and west of England, and on the small manors most typical of manorial forms. Thus, serfdom was 'widely prevalent but not predominant', and consequently it was not the main source of seigniorial revenues.[18] The most important conclusion from the computerised analysis of the Inquisitions Post Mortem is that the overwhelming majority of English manors were small and dominated by free tenures and free folk, and they were held by lay gentry lords of low status, some of whom were scarcely wealthier than the more prosperous peasants. Customary tenures represented a small proportion of the total landed resources on such manors and were even non-existent on some.

Despite their numerical importance, these manors scarcely feature in the published studies of serfdom for the simple reason that hardly any court rolls and accounts have survived from them. Kosminsky supposed that the lesser lords who ran these manors had no need for such documents, although later research has revealed that they did indeed draw up manorial surveys, court and account rolls in large quantities: they just have not been preserved as well as the manorial documents from the large manors of the great monastic and aristocratic lords, where servility featured prominently.[19] Serfdom on these small manors was usually low-profile and its management was light-touch, such as at Holywell (Oxfordshire).[20] Hence, our understanding of the mechanics of serfdom is based mainly on research into the large, classic manors of high-status landlords, whose records have survived in greatest quantities, even though these manors are atypical. The operation of serfdom is likely to have been weaker on the typical small English manor, where villeinage was a minority form of tenure and status, and where 'fundamental differences in landlord–tenant relations must have existed between small manors and large'.[21]

Freedom and unfreedom

Local practice followed legal theory in categorising land and people as either free or unfree. They were located on a continuum of obligations and services where the transitional zone from villeinage to freedom was blurred, in the sense that the personal and tenurial obligations associated with freedom shared some attributes with unfreedom. For example, freemen might owe labour services or tallage, and could pay fines to enter land, yet these obligations were also characteristic of unfree holdings. Likewise, the unfree on some estates did not render some of the defining incidents of servility.[22] Hence, identifying an incident exclusive to, and a definitive hallmark of, servility was problematic, because in practice there was no neat and tidy distinction between freedom and unfreedom, whatever contemporary lawyers might assert.[23] The differences between the free and unfree versions were matters of degree. In this section, we illustrate the blurring of the distinction between freedom and unfreedom through, first, the existence of intermediary forms of tenure – namely the 'privileged' villeinage of Ancient Demesne – and, second, the many shared characteristics between free and villein tenure. The latter point is exemplified through a detailed survey of mill suit, the most prominent 'economic monopoly' associated with servility, which, in reality, was not rendered by many serfs and was imposed on some freemen.

The Ancient (or 'royal') Demesne comprised those manors held as part of the estate of the king at the time of the Norman Conquest. Like most manors held by aristocratic and monastic lords, Ancient Demesne contained large areas of servile land held by villeins. However, these villeins enjoyed a privileged status that elevated them above the mass of ordinary or 'pure' villeins elsewhere.[24] The privileged villeins of Ancient Demesne were not 'serfs by blood' and they did not render merchet. Most important of all, they could make formal representations to their lord through the royal courts on issues relating to their landholdings.[25] In many respects, therefore, these villeins closely resembled freemen elsewhere.

The precise privileges of these villeins were not uniform across all Ancient Demesne manors, however, but instead varied according to the exact weight and type of services owed, and the ease with which they could access the king's courts. At one end of the spectrum, the villeins of Havering (Essex) enjoyed a rent package hardly distinguishable from freemen on other manors.[26] Likewise, although the villeins of Rothley held their land heritably 'at the will of the lord', the manor's extant documents contain no reference to them rendering servile dues such as merchet, tallage and chevage, probably because in 1245 these 'tenants at will' had agreed to the payment of an additional cash sum each year, at the fixed rate of 3s.' rent per carucate, in lieu of all other works and villein customs.[27] Heirs born within the soke of Rothley paid no entry fine on admittance to villein land, whereas outsiders paid an entry fine determined notionally by the lord.[28] Again, there was little difference between this package and that owed by many freemen. Indeed, in 1284 the villeins of Rothley attempted to argue that they were not required to attend the manorial court, echoing this claim of many freemen, although their new lord – the Knights Templar, to whom the king had granted the manor in 1231 – insisted successfully that they must do so.[29] At the other end of the spectrum of Ancient Demesne, the dues at Kings Ripton (Huntingdonshire) were much heavier and broader, and so were more reminiscent of the types of obligations owed by villeins on many monastic estates.[30]

Although the precise package of rent and servile incidents owed by the villeins of the Ancient Demesne varied from one manor to another, in general it tended to be light and to take the form of cash rather than labour rents. The main privilege of villeinage on Ancient Demesne manors was an explicit royal commitment to maintain the customs of the manor, even when it had been alienated to a private lord, and the ability to petition the king through a writ if any attempt was made to vary the customary rents and services on villein land.[31] It was once assumed that this privilege had been in force since at least the Norman Conquest, but detailed research has shown that it actually emerged around the same time as common law villeinage.[32] In other words, during the early decades of the thirteenth century the status of these privileged villeins and their relationship with the courts of common law were clarified and defined through case law, in the same way as the position of villeins elsewhere.[33] The argument was logical enough: villeins throughout England enjoyed a customary right to appeal a contentious issue to their lord, but where the lord was also the king then the appeal was to be made through the royal courts. Of course, this was comparable to the right of the freeman, which explains not only the 'privileged' nature of villeinage on these manors, but also reveals the primary motive of those villeins who claimed that their own manor had once been Ancient Demesne. Many of these legal claims were spurious, because either the manor had never been Ancient Demesne or it had been so before 1066, but the royal courts had to take them seriously because the king could not readily ignore alleged or potential infringements of his rights or responsibilities.[34]

Outside the royal estate, free tenure was distinguished from unfree tenures by the particular package of incidents attached to the land and the way in which each incident was managed, rather than by a single distinguishing incident, because free and unfree land owed similar types of dues. The tenants of both owed fines to enter their holdings, they could be subject to death duties of various kinds, and both paid 'aid' or tallage to their lords: what distinguished the free from the unfree incident was how they functioned and how lawyers regarded them (see pp. 27–33).[35] In many ways, this sharing of characteristics was inevitable, given that social relations at all levels of medieval society were based upon dependency, service and mutual obligations. All holders of land below the king owed obligations to the lord of that land. Hence, free tenure 'involved the notion of a personal concession quite as much as did the base tenure'.[36] Relief, death duty, aid, escheat, forfeiture and suit of court were requisites of all forms of tenure, each of which created some scope for profit, friction and perhaps abuse upon imposition.[37] Every lord and every peasant, free or unfree, was subject to some degree of seigniorial control.[38] As a result, as Freedman notes, 'it could be argued that serfdom was no more a unique form of bondage than anything else in [such] a society'.[39] So the range of obligations, and the constraints they imposed, were a matter of degree, although the extent of that degree was undoubtedly important.

Thus, in any part of England the rent and services owed on either free or unfree tenure could include a curious mixture of freeholding and servility, in which freeholders sometimes performed services usually regarded as servile. Indeed, even servile merchet – the most effective test of servility – bore a resemblance to a lord's rights over the marriage of a free but underage ward in the common law.[40] In the 1270s freemen of Eggington (Bedfordshire) owed merchet for women, heriot and harvest services, a combination that closely resembled the principal dues of villein tenure.[41] It is worth a more detailed exploration of this overlap of the obligations of free and unfree tenure through an examination of three such incidents: heriot, labour services on the lord's demesne and suit of mill.

Freedom and unfreedom: Heriot

Heriot is widely understood to have been a death duty payable to the lord of a manor from the estate of a deceased tenant. Indeed, its name derives from the Anglo-Saxon term for the armour given by a lord to a follower that was returnable at death, hence implying an incident on an individual of higher status.[42] It was mainly, but not exclusively, due from villein tenants. In Shropshire it was common for free tenants to owe heriot, and on some manors they alone were liable for it.[43] Wenlock priory (Shropshire) possessed the right to take one-third of the value of the goods of dead tenants, whether free or unfree.[44] Some free tenants on the estates of the bishopric of Ely, St Alban's abbey and Netley abbey (Hampshire) also owed heriot.[45] Even a few of the gentry were liable for heriot, such as the lady of Lyneal on land she held from the lords of Ellesmere (Shropshire), as were the lords holding land for fractions of a knight's fee from the bishopric of Hereford in south Shropshire.[46] Similarly, when Grace, lady [*domina*] of Salden, died in the plague epidemic of 1349 she 'freely' held three messuages and two 'virgates of free land' in Winslow (Buckinghamshire), for which she rendered one ox as heriot, whilst as late as 1521 Simon Mylborn, esquire, paid heriot to the almoner of Worcester priory for his holding.[47] As heriot could be owed from both free and unfree tenures, it was unsuitable as a legal test of villeinage.[48]

Local custom determined whether, when and what heriots were liable from villein tenants, so it was not imposed arbitrarily. In the overwhelming majority of cases across the country, heriot was due from the estate of a deceased servile tenant and took the form of the tenant's best beast.[49] There were local variants on this practice. In some places, as on some manors of St Albans abbey, heriot was due either on the death of a tenant or when a villein tenant relinquished his last parcel of villein land, and so it could be either a *post mortem* or an *inter vivos* payment (see Chapter 10). In much of East Anglia, heriot was strictly a *post mortem* render, but it was not due when an heir succeeded to the holding and paid an entry fine: furthermore, some tenants evaded payment through a deathbed transfer of the land to the heir.[50] Heriot was an incident of tenure and was seldom charged to landless serfs.

How affordable was heriot? The Wenlock priory example indicates that heriot might absorb up to one-third of the moveable goods of the deceased, a practice that was occasionally found elsewhere.[51] In the overwhelming majority of cases, the value of the heriot was the value of the outgoing tenant's best beast, although those without livestock rendered cash or a household item instead: on occasions, their heriot was waived. Unfortunately, we do not possess information about the annual income or assets of peasant households, so we cannot know how readily a villein household could absorb the loss of its most valuable beast. Very occasionally, however, some insight is possible when a source provides an exceptional amount of detail about peasant assets. Assessments for royal taxation in the 1280s and 1290s indicate that the average peasant household in southern England possessed one horse, three cattle, a pig and twelve sheep, whilst in much of the rest of the country the average was two cattle and five sheep.[52] In the 1290s an ox cost around 12s., a horse (affer) 11s., a cow 9s. and an adult male sheep (wether) 16d.[53] Thus, if we take these figures at face value, the heriot of a best beast would have absorbed around 10s. from total livestock assets worth around 26s.: close to one-third. Put another way, it was the equivalent of 60 days' unskilled labour. Yet royal taxation records focus only on certain types of moveable goods, and were likely to underestimate them, so they do not provide a full picture of peasant assets. Some indication of the real asset base of one serf is revealed through a unique inventory of the estate of William Lene of Walsham, following his death in a fire in 1328. His heir rendered as heriot an ox worth 13s. 4d. from an estate containing *inter alia* a total of fourteen bovines, four horses, two pigs, eight piglets and 120 sheep, which meant the heriot amounted to less than 3 per cent of the total value.[54]

Heriot is routinely cited as one of the principal burdens of serfdom and, by extension, one of the levers for extracting high levels of surpluses from the unfree. Yet the reality was more complex. Heriot was principally a condition of tenure, including some free tenures, and it was seldom an incident of personal servility. Custom determined its local character, but it was usually the best beast. Its affordability can be assessed against the objective reference point of a day's wage for an unskilled labourer (seventy-two days' work for an ox paid as heriot, eight days' for a sheep) in the 1300s. Alternatively, the best beast amounted to perhaps one-third of the livestock assets of most households, although the rare survival of an inventory of all William Lene's moveable assets reveals that wealthier servile households could comfortably absorb the payment of a heriot. The loss of the best beast must have been difficult for poorer households to bear, even though the value of the heriot tended to decline with the size of the holding.[55]

Freedom and unfreedom: Labour services

The requirement to perform some form of personal service was a standard element of medieval landholding, with the type of service distinguishing the particular form of tenure. Hence, knights performed military service or monks performed religious services in return for a grant of land, whereas peasants might perform manual labour on the lord's demesne. Any form of *labour* service was inferior to military, religious or administrative service, and was susceptible to connotations of servility.[56] Yet holders of free tenures were often required to render labour services on the manorial demesne – mainly light services in the harvest, known as boon-works, and perhaps a few ploughing and harrowing services – and so they could not be used as a test of villein status.[57] Occasionally, we even find manorial lords liable to labour services. Thus, Henry de Holnworth held one-quarter of Matley manor (Cheshire) for one knight's service, but was also required to find six men annually for one day to make hay and to labour on earthworks at nearby Tintwistle. Similarly, Richard de Eton held half of Hattersley manor (Cheshire), in return for which he was required to find reapers for three days in the harvest and undertake some ploughing works in Lent.[58] Of course, neither Henry nor Richard would have been expected to perform such work in person, and seigniorial labour services were exceptionally rare, but their existence underlines the fragility of the conventional distinction between the types of services lords and peasants were expected to perform.

Contemporary lawyers were aware of such untidiness and so attempted to distinguish the types of labour service associated with free tenure from those due from servile tenure by focusing on the nature of the work to be undertaken. They emphasised the association between free tenure and 'honourable' labour services, which were mainly light, seasonal and reciprocal (and the lord fed the workers), and contrasted these with the more onerous and 'dishonourable' labour services attached to villein tenure. They also posited a distinction between the 'nominated' labour services of the free tenant, such as rendering harvest boon-works, and the 'uncertain' duties of the villein, where the exact tasks to be performed as week works or winter works were not specified and usually featured the most menial and disagreeable types of agricultural work on the lord's demesne, such as spade work, swilling the sty or moving muck.[59]

The association between the unspecified nature of many villein labour services, the heavy demands of week works, and the most arduous and disagreeable agricultural tasks explains why some historians have portrayed labour services as being highly characteristic of serfdom and its exploitative nature.[60] To some extent, this view has been influenced by the importance placed on labour services in the work of early historians, whose research on villeinage focused tightly on the nature of labour rent and the chronology of its decline.[61] This is captured in Hilton's statement that 'the most important ... aspect of unfree tenure was the performance of heavy labour service as part of rent'.[62] Yet the persistence of this view also owes something to the way in which, during the 1970s and 1980s, ideological approaches to preindustrial societies continued to regard the extraction of surplus labour as a central element in the seigniorial capacity to control and to appropriate the wealth of peasants.[63] In the 1990s Brenner portrayed the large size of demesnes and their dependence on labour services as the driving force behind the systematisation of English serfdom in the early thirteenth century and its capacity to extract economic surplus from villeins. For him, 'villein labour services were very much alive in later thirteenth-century England'.[64]

Brenner's views on labour services had been shaped by the earlier work of Postan, although Postan's analysis had not drawn on a substantial evidentiary base.[65] He himself had been heavily influenced by pioneering studies of villeinage, which had presumed the importance of labour services and concentrated exclusively on accessible documents from the estate records of the greater landlords, for which manorial sources survive in relative abundance. These were, however, the most conservative and bureaucratic, and the least typical, landlords. Since then, systemic research that has avoided either presuming the importance of labour services or placing an excessive reliance on the records of monastic landlords has revealed unequivocally that labour services were relatively unimportant. Data from hundreds of small manors in the Inquisitions Post Mortem shows that labour services were one of the least valuable components of rent and that, throughout England as a whole, money rents were four times more valuable than labour services.[66] Campbell and Bartley have shown that customary services represented just 12 per cent of the value of rental income on thousands of lay manors throughout England.[67] Their analysis also reveals clear regional patterns in the relative importance of labour services, which is summarised in Map 2.2. They were least relevant, at less than 10 per cent of the total value of all rents and services, over large tracts of England – notably the north, the north and west Midlands, and the south-west. Labour services made up between

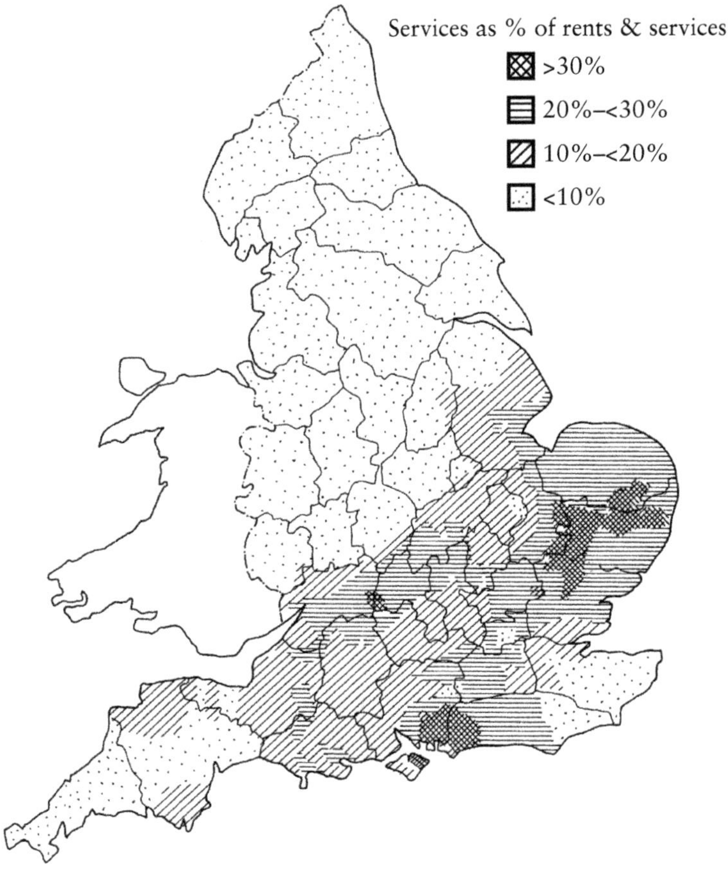

Map 2.2 Labour services expressed as a percentage of the value of all rents and services on lay manors in England 1300–48, from Inquisitions Post Mortem. Courtesy of B. M. S. Campbell, 'The agrarian problem in the early fourteenth century', *Past & Present*, 188 (2005): 3–70 (Map 4).

10 and 20 per cent in most of southern and south-central England, and were only consistently higher in East Anglia, the most populous region of the country.

The importance of labour services was also a function of the size and status of the manor. Heavy week works were mainly confined to the large classic manors of the most powerful landlords, especially Benedictine monasteries, bishoprics and aristocrats.[68] Where labour services were heavy, the cash component of the rent package was usually lower.[69] Labour services were lightest on the small lay manors.[70] For example, only five out of fourteen customary tenants on the small gentry manor of Walsham High Hall (Suffolk) rendered any week works, each owing on average sixteen half days over ten months: half a day in every nineteen days.[71] The discussion so far has been concerned with the liability for labour services, but in reality lords did not utilise all works available to them each year and instead allowed the tenant to pay a cash sum in lieu of any unused services (known as commutation). This was especially characteristic of week works, around half of which were commuted each year, although lords usually made fuller use of harvest services because this was the season when labour was most in demand.[72] The commutation of labour services further reduced the importance of labour services as a form of rent. An extensive assessment of these cash commutations has shown that they were largely fixed below market rates and affordable to the majority of villeins who owed them.[73] Indeed, the commutation rate for the half day work at Walsham was fixed at ½d. per work, equivalent to 1d. per day, which was half the prevailing market rate for unskilled labour.[74] Furthermore, serfs made choices about how hard to work when performing labour services for their lord.[75] Petty refusals to perform labour services and/or amercements for working badly are documented episodically in manorial court rolls. The productivity of customary labour in the performance of basic agricultural tasks was consistently lower than that of hired labour on those very rare occasions when the sources provide enough information for them to be compared directly.[76] Thus, serfs deployed tactics to reduce the value of labour services to lords even further, which may explain the latter's willingness to commute half of them to cash.

The strong association between heavier labour services, week works and the manors of the greater lords, and the relative absence of the first of these on the vast majority of the small manors of lesser lords, confirm the link between seigniorial power and the capacity to impose labour services.[77] But when all manorial types and the composition of seigniorial rental income are considered quantitatively, it is manifest that this classic incident of serfdom has acquired a higher profile than it deserves in the scholarship (Map

2.2). For all the attention devoted to labour services in the work of earlier historians, by the end of the thirteenth century they were neither 'the *raison d'être* of serfdom [nor] the principal form of rent'.[78] Labour services were unimportant as a form of rent throughout much of England and, even where they were regionally significant, such as in eastern England, they contributed little more than one-third of the rent on villein-holdings, even before commutations are factored into the equation.[79] There is no longer any doubt: in the pre-plague era, villein 'tenants did not face very heavy demands, and in particular owed relatively little labour service'.[80]

Freedom and unfreedom: Mill suit

The difficulties of separating servile from free obligations in any clean or decisive manner, and the complexities and contradictions that existed as a consequence, are powerfully illustrated by recent research into mill suit. The requirement for servile tenants to grind their corn at the mill of their lord (mill suit), and to render a fixed and non-negotiable toll (multure) for the privilege of doing so, was already established in eleventh-century England. Its origins are obscure, although in the generation or so after the Norman Conquest liability for mill suit was tightened and extended. Over the next two centuries the rights of lords to claim mill suit over their manorial tenantry (or sometimes the territory in which it was situated) were first clarified through customary usage, then reinforced through the expanding system of law. The legal status of mills and milling in medieval England was highly complex and intractable: it was mainly governed by customary law, but also featured in some convoluted contractual disputes in the common law.[81]

Regardless of the complex evolution of mill suit, by the late thirteenth century contemporaries associated it strongly with villein tenure.[82] This association resonated with Marxist historians, for whom a key characterisation of feudal class relations is the seigniorial control of economic monopolies backed by the legal system.[83] To them, mills and mill suit exemplified the view that serfdom involved extra-economic coercion and was the most lucrative of the monopolies of medieval lordship.[84] This perspective has endured. In the 1980s John Martin argued that the dominant ownership and control of grain mills by lords placed significant constraints on villeins, and in the 1990s Steven Justice believed that the existence of such widespread controls meant that 'milling rights were a perpetual irritant between tenants and landlords'.[85] Lucas has observed that for many historians mill suit is emblematic of the 'oppressive and privileged' nature of medieval ecclesiastical lordship.[86] Richard Holt argued that mill suit was largely confined to the villein sector, upon whom 'extortionate' rates of toll were imposed.[87] This viewpoint is apparently reinforced by research showing that mill revenues contributed a hefty 10 per cent of the total annual revenues of some ecclesiastical landlords.[88] Holt is certainly correct in his assessment that, in general, free tenants and outsiders paid lower rates of multure, probably determined by what the market would bear, whereas villeins paid at higher, fixed, rates.[89] Statute law recommended mill tolls of around 4–5 per cent, whereas villeins often paid between 5 and 8 per cent.[90]

Nevertheless, many of the claims about the ubiquity and onerousness of mill suit are no longer sustainable in the light of the most recent and wide-ranging research. This has revealed conclusively that the revenue from milling across most estates rarely exceeded 10 per cent, that it was usually under 5 per cent, and that lords did not monopolise milling: the most reliable estimate indicates that only 40 per cent of all English grain was milled in seigniorial mills, whose profitability depended not on enforcing suit of mill but on their ability to win a large share of the local market. The most valuable mills were located not in the south-east, where grain production was most commercialised, but in the north, where mills faced less competition for business and seigniorial controls over milling were strongest.[91] Mill suit was 'by no means uniform or straightforward in its application', and 'the extent to which suit of mill applied to, and was enforced upon, the tenants of a manor or a vill varied considerably throughout England'.[92] Hence English lords did not possess a monopoly on mills, mill suit was not confined to serfs or servile tenants, and its actual enforcement was variable even where tenants were theoretically liable for it.[93]

The demographic and commercial expansion of the twelfth and thirteenth centuries drove the construction of more mills, including the newly invented windmill as well as the traditional water, horse and hand mills.[94] This proliferation was also accompanied by some privatisation of ownership. In some cases, demesne mills had become alienated from seigniorial control and had passed into the hands of free and even villein tenants; in others, enterprising individuals had constructed their own mills, whose appearance was tolerated by their lords.[95] For example, of the 144 mills recorded in the Hundred Rolls of 1279 in Oxfordshire, sixty-eight (47 per cent) were held on free tenure and eleven (8 per cent) on customary tenure, leaving just sixty-five mills under direct seigniorial control; and an analysis of mills on the estates of twenty-eight ecclesiastical landlords estimates that around 40 per cent were in peasant hands.[96] These figures do not include peasant hand mills. The implications are clear: many mills did not have legal suit of mill attached to them; some lords had lost control of their own mills with suit attached; most seigniorial mills faced local competition for business; and, as a result, most consumers enjoyed a degree of choice over where to mill.[97] These forces weakened the seigniorial grip on, and capacity to enforce, mill suit.

Moreover, mill suit was not tightly attached to villeinage, which is why it was never deployed as a test of villein status. The post-Conquest redefinition of mill suit had resulted in some free tenants becoming liable for it, because it had been applied to areas of *territory* and not to a particular tenurial or personal status, especially in northern England.[98] By 1300 there is unequivocal evidence for liability for mill suit from free tenants on manors as far apart as Cheshire, Lancashire, Norfolk and Warwickshire, although examples are rarer in the south.[99] Even a handful of lower-status manorial lords were also required to perform suit of mill to their overlord, as when Sir John de Hyde and Lady Christina de Holyn of Mottram in Longdendale (Cheshire) both owed suit to their superior lord's mill.[100] Lords who owed suit of mill were expected to bring their own tenants with them, too.[101] Burgesses of some northern towns also owed mill suit.[102]

How rigorously did lords enforce their rights to mill suit? The only light on this issue is cast by the frequency of amercements for violating mill suit recorded in manorial courts. Langdon surveyed 1,318 court sessions between 1274 and 1347 from fifteen manors dispersed throughout England, discovering no evidence of violations on nine manors and fewer than one per annum on another three.[103] The absence of violations could mean either that every villein on these nine manors had observed and paid all mill suit in full, which seems highly unlikely, or that mill suit was either absent or weakly enforced: John Langdon preferred the latter interpretation and therefore deduced that on nearly 80 per cent of his sample mill suit was unimportant. Even on manors where violations did feature frequently, the levels of amercement were routinely low, usually 2d. or 3d. or a day's labour, and in some places lords commuted collective liability for mill suit to a negotiated cash sum.[104] On the basis of such wide-ranging and compelling evidence, Langdon concluded that 'coercion was never very strongly enforced'.[105] Other quantitative studies have confirmed the absence or insignificance of mill suit violations in the pre-plague period on smaller and lay manors in the south Midlands and East Anglia, while underlining that such breaches were altogether more frequent on monastic estates.[106] Lucas concurs that religious houses were especially attentive to their rights of mill, and he shows that monastic lords in the north of England were strictest: 'suit of mill violations were generally only considered to be an important issue in the north, with the exception of some of the more despotic religious houses in the south'.[107] Seigniorial ability to enforce suit of mill was stronger in the north of England and relatively weak in the south.[108] The latter – such as the great Benedictine abbeys of St Albans and Cirencester – did undertake periodic sweeps of enforcement, in which large numbers of tenants were fined for evasion.[109] The case studies later in this volume reveal, however, that even on three manors of St Albans abbey the total number of mill suit violations scarcely exceeded one per annum (see Table 3.1). Furthermore, the abbey did not maintain a consistent approach across all its manors, as is shown by the high frequency of violations at Norton as compared to their virtual absence from the much larger manor of Codicote (Chapters 8 and 9).

The complexities of mill ownership created some intriguing anomalies and potential conflicts in the enforcement of mill suit. Foremost among these was the existence of mills held by tenants on villein tenure, which were held heritably for a fixed annual rent with a variable entry fine payable on accession.[110] Most must have operated as commercial ventures, picking up business from free peasants and those villeins indifferent to evading mill suit. Furthermore, wherever a villein mill was the sole mill on the manor, it would have possessed the lord's rights to enforce suit of mill.

Where a demesne mill existed on manors where mills were also held on villein tenure, the lord was tacitly accepting that the competition would both divert some business from his own demesne mills and make breaches of mill suit more likely. The existence of such conflicts must explain why during the course of the thirteenth century some, especially ecclesiastical, lords made concerted efforts to recover mills on villein tenure.[111] Holt suggests that these powerful lords must have exerted legal and financial pressure on their servile tenants to return the mills.[112] This is certainly possible, but the most striking aspect of the process of mill recovery is the procedurally correct manner in which lords went about it. Lords did not seize the mills or eject the tenant arbitrarily, as was their right under the common law, but instead either purchased them or arranged a seemly transfer through a due process following the death of the existing tenant.[113]

From the early fourteenth century lords increasingly leased their own demesne mills to a third party for a term of years and at a fixed annual rent paid either in milled corn – 'multure' – or cash, rather than managing them directly through their officials.[114] In these circumstances, the lessee continued to receive the mill suit due from the manor's villeins, and the lord's officials would have supported the lessee by continuing to punish evasions in the manor court. This created another potentially odd situation, because if the lessee was a serf then one villein was demanding and enforcing mill suit from others. Villeins were not debarred from taking on the lease of a demesne mill: there are three unequivocal cases of this from the manor of Wakefield alone, where in the mid-1310s the mill of Rastrick (Yorkshire) was leased to a local man, Andrew Forester, who was a servile tenant of the manor.[115]

There is one further striking aspect to the changing seigniorial management of mill suit between the eleventh and thirteenth centuries. In the generation or so after the Norman Conquest, i.e. in the era *before* the development of the common law, lords enforced their will and imposed mill suit successfully on previously exempt sections of the population. In the early fourteenth century, i.e. in the era *after* the emergence of the common law, most of the evidence attests to seigniorial weakness, not strength. As we have seen, some landlords had alienated their mills, and many others were either unable or unwilling to enforce mill suit.[116] By this date, freemen and women could appeal to the royal courts if their lord attempted to impose mill suit on them. The lord's own manorial court sometimes heard pleas from local residents who claimed *not* to owe mill suit and, rather than dismiss such claims out of hand, it handled them according to a due process after which the lord's officials abided by the judgment (see Chapter 4).[117] Hence, the contrasting behaviour of lords in the pre- and post-common law eras is stark and instructive. If the common law of villeinage really had strengthened lordly powers over their dependent tenantry, then we would expect to find many examples of aggressive enforcement of mill suit and the seizure of mills on servile tenure recorded in early-fourteenth-century manorial courts. Yet such evidence is wanting. It would appear that the common law came to inhibit, not promote, arbitrary seigniorial behaviour (see Chapter 5)

This reappraisal of the relationship between English villeinage and the economic monopoly of milling has drawn on the latest research, based on large samples and rigorous quantification of the data. Mill suit was absent from many manors, and was not enforced very frequently even where it was present. Hence, Langdon's verdict from his extensive analysis of milling on hundreds of manors is that 'mill revenue always depended much more on consumer demand than the coercive efforts of lords ... customers generally came to mills because they wanted to, not because they were forced there'.[118] The most enthusiastic enforcers of mill suit were ecclesiastical landlords, but even on these estates Lucas concludes that, with few exceptions, 'the general attitude amongst the larger ecclesiastical lords was to maximise the income from the mills on their manors, rather than to ensure monopolistic control of them'.[119]

Of course, downplaying the role of coercion is not to deny the tensions surrounding mill suit, especially among villeins. Without doubt, mill suit and its fixed tolls were irritants to those subject to them. They were consequently worth evading and became the occasion (if not always the reason) for social unrest on some estates in the late thirteenth and early fourteenth centuries.[120] For example, early historians regarded St Albans abbey as an uncompromising enforcer of its seigniorial rights – drawing on prevailing stereotypes of serfdom – and cited its harsh policies on mill suit as a running source of tension with its tenants, and a contributing factor to the ferocity of the revolt there in 1381.[121] Yet the reality of mill suit on the St Albans estate is that its enforcement was inconsistent, highly variable from manor to manor, and, in general, infrequent (see Chapters 8–10). Some lords must have resorted to coercion to enforce their milling rights, in contravention of custom and norms of behaviour, but, in general, 'this kind of behaviour was the exception rather than the rule … it is very clear from the English evidence that no lord, no matter how powerful, could fully control their tenants' efforts … to avoid suit'.[122]

As we have seen, for some historians mill suit epitomised how economic monopolies extracted surpluses from serfs and symbolised the oppressions of villeinage. Yet these persistent stereotypes and generalisations are undermined when we examine how mill suit operated in practice. This reality also reveals two wider points about villeinage. First, as mill suit shows, it is difficult to disentangle the incidents of serfdom from the incidents of freedom in any clean and definitive manner, which, by extension, should warn against sweeping generalisations about how the condition of the serf contrasted with that of the free. Free tenure was not universally free of liability to economic monopolies, just as servile tenure was not universally liable to them. Second, mill suit exposes the dangers of crude generalisations about the weight of English serfdom, because the ameliorating effects of the variations in liability for mill suit were further enhanced by the wide variations in enforcement from manor to manor. The significance of these points for a reappraisal of our understanding of the dynamics of fourteenth-century society should not be understated. Mill suit was certainly an imposition, and where it existed it prevented households from seeking the cheapest rate for milling their grain. It was not, however, imposed on perhaps half of villein households and it was not even consistently enforced on the other half. In reality, liability for mill suit was not a universal condition of villeinage and, even among those liable, enforcement was often variable or lax.

Conclusion

On the eve of the Black Death servile land represented at most one-third of the arable in England, and half the rural population were hereditary serfs. Tenurial and personal servility were most prominent on the large manors held by high-status landlords, although the vast majority of manors were small and dominated by free tenures. As we saw in Chapter 1, contemporary lawyers were able to draw a line of sorts between the free and the unfree, but in practice this line was thin and porous, and represented an 'artificial crystallisation' of the differences between unfreedom and freedom.[123] As a result, the courts of common law 'never succeeded in forcing villeinage into any well-ordered, logical system'.[124] Statute law would have been a much better legal vehicle for creating watertight legislation to subjugate villeins (see Chapter 5), but it was never deployed in this way: in any event, the common law of villeinage established that relations between lords and villeins were a matter for lords to determine, not for the state.

The legal distinction between freedom and unfreedom was clear at both ends of the continuum, although the boundary line separating them was faint and interwoven. A handful of lords, and many more freemen, paid heriot and rendered labour services, both incidents traditionally associated with unfreedom. Freemen, especially in northern England, were routinely liable for the most prominent economic monopoly associated with unfreedom: the requirement to grind grain at the seigniorial mill at a fixed rate of toll. Indeed, the reality of mill suit illuminates how villeinage in general actually functioned on the eve of the Black Death: it was widespread, but 'riddled with exceptions and complications'.[125] Perhaps less than one-half of all villeins were liable to it, enforcement was variable and lax even where it was liable, some landlords had lost control over milling, and some villeins legitimately owned mills. Indeed, its history reveals how lords were able to wield considerable powers to subjugate and to impose their will on their dependent peasantry around 1100, i.e. *before* the creation of the common law, but in its wake they were decidedly constrained in their actions.

The practical reality of heriot, labour services and mill suit should caution against drawing clean and facile distinctions between the benefits of freedom and the burdens of unfreedom. They should also caution against considering serfdom as a discrete and separate entity from freedom, but instead encourage the contextualisation of serfdom within the wider institutional framework of manorial lordship. Serfdom was one, albeit important, element in the fabric of medieval society, and the way in which it operated raised costs, generated inefficiencies and created barriers to economic development. In this regard, it possessed both similarities with and differences from tenurial freedom. Their consequences for the welfare of the mass of English people, and for the development of the English economy, on the eve of the Black Death are considered in more detail in Chapter 6.

Notes

1 For recent surveys, see Rigby, *English Society*, pp. 17–144; Fryde, *Peasants and Landlords*, pp. 8–28; Briggs, 'English serfdom'; Hatcher, 'Lordship'; Schofield, *Peasants and Historians*, pp. 91–108; and Gibbs, *Lordship, State Formation*, pp. 117–20.

2 See, for example, the feather-light footnoting in Dimmock, *The Origin of Capitalism*, pp. 79–87.

3 Vinogradoff, *Villeinage*, pp. 134, 138–77; W. J. Ashley, *An Introduction to English Economic History and Theory*, Vol. I (London: Longmans Green, 1909), pp. 19–20, 38.

4 Rigby, *English Society*, pp. 29, 49–57; Hatcher, 'English serfdom', pp. 8–26; Hatcher, 'Lordship'; B. M. S. Campbell, 'The agrarian problem in the early fourteenth century', *Past & Present*, 188 (2005): 3–70 (pp. 37–44); Bailey, 'Villeinage in England'.

5 B. M. S. Campbell, 'The land', in R. Horrox and W. M. Ormrod, eds, *A Social History of England, 1200–1500* (Cambridge: Cambridge University Press, 2012), pp. 179–237 (p. 236).

6 B. M. S. Campbell and K. Bartley, *England on the Eve of the Black Death: An Atlas of Lay Lordship, Land and Wealth, 1300–49* (Manchester: Manchester University Press, 2006); J. Kanzaka, 'Manorialisation and demographic pressure in medieval England: An analysis of the Hundred Rolls of 1279–1280', *Journal of Historical Geography*, 60 (2018): 11–23.

7 Campbell, 'The agrarian problem', p. 36.

8 Bailey, *After the Black Death*, pp. 26, 298.

9 For this and what follows, see Campbell and Bartley, *England on the Eve*, pp. 69–96, 251–68; Campbell, 'The agrarian problem'; and Campbell, 'The land', pp. 190–5. This work is based mainly on the information contained within Inquisitions Post Mortem for 1,441 lay estates covering 4,090 manors between 1300 and 1349, plus ecclesiastical taxation from 1291 and 1341.

10 For the specific association between Benedictine monasteries and large manors dominated by villein tenure, see Campbell and Bartley,

England on the Eve, p. 205; Kosminsky, *Studies*, pp. 105, 107; and Kanzaka, 'Manorialisation', pp. 19–20.

11 Kosminsky, *Studies*, pp. 96–8. The average size of a manor was 507 acres of arable; the average large manor possessed 1,600 acres, medium 675 acres and small 224 acres.

12 Campbell and Bartley, *England on the Eve*, pp. 80–2; Kosminsky, *Studies*, pp. 99–101.

13 J. Kanzaka, 'Villein rents in thirteenth-century England: An analysis of the Hundred Rolls of 1279–1280', *Economic History Review*, 55 (2000): 593–618 (p. 598); B. Wells-Furby, *The Berkeley Estate 1281–1417: Its Economy and Development*, Bristol and Gloucestershire Monographs, 1 (n.p.: Bristol and Gloucestershire Archaeological Society, 2012), pp. 117–18.

14 Campbell and Bartley, *England on the Eve*, Map 14.7; Campbell, 'The agrarian problem', Maps 1 and 2; Kanzaka, 'Manorialisation'.

15 Larson, *Conflict and Compromise*, pp. 62–4; R. H. Britnell, C. Etty and A. King, eds, *The Black Book of Hexham: A Northern Monastic Estate in 1379* (Hexham: Hexham Local History Society, 2011), pp. 7–13.

16 Miller, *The Abbey and Bishopric*, map opposite p. 76.

17 B. M. S. Campbell, 'The complexity of manorial structure in medieval Norfolk: A case study', *Norfolk Archaeology*, 39 (1986): 225–61; Rigby, *English Society*, pp. 40–5; M. Bailey, ed., *The English Manor c. 1200 to c. 1500* (Manchester: Manchester University Press, 2002), pp. 5–10; M. Bailey, *Medieval Suffolk: An Economic and Social History 1200 to 1500* (Woodbridge: Boydell Press, 2007), pp. 27–34; Kanzaka, 'Manorialisation', pp. 16–23.

18 Campbell and Bartley, *England on the Eve*, p. 254.

19 Kosminsky, *Studies*, p. 269, but see R. H. Britnell, 'Minor landlords in England and medieval agrarian capitalism', in T. H. Aston, ed., *Landlords, Peasants and Politics in Medieval England* (Cambridge: Cambridge University Press, 1987), pp. 227–46 (pp. 227–8); and Bailey, *English Manor*, pp. 19–20. For a translated selection of material from the small lay manor of Walsham High Hall, see R. Lock, ed., *The Court Rolls of Walsham le Willows 1303–1350*, Suffolk Records Society, 41 (Woodbridge: Boydell Press, 1998); and A. McLaughlin and M. Bailey, eds, *Manorial Account Rolls and Rentals of Walsham le Willows, 1327 to 1559*, Suffolk Records Society, 68 (Woodbridge: Boydell Press, 2025).

20 Bailey, *The Decline of Serfdom*, pp. 115–16, 128–30, 137–40.

21 Campbell and Bartley, *England on the Eve*, p. 81.

22 E. Searle, *Lordship and Community: Battle Abbey and Its Banlieu 1066–1538* (Toronto: Pontifical Institute of Medieval Studies, 1974), pp. 170–4, 184.

23 Kosminsky, *Studies*, pp. 199–200.
24 Pollock and Maitland, *The History of English Law*, Vol. I, pp. 390–6; Vinogradoff, *Villeinage*, 89–126.
25 M. K. McIntosh, 'The privileged villeins of the English Ancient Demesne', *Viator*, 7 (1976): 295–328 (pp. 296–7, 303–12, 325).
26 Ibid., pp. 303–5.
27 V. McLoughlin, 'Medieval Rothley: Leicestershire manor, soke and parish' (PhD thesis, University of Leicester, 2006), pp. 76, 83–5, 94, 104.
28 Ibid., p. 115.
29 Ibid., pp. 99–101.
30 E. Miller and J. Hatcher, *Medieval England: Rural Society and Economic Change 1086–1348* (London: Longman, 1978), p. 119; Vinogradoff, *Villeinage*, 106–7.
31 Hilton, *A Medieval Society*, pp. 142–3.
32 R. S. Hoyt, *The Royal Demesne in English Constitutional History, 1066–1272* (New York: Greenwood Press, 1968), pp. 196–207.
33 McIntosh, 'Privileged villeins', pp. 316, 320–6.
34 Homans, *English Villagers*, pp. 276–83; Dyer, 'Memories of freedom', pp. 279–83, 286–8.
35 Pollock and Maitland, *The History of English Law*, Vol. I, p. 394.
36 Vinogradoff, *Villeinage*, pp. 371–2.
37 Hatcher, 'English serfdom', pp. 12–14.
38 Hyams, *King, Lords*, p. 234.
39 P. Freedman, *Images of the Medieval Peasant* (Stanford: Stanford University Press, 1999), p. 83.
40 Levett, *Studies*, p. 245; Poos and Bonfield, *Select Cases*, p. clxviii.
41 J. S. Thompson, ed., *Hundreds, Manors and Parishes*, Bedfordshire Historical Record Society, 69 (Bedford: Bedfordshire Historical Record Society, 1998), pp. 190–203.
42 Faith, *The English Peasantry*, pp. 257–8.
43 G. C. Baugh, ed., *Victoria County History, Shropshire*, Vol. IV, *Agriculture* (London: Institute of Historical Research, 1989), p. 36; M. Clough, ed., *Two Estate Surveys of the Fitzalan Earls of Arundel*, Sussex Record Society, 67 ([Lewes]: Sussex Record Society, 1969), pp. xxxi, 77.
44 Baugh, *VCH, Shropshire*, Vol. IV, p. 113.
45 For the Ely estate, see Salzman, *Victoria County History, Cambridgeshire*, Vol. II, p. 64; and Cam, *Selected Historical Essays*, p. 17. For St Albans, see D. Noy, ed., *The Winslow Manor Court Books, 1322–1377*, Buckinghamshire Record Society, 35 ([Aylesbury]: Buckinghamshire Record Society, 2011), pp. 124, 239, 241, 365, 367, 375, 441; and Levett, *Studies*, p. 193. For the Netley abbey manor of Totton (Hampshire), see TNA, SC2/201/55.

46 U. Rees, 'The leases of Haughmond abbey, Shropshire', *Midland History*, 8 (1983): 14–28 (p. 22).

47 Noy, *The Winslow Manor Court Books, 1327–1377*, p. 248; J. M. Wilson, ed., *Account Rolls of the Priory of Worcester, 1521–2*, Worcestershire Historical Society, 24 (Oxford: J. Parker, 1907), p. 10.

48 Vinogradoff, *Villeinage*, pp. 160–2; Hyams, *King, Lords*, pp. 77–8.

49 Textbooks and estate studies reinforce this point. For example, this was the practice on the vast estate of the bishop of Winchester; P. Arthur, 'The Black Death and mortality: A reassessment', in C. Given-Wilson, ed., *Fourteenth-Century England*. Vol. VI (Woodbridge: Boydell Press, 2010), pp. 49–72 (pp. 60–2); Miller and Hatcher, *Medieval England: Rural Society*, p. 130.

50 Bailey, *Medieval Suffolk*, pp. 56–7.

51 W. Farrer, ed., *Some Court Rolls of the Lordship, Wapentakes and Demesne Manors of Thomas, Earl of Lancaster 1323–4 in County of Lancaster* ([Manchester]: Record Society of Lancashire and Cheshire, 1901), pp. 91–3; H. P. R. Finberg, *Tavistock Abbey: A Study in the Social and Economic History of Devon* (Newton Abbot: David and Charles, 1969), pp. 76–7.

52 P. Slavin, 'Peasant livestock husbandry in late-thirteenth-century Suffolk: Economy, environment and society', in Kowaleski et al., *Peasants and Lords*, pp. 3–26 (p. 9).

53 D. L. Farmer, 'Prices and wages', in H. E. Hallam, ed., *The Agrarian History of England and Wales*, Vol. II, *1042–1350* (Cambridge: Cambridge University Press, 1988), pp. 716–817 (p. 748).

54 Lock, *The Court Rolls 1303–1350*, pp. 132–5. The accidental death of William in a fire explains the compilation of an inventory of his goods on the day he died, which just happened to be enrolled in the court rolls. This represents an exceptional survival of a villein's moveable goods.

55 Kanzaka, 'Villein rents', p. 613 n. 63.

56 Hyams, *King, Lords*, p. 197.

57 DeWindt, *Land and People*, pp. 68–9; Faith, *The English Peasantry*, p. 262.

58 J. Harrop, P. Booth and S. Harrop, eds, *Extents of the Lordship of Longdendale, 1360*, Record Society of Lancashire and Cheshire, 140 (n.p.: Record Society of Lancashire and Cheshire, 2005), pp. 19, 21, 65, 67.

59 For seasonal labour services on free tenures, see Homans, *English Villagers*, pp. 249–50; and Clough, *Two Estate Surveys*, pp. xxxi, 6. For more menial and regular works attached to villein tenure, see Vinogradoff, *Villeinage*, pp. 170–1; Pollock and Maitland, *The*

History of English Law, Vol. I, pp. 370–2; and Faith, *The Moral Economy,* pp. 202–4.

60 For a general survey of labour services, see Miller and Hatcher, *Medieval England*, pp. 121–8. For the association between week works and villeinage, see Hilton, *Medieval Society*, pp. 131–40, 154; P. Franklin, 'Politics in manorial court rolls: The tactics, social composition, and aims of a pre-1381 peasant movement', in Razi and Smith, *Medieval Society*, pp. 162–98 (pp. 175–9); Miller and Hatcher, *Medieval England*, p. 117; Miller, *The Abbey and Bishopric*, p. 129; and Kosminsky, *Studies*, pp. 130, 330.

61 For a survey, see Bailey, *The Decline of Serfdom*, pp. 48–52.

62 Hilton, *Medieval Society*, p. 129.

63 J. E. Martin, *Feudalism to Capitalism: Peasant and Landlord in English Agrarian Development* (Basingstoke: Macmillan, 1983), pp. 8–12, 19.

64 Brenner, 'Rises and declines', pp. 263–8 (quotation p. 264).

65 Brenner, 'Agrarian class structure', pp. 20–2, and 'Rises and declines', p. 264, are based on Postan, 'Medieval agrarian society', pp. 603–8, and M. Postan, 'The chronology of labour services', *Transactions of the Royal Historical Society*, 4th series, 20 (1937): 169–93.

66 Campbell and Bartley, *England on the Eve*, pp. 253–4, 265.

67 Ibid., pp. 253–4, Graph 14.2(b).

68 Kosminsky, *Studies*, pp. 599–607; Kanzaka, 'Villein rents', pp. 605–6; Dyer, 'Villeins, bondsmen', p. 426; Bailey, 'Villeinage in England', 436; Bailey, *The Decline of Serfdom*, pp. 48–52.

69 Kanzaka, 'Villein rents', pp. 607–8.

70 Rigby, *English Society*, pp. 42–3.

71 McLaughlin and Bailey, *Manorial Account Rolls*, pp. 4–5, 15. This example is provided because of the rarity of such detail surviving from such manors.

72 Rigby, *English Society*, p. 75; Raftis, *Peasant Economic Development*, pp. 47–62; Campbell, 'The agrarian problem', pp. 36–8; Bailey, 'Villeinage in England', p. 438.

73 Kanzaka, 'Villein rents', pp. 598–608, 614–17.

74 Bailey and McLaughlin, *Manorial Account Rolls*, p. 32.

75 Ogilvie, 'Economics and history', pp. 332–3.

76 D. Stone, 'The productivity of hired and customary labour: Evidence from Wisbech Barton in the fourteenth century', *Economic History Review*, 50 (1997): 640–656.

77 Martin, *Feudalism to Capitalism*, pp. 33–4.

78 Campbell, 'The agrarian problem', p. 38; Campbell, 'The land', pp. 212–13.

79 Hatcher, 'English serfdom', pp. 10–12; Campbell, 'The agrarian problem', pp. 37–40.
80 Dyer, 'Memories of freedom', p. 289.
81 The most comprehensive and recent introduction is Lucas, *Ecclesiastical Lordship*, pp. 269–82.
82 J. Langdon, *Mills in the Medieval Economy: England 1300–1540* (Oxford: Oxford University Press, 2004), p. 275; Lucas, *Ecclesiastical Lordship*, p. 279; Bailey, *The Decline of Serfdom*, pp. 55–6.
83 Rigby, *English Society*, p. 26.
84 For overviews, see ibid., pp. 33–4; Holt, *The Mills*, pp. 36–53; Bennett, *Life on the English Manor*, pp. 130–3, 137; Levett, *Studies*, pp. 202–5; and M. Bloch, 'Avènement et conquêtes du moulin à eau', *Annales*, 7 (1935): 538–63.
85 Martin, *Feudalism to Capitalism*, pp. 27–8, 41, 43; S. Justice, *Writing and Rebellion: England in 1381* (Berkeley: University of California Press, 1984), p. 136.
86 Lucas, *Ecclesiastical Lordship*, p. 45; see also Dimmock, *The Origin of Capitalism*, p. 65.
87 Holt, *The Mills*, pp. 50–2.
88 Ibid., pp. 82–3; Rigby, *English Society*, pp. 33–4; Lucas, *Ecclesiastical Lordship*, pp. 269, 312.
89 Holt, *The Mills*, pp. 50–2, 80–1.
90 Although John Langdon argues that villeins would take their business elsewhere if the lord attempted to impose higher rates than these on villeins; Langdon, *Mills*, pp. 261, 277–85.
91 J. Langdon, 'Lord and peasant consumerism in the milling industry of early fourteenth-century England', *Past & Present*, 145 (1994): 3–46 (pp. 5, 31, 22–5); Lucas, *Ecclesiastical Lordship*, pp. 312–3; Campbell and Bartley, *England on the Eve*, pp. 279, 288–95.
92 First quote from Langdon, *Mills*, p. 257; the second is from Lucas, *Ecclesiastical Lordship*, p. 282.
93 See, for example, Bailey, *The Decline of Serfdom*, pp. 107, 115, 124, 129, 138–9, 201–2, 223, 262; and Woods, *Medieval Hadleigh*, p. 119.
94 For the general background, see Holt, *The Mills*, pp. 107–16; and Langdon, *Mills*, pp. 8–20, 34–40.
95 Holt, *The Mills*, pp. 57–8; Langdon, *Mills*, pp. 55–6, 218–27; Lucas, *Ecclesiastical Lordship*, pp. 322–5.
96 Holt, *The Mills*, pp. 54–5; Lucas, *Ecclesiastical Lordship*, p. 319, Table 10.2.
97 Langdon, *Mills*, pp. 17–19, 286–7; Lucas, *Ecclesiastical Lordship*, pp. 319–20; Bailey, 'Villeinage', pp. 446–7.

98 Lucas, *Ecclesiastical Lordship*, pp. 272–83; Langdon, *Mills*, pp. 274–6.
99 Langdon, *Mills*, p. 276; Lucas, *Ecclesiastical Lordship*, pp. 282–3.
100 Harrop et al., *Extents*, pp. 48–9, 67.
101 Langdon, *Mills*, pp. 261, 265.
102 Lucas, *Ecclesiastical Lordship*, p. 272 n. 23.
103 Langdon, *Mills*, p. 284, Table 6.5; Bailey, 'Villeinage', pp. 447–8.
104 Holt, *The Mills*, pp. 45–6.
105 Ibid., p. 286.
106 Bailey, *Medieval Suffolk*, p. 57; Bailey, *The Decline of Serfdom*, pp. 108, 115, 129, 139, 202, 262, 446–7.
107 Lucas, *Ecclesiastical Lordship*, p. 285.
108 Campbell and Bartley, *England on the Eve*, p. 290.
109 Langdon, 'Lord and peasant consumerism', pp. 23–4.
110 Holt, *The Mills*, 58, 60; Langdon, *Mills*, 190.
111 Holt, *The Mills*, pp. 61–8; Langdon, *Mills*, pp. 55–6.
112 Holt, *The Mills*, pp. 60–1. Although not all ecclesiastical landlords either attempted to recover mills in customary tenure or succeeded in doing so; Lucas, *Ecclesiastical Lordship*, p. 320.
113 Holt, *The Mills*, pp. 60, 66.
114 Ibid., pp. 71–7.
115 Lister, *Court Rolls 1315–1317*, pp. 18, 155 (for the lease of the mill for £21 per annum), and pp. 83–4, 105, 109, 118, 193 (juror and hereditary tenant of customary land for services). In 1351 Thomas Culpon, villein tenant, leased three mills around Warley (Yorkshire) from the lord, and in 1360 another villein tenant, John del Fery, leased the demesne mill at Horbury (Yorkshire) with suit of mill. M. Habberjam, M. O'Regan, B. Hale and C. M. Fraser, eds, *The Court Rolls of the Manor of Wakefield from October 1350 to September 1352*, Yorkshire Archaeological Society, Wakefield Court Roll Series, 6 (Leeds: Yorkshire Archaeological Society, 1985), pp. 34, 36, 56. C. J. Watson, ed., *The Court Rolls of the Manor of Wakefield from 5 October 1360 to 28 September 1361*, Yorkshire Archaeological and Historical Society (Leeds: Yorkshire Archaeological and Historical Society, 2019), p. 38 for the lease and p. 124 for his status as a tenant of unfree land.
116 Lucas, *Ecclesiastical Lordship*, pp. 276–87 (quotation p. 286).
117 Lister, *Court Rolls*, p. 192; Troup, *The Court Rolls*, pp. 239, 244, 251.
118 Langdon, *Mills*, pp. 286–7.
119 Lucas, *Ecclesiastical Lordship*, p. 321.
120 Holt, *The Mills*, pp. 40–5; Lucas, *Ecclesiastical Lordship*, pp. 284–7.

121 For a fuller discussion of this point, see Chapters 8 and 9; for a brief summary of the conventional narrative around St Albans abbey, its tenants and mill suit, see Lucas, *Ecclesiastical Lordship*, pp. 40–1.
122 Ibid., p. 286.
123 Vinogradoff, *Villeinage*, p. 130; see also Eldridge, *Law and the Medieval Village Community*, p. 108.
124 Hyams, *King, Lords*, p. 81; see also Vinogradoff, *Villeinage*, p. 177.
125 Langdon, *Mills*, p. 278.

3

Serfdom in practice: Certainty and uncertainty

In the Middle Ages common law lawyers stressed that the various exactions associated with free tenure were known and fixed, whereas those associated with villein tenure were precarious because the latter was held at the will of the lord.[1] Britton, the late-thirteenth-century commentator, stated 'the very essence of villeinage is uncertainty ... serfs hold only from day to day at the will of their lords and for no certain services', and the early-fourteenth-century *Mirror of Justices* agreed: 'there is nothing certain in their services'.[2] To reinforce this distinction between the certainty of freedom and the uncertainty of unfreedom, the rent for free tenures was sometimes described as *servicia certa et nominata* ('services certain and named'), whereas the villein tenures were held in return for *servicia debita et consueta* ('services owed and customary') or *pro serviciis et consuetudinibus faciendis* ('for rendering services and customs').[3] Contemporary lawyers emphasised the contrast between the certainty of the 'nominated' labour services of the free tenant, such as rendering specific harvest boon-works, and the uncertainty faced by the villein who did not know what agricultural tasks would have to be performed as 'week works'.[4] The ostensibly pliable and unfixed nature of villein services is captured in a well-known passage in the mid-thirteenth-century legal treatise known as Bracton: 'where one cannot know in the evening the service to be rendered in the morning, that is where one is bound to do whatever one is bid'.[5]

Those historians who focus on the social and cultural dimension of serfdom in preference to its economic implications regard this issue of 'uncertainty' – meaning the precariousness of the villeins' rent, services and relationship with their lord – as being central to understanding the lived experience of serfs.[6] Freedman, for instance, associates uncertainty with arbitrary and oppressive lordship (whether real or potential), and sees it as the distinguishing characteristic of serfdom in medieval Europe.[7] If we apply this to early-fourteenth-century England, the main possible sources of precarity were the absence of any legally secure rights of possession in villein land and the lord's theoretical ability to increase its rent and services; the lord's scope to impose variable servile exactions or to charge large sums for them without warning; and, finally, the villein's lack of legal recourse in the event of a dispute.[8]

Brenner pointed repeatedly to the 'arbitrary' dues and fines imposed on the unfree, and likewise Hilton regarded 'heavy and arbitrary monetary exactions' as the essence of seigniorial power and the primary source of tension between lords and villeins.[9] According to Phillipp Schofield, the main threat to serfs from lordship lay in the political nature of rent in general, and the existence of these 'unfixed customs' in particular.[10] Dyer, too, noted 'that rents depended upon the lord's power, and that therefore lords were able to demand payments according to their needs and above market rates':[11] consequently, 'there was always the nagging fear, which was occasionally justified, that a lord would make an abrupt demand for [for example] a very high entry fine'.[12] He places particular emphasis on the fact that the sums payable for 'variable, uncertain and occasional dues', notably as tallage, entry fines, merchet, chevage, leyrwite and licences to educate, were not specified anywhere, with the implication that they could be hiked to exceptional levels: 'these unfixed payments were dangerous areas for villeins ... lords' arbitrary powers increasingly took the form of financial penalties ... better off tenants feared that their savings would disappear in large fines'.[13] Edmund Fryde argued that 'it was the essence of servile tenure and status that anything that suited the lord's interest might be demanded ... villeins were left without any rights in the relations with their lords'.[14] Dimmock states that many servile dues 'could be imposed arbitrarily at the will of lords ... armed with these arbitrary powers, lords were able to increase the proportion of their income at the expense of the peasants, and this ability was backed by the threat of military force': he asserts that 'entry fines and marriage fines offered lords the best source for profit and these rose in the 1310s when peasants could least afford them'.[15] Thus, historians who stress the uncertainty of villeinage see villeins as being ensnared within a system of extra-economic extraction, in which, as Brenner put it, 'the villein as the lord's property was subject to the lord's arbitrary levies and was unable to leave the manor without the lord's permission'.[16] Vulnerable to uncertain levies and unable to run away, the villeins' best chance was thus to agitate for greater certainty in the levying of such incidents.[17]

Here we assess these views by establishing the extent and degree of precarity in these areas, drawing on the large corpus of research into the practice of villeinage. First, we examine the types of villein tenure, the degree of certainty of the head rents owed for the land – mainly labour services and the cash rent – and the security of the tenancy, including the ability of the tenant to pass the land onto heirs after his death (a *post mortem* transfer) or to sell it to anyone else during his lifetime (an *inter vivos* transfer). Then we consider how variable, precarious and affordable were the sums levied through occasional and 'uncertain' incidents. Particular attention is devoted here to the entry fines payable on admission to villein land, because they provided a means by which lords could raise rents and increase levels of extraction from serfs. Our analysis is based on large samples and averages drawn from as many data points as possible, in contrast to the approach of some historians who have preferred to cherry-pick specific anecdotes from the sources and invite us to judge serfdom from extreme examples of its practice. But neither the economic implications nor the social experience of serfdom can be properly assessed without establishing norms – what was typical – securely.[18]

A recurrent feature of the scholarship is a tendency to describe the behaviour of lords who appear to have raised large sums for variable incidents as 'extortionate', 'oppressive', 'rapacious' and 'exorbitant', without actually clarifying or defining what thresholds had to be reached to be so adjudged.[19] One possible threshold might be to regard any rent paid to a landlord by a serf as exploitative, since it would represent the 'surplus labour' of the peasant whether rendered directly as labour services or indirectly as labour invested in generating produce for sale in order to pay cash fines and rent.[20] A second possibility is to regard a certain level of rent as being justified, because landlords provided the public goods of defence and justice in exchange for land and personal subjection: in this scenario, only the rent set above the cost of those public goods could be deemed exploitative.[21] Quantifying the value of these public goods is, of course, problematic, and contemporaries did not attempt to match the level of rents on the holdings of their serfs with some assessment of the price of public goods. A third possibility is to accept that landlords possessed land as 'private property', irrespective of the provision of justice and defence, and therefore were entitled to charge rent: in this scenario the level of rent would be exploitative only if it was above the economic level set by supply and demand. Adopting this threshold, however, throws up some interesting challenges. We can seldom be certain what *was* the level of economic rent at any place and time, and if serfs paid *below* the level would we then be forced to conclude that they were 'exploiting' their lords or that their lords were 'philanthropic'?

There are thus many pitfalls in attempting to define what threshold has to be reached in order for rents and fines to be regarded as 'exploitative' and 'rapacious', or indeed 'reasonable'. Framing discussions of the level of servile rents and incidents through such labels involves a moral judgement, which arguably reveals more about the historian making it than the institution being judged. In order to avoid such pitfalls, wherever possible I will seek to compare the level of villein rents, entry fines and payments for licences to sublet with the prevailing market value for land, i.e. the level that others would be willing to pay through the price mechanism of the time. For those variable incidents where the competitive price mechanism did not apply, such as merchet, leyrwite and chevage, I will seek to establish the average or standard charge, rather than dealing with exceptional outliers, and to compare this with the mean day wage for a labourer or, where available, the value of a serf's total assets. This approach provides the reader with some degree of contextualisation based on a quantifiable, contemporary reference point.[22]

Villein tenures

As we have seen, around 35 per cent of the arable land in pre-plague England was designated servile (also known as villein, customary, native, bond). It was widely distributed, but it predominated on certain types of manors (such as large manors held by Benedictine monasteries) and certain areas of the country (such as the north). Some manors had no villein land, and the most typical form of English manor – small and held by a lesser lay lord – was dominated by free tenures. Customary tenure was not the universal norm, and rents from villein land accounted for under half of all estimated seigniorial income.[23] This provides an important context to the following discussion.

Head rents

In the period 1280–1348 the majority of unfree land was held for 'services', or what I shall call villein service tenure. This comprised a mixed annual rent package made up of various elements in different combinations: labour services; renders in kind (such as grain, Easter eggs, hens at Christmas); cash payments; and a range of occasional dues such as a fine to enter the holding, a fine to marry (merchet), a death duty (heriot), suit of mill and tallage.[24] According to one recent estimate, in the 1340s perhaps 80 per cent of all servile land was held on a service tenancy.[25]

To what extent could the lord increase the rent package of the service tenancy at will? The occasional levies – such as merchet and entry fines – are considered later on (pp. 94–112), and so here we concentrate on the annual 'head' rent of renders in cash, kind and labour services. A few historians have adopted the Bractonian view of services and so suppose that a lord could impose additional labour services on the villein-holding without warning.[26] There are some examples of lords increasing the level of labour services on villein-holdings, although these date mainly from the early thirteenth century, when many were taking their demesnes back into direct management and consequently were clarifying the nature and extent of labour services owed to them.[27] For example, the reorganisation of tenurial structures and dues in the early thirteenth century on the five Polden Hill (Somerset) manors of Glastonbury abbey involved an increase in labour services between the 1180s and the 1230s, although thereafter there was little change.[28] In general, after the mid-thirteenth century attempts to increase levels of labour services were rare and usually provoked confrontation with, and serious resistance from, villeins.[29]

In the same vein, the principal cash rents, renders in kind and labour services due from villein-holdings (often called 'rents of assize') throughout England were largely fixed and ossified after the middle of the thirteenth century, and this was even the case on the estates of the most powerful landlords.[30] Estate studies provide many illustrations of this phenomenon.[31] For instance, the level of cash assize rents and labour services due from villein-holdings on the East Anglian manors of Canterbury Cathedral Priory hardly changed between the mid-thirteenth century and the 1320s.[32] Thus, the head rents on villein service tenancies were, to all intents and purposes, fixed and certain (I consider the cause of that fixity in Chapter 5). As A. W. B. Simpson states, 'in general the services due from a villein tenant were as rigidly fixed and probably as generally observed as those from free tenants'.[33] This state of affairs persisted even though the period between the mid-thirteenth century and the 1320s was characterised by rising population, acute demand for land and rising agricultural prices, which meant that these fixed rents were being devalued in real terms.

The second main category of villein tenure involved the grant of land primarily for an annual money rent, and these monetary tenancies were sometimes described as *ad gabulum*, *ad arentatum* or *ad censum*.[34] The key difference between a service tenancy and a money tenancy was the absence of labour services, renders in kind and liability to serve in manorial offices such as reeve: the monetary tenure still owed suit of court and an entry fine, and also a reduced range of occasional levies such as heriot and tallage 'according to the custom of the manor'. The level of the annual cash rent on monetary tenancies was usually set close to or at the prevailing competitive rent at the time of the initial grant, but it was ossified thereafter. Once set, the rental terms were protected by local custom for as long as there was continuity of tenancy, so the lord could not unilaterally impose new terms, such as increasing the annual rent or altering its composition, on a sitting tenant or an heir.[35]

These monetary tenures usually existed alongside service tenancies on the same manor, and indeed became increasingly common. From the middle of the thirteenth century many grants of newly created villein land and cottages, colonised from the waste or carved from the demesne in response to rising population pressure, were issued as a monetarised rather than a service tenure.[36] For example, when small parcels of waste were being ploughed for cultivation in the early 1330s in the uplands west of Halifax (Yorkshire), the lord granted them as customary tenure for a fixed annual rent (of around 4d. per acre) and an entry fine.[37] Similarly, the rapid growth of Hadleigh (Suffolk) between the 1270s and 1340s is reflected in the expansion of income from 'new' rents from 14s. 4d. per annum to £20 12s. in 1347, which was mainly attributable to the creation of dozens of new cottages paying money rents on villein tenure.[38] The increased income was driven by house building and newly ploughed land, not by any upward renegotiation of the cash head rent on individual grants. Overall, then, the proportion of villein land held on monetary tenures grew in the late thirteenth century, as wasteland was colonised in response to the acute demographic pressure and lords increasingly sought straight cash income from their tenancies.[39] As a result, by the early fourteenth century customary 'service' tenancy was on the wane, and after 1350 the swing to monetary tenures accelerated.[40]

The third type of tenure on which villein land was held comprised the grant of land for a straight cash rent for a stipulated fixed term, after which the land reverted to the lord. These were either leaseholds, issued for a term of years on stipulated terms, or a tenancy-at-will, which literally could be terminated by either party without notice. In both cases, the rent to be paid annually was fixed at the outset as a straight cash rent at the prevailing market value of land. Entry fines were uncommon on these fixed-term tenancies, and the only other requirement was attendance at the manor court. In other words, leasehold swept away liability for heriot, merchet and the rest. On expiry of the term, the lord was able to renegotiate the level of the cash rent, and so was able to adjust the level of head rent in line with market forces: alternatively, the lord might decide to convert the land to a fixed monetary or service tenancy. Before the Black Death it was unusual for villein land to be issued at leasehold or at will, although thereafter it became more common. Prior to 1348–49, leasehold was commonly used to grant demesne land and other demesne resources on short-term contracts. An exception is 'conventionary' tenure – effectively a leasehold – which was already widespread in Cornwall and used for both free and unfree land, thus blurring the distinction between the two.[41] According to one estimate, in the

1340s at least 20 per cent of villein land in England was held on monetary tenancies and leaseholds.[42]

Overall, then, by the end of the thirteenth century the head rents on the vast majority of villein tenure were overwhelmingly fixed and certain. The traditional service tenancy was most strongly associated with the uncertainty of common law villeinage. In contrast, monetarised rents enhanced the status of villein land and contemporaries associated them with free tenure.[43] The grant of villein land for a cash rent eroded the distinction between villein and free tenure to such an extent on the Berkeley estate in Gloucestershire that villein land held on life tenancies for cash was included with the listings of free tenures.[44] The fifteenth-century lawyer Littleton captured this distinction when contrasting the lowliness of the traditional villein tenure for services with the superior copyhold for money, which he regarded as the tenure of choice for freemen holding villein land.[45] Historians of medieval England have also accepted this distinction. Hyams observes that 'to most minds the most certain service of all was express money rent ... [which] carried absolutely no connotation of servility', and, in a similar vein, Vinogradoff observed that rent paid in labour was associated with villeinage, and money rent with freedom.[46] The fact that on the eve of the Black Death monetary tenures had already obtained good traction on villein land was a significant factor in their rapid spread thereafter.

The significance of the fixed and certain nature of head rents on villein service and monetary tenancies after c. 1250 is that their level dropped further and further below the commercial value of land, given that the population continued to rise to unprecedented levels and that land became increasingly scarce.[47] As Dyer observes of the bishop of Worcester's estates, rents that had been set by 1230 were thereafter 'rapidly overtaken by inflation and so seemed very cheap in the late thirteenth century'.[48] Even conservative ecclesiastical lords in Huntingdonshire were 'reluctant to exercise their economic muscle' by increasing head rents, and consequently, as Sandra Raban states, 'older notions of harshly exploitative ecclesiastical landlords can no longer be sustained'.[49] The only realistic option available to lords seeking to charge rents at competitive rates would have been to convert the land to a renewable leasehold tenancy, where the annual cash rent could be adjusted at the expiry of each short term to reflect the prevailing commercial value of land. A handful of lesser gentry landlords certainly did this – for example, by such means in the 1340s Lionel de Bradenham increased the rent roll from around £8 per annum to nearly £15 on the manor of Langenhoe (Essex) – but in general this tactic was not widely adopted before the Black Death.[50]

Thus, there is no question that the fixed head rents liable from villein land held on service and monetary tenures meant that servile tenants enjoyed some measure of protection from the effects of rising agricultural prices and the surging demand for land.[51] Overall, by c. 1300 villein head rents per acre were below both the market rent and freehold rents, prompting Junichi Kanzaka to observe that 'villeins held lands on highly advantageous tenure', even when allowance is made for additional dues such as heriot and entry fines.[52]

Security of tenure

The evolution of the common law between the 1180s and the 1220s, reinforced by bureaucratic action and political pragmatism, resulted in the emergence of relatively secure property rights in freehold land in England.[53] Simultaneously, and in stark contrast, it was established that in strict legal terms the ownership ('seisin') of servile land was invested in the lord, so that the villein tenant occupied it entirely at the lord's will with no legally secure rights to inherit or alienate, and no protection in the common law against eviction.[54] The reality of the latter, however, was very different. By the end of the thirteenth century, not only did villein tenants enjoyed secure de facto rights of inheritance within service and monetary tenures, but also they sold, bought, sublet and managed servile land with limited interference from the lord.[55] Briggs has shown how villeins were free to make legally enforceable agreements with strangers and even did so with their own lord, as when leasing demesne land or the demesne mill, even though strictly speaking this meant that they were alienating the lord's own property when paying rent to him.[56] Ironically, the reason for this growing gap between restrictive legal theory and permissive practice was that some of the basic common law practices relating to the ownership and alienation of free land in the royal courts were now being applied to unfree land in manor courts.[57]

Thus, although the legal title to servile land remained firmly with the lord, in practice most service and monetary villein tenures were held heritably, i.e. they could be transferred on their existing terms to an heir, and local custom – not the manorial lord – determined the exact rules of inheritance.[58] In c. 1300 the most common arrangement was primogeniture (i.e. the eldest son as sole heir) and occasionally ultimogeniture (the youngest son), although partible inheritance among all progeny was sometimes found in the south-east. Local custom also dictated the age of majority and the rules of succession that were to be followed in cases where there was no heir. Lords not only respected these customary rights of inheritance, but also their manorial courts ensured that they were properly observed. A minority of monetary and service tenancies were held for the life of the tenant, or indeed of the lord, or for a specified number of lives (father, wife and son), when the land would theoretically revert to the lord. Tenures for a life or lives were most in evidence in western England.[59]

The security of villein tenure was also reflected in the growing consistency and frequency of the record of villein land transfers in manorial courts across the country by the end of the thirteenth century, as common law procedures were adopted and regularised. There had emerged 'a sharply defined regularisation in the form of land transfers in the manorial court', and manorial courts were now careful to follow prescribed forms of conveyancing, 'observance of which was clearly important in safeguarding claims to the property'.[60] The wording of land transfers in the court rolls (effectively the conveyance of the land from one person to another) came to assume a relatively consistent format across the country, and a peasant entering villein land was regularly described as holding it 'to use to him/her and his/her heirs'. This phrasing was based directly on that for livery of seisin in the common law and closely resembled the forms of transfer used for free tenures in royal courts.[61] Such developments were fundamental to strengthening and upholding customary rights to hold and inherit servile land.

During the early fourteenth century individual manor courts further tightened the vocabulary of land transfers to ensure the accurate use of the phrases of surrender and admittance, in a manner that openly imitated common law formulae. Such rigour benefited both the lord and the villein by reducing the chances of a subsequent challenge to the transfer and ownership of the land.[62] For example, many conveyances came to include a variation on the phrase 'saving the right' (such as *salvo tamen iure cuiuslibet*), which enshrined a simple form of due process and recognised the rights of tenants as long as they adhered to the terms of the tenancy.[63] In the 1290s the wording of conveyances in villein land charters on the estates of Peterborough abbey was quickly adjusted to reflect recent changes brought about through the statute *Quia emptores* (1290), which related to free tenures.[64] Similarly, some manorial courts introduced devices imported from the common law to cases concerning villein land, such as the use of entail and jointure, and deathbed transfers.[65] In practice, then, 'villeins were allowed much the same kinds of transfers as anyone of free status and their title was protected by a written record that would be recognised by the [manorial] court in the event of a dispute'.[66] Indeed, to casual onlookers a villein land transaction in c. 1300 closely resembled ordinary grants of free land.[67] Slota even suggests that in some respects manorial courts handled villein land transactions more efficiently than the royal courts handled freeholds, because, although the technical process was similar in both, local manorial courts handled cases more quickly, cheaply and conveniently.[68]

Thus, whatever lawyers wrote about the lord's theoretical control of customary land, in practice servile peasants owned their holdings and could alienate them to their heirs or could sell them to anyone else during their lifetime. Long before the arrival of plague, some villeins were obtaining charters of their acquisition of land and others were provided with 'copies' of the record of a grant of servile land contained within the manorial court roll, both of which testify to the de facto ability of serfs to hold and to transfer land.[69] As early as 1274 one Wakefield villein sold a parcel of unfree land to another *per cartam* ('by a charter'), which emulated the free tenant's charter and anticipated the eventual emergence of 'copyhold' tenure.[70] In the early fourteenth century copies and the written details of transfers in manorial court rolls were sufficient for a serf to establish his title to servile land on the estates of Ely abbey.[71] Lords did not seize villein land arbitrarily, and the practices recorded in manorial courts confirm that those seizures which did occur followed established lapses or breaches in the terms of the tenure on the part of the tenant, and took place only after the exhaustion of an established process leading to seizure that offered the tenant the possibility of recovery of the land.[72] Lords might on occasions intervene if they were concerned that a particular villein tenant was incapable of managing the holding, or might compel the community to find a tenant for an empty and heirless holding.[73] As Lawrence Poos and Lloyd Bonfield conclude, based on the evidence of thousands of court rolls, there were 'only limited circumstances in which the lord would ordinarily be prepared to deprive a tenant of customary land'.[74]

Thus, on the eve of the Black Death the manorial court was the principal locus for the transfer and disposal of, and the protection of rights to, customary land, and it did so deploying procedures closely resembling those which had previously been developed in the common law for free land.[75] Disputes over ownership were routinely resolved through the scrutiny of earlier court rolls or the inspection of copies of land transfers, and by means of complex and technical legal arguments. The issuing of copies of conveyances and the inclusion of written details of transfers within manor court rolls were advantageous to lords, not just their villein tenants, because they provided robust proof of the servile status of the land and greatly reduced the earlier reliance on tests such as merchet and tallage.[76] The practice of carefully recording transfers of villein land was commonplace everywhere, whether on the Battle abbey and St Albans manors in southern England or on northern manors such as Wakefield.[77] Manorial juries were routinely convened to determine disputes over the ownership of unfree land and consulted the record of the court rolls as part of their decision-making process (see Chapter 4).[78] Successful litigants sometimes opted to pay to have their decision recorded formally in the court roll following a dispute. For example, in 1317 a Wakefield serf who had purchased freehold land also paid to have the charter recording the acquisition copied into the manor court roll as proof of his ownership, while a freeman whose status had been disputed had the jury's confirmation of his personal freedom entered formally in the rolls.[79]

An important consequence of the de facto security of villein tenure was an increased confidence in buying and selling parcels of unfree land, so that a customary land market developed extensively in south-east and eastern England, and also, to varying degrees, elsewhere in the country.[80] The villein land market was especially advanced in East Anglia.[81] For example, between 1300 and 1309 368 customary land transfers, averaging a mere half an acre in size, were recorded in the Redgrave (Suffolk) court, whilst between 1330 and 1339 200 similar-sized transfers took place at Coltishall (Norfolk), many of which were granted *inter vivos* to non-kin rather than being transferred to heirs *post mortem*.[82] Lords insisted on registering such transfers in their courts, and received entry fines on each occasion, so that the existence of a villein land market actually benefited them too: for example, the abbot of Bury St Edmunds received over £30 from those 368 transfers at Redgrave.[83] The *inter vivos* sale of small parcels of land tended to cause the break-up of the large standardised landholdings characteristic of villeinage, thereby requiring the head rent of the holding to be allocated proportionately among the new co-parceners.[84] The ability to transfer villein land permanently or temporarily meant that it could also serve as security for loans, fuelling the development of a rudimentary credit market in rural communities.[85] Another consequence of an active land market in villein land – albeit under the pressure of population and high grain prices – was the fragmentation of holdings and pitifully small average holding size, a tendency that was most evident in East Anglia. The wider implications of the extreme fragmentation of holdings are considered in Chapter 6.

By contrast, the villein land market was far less active in other areas of the country. The volume of land sales was low and the large standardised villein-holdings tended to remain intact and to be passed onto the heir after the death of the tenant, rather than broken up into smaller parcels and sold to non-heirs during the tenant's lifetime.[86] Where sales and exchanges of land *inter vivos* did occur, they tended to involve cottages or slivers of arable carved from the waste.[87] Average landholding size did not fall as far as it had in, say, East Anglia, but the shortage of land was still evident in a long tail of landless residents and a fall in mean holding size: for example, in 1279 around two-thirds of all documented holdings in the four Midland counties covered by the Hundred Rolls comprised less than six acres.[88]

Many manorial lords allowed their villein tenants to lease small parcels of their holding to others for a fixed term.[89] The general practice of subletting for fixed terms helped to redistribute some property from the land-sufficient to the land-deficient, and also to increase the flow of smaller land parcels onto the market, which was especially important on manors where the large standardised villein-holdings remained mostly intact.[90] The principal interest of lords lay in insisting that such arrangements should be recorded in the court rolls and a fee should be paid for a licence to sublet, although some lords also sought to prevent subletting to people of free status.[91] Hence, the Wakefield court routinely amerced individuals who had not obtained a licence to sublet servile land.[92] The size of such amercements was not prohibitive. For example, between 1316 and 1348 sixteen licences to sublet at Walsham were obtained for one-off charges averaging 2½d. per acre, when entry fines on the same manor were being levied at 40d. per acre.[93] Knowing the size of seigniorial licences is of limited value without knowledge of the subrents being charged and the length of the lease, but unfortunately these details are almost never included in the court rolls, because these were matters for the two parties involved, not the court. In the tiny number of cases where such information is given, the licence was equivalent to 3 per cent of the total value of the lease (Chapter 8). Court rolls occasionally handled disputes over the terms of a sublease, such as whether the head tenant or the sub-lessor was liable for the labour services attached to the land.[94] For example, in 1317 a tenant of Sutton (Cambridgeshire), held by the prior of Ely, sublet 2 acres and 1 rood of servile land to a freeman, although the freeman insisted that the head tenant continued to render the labour services attached to the land.[95]

Once the villein lessor had paid a fine to the lord for a licence to sublet, he was then free to negotiate and collect an agreed rent from the lessee.[96] We know very little about the terms of these subleases, although historians have presumed that the rent was charged at the prevailing market rate, whereas the licence (payable to the lord) was nominal.[97] Confirmation of this presumption comes from two exceptionally rare and detailed subleases documented in the court rolls of Codicote (Hertfordshire), whose subrents were charged at least 50 per cent above the prevailing customary head rent for villein land.[98] In such cases, lords were not recouping the true value of villein land, and therefore the profits of subletting in these land-hungry years accrued to their villeins.

Lords were able to exercise some influence over the servile land market. They kept a close track of villein land transfers by insisting that they should be recorded in the manor court rolls, and they also required the acquisition of free land by serfs to be registered, although they did not prohibit it.[99] They preferred where possible to maintain the integrity of the standardised villein-holdings, and it is no coincidence that these were protected most effectively on the manors of the highest-status landlords, and especially on the great ecclesiastical estates.[100] As we have seen, lords tolerated the short-term subletting of villein land as long as leases of more than a couple of years, and sublets to freemen, were licensed in the manorial court.[101] In effect, lords could not suppress the pressure of market forces to sublet and subdivide, but they could extract some profit from them.[102] Where shortages of arable land and population densities were greatest, where many freemen were present and where an active market in free land existed, not even the most powerful monastic landlords could withstand the pressures to fragment villein-holdings and the associated development of a market in villein land.[103] Put another way, no lord could dictate that villein landholdings remain intact across the whole of his estate in defiance of local circumstances, which explains why the extent of villein land market activity varied enormously from one manor to another across the large estate of the bishopric of Winchester.[104] The nature of the servile land market on a given manor was determined primarily by variations in local custom, land availability, population pressure and market forces, and to a much lesser degree by seigniorial policy.[105]

Variable incidents

Entry fines

The fixed and ossified nature of the rent package on the traditional service tenure meant that the only real scope for lords to extract extra sums of money from their servile population lay in occasional levies, where the sum payable was variable. The two most prominent of these were tallage (considered in the next section) and entry fines. Entry fines were payable everywhere by an incoming tenant whenever villein land changed hands, and in the pre-plague era they were enforced and paid in the overwhelming majority of cases.[106]

A persistent theme in the scholarship is that entry fines were one of the most powerful and accessible instruments of extra-economic coercion available to English lordship under villeinage, because they were uncertain and determined at the will of the lord. For Kosminsky, 'the arbitrary nature of entry fines … in practice meant an increase in rent'.[107] Similarly, Fryde claimed that since the lord possessed the right 'to fix according to his arbitrary wishes the fines demanded from new tenants as a condition of admitting them to these servile tenements', the result was that the latter often paid 'exorbitantly large entry fines' as a consequence of their vulnerability to the 'arbitrary will of determined and unscrupulous lords'.[108] For Dimmock, 'entry fines were arbitrary and not fixed, and they remained burdensome to peasants'.[109] Similarly, Dyer observed that entry fines 'depended on the demand for land and the will of the lord' and they were 'often adjusted according to the lord's judgement of [the serf's] capacity to pay', and therefore 'offered the best chance of profit to lords': villeins 'were put in a dangerous position, as custom gave them no protection and fines could in theory rise to the maximum that the lord thought the would-be tenant could pay'.[110]

Some credence to these claims about the burdens of entry fines is provided by the contrast between them and the equivalent fine to enter freehold land, which was 'certain' in the sense that precedent and the common law had fixed it at a predictable and artificially low level, usually a year's rent.[111] According to Dyer, 'the enviable characteristic of free tenure lay in the certainty of the obligations as well as their overall low level'.[112] The claims are further supported by select examples demonstrating the highly variable nature of servile entry fines.[113] For example, Edward Miller observed that between 1304 and 1314 tenants entering 'cotlands' at Sutton (Cambridgeshire) paid entry fines varying from 1s. to 10s. for essentially the same standardised unit of landholding, and he concluded that such variability must have been the result of the lord's 'arbitrary' decision about the amount to be rendered.[114] Hilton made a similar point when noting that between the 1290s and 1320s 'fines seem to have increased considerably' at Minchinhampton (Gloucestershire) and on the estate of Worcester priory.[115] Likewise, Zvi Razi showed how during the thirteenth century the abbot of Halesowen doubled the rates of entry fine per virgate payable at Halesowen, whilst Dyer cites the threefold rise in entry fines for virgates on the Ramsey abbey estate in the second half of the thirteenth century to demonstrate the power of the lord to determine and alter the level of fine.[116]

The variable nature of entry fines within and between manors, and their tendency to rise over the course of the late thirteenth century, are indisputable.[117] This does not mean, however, that they were 'arbitrary' impositions or that they constituted 'exorbitant' (to use Fryde's expression) rent increases. Variety is not necessarily or exclusively a function of arbitrariness, because it could also be the result of a range of other considerations. We cannot be certain, however, what exactly caused those variations or increases in entry fines, because court rolls seldom offer any explanation.[118] Furthermore, we seldom have a precise indication of the prevailing market rate for land against which the scale of any rise in entry fines could be measured objectively.[119] So when historians state that different charges or sizeable hikes reflect the 'arbitrary' will of the lord, and when they state that fines rose to 'exorbitant' and 'extortionate' levels, these represent their own opinions, interpretations and explanations for such changes, not the reasons given by contemporaries. This also explains why other historians have interpreted similar or even the same evidence very differently. For example, Dyer uses the threefold hike in the standardised entry fine for a virgate from 20s. to 66s. 8d. between the 1250s and 1300s on the Ramsey abbey estate to illustrate how seigniorial power and market forces could combine to place onerous demands on villeins.[120] In contrast, Raftis compares the 66s. 8d. entry fine to the capital value of one of these virgates, which he calculates at £10, and concludes that this was a relatively modest one-off payment and that 'there is no evidence that entry fines ... debilitated the family enterprise'.[121] So, in the absence of a definitive contemporary explanation for the threefold increase in the fine, or indeed a contemporary judgement on its affordability to the villein, these two leading historians interpret the same evidence very differently. No wonder the treatment of entry fines in the scholarship can appear misleading, confusing and contradictory.

Misunderstandings about the nature of entry fines can also derive from an overdependence on sample sizes that are too small to be reliable or representative. For example, Hole has recently drawn on the evidence for entry fines in Razi's study of Halesowen (Warwickshire) between 1270 and 1348, and the evidence from two Wakefield courts held in November 1331, to assess whether English lords were 'reasonable' or 'rapacious' in their demands. Hole argues that at Halesowen incoming non-heirs were charged a 'dramatically' higher rate of entry fine than heirs at Halesowen, whereas at Wakefield non-heirs paid low rates similar to those paid by heirs, and so concludes that the secular lord of Wakefield was 'less rapacious than the abbot' of Halesowen.[122] By implication, the abbot of Halesowen was deploying seigniorial power to impose fines at extortionate levels on new tenants who had bought, rather than inherited, land. Hole then states that this rapacious policy 'had consequences ... some tenants who were unable to afford them left Halesowen: some 67 departed between 1270 and 1348'.[123] Yet it is unclear how charging non-heirs a higher rate for entry to a servile holding therefore constitutes 'rapacious' behaviour, and presumably this is Hole's opinion, not that of the lord or the non-heirs. Furthermore, Hole's assessment of the Wakefield material is based on a very small sample: just two courts and a handful of examples from November 1331. In fact, 515 court sessions involving thousands of entry fines from the period 1274–1340 are available in print, and a brief scan of this larger sample provides clear evidence that non-heirs in Wakefield were routinely charged higher fines than heirs.[124] Finally, Hole's assertion of a direct causal link between the high entry fines and the departure of peasants from Halesowen is pure supposition: Razi neither claimed nor implied any causal link between the two, and even noted that the population of Halesowen increased 46 per cent between 1270 and 1348, despite the general conditions of destitution and chronic land shortages.[125]

To some extent, Hole's approach epitomises the recurring tendency for discussions about entry fines to feature broad generalisations from small samples, a lack of quantification, and value judgements about what constituted exploitation.[126] An accurate understanding of the mechanics of entry fines can only be obtained through quantitative research into how entry fines operated across many manors, preferably based on unit rates of entry fine (i.e. per virgate or per acre) from large samples over long timeframes.[127] Studies adopting such an approach have identified some consistent patterns across manors held by different lords throughout

England: fines for transfers *inter vivos* to third parties were higher than for hereditary transfers; fines were adjusted according to the ability of the incoming tenant to pay (including being waived because of poverty or old age); fines broadly reflected the quality of the arable land or the size of the messuage; fines might be waived entirely if heriot was paid instead on a post mortem transfer to an heir; fines tended to rise in the early fourteenth century as land shortages became acute; and fines were higher for males entering the landholding of heiresses or for remarrying widows.[128]

In addition to these observed general trends, the level of entry fines also conformed to broad regional patterns. Dyer has shown unequivocally that in the period 1270–1348 entry fines on many manors in Hampshire, northern England and the west Midlands were often below 12d. per acre, regardless of lordship, whereas in parts of Somerset and East Anglia they reached over 40d. per acre.[129] Regions experiencing a high demand for land and with an active servile land market, access to urban markets and good quality arable tended to have higher entry fines per acre than those with a lower demand for land, a limited land market, few commercial opportunities and poorer-quality arable. Furthermore, in case studies where entry fines per unit area have been quantified from numerous data points over a long period, the general levels of entry fine over time were broadly reflective of the general trends in the market value of servile land. For example, entry fines peaked in the first quarter of the fourteenth century on the bishop of Winchester's estates, but then dipped slightly in the 1330s and early 1340s in response to a deflationary shortage of coin and a short-term economic downturn.[130] Similarly, in the 1350s entry fines throughout England fell sharply following the arrival of plague, and they were universally low in the depressed conditions of the fifteenth century.[131] The direction of entry fines over the course of the fourteenth century on the three manors in our case studies (Chapters 8–10) reinforces these general observations.

These findings confirm that market forces were an important determinant of the level of entry fines temporally and spatially: indeed, Dyer concluded that 'the market for land was the main factor'.[132] Yet on other occasions Dyer has also argued that the coercive power of lordship was 'of prime importance' in driving up the level of entry fines.[133] His principal evidence for the latter assertion is the 'failure of entry fines to fall immediately after the Black Death, when we would expect demand for land to plummet'. Dyer states that 'many researchers report individual fines at a very high level' in the third quarter of the fourteenth century and he attributes their existence after the loss of half the population to seigniorial coercion against prevailing market forces.[134] However, no reference is supplied to identify the 'many researchers' who had reported high fines after 1350, and the only concrete examples that Dyer himself supplies are from Bredfield (Suffolk) and Ingatestone (Essex). In reality, after 1350 the level of entry fines collapsed almost everywhere, as Dyer himself has recently confirmed for two manors in the west Midlands.[135] Hence, there is very little conclusive evidence of seigniorial intervention to impose very high entry fines either before or after the Black Death.[136] The only convincing evidence so far presented for a lord imposing a sharp increase in entry fines is that which occurred in the immediate aftermath of successive abbatial vacancies in the early fourteenth century on two manors held by St Albans abbey. The correlation between the two factors is so strong that a causal link is imputed between them, which Slota interprets as an aggressive act of estate policy to help defray a short-term surge in monastic expenses incurred by the election process. He concludes that while entry fines did not display signs of seigniorial pressure in most years, the abbey did indulge itself in 'the luxury of an occasional arbitrary act'.[137]

Another factor that tended to inhibit the ability of the lord to intervene and direct the level of entry fines was the role of manorial officials elected from the ranks of villein tenants in adjudicating what constituted an acceptable level for such fines based on previous precedents (see Chapter 4).[138] This was certainly the case on the Taunton (Somerset) manor of the bishop of Winchester, which in the early fourteenth century was charging some of the highest fines in the country. According to Titow, 'far from representing an arbitrary exaction of a rapacious landlord, [these fines] represent the villagers' own assessment of what was "reasonable" in the circumstances'.[139] These examples emphasise how customary conventions were also influential in determining the level of entry fines, as a result of which they were charged below the prevailing market value of land.[140] Ascertaining the market value for villein land from the sources is difficult, because head rents were fixed by custom and because the sum payable by the purchaser to the vendor for the sale was a private agreement, seldom recorded in the manor court rolls. Very occasionally, however, the sale price *was* documented, which provides a reasonable indication of the market value of land compared with the level of entry fines. For example, between the 1260s and 1280s arable land in various villages in north-east Norfolk was being sold for between 35s. and 59s. per acre, when entry fines averaged around 40d. per acre (between 6 and 10 per cent of the sale value).[141] Similarly, in early-fourteenth-century Redgrave (Suffolk) villein land selling at around 14s. per acre rendered entry fines to the lord at around 6–12d. per acre (7 per cent of the sale value).[142] A similar picture emerges when we are able to compare directly the sale price of land with the entry fine paid to the lord for the same parcel. For example, in 1361 a tenant paid an entry fine of 2s. to obtain 2 acres of servile land in Alverthorpe (Yorkshire), having bought the land for at least 40s., which represents 5 per cent of the market value.[143] At Winslow (Buckinghamshire) in 1345 one villein paid 56s. for 6 roods of land to another villein when the mean entry fine was 28d. per acre (6 per cent), and in 1430 a couple undertook to pay the existing villein tenant £9 6s. 8d. for the purchase of a messuage and 12 acres, whereas they paid only 13s. 4d. to the lord as an entry fine (7 per cent).[144]

How affordable were entry fines to villeins? The majority of fines amounted to around two to three times the annual rent payment on the holding.[145] Obtaining the lump sum could have been demanding for the villein in a world where credit and loans involved risk and challenges of availability, especially to the poorer sections of society. Yet the sums appear more manageable when contextualised over a longer term. Kanzaka calculates that even an entry fine charged at the upper end of the range at 32d. per acre would equate to 1.3d. per acre per annum.[146] We have seen how entry fines on Ramsey abbey virgates were equivalent to approximately one-third the capital value of the holding.[147] Of course, villein tenants possessed other sources of wealth and income. The entry fine paid by William Lene's heir for all his villein-holdings in Walsham in 1328 was equivalent to 8 per cent of the value of William's documented moveable goods.[148] There are parallels here with the low level of the licences charged for subletting villein land, which represented just a couple of per cent of the value of the lease.

Thus, the primary determinants of the level of the fine were a combination of customary considerations and market forces, although custom ensured that the level of fine in the overwhelming majority of cases was considerably below that of the commercial value of land. On the exceptionally rare occasions when we can compare the sale value of land with the level of entry fines, the latter were remarkably consistent in ranging between 5 and 10 per cent of the true commercial value. Lords obtained a steady stream of revenue from entry fines, although variations in their level were due principally to a range of market and customary forces. Lords could manipulate them to exploit their servile tenants, but the evidence indicates such practice was exceptional.

Tallage

Contemporary disputes about servile tallage in the royal courts usually asserted that it was paid 'at the will of the lord' and charged 'high and low', indicating that the lord could arbitrarily vary how much was demanded and when.[149] For example, in 1350 the abbot of Vale Royal (Cheshire) claimed the right 'to tallage his villeins high and low (*alto et basso*) at will, and by them to have all the profit and progeny of those same villeins', whilst in 1402 the prior of Coventry was still asserting the legal right to charge tallage 'at will' in estate documents.[150] Such claims seem to support the view that lords could increase the frequency and sums paid as tallage as a means of raising money rents without any breach of their legal rights or customary norms.[151] For example, Hole has recently stated that the amounts paid as tallage 'could be altered', no less than 'rises in rents and entry fines before the Black Death', and argues that ecclesiastical lords were most likely to exploit this to the disadvantage of their servile peasants.[152] But was tallage as 'uncertain' in practice as it was in theory?

The evidence from a wide range of estates throughout England confirms that tallage-at-will was seldom demanded according to the lord's will, but instead was largely fixed in its frequency and amount, including a cap on the contribution of any one individual.[153] Likewise, occasional recognition payments, made at the accession of a new lord of the manor and a variant on tallage, were largely fixed.[154] Arbitrary tallage literally imposed at the will of the lord was virtually unknown.[155] The precise frequency and nature of payments varied from manor to manor, even on the same estate, although once a particular practice was established it was fixed by custom and seldom changed thereafter. On some manors tallage was charged annually; on some it was charged in most, but not all, years. Others did not charge tallage at all, whilst others required the payment of a 'recognition' (of overlordship) fine only on the accession of a new lord to the manor. Half of the manors on the estates of the earls of Devon and Cornwall in south-west England did not render tallage, and tallage is not recorded on fifteen out of sixteen manors held by lesser lay lords in East Anglia.[156] At least one-half of all English manors probably did not render annual tallage.

Did tallage generate sufficient cash to close the considerable gap that had emerged between the low rent levels received for villein land and the high market value for land? Postan supposed that it did and portrayed it as the most onerous of all servile incidents.[157] Yet a more accurate way of answering this question is to express the sums received for tallage as a percentage of the total annual revenue from fixed rents on the same manor. For example, this 'extraction rate' averaged 43 per cent on ten estates belonging to aristocratic and monastic lords spread across southern and eastern England and the Midlands, which charged tallage annually, although the rate was much lower on the majority of manors.[158] In other words, even the greatest lords – those who extracted the most cash from tallage-at-will – were still not recouping anything like the real value of land each year now that tallage had become a fixed, not routinely variable, charge. The local arrangements for determining the contribution of individual villeins were customary, fixing a set rate either per unit of landholding or in proportion to the number of livestock each tenant possessed, and the sum paid by any one individual was capped. Alternatively, tallage was a fixed sum charged collectively to the villeins of the manor, with the individual contributions being determined among themselves.[159]

Four main conclusions emerge from studies of the way in which tallage-at-will operated in practice. First, local custom was the primary influence in determining whether tallage was rendered annually and whether recognition was charged as well as or instead of tallage, or indeed whether either were charged at all. Perhaps one-half of all manors did not levy tallage. Second, custom also standardised the frequency of, and amount paid as, tallage, and how the amounts owed by each villein were determined: landlords did not deploy their legal power to override these customary arrangements. Third, where tallage was imposed, by the early fourteenth century it did not cover the shortfall between the artificially low level of fixed rents and the commercial value of land. Fourth, given that tallage was neither uncertain in frequency nor size, then the phrase 'at the will of the lord' was not meant literally: rather, it was deployed to signal the servile status of the land or person in question and as a reminder of the lord's theoretical power.[160]

Establishing the affordability of tallage is difficult, given all the variables associated with its form and frequency, and the rate of its extraction, from one manor to another. Furthermore, the documents tend to state collective sums rather than the contributions of each individual and, where the latter are stated, individual contributions were capped and poorer serfs were excused payment.[161] In a few exceptional cases, the extant sources provide explicit details of how the individual payments were calculated. On manors charging annual tallage according to the size of the landholding, the rate varied from 10d. per virgate (five days' wages) to 48d. per virgate (24 days' wages).[162] On manors charging occasional recognition payments, the contribution of an individual serf was usually graded according to ability to pay. For example, in 1277 the lowest individual charge at Norton was 6d., the highest 6s. 8d., and the mean 21d. (Chapter 10), whereas in 1302 on two manors held by the abbot of Bury St Edmunds the mean charge was 23d. at Elmswell (Suffolk) and 17d. at Coney Weston (Suffolk), with a range of individual payments from 3d. to 40s.[163] So recognition occurred once every ten-to-twenty years and, when it was due, it cost the average serf around ten days' wages. The Coney Weston return also includes the number of livestock held by each serf, on which the assessment for recognition was based, revealing that the total sum paid to the lord was equivalent to 5 per cent of the value of all the servile livestock on the manor.[164]

Merchet

Merchet – a financial levy on the marriage of hereditary serfs and villein tenants – was routinely charged on manors across England

and it possessed an especial significance as one of the two key tests of servility under the common law. Three principal features characterised its implementation on the ground. First, seigniorial interference in the marital choices of their serfs was rare, so lords seldom prohibited servile marriages or dictated marriage partners.[165] Second, on most manors only females were liable, but males were also charged on a sizeable minority.[166] Finally, and most importantly, merchet was not imposed on all liable villeins: detailed research has shown beyond any doubt that it was not levied on the marriages of every personal serf or villein tenant, because lords targeted certain individuals for particular reasons.[167] For the most part, as Paul Brand and Hyams have argued, merchet was an incidental source of revenue worth collecting only from the wealthier villeins, although poorer serfs sometimes featured if they were marrying freemen (and therefore became free themselves for the duration of marriage) and leaving the manor, or if the lord wished to create a written record of their servility.[168] As a result of such exceptions, the majority of servile women did not pay merchet in Wisbech (Cambridgeshire).[169] Just eleven merchets are recorded in 193 manorial court sessions held at Wakefield between 1322 and 1333 on a manor containing hundreds of people (see above, p. 5). Just two merchets were rendered in the whole of 1323–24 at Clitheroe (Lancashire).[170] Merchet was rarely levied on two of Canterbury Cathedral Priory's distant manors and, similarly, was relatively uncommon across much of Worcestershire.[171] Rates of omission were often high among males on those manors where they were also liable. One reconstruction estimated that 23 per cent of married male serfs had not paid merchet at Hinderclay and just under one-half had not paid it at nearby Redgrave.[172] Thus, taking England as a whole, merchet was probably paid by only one-third of those who were theoretically liable for it.[173]

What sums were charged for merchet? A few manorial surveys state explicitly that the sum was determined 'at the will of the lord', which might suggest that it could be varied arbitrarily.[174] Certainly, in most places there was no set fee, and payments varied according to individual circumstance.[175] The level of payments was usually higher for widows and those marrying outside the manor, and was also linked to the ability of the individual to pay based principally on their landed assets: in many ways, therefore, it was akin to a stamp duty as a means of controlling inheritance, and hence a tax on the marriages of the wealthier villein families.[176] For example, at Sutton most payments fell between 2s. and 10s., although the highest reached 100s. – an exceptional outlier charged on the remarriage of a wealthy widow.[177] Likewise, Crowland abbey occasionally intervened in the remarriages of widows to charge high sums for merchet at Cottenham (Cambridgeshire).[178]

High fines were unquestionably levied for merchet, but, as with entry fines, the focus must be on norms rather than exceptions. The mean charge varied from those manors imposing a relatively high fine, such as 6s. 8d. at Walsham, to manors with lower averages of 3s. at Sutton, 2s. on the Polden Hill (Somerset) manors of Glastonbury abbey, 2s. on the Worcester priory manors, 2s. at Alrewas (Staffordshire), 1s. 8d. at Dunningworth (Suffolk), 1s. 3d. on the manors of Tavistock abbey, 12d. on the manors of the bishopric of Durham and 12d. at Chedzoy (Somerset).[179] In the case studies later in this volume, the average merchet before 1348 was around 1s. 10d. at Codicote, 2s. 3d. at Norton and closer to 2s. 6d. at Winslow. Taking all such variations into consideration, on most manors the average fine for merchet in pre-plague England was between 2s. and 3s.[180] A handful of manors routinely charged higher fines for serfs who had 'married without licence' (i.e. without first checking whether they would be required to pay a merchet), such as at Winslow (Chapter 9), which would have served as a disincentive to evade merchet. On most manors, however, unlicensed marriages attracted much lower fines, probably because they were paid predominantly by the poorer serfs. For example, fines for unlicensed marriages averaged 11d. between 1308 and 1319 at Sutton (merchet 3s.), 10d. at Norton (merchet 2s. 3d.) and 12d. at Codicote (merchet 1s. 10d.).[181]

How affordable were these merchet fines? Again, historians have offered conflicting answers to this question, such as Dyer's conflicting claims that the sums 'were a burden ... and in bad years they would cause real hardship' in one article and, in another, that they were 'not a crippling charge'.[182] Many such judgements are subjective. One way of offering a more objective reference point is to take the modal sum and express it against prevailing wage rates. If we take the merchet of 2s. as a rough and ready mean, then the money could be raised through just over two weeks of unskilled labour, reckoned at 2d. per day.[183] Thus, we can reasonably conclude that merchet fines for the majority of those serfs required to pay them were neither a major impediment to marriage nor an onerous financial burden.[184]

Leyrwite

The exact origins and purpose of leyrwite are obscure. It was essentially a monetary fine imposed on some servile women for fornication, although in East Anglia the incident was known as 'childwite' and paid following illegitimate childbirth.[185] Leyrwite was uncommon in many parts of southern England. For example, it was recorded on just three of the bishopric of Worcester's manors and only sporadically on the estate of Worcester priory.[186] Leyrwite was not imposed on all extra-marital sexual activity even on those manors where it was found, but instead certain females were targeted for specific reasons that varied locally, such as being especially wealthy or involved in prostitution.[187] As Judith Bennett observes, in general 'leyrwite netted so few offenders and ... little profit': for example, just six cases at Wakefield between 1322 and 1333, and once in every three years on average on the manor of Park (Hertfordshire) between 1300 and 1340.[188] It often appears in court rolls in clusters and so seems to have been subject to enforcement waves.[189] Such patterns suggested to P. J. P. Goldberg that leyrwite was deployed more as an instrument of community control over sexual behaviour than as an instrument of seigniorial control over serfs.[190] As Dyer states, the language of leyrwite was powerful in signalling social control, because it conveyed subjugation and humiliation.[191]

The fine for leyrwite was variable, but it seldom exceeded 6s. 8d. and the most common fine was 6d.[192] The average fine was between 4d. and 6d. on three St Albans manors (Chapters 8– 10). Again, the reasons for such variations are seldom stated, although poorer women certainly paid less. Higher fines appear to have been sometimes imposed on those who formicated with either more than one man or with a cleric.[193] The fine for East Anglian childwite was paid at the higher level of 2s. 8d. (sixteen days' labour) on manor after manor regardless of lordship, probably reflecting a tough line on illegitimate births in a region of very high population density with a long tail of landless and poor.[194] Leyrwite was unquestionably demeaning, and some communal moral judgement was applied to decide who was fined or not. Three days of unskilled labour would cover the modal fine of 6d.

Chevage

In theory, as we saw in Chapter 1, serfs were not supposed to leave their home manor without permission, and other lords were supposed to return any who did so. In practice, hereditary serfs could come and go from the manor on a casual and daily basis without any restriction, although those who remained away from the manor for more than a year at a time were required to pay chevage for each absent year, effectively a seigniorial licence to migrate. By the late thirteenth century other lords seldom returned unlicensed emigrants, and the royal courts and its officials offered little if any help to lords attempting to retrieve flown serfs: consequently, the lord was thrown back on his own initiative with few practical options for enforcing their return.[195]

How frequently was chevage imposed and how uncertain was the levy? Manorial juries were supposed to name all those who were resident away from the manor, and some court rolls did note the names and sometimes the destination of flown serfs among 'presentments for absence', while others recorded the payment of chevage for a licence to be absent for a year. Early historians, such as E. P. Cheyney, portrayed manor court rolls as 'full of presentments that villeins have fled', and Hilton observed that a lord 'always made [the effort] to fix the peasant to his holding'.[196] In his later works, Brenner stressed the importance of mobility restrictions on English serfs in enabling lords to extract surpluses from them by force.[197] It is certainly the case that the pre-plague estate records of some high-status landlords, such as Ramsey abbey, Crowland abbey, Halesowen abbey and the duchy of Cornwall, routinely contain lists of flown serfs.[198] Most of these are presentments for absence rather than chevage payments, however, and few of these estates converted their conscientious recording of migrants into regular chevage payments or actual retrievals. Consequently, even on those manors where departures were recorded, the management of servile flight was 'innocuous'.[199]

On the majority of manors, however, lords proved indifferent to serf migration, because their courts rolls contain very little record before the Black Death of either chevage payments or presentments for absence.[200] For example, an average of only 0.2 chevage/presentments for absence are recorded per court between 1249 and 1348 in a sample of five manors across southern England with a combined total of over 400 extant court sessions.[201] At Layham (Suffolk) just one case of chevage, and no presentments for absence, are recorded in eighty-five extant court sessions between 1330 and 1375.[202] In the period 1258–1351 there are just eleven references to fugitive serfs on the five Polden Hill manors of Glastonbury abbey (Somerset), and between 1327 and 1348 a mere five people paid chevage on the nearby lay manor of Chedzoy.[203] In 515 courts of Wakefield (Yorkshire) between 1274 and 1340 there are twenty presentments for absence and no chevage payments. This widespread seigniorial indifference enabled many villeins to move around in search of work or a landholding with relative impunity. Such indifference was probably pragmatic, because by c. 1300 sustained population pressure ensured full rent rolls and an abundance of cheap labour in almost every manor.[204]

An assumption persists that fines for movement were uniformly high across medieval Europe: for example, according to Peters 'while serfs could move if they paid a fee, these fees were often relatively high, limiting mobility'.[205] Was this true of chevage before 1348 in England? Here, the level of fine was variable, but in general it amounted to between 1d. and 6d. per annum. In a sizeable minority of cases the annual charge was fixed at one or two capons rather than cash, a practice evident on a sufficient scale across manors held by different lords to be suggestive of customary practice.[206] These charges were 'trifling', as Vinogradoff pointed out long ago, and could be raised from the wages of a couple of days of unskilled labour.[207] Of course, we should emphasise again that most flown serfs did not pay chevage. It is likely that the few who did pay were opting to do so for particular reasons, such as maintaining an interest in an inheritance.[208] Thus, mobility restrictions were very lightly applied to English villeins. This finding is a major corrective to the narratives that place great emphasis on the importance of controls over migration in systems of serfdom.[209]

Licences to educate

A variation on restricting the mobility of serfs, especially adult males, was to prohibit them from being educated for clerical orders or from taking up a trade without licence, because both activities would involve the serf becoming free and therefore a notional loss to the asset base of the manor. In practice, however, both incidents were enforced only very infrequently, and the restriction on educating serfs for clerical orders was only found on a handful of monastic estates.[210] Case studies of individual manors or estates seldom comment explicitly on the *absence* of this incident, but its rarity is apparent whenever such nil returns are recorded.[211] On those manors where it was imposed, the scale and frequency of exactions were low. For example, licences to educate were a feature of servility on the estate of St Albans abbey, where an average fine of 6d. was charged on its manor of Norton and 16d. at Winslow. An average of 0.4 cases per annum are recorded at Norton, whereas at Codicote the rate was even lower at 0.1 per annum, and it was last levied in 1336 (Chapters 8–10). The average charge for this licence, when it was paid, was equivalent to three days' unskilled labour. Hence, restrictions either on taking up a trade or being educated were even rarer than chevage, underlining the conclusion that mobility restrictions under English villeinage were very limited.

Summary

This extensive survey of the management of the 'uncertain' servile dues of merchet, leyrwite, chevage and licences to educate – which were occasional and variable, and whose fine was not stipulated in custumals – has established that they were relatively infrequent and were not levied on a sizeable proportion of the population who were theoretically liable to them. This conclusion can be illustrated by expressing their frequency on a given manor as total cases per annum, although such calculations are only meaningful for manors with an almost complete series of court rolls and for which we have a reliable sense of the size of the population. This exercise is attempted for six manors: Bredfield, Codicote, Norton, Walsham, Walsham High Hall and Winslow (Table 3.1). The infrequency of

Table 3.1 Total number of servile merchets, leyrwite, absences, licences to educate and mill suit violations (also expressed per annum) on six manors, 1320–49

Manor	Years of surviving courts	Merchets	Leyrwite	Absence	Licence to educate	Mill suit	Population (estimate) in 1300
Bredfield	1330–48	25 (2.2)	8 (0.4)	25 (1.3)	0	0	400
Codicote	1327–48	38 (1.7)	6 (0.3)	29 (1.3)	2 (0.1)	13 (0.6)	600–700
Norton	1325–49	73 (2.9)	29 (1.2)	40 (1.6)	9 (0.4)	88 (3.5)	300
Walsham	1325–48	53 (2.2)	29 (1.2)	24 (1.0)	0	0	1,400
Walsham High Hall	1325–48	7 (0.3)	4 (0.2)	16 (0.7)	0	0	as above
Winslow	1320–49	137 (4.6)	42 (1.4)	3 (0.1)	4 (0.1)	51 (1.7)	1,000

Sources: Chapters 8–10, this volume; Bailey, *The Decline of Serfdom*, pp. 104–18; SA/I HA91/1; Foden, *Records of the Manor of Norton*, p. xlix; Lock, *The Court Rolls 1303–1350*, p. 1.; R. Toepfer, 'The abbey at St Albans and its relationship with its lordship in the late Middle Ages' (PhD thesis, University of Southampton, 2017), p. 90.

these incidents becomes abundantly clear when expressed in this format: an average in each manor of around just one leyrwite, one absence and two merchets a year from communities with populations of hundreds of people.

The levels of exaction taken from the 'uncertain' incidents of merchet, leyrwite, chevage and licences to educate certainly varied from one individual case to another, and large sums were sometimes charged for merchet. However, the average payment for each of these exactions was generally low and was conditioned by local custom. Overwhelmingly, these incidents were not manipulated according to seigniorial need and they did not significantly alter the rent burden on villeins. By one calculation based on data from the 1270s the total annual rent burden on villein-holdings – i.e. taking both the fixed head rent and tallage, heriot and merchet into account – remained 'well below the competitive rent'.[212] Once more, the contemporary statement that these payments were determined 'at the will of the lord' cannot be taken literally.[213] On the contrary, villeins enjoyed a degree of certainty about the nature, frequency and size of exactions they faced.

Villeins did, however, face uncertainty in two areas. The first is whether they would be charged for an incident such as merchet or chevage or not, given that a majority of those liable did *not* pay such fines. The second, and most significant, area was their lack of any independent legal redress on those rare occasions when their lord did behave aggressively and unreasonably. This cuts to the heart of the real meaning of uncertainty in the context of common law villeinage. When Bracton argued that villein services were 'uncertain and indeterminate', he was well aware that in reality there was little uncertainty about their frequency or duration.[214] Rather, he used the phrase within a specific context, i.e. when contrasting the privileged villeinage of royal demesne with the pure villeinage of ordinary villein tenure. Bracton's point was that villeins on the royal demesne had some legal protection against ejection and rent increases, whereas all other villeins did not. Their tenure was uncertain not in the sense of unpredictable and variable rent levels, but in not having any legal redress within the common law.

The reality of English serfdom in the pre-plague era provides support for adopting Ogilvie's interpretative framework for European serfdom. Instead of focusing narrowly on how serfdom suppresses the choices available to peasants, she advocates exploring the broad interplay between those forces promoting peasant choice (autonomy, individualism, rationality) and those generating constraints (lordship, exploitation, coercions, institutions, even field systems).[215] Constraints under English serfdom were highly varied from manor to manor, and they mainly took the form of the payment of licences and fines, or alternatively the costs of evading such payments, rather than outright compulsion or prohibition. Similarly, some serfs may have been deterred from following a course of action by either the threat of seigniorial intervention or the possibility of confrontation with the lord's officials, or the prospect of a licensing fine, or of pressure being placed on close family members (Chapter 6). Just because the lord could not compel a serf to remain on the manor, or did not monitor departures routinely, does not necessarily mean that his lack of action had no effect on peasant choice.[216] The effects of these constraints are difficult to measure directly, but they must be factored into any evaluation of the impact of serfdom on economic development (see Chapter 6).

Villeins and commodity markets

If many, let alone all, of the theoretical constraints on serfs under common law villeinage had applied in practice, it would have true that, as Ralph Evans put it, seigniorial demands on English villeins 'may have left little room for a free economic market in land, labour or produce'.[217] Yet all the evidence presented above shows that such an assessment would be wrong. English serfs possessed far greater freedom of time and action than the strict theory of common law villeinage allowed, something that was entirely consistent with the abundant evidence on the eve of the Black Death for the existence of land; labour; and, to a lesser extent, capital markets. We have seen how villeins were engaged in land markets to varying degrees. Labour services absorbed less than 10 per cent of productive labour in England and villeins could access the sizeable open market in hired labour with few restrictions.[218] Likewise, villeins were heavily involved in rudimentary rural credit markets.[219] Dyer has consistently and persuasively argued that we should regard the English peasantry, including serfs, as a dynamic and resilient group who, far from retreating into oppressed misery, shaped the economy and the countryside through their decisions and actions.[220]

The evidence for the immersion of villeins in commodity markets is overwhelming.[221] The very fact that most rents and almost all servile dues were paid in ready cash provides a sure sign of commercialisation spreading throughout society.[222] Tax assessments reveal the presence of relatively wealthy villeins who possessed large stocks of animals that far exceeded their subsistence needs and were manifestly being reared for commercial purposes.[223] These indicate that peasant-holdings were more densely stocked with livestock than demesnes, indicating that they dominated this sector of agriculture.[224] Most of England's prodigious output of wool was sourced from peasants, many of whom were villeins such as William Lenne of Walsham, who in 1328 had over 120 sheep in his flock.[225] In the 1290s the borough of Ipswich required villeins to pay tolls on merchandise traded in its markets, and the citizens of Norwich were in dispute with rural villeins from the manors of the bishop of Ely over the payment of tolls for selling large quantities of agricultural produce in the city: proof both of the established presence of villeins in commodity markets and of the additional costs they faced.[226] In the early fourteenth century villeins in the east Midlands possessed sufficient resources to cart large quantities of agricultural produce to local and regional markets, and the peasants of Brigstock (Northamptonshire) were deeply immersed in local labour markets, trades and commercial enterprise, irrespective of status.[227] Many active traders held plots, shops and stalls in marketplaces on villein tenure.[228] For example, the smithy, shops and stalls in the market place of Codicote (Chapter 8), and some commercial plots in the market at Winslow, were held on villein tenure (Chapter 9). Much of this is familiar, but its implications for our understanding of the nature of serfdom needs to be emphasised: i.e. that the routine and deep immersion of villeins in commodity markets are incompatible with the legal theory of villeinage.

Given that villeins regularly engaged in commodity markets, did their lords profit directly from their tenants' commercial activities by means of the restrictions of villeinage? The short answer is that they did so only to a very limited extent. Villeins who owed suit at their lord's mill were occasionally required to pay a higher rate of multure for grain destined for market than for corn ground for domestic purposes.[229] Dyer has portrayed the seigniorial right to levy a toll on the sale of draught animals as one of the defining features of English serfdom, and lists it as one of the incidents whereby lords might raise sizeable sums from their villeins, implying it was a standard practice.[230] In reality, however, it was only found on the estates of a handful of ecclesiastical lords and its enforcement was patchy.[231] For example, a survey of 1251 does state that villeins on the estate of the bishopric of Ely should not sell their ox or colt (i.e. their beasts of burden) without the lord's licence.[232] Even here, however, evidence for its enforcement is thin. For example, a mere handful of cases with petty fines are recorded when court rolls survive from the bishop's manor of Downham (Cambridgeshire) in the fourteenth century.[233] The fee charged for licences to sell seldom exceeded 2d., and punishments for failure to comply with this requirement are exceptionally rare.[234]

There are some examples of manorial authorities attempting to place some very specific restrictions on the consumption habits of villeins. Between 1321 and 1324 the manor court of Balsham (Cambridgeshire) elected special wardens whose role was to ensure that its villeins did not sell in any outside market, although this was a temporary measure to ensure that local food supplies were protected in response to the recent famine conditions.[235] In 1338, as part of a package of wider measures to deal with public order issues, the cellarer of St Albans abbey prohibited his villein tenants of Norton from 'expending and wasting their goods and chattels' in taverns in nearby Baldock (Hertfordshire), insisting instead that they brew and consume ale on the manor itself, but there is no evidence that this unusual ordinance was actually enforced.[236] Similarly, in 1339 two Cottenham (Cambridgeshire) villeins were amerced for wasting their goods at taverns, although in another entry in the same court these two were also amerced for wasting their tenements: no other villeins were amerced for their drinking habits, so it seems that some specific context relating to the behaviour of these two men lay behind this presentment.[237] Special restrictions such as these were very unusual.[238]

In general, then, English serfdom neither prevented villeins from entering commodity markets nor offered lords much opportunity to profit from such activity. We have seen how villeins leased and ran demesne water mills for profit, and some even ran market franchises.[239] Indeed, villeins could be among the wealthiest peasants and highest taxpayers in their communities.[240] In the 1320s the servile Jop family controlled around 10 per cent of the customary land in Redgrave, and featured prominently in the 1327 lay subsidy there, as, too, did the established villein families of Osborn, Cranmer, Hawys and Spileman in nearby Walsham.[241] Indeed, Walter Osborn and William Hawys – prominent villein tenants in Walsham – paid 4s. in tax, the same as the local lord of High Hall manor, Nicholas de Walsham.[242] Villeins served as royal tax assessors and collectors.[243] As Briggs states, 'in most circumstances the rules of villeinage allowed villeins to travel around to market, to possess rights in the property they bought and sold, and to make enforceable contracts'.[244]

Conclusion

The strict theory of common law villeinage excluded serfs from the royal courts, denied them ownership of land and goods, and prevented them from leaving the manor or bequeathing assets to their heirs. If applied, this theory would have left them vulnerable to seigniorial will and whim, enabling lords to alter rents arbitrarily on servile land; to seize the land itself at any time; and to vary the frequency and weight of seigniorial monopolies such as suit of mill, and of servile incidents such as tallage, merchet and entry fines. Some historians have regarded this theory as a guide to actual practice, arguing that villeins were vulnerable and exploited, wracked by uncertainty over the scale or frequency of their burdens, and impoverished by extortionate demands. In the words of Brenner, 'the construction of a unified system of law and administration of justice buttressed and enforced surplus extraction from peasant unfreedom'.[245] Such interpretations are compelling in their clarity and cogency, but tend to be long on presumption and short of convincing evidence.

Thirteenth-century lawyers asserted the 'uncertainty' of villeinage, and historians have debated what this might have meant for serfs. In practice, villeins enjoyed security of tenure and rights of inheritance, and after the mid-thirteenth century their rent package was largely ossified and fixed. Lords only seized servile land following clear breaches of customary norms and in accordance with an established due process. Villeins could sell their land to a third party, and the proceeds from any land sales accrued largely to them rather than their lord. Entry fines were routinely charged for entry to villein land, but represented less than 10 per cent of its commercial value. Licences paid to lords for permission to sublet villein land cost less than 3 per cent of the value of the lease. Tallage-at-will was not levied annually on perhaps half of all English manors: where it was levied, its size was calculated proportionate to certain assets (landholding or livestock) and fixed by custom, and the contribution of any one serf was capped. Lords did not recoup the market rental value of villein land from either annual tallage-at-will or entry fines, which has prompted the observation that in the early fourteenth century villein 'tenants rather than lords largely had the upper hand'.[246] Despite the legal theory of villeinage, arbitrary seigniorial power was not a major influence on the frequency and size of the main servile incidents of tallage and entry fines.

The other servile incidents that were theoretically variable at the will of the lord – merchet, leyrwite, chevage and permission to educate – were, in reality, largely fixed in frequency, modest in weight and not levied on all those liable for them. Variations in the levels of fines occurred for a set of consistent reasons and seldom because lords were intervening to extort their serfs. Although all villein tenants and hereditary serfs were liable for merchet, in reality only around a third actually paid it, and few serfs paid leyrwite or chevage. Leyrwite was imposed selectively and infrequently outside East Anglia and it was virtually unknown in southern England. A very small proportion of flown serfs rendered chevage, and many lords hardly bothered to track emigrant serfs. The will of the lord was exercised more often in determining whom not to charge than in manipulating the level of charges upwards. In this chapter I have attempted to deal with norms – with the frequency of payments over time and with the average level of payments rather than extreme individual cases – and to provide a sense of the affordability of mean payments. Even on three populous manors of a highly conservative and supposedly uncompromising landlord such as St Albans abbey, there was around one fine for absence, one for leyrwite and a couple for merchets recorded annually on each of them: chevage was charged at the equivalent of a couple of days' wages, leyrwite three days', and merchet around three weeks'. Such light touch impositions explain Raftis's view that Ramsey abbey encouraged its substantial villein tenants to develop their resources commercially for mutual benefit.[247] There is no doubt that villeins participated extensively in commodity markets and some of them could be among the wealthiest taxpayers in their communities. Hence, the enduring stereotype that English lords were able to extract through rents and dues the entire surplus of serfs beyond that required for subsistence is entirely without foundation.[248]

The reasons for this fixity of rents, dues and incidents – and the associated seigniorial restraint in their relations with their serfs – are explored in Chapter 5. The point here is that the economic and social disabilities of villeinage were not as severe or constraining as the legal theory of the time, and the views of some modern historians, would indicate. When evidence from large samples of data and numerous detailed case studies is carefully assessed, it is apparent that the gap between the nature of villein status as set out in the common law and the reality in practice was unquestionably wide.[249] It was certainly possible and feasible for a lord to demand suddenly additional labour services or to impose a very heavy entry fine well above the market value of land. But, as my survey of the scholarly literature and the case studies has revealed, such events were exceptionally rare. This discovery carries far-reaching implications for our understanding of the economic significance of serfdom and for how we attempt to reconstruct the social experience of serfs.

The incidents of serfdom were overwhelmingly predictable, rather than uncertain, in their frequency: although the sums charged were variable, the amounts collected normally fell within customary bands that, by and large, were affordable to most households. Thus, the 'uncertainty' of villeinage did not mean that the incidents of serfdom were literally variable at the will and whim of the lord. In the vast majority of cases their application was conditioned by precedent and customary usage. If a lord did attempt to introduce new services and impositions, serfs had some scope for defending their position in the manor court (see Chapter 4), but otherwise had no formal legal redress against the lord. Instead, their only remaining options were to protest, drag their feet, strike, attempt to litigate in the royal courts, accept the burdensome imposition or leave. Here was the essence of 'uncertainty' under villeinage.

While serfdom was not as onerous in its practice as in its theory, some serfs did still seek to be free of it. The existence of cases of conflict with manorial lords over servile services, the presence of low-level resistance and non-compliance, the out-migration of serfs, the claims of some villeins to be part of the Ancient Demesne, and the reluctance to hold unfree land on the old service tenancies when land became more freely available after 1348–49 all testify to the dislike of serfdom among serfs and villein tenants. Denying villeins access to the royal courts meant that they had no court of appeal if relations with their own lord deteriorated badly, and their exclusion was a source of social stigma.[250] Serfs faced a wider range of potential exactions than did free tenants. Some lords maintained the language of serfdom to discriminate and to humiliate, and they were not beyond intimidating their serfs.[251] Serfdom was irksome, and occasionally worth rejecting, but it was not sufficiently burdensome to prevent freemen from routinely occupying and rendering the full dues on villein land: holding villein land was better than having no land at all.[252] As Briggs argues, villeinage was 'a set of rules of conduct which resulted in penalties if the villein infringed and was detected'.[253] The principal objections to serfdom lay in its dishonour and discrimination; the theoretical vulnerability in law; and in the inefficiencies, constraints, obstacles and additional costs it created to serf agency.

Notes

1 Hyams, *King, Lords*, pp. 185–6, 193–4.
2 Cited in Hatcher, 'English serfdom', p. 8; and Hatcher, 'Lordship', p. 115.
3 Pollock and Maitland, *The History of English Law*, Vol. I, p. 393.
4 Faith, *The English Peasantry*, pp. 260–2. Of course, this interpretation of 'uncertainty' is improbably elastic. Arguing that the free tenant who owed six eggs at Christmas and ten boon-works in the harvest enjoyed materially greater certainty than the villein tenant owing six eggs at Christmas and forty week works on unspecified tasks throughout the year is a pedantic legal abstraction, because both requirements were certain enough. From this perspective, it is nonsense to argue that villein services were 'uncertain' in any literal sense, which is confirmed by the manner in which medieval lawyers quickly dropped labour services as a test for villeinage. Hatcher, 'English serfdom',

p. 9; Simpson, *A History of the Land Law*, p. 159; Hyams, *King, Lords*, pp. 185–6, 194.

5 Hyams, *King, Lords*, p. 200; Vinogradoff, *Villeinage*, pp. 77, 82–3; Faith, *The English Peasantry*, p. 261.

6 Dyer, *From Slavery to Freedom*, pp. 5, 11–15.

7 Freedman, *Images*, pp. 83–4.

8 Dyer, 'Villeins, bondsmen', p. 423; Hilton, *The Decline of Serfdom*, pp. 25–6.

9 Brenner, 'Agrarian class structure', pp. 47–8; Brenner, 'The agrarian roots', pp. 235–6, 252, 295; Hilton, *Medieval Society*, pp. 145–8; Hilton, *Class Conflict*, pp. 50–60. See also Schofield's summary, *Peasants and Historians*, pp. 92–8.

10 P. R. Schofield, 'Lordship and the peasant economy, c. 1250 c. 1400: Robert Kyng and the abbot of Bury St Edmunds', in Dyer et al., *Rodney Hilton's Middle Ages*, pp. 57–8.

11 Dyer, *Standards of Living*, p. 136.

12 Dyer, 'Villeins, bondmen', p. 428.

13 Dyer, 'Memories of freedom', pp. 290–1. Liability for dues such as tallage, merchet, leyrwite, tolls on animal sales, heriot, and entry fines are not always recorded in thirteenth-century custumals, and the sums payable are rarely stated; J. Birrell, 'Manorial custumals reconsidered', *Past & Present*, 224 (2014): 3–37 (pp. 27–30).

14 Fryde, *Peasants and Landlords*, pp. 33, 39.

15 Dimmock, *The Origin of Capitalism*, pp. 65–6, 85.

16 Brenner, 'The rises and declines', p. 263.

17 Scase, *Literature and Complaint*, pp. 6–8, 26; Dyer, 'Memories of freedom', p. 291.

18 Dyer, 'From slavery to freedom', pp. 11–18.

19 For discussions of this point, see Dyer, 'The language of oppression', pp. 71–86; Hatcher, 'Lordship', p. 131; Rigby, *English Society*, pp. 56–7.

20 R. H. Hilton, 'Introduction', in Aston and Philpin, *The Brenner Debate*, pp. 1–9 (pp. 5–6); S. H. Rigby, *Marxism and History: A Critical Introduction* (Manchester: Manchester University Press, 1998), pp. 20–1, 209–14; Hatcher, 'Lordship', p. 131.

21 D. C. North and R. P. Thomas, 'The rise and fall of the manorial system: A theoretical model', *Journal of Economic History*, 31 (1971): 777–803.

22 Hatcher, 'Lordship', p. 131.

23 Campbell and Bartley, *England on the Eve*, pp. 254, 261–3.

24 See, for example, Vinogradoff, *Villeinage*, pp. 304–12; Miller and Hatcher, *Medieval England: Rural Society*, pp. 111–33.

25 Bailey, *After the Black Death*, p. 27.

26 Kosminsky, *Studies*, pp. 330, 347–50.
27 Postan, 'Medieval agrarian society', pp. 607–8; Dyer, 'Memories of freedom', p. 292; Birrell, 'Manorial custumals', pp. 21–4. For a rare example from the early fourteenth century, see Dyer, 'From slavery to freedom', p. 17.
28 M. G. Thompson, 'The Polden Hill manors of Glastonbury Abbey: Land and people c. 1260–1351' (PhD thesis, University of Leicester, 1996), pp. 79–80, 107–8, 117; see also Wells-Furby, *The Berkeley Estate*, pp. 90–2.
29 Homans, *English Villagers*, pp. 276–83; Searle, *Lordship and Community*, pp. 188–94; Miller and Hatcher, *Medieval England: Rural Society*, p. 117; Dyer, 'Memories of freedom', pp. 288–9; Birrell, 'Manorial custumals', pp. 15–24.
30 Hatcher, 'English serfdom', pp. 22–3; L. Bonfield, 'The nature of customary law in the manor courts of medieval England', *Comparative Studies in Society and History*, 31:3 (1989): 514–34 (pp. 519–20); Campbell, 'The agrarian problem', pp. 7–8, 22–4, 42; Dyer, 'Memories of freedom', pp. 289–90; Campbell, 'The land', p. 236; Campbell and Bartley, *England on the Eve*, pp. 251–3; Eldridge, *Law and the Medieval Village Community*, p. 114.
31 Miller, *The Abbey and Bishopric*, p. 103; Hatcher, *Rural Economy*, pp. 60–1, 81–2, Table 4; Titow, *English Rural Society*, pp. 73–4; B. Harvey, *Westminster Abbey and Its Estates in the Middle Ages* (Oxford: Oxford University Press, 1977), pp. 219–23; P. D. A. Harvey, *A Medieval Oxfordshire Village: Cuxham, 1240 to 1400* (Oxford: Oxford University Press, 1965), pp. 82, 130; P. D. A. Harvey, 'Introduction', in P. D. A. Harvey, ed., *The Peasant Land Market in Medieval England* (Oxford: Oxford University Press, 1984), pp. 1–28 (pp. 7–19); Bailey, 'Villeinage in England', pp. 435–6; S. Raban, *A Second Domesday? The Hundred Rolls of 1279–80* (Oxford: Oxford University Press, 2004), pp. 133–6; Wells-Furby, *The Berkeley Estate*, pp. 107–114; Birrell, 'Manorial custumals', p. 29.
32 Woods, *Medieval Hadleigh*, p. 95. For example, assize rents at Monks Eleigh were £8 9s. in c. 1250, £8 13s. in c. 1270, and £8 13s. in 1330. Likewise, in the 1270s around 1,886 works were owed from the villein-holdings, and the same in 1330; V. Aldous, ed., *Monks Eleigh Manorial Records, 1210–1683*, Suffolk Records Society, 65 (Woodbridge: Boydell Press, 2002), pp. 32–5, 38, 61, 67.
33 Simpson, *A History of the Land Law*, p. 159.
34 DeWindt, *Land and People*, pp. 69–71; M. Bailey, 'The transformation of customary tenures in southern England 1350–1500', *Agricultural History Review*, 62 (2014): 210–30 (pp. 212–16).

35 Hatcher, 'English serfdom', pp. 20–2; Kanzaka, 'Villein rents', pp. 616–17; Bailey, *After the Black Death*, pp. 27, 90–2.

36 See, for example, Hatcher, *Rural Economy*, pp. 85–6; N. J Tringham, ed., *Three Thirteenth- and Fourteenth-Century Surveys of Burton Abbey Manors*, Collections for a History of Staffordshire, 4th series, 20 ([Stafford]: Staffordshire Record Society, 2004), pp. 19–22 (Stretton, Staffordshire); and Raban, 'Landlord returns on villein rents in north Huntingdonshire in the thirteenth century', *Historical Research*, 66 (1993): 21–34 (p. 31).

37 Walker, *The Court Rolls 1331–3*, pp. 65–7, 75, 77, 85.

38 Woods, *Medieval Hadleigh*, pp. 97–8.

39 Miller, *The Abbey and Bishopric*, pp. 142–3, 152–3; DeWindt, *Land and People*, p. 71; Hatcher, *Rural Economy*, pp. 80–101; Hatcher, 'English serfdom', pp. 15–18.

40 Campbell and Bartley, *England on the Eve*, p. 263; Bailey, 'The transformation', pp. 216–26; Bailey, *After the Black Death*, pp. 90–102.

41 Hatcher, *Rural Economy*, pp. 52–5, 87.

42 Bailey, *After the Black Death*, p. 301 n. 107.

43 Vinogradoff, *Villeinage*, p. 186. Homans, *English Villagers*, pp. 234–5: 'socage tenure was used occasionally to describe villein tenure held for cash rather than for services'.

44 Wells-Furby, *The Berkeley Estate*, pp. 96–8.

45 Simpson, *A History of the Land Law*, p. 161.

46 Hyams, *King, Lords*, pp. 196–7; Vinogradoff, *Villeinage*, pp. 216, 309.

47 Kanzaka, 'Villein rents', pp. 612–13; Campbell, 'The agrarian problem', p. 40; Raban, *A Second Domesday?*, pp. 132–7; Wells-Furby, *The Berkeley Estate*, pp. 107–8.

48 C. Dyer, *Lords and Peasants in a Changing Society: The Estates of the Bishopric of Worcester, 680–1540* (Cambridge: Past & Present Publications, 1980), p. 99.

49 Raban, *A Second Domesday?*, pp. 136–7.

50 Ibid., pp. 137–8; Raban, 'Landlord returns', pp. 25–6; R. H. Britnell, 'Production for the market on a small fourteenth-century estate', *Economic History Review*, 19 (1966): 380–7; Bailey, *After the Black Death*, p. 27.

51 Hatcher, 'English serfdom', pp. 6–26; R. H. Britnell, *The Commercialisation of English Society, 1000–1500* (Manchester: Manchester University Press, 1996), pp. 126–7; Kanzaka, 'Villein rents', pp. 608–14.

52 Kanzaka, 'Villein rents', pp. 610–13; Wells-Furby, *The Berkeley Estate*, pp. 89, 108–10; Campbell, 'The agrarian problem', pp. 52–3; Campbell, 'The land', pp. 228–30; Briggs, 'English serfdom', p. 19.

53 Palmer, 'The origins'; Palmer, 'The economic and cultural impact', pp. 375–96.

54 See, for example, Martin, *Feudalism to Capitalism*, p. 39.

55 Two of the best, and well informed, surveys are R. M. Smith, 'The English peasantry 1250–1650', in T. Scott, ed., *The Peasantries of Europe from the Fourteenth Century to the Eighteenth Century* (London: Longman, 1998), pp. 341–7; and Poos and Bonfield, *Select Cases*, pp. lxxiii–cvii.

56 Hyams, *King, Lords*, pp. 145–7.

57 R. M. Smith, 'Some thoughts on "hereditary" and "proprietary" rights in land under customary law in thirteenth and early fourteenth century England', *Law and History Review*, 1 (1983): 95–128; Harvey, *The Peasant Land Market*; Slota, 'Law, land transfer', pp. 120–6; Hyams, 'What did Edwardian villagers mean?', pp. 80–3; Smith, 'The English peasantry' pp. 347–60.

58 Poos and Bonfield, *Select Cases*, pp. cvii–cxii. For example, inheritance of villein-holdings varied locally according to custom on the sixty manors held by the bishopric of Winchester; M. Page, 'The peasant land market in Southern England: The estate of the bishops of Winchester, 1260–1350', in Feller and Wickham, *Le marché de la terre*, pp. 315–40 (pp. 318–19).

59 For evidence of villein land held for lives before 1350, see G. C. Baugh, ed., *Victoria County History, Shropshire*, Vol. XI (London: Institute of Historical Research, 1985), pp. 117–18, 223; G. C. Baugh, ed., *Victoria County History, Shropshire*, Vol. X (London: Institute of Historical Research, 1998), pp. 183, 227; Baugh, *VCH, Shropshire*, Vol. IV, pp. 110–11; Rees, 'The leases', pp. 17–20; and Hatcher, *Rural Economy*, pp. 70–1.

60 Smith, 'Some thoughts', p. 106. See also Hyams, 'What did Edwardian villagers mean?', pp. 80–3; Razi and Smith, 'The origins', pp. 53–6; and Poos and Bonfield, *Select Cases*, pp. lxxxiv–lxxxv.

61 Harvey, *Westminster Abbey*, p. 279; Hyams, *King, Lords*, p. 69; Smith, 'Some thoughts', pp. 108, 110; Slota, 'Law, land transfer', pp. 121–3; J. S. Beckerman, 'Toward a theory of medieval manorial adjudication: The nature of communal judgments in a system of customary law', *Law and History Review*, 13 (1995): 1–22 (p. 12); Hyams, 'What did Edwardian villagers mean?', pp. 81–2; Poos and Bonfield, *Select Cases*, pp. lxxvi–lxxxv, cliv–clv.

62 Phillips, 'Collaboration and litigation', pp. 66–8.

63 Beckerman, 'Toward a theory', p. 17.

64 King, *Peterborough Abbey*, pp. 103–4.

65 Smith, 'Some thoughts', pp. 110–11; Razi and Smith, 'The origins', pp. 54–6; Poos and Bonfield, *Select Cases*, pp. cxxi–cxlv.

66 Slota, 'Law, land transfer', p. 131; Poos and Bonfield, *Select Cases*, p. lxxvi.
67 Hyams, *King, Lords*, p. 44; Slota, 'Law, land transfer', p. 123.
68 Slota, 'Law, land transfer', p. 131; Hyams, *King, Lords*, p. 49.
69 Poos and Bonfield, *Select Cases*, p. lxx; Hyams, 'What did Edwardian villagers mean?', pp. 81–3; Bailey, 'The transformation', p. 220.
70 Baildon, *Court Rolls 1274 to 1297*, pp. 88, 129.
71 Miller, *The Abbey and Bishopric*, pp. 148–9; see also McGibbon Smith, 'Reflections', pp. 78–9. For an example from Stanley (Yorkshire) in 1332, see Walker, *The Court Rolls 1331–3*, p. 39.
72 R. M. Smith, 'Some issues concerning families and their property in rural England 1250–1800', in R. M. Smith, ed., *Land, Kinship and Life-Cycle* (Cambridge: Cambridge University Press, 1984), pp. 1–86 (p. 64); Slota, 'Law, land transfer', p. 132; Eldridge, *Law and the Medieval Village Community*, p. 187. All the examples of arbitrary seizures of customary land cited in, for example, Miller and Hatcher, *Medieval England: Rural Society*, p. 117, are from the twelfth century.
73 R. Evans, 'Merton College's control of its tenants at Thorncroft, 1270–1349', in Razi and Smith, *Medieval Society*, pp. 199–259 (pp. 239–40); M. Page, 'The peasant land market on the estates of the bishop of Winchester before the Black Death', in R. H. Britnell, ed., *The Winchester Pipe Rolls and Medieval English Society* (Woodbridge: Boydell Press, 2003), pp. 61–80 (p. 77).
74 Poos and Bonfield, *Select Cases*, p. xcvi.
75 Smith, 'Some thoughts', pp. 100, 111–12; Poos and Bonfield, *Select Cases*, pp. cliv–clv; Eldridge, *Law and the Medieval Village Community*, pp. 176–8, 186.
76 Slota, 'Law, land transfer', pp. 125–6; Poos and Bonfield, *Select Cases*, pp. lxxvi–lxxxv, cliv.
77 Searle, *Lordship and Community*, pp. 135–9; Lister, *Court Rolls 1315–1317*, pp. 40, 195, 198; Walker, *Court Rolls 1331–3*, pp. 66–7, 205; Troup, *The Court Rolls*, pp. 64, 95–6, 101–2, 175–6, 196. See also Lock, *The Court Rolls 1303–1350*, pp. 5, 80, 105, 107, 126, 140, 168, 171, 259.
78 Ibid., pp. 64, 120, 196, 261.
79 Lister, *Court Rolls 1315–1317*, p. 201; Troup, *The Court Rolls*, pp. 183–5, 254.
80 Hatcher, *Rural Economy*, pp. 56, 98–9; Slota, 'Law, land transfer', pp. 126–7; Harvey, 'Introduction', pp. 19–28; J. Williamson, 'Norfolk: Thirteenth century', in Harvey, *The Peasant Land Market*, pp. 30–105; Smith, 'The English peasantry', pp. 341–69; Poos and Bonfield, *Select Cases*, pp. ci, cxxi–cxxvii; Campbell, 'The agrarian

problem', pp. 51–3; C. Dyer, 'Seigniorial profits on the land market in late medieval England', in Feller and Whickham, *Le marché de la terre*, pp. 219–36; Smith, 'Some issues', pp. 13–21, 65–8; B. M. S. Campbell, 'Population pressure, inheritance and the land market in a fourteenth-century peasant community', in Smith, *Land, Kinship*, pp. 87–134 (pp. 107–20); R. M. Smith, 'Families and their land in an area of partible inheritance: Redgrave, Suffolk 1260–1320', in Smith, *Land, Kinship*, pp. 135–96; Page, 'The peasant land market', pp. 61–80; Bailey, 'Villeinage', pp. 442–3; M. Page, 'The smallholders of Southampton Water: The peasant land market on a Hampshire manor before the Black Death', in S. Turner and B. Silvester, eds, *Life in Medieval Landscapes: People and Places in the Middle Ages. Papers in Memory of H. S. A. Fox* (Oxford: Oxford University Press, 2012), pp. 181–97 (pp. 186–90); P. R. Schofield, 'Lordship and the early history of peasant land transfer', in Kowaleski et al., *Peasants and Lords*, pp. 201–24 (pp. 206–20).

81 An important discussion is Schofield, 'Lordship and the early history'.

82 Smith, 'Families and their land', Table 3.7; Campbell, 'Population pressure', Table 2.11. Also around 150 per decade at Hinderclay; P. R. Schofield, 'The social economy of the medieval village in the early fourteenth century', *Economic History Review*, 61 (2008): 38–63 (p. 46); Bailey, *The Decline of Serfdom*, pp. 25–32.

83 Smith, 'Families and their land', Table 3.10; Smith, 'Some thoughts', pp. 116–18. See also P. R. Schofield, 'Dearth, debt and the local land market in a late thirteenth-century village community', *Agricultural History Review*, 45 (1997): 1–17 (pp. 4–5).

84 For examples of allocating head rents among the tenants of a subdivided holding, see Smith, 'Families and their land', pp. 141–5; and M. Bailey, *A Marginal Economy? East Anglian Breckland in the Later Middle Ages* (Cambridge: Cambridge University Press, 1989), pp. 48–50.

85 Dyer, 'Seigniorial profits', pp. 73–4.

86 J. Whittle, 'Individualism and the land–family bond: A reassessment of land transfer patterns among the English peasantry, 1270–1580', *Past & Present*, 160 (1998): 25–67; Dyer, 'Seigniorial profits', pp. 226–9; Thompson, 'The Polden Hill manors', pp. 89–95; Campbell, 'The agrarian problem', pp. 48–50; Page, 'The peasant land market', pp. 329–32; Mullan and Britnell, *Land and Family*, pp. 44–8; M. Müller, 'Seigniorial control and the peasant land market in the 14th century', in Feller and Wickham, *Le marché de la terre*, pp. 297–313.

87 See, for example, Page, 'The peasant land market', pp. 329–30.

88 Kanzaka, 'Villein rents', Table 2.

89 Hatcher, *Rural Economy*, p. 58; Harvey, *Westminster Abbey*, pp. 214, 242, 307–11; Levett, *Studies*, p. 188; Raftis, *Tenure and Mobility*, pp. 74–81, 90; Page, *The Estates*, pp. 112–13; Page, 'The peasant land market', pp. 331–2; McGibbon Smith, 'Reflections', pp. 76–8, 127; M. Page, 'Town and countryside in medieval Ivinghoe', *Records of Buckinghamshire*, 51 (2011): 189–203.

90 Harvey, *Westminster Abbey*, pp. 302–3, 317; R. Faith, 'Fourteenth century: Berkshire', in Harvey, *The Peasant Land Market*, pp. 106–77 (pp. 123, 125–6); Dyer, *Standards of Living*, p. 120.

91 Schofield, 'Lordship and the early history', pp. 219–20.

92 For example, Walker, *The Court Rolls 1331–3*, pp. 161–2, 174.

93 Most of the land was arable, with some meadow and pasture; Lock, *The Court Rolls 1303–1350*, pp. 43, 144, 149, 157, 182, 186, 227, 254, 256–7, 271, 278, 297, 300; Bailey, *The Decline of Serfdom*, p. 109.

94 Walker, *The Court Rolls 1331–3*, p. 212; Troup, *The Court Rolls*, p. 51, 55, 145; Watson, *The Court Rolls*, p. 62. See also D. Noy, ed., *The Winslow Manor Court Books, 1423–1460*, Buckinghamshire Record Society, 36 ([Aylesbury]: Buckinghamshire Record Society, 2011), p. 530.

95 McGibbon Smith, 'Reflections', pp. 73–9; for a similar case in Wakefield, see Baildon, *Court Rolls 1274 to 1297*, p. 81.

96 Briggs, 'English serfdom', pp. 25–6.

97 C. Dyer, *Making a Living in the Middle Ages: The People of Britain 850–1520* (London: Yale University Press, 2002), pp. 176–7; Kanzaka, 'Villein rents', pp. 600 n. 27, 612; Campbell, 'The agrarian problem', pp. 54–9.

98 Head rents on customary holdings at Codicote were ossified at 3d. per acre, whereas one sublessee paid 4.6d. per acre and another 4.8d. per acre; see Chapter 8.

99 Briggs, 'English serfdom', pp. 24–8.

100 Kanzaka, 'Villein rents', pp. 598–601; Page, 'The peasant land market', pp. 329–34.

101 Campbell, 'The agrarian problem', pp. 56–7.

102 Dyer, 'Seigniorial profits', p. 73; see also Evans, 'Merton College's control', p. 245.

103 P. R. Schofield, 'The market in free land on the estates of Bury St Edmunds, c. 1086–c. 1300', in L. Feller and C. Wickham, eds, *Le marché de la terre*, pp. 273–95 (pp. 281–90); Schofield, 'Lordship and the early history', pp. 201–24; Phillips, 'Collaboration and litigation', pp. 61–2.

104 Page, 'The peasant land market', pp. 329–33.

105 Mullan and Britnell, *Land and Family*, pp. 37–56; Page, 'The peasant land market', p. 65; Schofield, 'Lordship and the early history', pp. 206–8, 220.
106 For a brief introduction, see Bailey, *The Decline of Serfdom*, pp. 53–5.
107 Kosminsky, *Studies*, pp. 346–7, although no evidence is supplied to support this contention. Similarly, see Martin, *Feudalism to Capitalism*, pp. 235–6.
108 Fryde, *Peasants and Landlords*, pp. 14, 16.
109 Dimmock, *The Origin of Capitalism*, p. 83, although this assertion is not footnoted.
110 Dyer, *Standards of Living*, pp. 135–6; Dyer, *Making a Living*, pp. 141, 242; Dyer, 'Seigniorial profits', p. 223. See also Hilton, *A Medieval Society*, p. 145.
111 Faith, 'Fourteenth century: Berkshire', p. 147; Dyer, 'Seigniorial profits', p. 233; Kanzaka, 'Villein rents', pp. 613–14.
112 Dyer, *Standards of Living*, p. 138.
113 See, for example, Hilton, *A Medieval Society*, p. 145. Likewise, Fryde supports his statements about 'extortionate' entry fines with one short paragraph of anecdotal examples from three manors; *Peasants and Landlords*, pp. 14, 16.
114 Miller, *The Abbey and Bishopric*, p. 139.
115 Hilton, *A Medieval Society*, p. 145.
116 Z. Razi, *Life, Marriage and Death in a Medieval Parish: Economy, Society and Demography in Halesowen 1270–1400* (Cambridge: Past & Present Publications, 1980), p. 9; Dyer, *Standards of Living*, p. 138.
117 For evidence of wide variations within a given manor, and also for increasing rates of fine over the course of the thirteenth and early fourteenth centuries, see Dyer, 'Seigniorial profits', pp. 224–5, 227.
118 Page, 'The peasant land market', p. 338.
119 Hatcher, 'English serfdom', pp. 20–2; Kanzaka, 'Villein rents', pp. 609–12.
120 Dyer, *Standards of Living*, p. 138; Dyer, *Making a Living*, p. 242.
121 Raftis, *Peasant Economic Development*, pp. 15–17.
122 Hole, *Economic Ethics*, pp. 180–2.
123 Ibid., pp. 181–2; see Razi, *Life, Marriage*, p. 30.
124 For instance, in 1333 the court recorded the grant of 2 roods of servile land to a non-heir, who was charged a high entry fine of 6s. 8d. (i.e. 40d. per rood), whereas in a separate transaction another 2 roods were granted to an heir for an entry fine of 12d. (i.e. only 6d. per rood), whilst in the same year two female heirs to a messuage and 16

acres of land paid an entry fine of 5s. 6d. (i.e. less than 1d. per rood). Walker, *The Court Rolls 1331–3*, pp. 161, 165–6, 175. For some broad generalisations on the determinants of entry fines at Wakefield, see Hole, *Economic Ethics*, p. 180.

125 Razi, *Life, Marriage*, pp. 30–1.

126 Rigby, *English Society*, pp. 56–7; Hatcher, 'Lordship', p. 131.

127 There are, for example, 36,000 entry fines recorded in the pipe rolls relating to the bishopric of Winchester between 1263 and 1349; Page, 'The peasant land market', p. 316.

128 See, for example, J. A. Raftis, *The Estates of Ramsey Abbey: A Study in Economic Growth and Organisation* (Toronto: Pontifical Institute of Medieval Studies, 1957), pp. 238, 248; Titow, *English Rural Society*, pp. 73–8; Hatcher, 'English serfdom', 18; A. Jones, 'Bedfordshire: Fifteenth century', in Harvey, *The Peasant Land Market*, pp. 178–251 (pp. 211–12, 244–5); Raftis, *Peasant Economic Development*, pp. 15–17; Bolton, *The Medieval English Economy*, pp. 109–10; Kanzaka, 'Villein rents', pp. 613–14; Page, 'The peasant land market', pp. 78–9; Campbell, 'The agrarian problem', pp. 41–2; P. R. Schofield, 'Seigneurial exactions in eastern England, c. 1050–1300', in Bourin and Martínez Sopena, *Pour une anthropologie*, pp. 383–409 (pp. 400–1); Page, 'The peasant land market', pp. 338–40; Dyer, 'Seigniorial profits', pp. 219–36; Bailey, 'Villeinage', p. 444; Mullan and Britnell, *Land and Family*, pp. 74–5; Bailey, *The Decline of Serfdom*, pp. 53–5, 109, 126, 139, 175, 193, 208; Faith, 'Fourteenth century: Berkshire', pp. 114–18, 124, 132; J. Ravensdale, 'Population changes and the transfer of customary land on a Cambridgeshire manor in the fourteenth century', in Smith, *Land, Kinship*, pp. 197–226 (pp. 210–11); and J. Whittle, *The Development of Agrarian Capitalism: Land and Labour in Norfolk 1440–1580* (Oxford: Oxford University Press, 2000), pp. 79–82.

129 Titow, *English Rural Society*, pp. 73–8; Dyer, 'Seigniorial profits', Fig. 2; Bailey, *The Decline of Serfdom*, pp. 109, 208. Higher entry fines in East Anglia may also reflect the fact that inheriting tenants did not usually pay a heriot for the deceased's estate.

130 Mullan and Britnell, *Land and Family*, pp. 74–80. See also Titow, *English Rural Society*, pp. 73–8; and Hatcher, *Rural Economy*, p. 57.

131 Titow, *English Rural Society*, p. 78; Faith, 'Fourteenth century: Berkshire', pp. 115–17; T. Lomas, 'Fifteenth century: Durham', in Harvey, *The Peasant Land Market*, pp. 252–327 (pp. 307–8); Ravensdale, 'Population changes', p. 210; Dyer, *Making a Living*, pp. 295, 335; Dyer, 'Seigniorial profits', pp. 225–6, 231; Bailey, *The Decline of Serfdom*, pp. 109, 175, 193, 208; M. Yates, *Town*

and Countryside in Western Berkshire, c. 1327–c. 1600: Social and Economic Change (Woodbridge: Boydell and Brewer, 2007), pp. 144–5; Bailey, *After the Black Death*, p. 87; C. Dyer, *Peasants Making History: Living in an English Region 1200–1540* (Oxford: Oxford University Press, 2022), pp. 60–4.

132 Dyer, 'Seigniorial profits', p. 234.

133 Ibid., p. 230.

134 C. Dyer, *Everyday Life in Medieval England* (London: Hambledon Press, 1994), p. 206; Dyer, 'Seigniorial profits', pp. 225–6, 231.

135 Summarised in Bailey, *After the Black Death*, p. 87; this volume, Chapters 7– 10; and Dyer, *Peasants Making History*, pp. 61–2.

136 Kanzaka, 'Villein rents', pp. 613–14; Wells-Furby, *The Berkeley Estate*, p. 110.

137 Slota, 'Law, land transfer', pp. 132–4. Slota acknowledges the security of villein tenure and the fixity of rents on the estate of St Albans abbey, and the limitations placed on arbitrary seigniorial action by formal processes, but also states that the lord changed the rules and increased entry fines 'when it suited him' and notes 'the continuing potential for arbitrary action by the lord'. Yet he provides no other examples of arbitrary action, simply stating that arbitrary acts were 'not non-existent'.

138 Mullan and Britnell, *Land and Family*, pp. 74–5; Page, 'The peasant land market', pp. 78–9.

139 Titow, *English Rural Society*, p. 76.

140 Hatcher, 'English serfdom', pp. 18–19; Dyer, 'Seigniorial profits', pp. 233–5; Dyer, *Making a Living*, p. 175.

141 Campbell, 'The agrarian problem', p. 52; Dyer, 'Seigniorial profits', p. 229.

142 Smith, 'Some thoughts', p. 118; Bailey, 'Villeinage', pp. 444–5.

143 Watson, *The Court Rolls*, p. 145.

144 Noy, 'Winslow', p. 142; and see p. 000, this volume. D. Noy, ed., *The Winslow Manor Court Books, 1423–1460*, p. 528.

145 Dyer, 'Seigniorial profits', p. 233; C. Dyer, 'The language of oppression', p. 83; Finberg, *Tavistock Abbey*, p. 250.

146 Kanzaka, 'Villein rents', p. 614.

147 Raftis, *Peasant Economic Development*, pp. 15–17.

148 A 40s. fine on an estate valued at £26 9s. 11d.; Lock, *The Court Rolls 1303–1350*, pp. 132–5.

149 Dyer, 'The language of oppression', p. 83.

150 J. Brownhill, ed., *The Ledger-Book of Vale Royal Abbey*, Record Society for Lancashire and Cheshire, 68 ([Manchester]: Record Society of Lancashire and Cheshire, 1914), p. 134. Dyer, *Peasants*

Making History, p. 79, cites the Coventry reference and seems to imply that in 1402 the priory was still asserting and enforcing this right, and therefore continuing to implement villeinage, without providing any evidence that the priory was collecting tallage at this date or that it was charging tallage arbitrarily.

151 Kosminsky, *Studies*, pp. 346, 355. For a survey of similar views, see Bailey, 'Tallage-at-will', p. 25.

152 Hole, *Economic Ethics*, pp. 190–1, 193, 195.

153 Hatcher, *Rural Economy*, p. 61; Miller and Hatcher, *Medieval England: Rural Society*, p. 130; Britnell, *The Commercialisation*, p. 144; Kanzaka, 'Villein rents', p. 613; Campbell, 'The agrarian problem', pp. 41–2; Bailey, 'Tallage-at-will', pp. 25–48.

154 Bailey, *The Decline of Serfdom*, pp. 47–8, 178, 189, 263; Birrell, 'Manorial custumals', p. 27; Bailey, 'Tallage-at-will', p. 39.

155 Bailey, 'Villeinage', pp. 449–51; Bailey, *The Decline of Serfdom*, pp. 47–8.

156 Bailey, 'Tallage-at-will', p. 34.

157 Postan, 'Medieval agrarian society', pp. 603–4.

158 Figure calculated from the eight estates in Tables 7 and 8, plus Westminster abbey, Lenton priory and Worcester cathedral priory, in Bailey, 'Tallage-at-will', pp. 43, 45–7.

159 Ibid., pp. 25–48.

160 Dyer, *From Slavery to Freedom*, p. 16.

161 Bailey, 'Tallage-at-will', pp. 34, 39; E. Powell, ed., *A Suffolk Hundred in the Year 1283* (Cambridge: Cambridge University Press, 1910), p. 79.

162 Bailey, 'Tallage-at-will', pp. 37–8.

163 Powell, *A Suffolk Hundred*, pp. 78–82.

164 There were fifty-six horses, 340 sheep, ninety-two cows, fifty pigs and twenty-two oxen. Their value was calculated from the average price for each across both 1301–2 and 1302–3, as supplied by Farmer, 'Prices and wages', pp. 804–5, which works out at 11.3s. per ox, 9.31s. per horse, 8.44s. per cow, 1.36s. per sheep and 2.62s. per pig: grand total £106 19s. 10d. The amount paid as recognition on all this livestock was 97s. 10d.; Powell, *A Suffolk Hundred*, pp. 78–80. In 1302 the recognition payments at Culford were based on just sheep ownership, where 188s. was paid on 427 sheep valued at 580s., or 32 per cent of the total value.

165 Poos and Bonfield, *Select Cases*, pp. clxix, clxxv; Larson, *Conflict and Compromise*, p. 93.

166 Females only on the Crowland estate; Page, *The Estates*, p. 137; Bailey, *The Decline of Serfdom*, pp. 111, 116, 139, 188, 203, 223, 265.

167 For a summary, see R. M. Smith, 'Moving to marry among the customary tenants of late thirteenth-century and early fourteenth-century England', in P. Horden, ed., *Freedom of Movement in the Middle Ages: Proceedings of the 2003 Harlaxton Symposium* (Donington: Shaun Tyas, 2007), pp. 169–85; Poos and Bonfield, *Select Cases*, p. clxxiii; and Bailey, *The Decline of Serfdom*, pp. 37–40. The main literature comprises Scammell, 'Freedom and marriage'; E. Searle, 'Freedom and marriage in medieval England: An alternative hypothesis', *Economic History Review*, 29 (1976): 482–6; E. Searle, 'Seigniorial control of women's marriage: The antecedents and function of merchet in England', *Past and Present*, 82 (1979): 3–43; Hyams, *King, Lords*, pp. 187–90; J. M. Bennett, 'Medieval peasant marriage: An examination of marriage license fines in the *Liber Gersumarum*', in J. A. Raftis, ed., *Pathways to Medieval Peasants* (Toronto: Pontifical Institute of Medieval Studies, 1981), pp. 193–246; P. A. Brand and P. R. Hyams, 'Seigneurial control of women's marriage', *Past & Present*, 99 (1983): 123–32; E. Searle, 'A rejoinder', *Past & Present*, 99 (1983): 148–60; L. R. Poos, Z. Razi, and R. M. Smith, 'The population history of medieval English villages: A debate on the use of manor court rolls', in Razi and Smith, *Medieval Society*, pp. 298–368 (pp. 316–33); E. D. Jones, 'Medieval merchets as demographic data: Some evidence from the Spalding priory estates, Lincolnshire', *Continuity and Change*, 11:3 (1996): 459–70; and Poos and Bonfield, *Select Cases*, pp. clxvii–clxxxi.

168 Brand and Hyams, 'Seigneurial Control', pp. 131–3. See the discussions in Smith, 'Moving to marry', pp. 175–6, 182–5; K. Parkin, 'Courts and the community: Reconstructing the fourteenth-century peasant society of Wisbech Hundred, Cambridgeshire, from manor court rolls' (PhD thesis, University of Leicester, 1998), pp. 151–6; R. M. Smith, 'Further models of medieval marriage: Landlords, serfs and priests in rural England, c. 1290–1370', in C. Duhamel-Amado and G. Lobrichon, eds, *Georges Duby: L'écriture de l'histoire* (Brussels: De Boeck Université, 1992), pp. 161–74; M. Müller, 'The function and evasion of marriage fines on a fourteenth-century English manor', *Continuity and Change*, 14 (1999): 169–90; Jones, 'Medieval merchets', p. 461; and Bailey, 'Villeinage', pp. 439–40.

169 Parkin, 'Courts and the community', pp. 140, 152.

170 Farrer, *Court Rolls*, p. 31.

171 Merchet was rare at Hadleigh and last enforced in 1344 (Woods, *Medieval Hadleigh*, p. 113), even though liability for merchet was recorded as a condition of tenure in a survey of 1305; Birrell, 'Manorial custumals', p. 18. Just two merchets are recorded in the

twenty-four extant court rolls of Monks Eleigh between 1305 and 1422; Aldous, *Monks Eleigh*, pp. xxvii, 138. Dyer, 'From slavery to freedom', p. 28.

172 Phillips, 'Collaboration and litigation', p. 185; Bailey, 'Villeinage', p. 439; McGibbon Smith, 'Reflections', pp. 39–40.

173 Smith, 'Further models', pp. 161–174, 173; Smith, 'Moving to marry', pp. 182, 185.

174 For an example in a survey, see Tringham, *Three Thirteenth- and Fourteenth-Century Surveys*, pp. 12–13. For historians citing its arbitrariness, see Hilton, *A Medieval Society*, p. 145; Martin, *Feudalism to Capitalism*, pp. 235–6; and Dyer, 'Memories of freedom', pp. 290–1.

175 Although some Ramsey abbey manors stipulated a cap of 5s.; Birrell, 'Manorial custumals', p. 30; E. D. Jones, 'The Spalding priory merchet evidence from the 1250s to the 1470s', *Journal of Medieval History*, 24:2 (1998): 155–75 (p. 158).

176 Poos, *A Rural Society*, p. 134; Smith, 'Further models', pp. 169–73; Parkin, 'Courts and the community', pp. 154–6.

177 McGibbon Smith, 'Reflections', p. 95 n. 19.

178 Ravensdale, 'Population changes', pp. 203, 209.

179 Lock, *The Court Rolls 1303–1350*, p. 15; Thompson, 'The Polden Hill manors', pp. 153–4; Dyer, 'From slavery to freedom', p. 16; Bailey, *The Decline of Serfdom*, pp. 111, 116, 202, 265; Birrell, 'Manorial custumals', p. 30; Finberg, *Tavistock Abbey*, pp. 77–8; Larson, *Conflict and Compromise*, pp. 93–4; M. Stock, 'The exercise of manorial lordship on the manor of Chedzoy, Somerset, 1327–1377' (MSt thesis, University of Cambridge, 2023), p. 26.

180 Smith, 'Further models', p. 172, Table 6a; Dyer, 'Memories of freedom', p. 42; Dyer, 'Ineffectiveness', p. 74; Dyer, 'Language of oppression', p. 83; Bailey, *Decline of Serfdom*, pp. 38–9.

181 McGibbon Smith, 'Reflections of reality', pp. 38–9, 93.

182 Dyer, 'The ineffectiveness of lordship', p. 74; Dyer, 'The language of oppression', 83.

183 Farmer, 'Prices and wages', pp. 766–7.

184 See also Jones, 'The Spalding priory merchet', p. 164; and Stock, 'The exercise', pp. 30–1.

185 For a recent summary, see Bailey, *The Decline of Serfdom*, pp. 40–1. The main literature comprises T. North, 'Legerwite in the thirteenth and fourteenth centuries', *Past & Present*, 111 (1986): 3–16; E. D. Jones, 'The medieval leyrwite: A historical note upon fornication', *English Historical Review*, 107:425 (1992): 945–53; Poos and Bonfield, *Select Cases*, pp. clxxxi–clxxxiv; and J. M. Bennett, 'Writing

fornication: Medieval leyrwite and its historians', *TRHS*, 6th series, 13 (2003): 131–62.

186 Bennett, 'Writing fornication', p. 141; Dyer, *Lords and Peasants*, p. 104; Dyer, 'From slavery to freedom', p. 27.

187 Jones, 'The medieval leyrwite', p. 948; Bennett, 'Writing fornication', pp. 138–40; Parkin, 'Courts and the community', pp. 163–4; J. M. Bennett, 'Married and not: Weston's grown children in 1268–1269', *Continuity and Change*, 34 (2019): 151–82 (p. 157); A. Raw, 'Life after leyrwite: Sexual subjectivity on the medieval manor, c. 1270–c. 1330', in G. Dodd and H. Lacey, eds, *Fourteenth Century England*, Vol. XIII (Woodbridge: Boydell Press, 2025), pp. 1–18 (pp. 1–6).

188 Bennett, 'Writing fornication', pp. 136–7; for Wakefield, see this volume, p. 5; P. Foden, trans., *Records of the Manor of Norton in the Liberty of St Albans 1244–1539*, Hertfordshire Record Publications, 29 (n.p.: Hertfordshire Record Society, 2014), p. xlvi.

189 McGibbon Smith, 'Reflections', pp. 42–3.

190 P. J. P. Goldberg, *Medieval England: A Social History 1250–1550* (London: Hodder Arnold, 2004), p. 90.

191 Dyer, 'From slavery to freedom', pp. 13, 21.

192 Bennett, 'Writing fornication', pp. 151–2; North, 'Legerwite', p. 11; Larson, *Conflict and Compromise*, p. 103; Jones, 'The medieval leyrwite', p. 948; Ravensdale, 'Population changes', p. 211; Parkin, 'Court and community', 165; McGibbon Smith, 'Reflections', p. 43. For higher fines of around 5s., see Finberg, *Tavistock Abbey*, p. 78; and Dyer, *Lords and Peasants*, p. 273.

193 McGibbon Smith, 'Reflections', p. 43.

194 Bailey, 'Villeinage', pp. 440–1.

195 Hyams, *King, Lords*, pp. 25–37; Hatcher, 'English serfdom', pp. 30–2.

196 Cheyney, 'The disappearance', p. 28; Hilton, *Class Conflict*, p. 52.

197 Brenner, 'The rises and declines', pp. 248, 263; Brenner, 'Property and progress', p. 64.

198 Raftis, *Tenure and Mobility*, pp. 129–50; Briggs, 'English serfdom', p. 29; Razi, *Life, Marriage*, 30–1; Hatcher, *Rural Economy*, pp. 78, 101.

199 Raftis, *Tenure and Mobility*, p. 141.

200 Poos, *A Rural Society*, p. 160; Evans, 'Merton College's control', p. 245; Bailey, *Medieval Suffolk*, pp. 57–8; Briggs, 'English serfdom', p. 29; Bailey, *The Decline of Serfdom*, pp. 42–6; Dyer, *The Age of Transition?*, p. 94; Larson, *Conflict and Compromise*, pp. 64–5; Bailey, 'Servile and gender migration', pp. 58–61, Tables 1 and 2; Gibbs, *Lordship, State Formation*, Table 3.3.

201 Bailey, 'Servile and gender migration', Table 1.

202 Suffolk Archives (SA), E3/1/2.1–2.7 and HD526/92/1. The chevage case is 'Thomas Hankyn took his oath for 1d annually at the feast of St Michael for paying chevage and for one court appearance at the feast of St Michael', court held September 1330, SA, E3/1/2.2.

203 Thompson, 'The Polden Hill manors', p. 154; Stock, 'The exercise', pp. 43–4. For another west country example, see Franklin, 'Politics', pp. 94–5.

204 Vinogradoff, *Villeinage*, pp. 157–9; Campbell, 'The agrarian problem', pp. 61–2.

205 Peters, 'Government finance', p. 150.

206 Raftis, *Tenure and Mobility*, pp. 139–40; Briggs, 'English serfdom', pp. 29–30; Bailey, *The Decline of Serfdom*, p. 43.

207 Vinogradoff, *Villeinage*, p. 157.

208 Bailey, *The Decline of Serfdom*, p. 45.

209 E. D. Domar, 'The causes of slavery or serfdom: A hypothesis', *Journal of Economic History*, 30 (1970): 18–32 (pp. 20–1); Brenner, 'The rises and declines', pp. 248, 263; Brenner, 'Property and progress', p. 64; Peters, 'Government finance', Map 1.

210 Bailey, *The Decline of Serfdom*, p. 46.

211 See, for example, Bailey, 'Servile and gender migration', Tables 1 and 3.

212 Kanzaka, 'Villein rents', pp. 612–14; Hatcher, 'English serfdom', p. 15.

213 Hyams, *King, Lords*, p. 185; Hatcher, 'English serfdom', p. 23; Poos and Bonfield, *Select Cases*, p. lxxiv; Bailey, 'Tallage-at-will', pp. 52–6.

214 Hatcher, 'English serfdom', p. 9.

215 Ogilvie, 'Choices and constraints', pp. 269–76.

216 Ibid., pp. 278–81.

217 Evans, 'Whose was the manorial court?', p. 155. See also Martin, *Feudalism to Capitalism*, p. 43.

218 Bailey, *After the Black Death*, pp. 32–8; M. Bailey, 'The regulation of the rural market in waged labour in fourteenth century England', *Continuity and Change*, 38 (2023): 137–62.

219 C. Briggs, *Credit and Village Society in Fourteenth-Century England* (Oxford: Oxford University Press, 2009).

220 C. Dyer and P. R. Schofield, 'Recent work on the agrarian history of medieval Britain', in I. Alfonso, ed., *The Rural History of Medieval European Societies: Trends and Perspectives* (Turnhout: Brepols, 2007), pp. 21–56 (pp. 44–5); Dyer, *Peasants Making History*, pp. 1–9, 342–5.

221 For general overviews, see Masschaele, *Peasants, Merchants*, pp. 161–225; Dyer and Schofield, 'Recent work', pp. 33–7; Schofield,

Peasants and Historians, pp. 117–47; Bailey, *After the Black Death*, 39–44; and Dyer, *Peasants Making History*, pp. 159–63, 222–3.

222 Campbell, 'The agrarian problem', p. 37; Ghosh, 'Rural economies', pp. 257–61.

223 Masschaele, *Peasants, Merchants*, pp. 45–6; Raftis, *Peasant Economic Development*, pp. 12–18.

224 Slavin, 'Peasant livestock husbandry', pp. 13, 22–3.

225 E. Power, *The Wool Trade in English Medieval History* (Oxford: Oxford University Press, 1941), pp. 29–40; R. H. Britnell, *Britain and Ireland 1050–1300: Economy and Society* (Oxford: Oxford University Press, 2005), pp. 214–17; Slavin, 'Peasant livestock husbandry', p. 22; Lock, *The Court Rolls 1303–1350*, p. 135. The rare survival of tithe accounts at Lakenheath (Suffolk) shows that in the 1340s the total number of peasant sheep (c. 2,300) outnumbered those of the demesne (c. 2,200); Bailey, *A Marginal Economy?*, Tables 4.14 and 4.15.

226 Masschaele, *Peasants, Merchants*, pp. 134–5, 151.

227 Ibid., p. 205; J. M. Bennett, *Women in the Medieval English Countryside: Gender and Household in Brigstock before the Plague* (Oxford: Oxford University Press, 1987), pp. 54–8.

228 R. M. Smith, 'Families and their land', pp. 170–1; Bailey, *Medieval Suffolk*, p. 142; J. Davis and J. Sear, eds, *Records of Medieval Newmarket: Manor Court Rolls 1399–1413 and Manor Account Rolls 1403–1483*, Suffolk Records Society, 66 (Woodbridge: Boydell Press, 2023), pp. 42, 49, 62, 64, 66, 69–70, 74, 76, 79, 140–4.

229 J. Birrell and D. Hutchinson, 'An Alrewas rental of 1341', *Collections for a History of Staffordshire*, 20 (2004): 59–81 (p. 81) reveals 1/24th for commercial tolls, 1/30th for domestic.

230 Dyer, *Standards of Living*, p. 136; Dyer, 'Memories of freedom', p. 423; Hilton, *Class Conflict*, p. 52.

231 Hilton, *A Medieval Society*, p. 134; Thompson, 'The Polden Hill manors', p. 109; H. E. Salter, ed., *The Cartulary of the Abbey of Eynsham*, Vol. II, Oxfordshire History Society, 51 (Oxford: Clarendon Press, 1908), pp. 62–4.

232 Miller, *The Abbey and Bishopric*, pp. 127, 139.

233 Gibbs, *Lordship, State Formation*, p. 134; Briggs, 'English serfdom', p. 20.

234 D. L. Farmer, 'Marketing the produce of the countryside', in E. Miller, ed., *The Agrarian History of England and Wales*, Vol. III, *1348–1550* (Cambridge: Cambridge University Press, 1991), pp. 324–430 (p. 385 n. 190).

235 C. Briggs, 'Peasant, lords and commerce: Market regulation at Balsham, Cambridgeshire, in the early fourteenth century', in Kowaleski et al., *Peasants and Lords*, pp. 247–72 (pp. 262–3). The same estate, the bishopric of Ely, also prohibited villeins from selling their bulls or male horses without the lord's permission according to a survey of 1251, but it was seldom enforced in manor courts; Bailey, *The English Manor*, p. 52.
236 Foden, *Records of the Manor of Norton*, pp. 114–15.
237 Page, *The Estates*, p. 374.
238 Briggs, 'English serfdom', pp. 19–20.
239 Bailey, *After the Black Death*, pp. 48–50.
240 Miller, *The Abbey and Bishopric*, pp. 150–1; Raftis, *Peasant Economic Development*, pp. 12–18; DeWindt, *Land and People*, pp. 196–7.
241 Smith, 'Families and their land', 165–70; Lock, *The Court Rolls 1303–1350*, 89–138; S. H. A. Hervey, ed., *Suffolk in 1327: Being a Subsidy Return* (London: G. Booth, 1906), pp. 39, 183; Bailey, *Medieval Suffolk*, pp. 59–61.
242 See, for example, Lock, *The Court Rolls 1303–1350*, pp. 55, 60, 62, 103, 122–3; and Hervey, *Suffolk in 1327*, p. 183.
243 W. S. Thomson, ed., *A Lincolnshire Assize Roll for 1298*, Lincoln Record Society, 36 (Hereford: Hereford Times, 1944), p. xlvi n. 3.
244 Briggs, 'English serfdom', p. 23.
245 Brenner, 'The rises and declines', p. 258.
246 Campbell, 'The agrarian problem', p. 69.
247 For the attitudes to serfdom of monastic lords in general and Ramsey in particular, see Dyer, *Standards of Living*, p. 136; Kosminsky, *Studies*, p. 112; and Raftis, *Peasant Economic Development*, pp. 12–27, 118–23.
248 Jedwab et al., 'The economic impact', p. 163.
249 Hyams, 'What did Edwardian villagers mean?', p. 71.
250 Bailey, 'Tallage-at-will', pp. 56–7.
251 Dyer, 'From slavery to freedom', pp. 12–15, 20–7.
252 Raftis, *Peasant Economic Development*, pp. 21, 28–32, 47–8.
253 Briggs, 'English serfdom', p. 17.

4

Serfdom in practice: Access to the law

A major theme in the scholarship on English serfdom is the demeaning exclusion of hereditary serfs and tenants of servile land from the common law, and their consequent vulnerability in legal theory to seigniorial whim, coercion and exploitation. Such a view is consistent with the stereotypes that in feudal societies serfs were reliant on their lords for the provision of justice and that emerging legal systems served to codify and reinforce the interests of tiny ruling elites over the massed lower orders of society.[1] In this chapter I explore the actual practice of the lord's manorial court in order to determine if it did serve as an instrument of seigniorial will or whether it regulated the lord's relationship with the villein in more nuanced ways. I then consider the standing of villeins more broadly within the hierarchical and overlapping systems of English statute, common, canon and mercantile law.

From the outset, it is important to stress that the lord's manor court was not simply a court in the narrow modern sense of a legal tribunal, because alongside its legal role it also performed functions that were political (such as enforcing seigniorial rights over the peasantry) and administrative (such as regulating the agricultural practices of the community as a whole), as well as bestowing on lords the status associated with dispensing justice.[2] The challenge is to disentangle these different strands to establish the extent to which lords dominated the business of their courts for their own personal benefit and directed the judgments made there at their own discretion, and to examine whether villeins used the courts for their own purposes or even to restrict the lord's freedom of action.

As we shall see, an examination of the operation of manorial courts reveals that their business and decision-making were not driven by the arbitrary will and judgement of the lord, and that their procedures were heavily influenced by customary law and were increasingly standardised along common law principles. Disputes between lords and their villeins were rare, and those which occurred were most often resolved through an established due process with regard to custom and written precedents, whereby decisions might fall in favour of the latter. Fines in the courts were determined by peers, not the lord. Furthermore, serfs were also able to seek justice in tribunals outside the control of their own lord, subject to some minor constraints. The immersion of serfs in an emerging English legal system and culture helped to protect their ownership of moveable goods, enabled them to make enforceable contracts and to obtain rudimentary access to credit. Indeed, serfs themselves were heavily invested in the operation and success of the legal system, serving as the curial jurors and officials who upheld and enforced customary, statute and merchant law. Serfs even ran market franchises themselves, pursued litigation in tribunals beyond their home manorial courts, and utilised some of the royal courts, all of which reflected their widespread involvement in commodity markets, reduced some of the risk in their commercial transactions, and enabled some serfs to become among the wealthiest residents of their communities.

The manor court

According to the common law of villeinage, serfs were entirely subject to the will of their lord and could not plead against their lord in matters relating to tenure in the royal courts. Furthermore, as their goods and chattels theoretically belonged to their lord, they were open to the charge of wasting their lord's assets if they spent money litigating in other courts or suffered seizures of their goods while trading. Various historians have stressed how this legal theory placed severe limitations on serfs in practice.[3] Hence, for Cheyney, 'the only court in which [the villein] possesses a standing is his lord's own court on the manor', an interpretation echoed in Dimmock's recent statement that serfs were 'entirely subjected to their lord's jurisdiction'.[4] For historians in the Marxist tradition, this legal constraint worked to the profound detriment of the serf, because they tend to see legal and political power in instrumentalist terms as a means of buttressing the lords' property rights and social supremacy.[5] Kosminsky, for example, characterised the exclusion of villeins from the royal courts as tantamount to 'abandoning villeins to the lord's will', so that the manor court 'became more and more a purely villein court': as such, it 'was to a far greater extent an apparatus for the maintenance of servile discipline among the peasants and for the extraction of additional rent, than an organ for protecting their personal and property rights'.[6] For Brenner the emergence of the common law consigned serfs 'explicitly to their lord's jurisdiction', which constituted 'a mobilisation of the power of the monarchical state behind the efforts of lords to dominate, and thereby to exploit, their unfree tenants'.[7] Martin believes that the manor court imposed an 'oppressive legal framework within which the full extent of feudal landlord power could be mobilised. The economic subsumption of the community was ensured by its political subsumption through the manorial courts.'[8] For Dimmock, these 'private law courts' were the main medium for the 'extra-economic coercion' of the peasantry, free as well as unfree, applying 'extra-economic compulsion by feudal powers' that 'represented a serious disability' to serfs.[9]

It is not only Marxists who regard the operation of the manor court as fundamentally detrimental to serfs. Thus, for Dyer, 'the dramatic extension of the scope of royal justice and of the common law' in the early thirteenth century brought about 'a sudden and profound strengthening of lordly control over much of the peasantry' and cast 'the servile population under private jurisdiction': for him, 'seigniorial courts were the key instrument for the maintenance of lordly control'.[10] Similarly, Evans viewed the manor court as the central 'instrument of seigniorial control' in a relationship characterised by 'exploitation', whose mechanics 'consistently secured eventual compliance' to the lord's will.[11] Slota has depicted the manor court as a means of maintaining the social order in general and villeinage in particular: landlords improved the 'law and practice of manor courts to reinforce the institution of villeinage'.[12] For Fryde, 'anything that hurt the lord was sure to be prohibited', with manorial courts revealing the 'oppressive interference of the lords with the lives and conduct of their servile dependants'.[13] Consequently, the profits from the operation of manor courts are presented as an important source of income to lords: a single court could yield between £10 and £20 per annum, and the combined income of all courts on a single estate could contribute over 10 per cent of total seigniorial revenues.[14]

If these views are correct, then serfs' experience of the law and justice was bleak. Since they were unable to plead in any court other than their lord's manor court, their dependence on the quality of justice there was total. Yet they were unlikely to receive fair justice in a seigniorial jurisdiction run by the lord or his appointed officials, whose business and, especially, decision-making were an extension of the preferences and interests of the lord, and when villeins possessed no scope to appeal against its judgments. If this was the reality for villeins, then, as Hyams points out, they could harbour 'slim hopes of seigniorial grace': even worse, they could not personally pursue a wrong by a third party outside their manor, in which case their only hope was to persuade their lord to take up the wrong on their behalf.[15]

Yet many other historians have rejected such views of the function of manorial courts. Vinogradoff argued long ago that 'it would be very wrong to assume' that it 'could act only in the interest of the lord', while Maitland stated that the court primarily administered the custom of the manor, which was broader than the lord's narrow interests and also tempered the will of the lord.[16] Aggregate analysis of thousands of Inquisitions Post Mortem has revealed the relative unimportance of curial revenues to most lords, thereby diminishing their significance as an instrument of extraction and control: the vast majority of manor courts generated less than 16s. per annum, and contributed less than 2 per cent of estate income.[17] The Toronto School of historians has focused on the communal role of manorial courts, concluding that they promoted mutual interests between lords and villeins, while facilitating greater social and economic cooperation among peasants.[18] Viewed from this perspective, manorial courts provided a forum for an ongoing dialogue and collaborative relationship between lords and tenants, characterised by negotiation, consensus and 'mutual formation' of common interests. Villeins had a vested interest in the administration and recording of the business of the manor court, which they believed would improve their social and economic position within the existing framework of rural social relations. In extreme cases, 'the body of customary tenants were, in a manner of speaking, lords in their village'.[19]

The existence of such strongly opposing interpretations of the operation of the manor court is yet another powerful illustration of the conflicting and confusing array of views that continue to characterise the academic literature about English serfdom. In this section, we draw on the expanding body of research over the last four decades into the mechanics, business, procedures and decision-making of manorial courts, in order to resolve these conflicting views.

Attendance

In theory, all villeins owed 'suit' to the manor court of their lord, meaning they were to attend and to contribute to its business as required. The requirement to perform suit was usually stated explicitly as part of the terms of landholding and in manorial custumals. It was an indisputable obligation of servile status. The extent to which, and the grounds on which, free tenants owed suit to the manor court is less certain.[20] In the mid-thirteenth century these uncertainties became a bone of contention between them and their lords, and as a consequence in 1259 attracted considerable attention in the Provisions of Westminster.[21] In 1267 the Statute of Marlborough established that a freeholder was only bound to perform suit to the manor court if this obligation was explicitly stated in the grant of land to them or if it had been required of them personally before 1230.[22] A few high-status landlords, such as Durham priory, held separate courts for their free tenants.[23] From the end of the thirteenth century manorial surveys tended to state explicitly whether any free tenants owed suit of court, although, even then, they were not usually required to attend every session.[24] For example, freemen were only required to attend the manor courts of both Redgrave and Rickinghall once a year, unless directly involved in a case.[25] Few free tenants were as onerously burdened as those of Eggington (Bedfordshire), who were required to perform suit of court every three weeks and to record their land transfers in its rolls.[26] In general, it is clear that freemen were, at best, irregular attendees of manorial courts. Of course, freemen who held some customary land were obliged to attend the manor court as part of the terms of their tenure.[27]

Hence, villeins were the only category of people obliged to attend the manor court routinely, whereas free people did so to varying degrees, which could be interpreted as a coercive and onerous requirement of villeinage. Indeed, given that by 1300 most courts met every two or three months, and a few met every three weeks, and given that attendance also implied the liability to serve on manorial juries or to be elected to various manorial offices, such as reeve, hayward and rent collector, then the obligation becomes even more onerous.[28] Yet the reality was rather different. The court rolls never list the attendees or the absentees at each session, so we can never know definitively how rigorously attendance was enforced. The courts only paid consistent attention to tenants who were habitual absentees and to absentees who were actively engaged in ongoing cases, any of whom could formalise their absence from a given court session through the payment of a small sum (a couple of pennies, equivalent to one or two days' wages). Thus, the internal evidence of the court implies that a degree of non-attendance was tolerated, particularly from serfs who were not heads of households. One detailed analysis – based on the painstaking evaluation of thousands of individuals and cases in the courts of Redgrave and Hinderclay between 1289 and 1364 – suggests that only 15 per cent of villein landholders attended the manor court in any given year.[29] The regular attendees at manor courts were the heads of villein households. Although they were obliged to attend, their presence offered opportunities to contribute to and influence the business of the court and its decision-making. As we shall see, they had a stake of sorts in the running of the court.

Procedure

How manor courts were run provides an insight into the weight given to seigniorial power, will and discretion on the one hand, and to an adherence to some form of established due process on the other. As manor courts were essentially the private court of the manorial lord, then in theory they were free to develop their own idiosyncratic procedures in splendid isolation from other courts.[30] Indeed, if they were run predominantly as the personal instrument of the lord's will, then we would expect their procedures to differ greatly from one court to another. There is some evidence of procedural idiosyncrasy in the earliest extant manor court rolls – i.e. those dating from the third quarter of the thirteenth century – where the modes of recording business are rather haphazard. After 1275, however, there emerged a remarkable degree of uniformity in the formats and procedures of manorial courts held by different landlords, even in far-flung regions of England.[31] In effect, some common law procedures and processes had been grafted onto the customary law that had long been the basis of practice in village-based assemblies. Legal historians have been engaged in a debate about the character of customary law, its relationship with the common law and whether its principles were fixed or flexible.[32] The important point in this context is that customary practices, alongside other practices adapted and imported from the common law, were the primary influences on how manorial courts were run and what business they transacted (see pp. 151–8): seigniorial power and discretion had some influence, but it was a secondary factor.

The standardisation of the procedures is most apparent in how cases were brought to the manor court and how they were determined. Only the lowest-status lords would have routinely attended the manorial court sessions in person, although higher-status lords might attend occasionally, and so courts were usually administered by an estate steward and by the lord's paid or elected officials.[33] The person presiding over the court acted 'more as moderator than judge'.[34] The steward and manorial officeholders could bring cases to the court on the lord's behalf, and they could be punished by the court for failing to discharge their duties to the lord properly. In this sense, the court was manifestly the lord's, and his jurisdictional interests were strongly evident in its business, as we shall see.[35] Yet the suitors – those required to attend the court – were responsible for bringing and determining the majority of cases, and they did so through one of two standardised mechanisms: either by an elected and sworn jury of presentment or by individuals pursuing private litigation.[36] In addition, an inquisition jury might be empanelled to deal with specific cases.[37] The presentment jury was responsible for both initiating and determining cases. Its testimony was given under oath and it was also compelled to report against a proscribed list of potential offences, including those which infringed the lord's jurisdictional interests.[38] These procedural developments indicate how a basic notion of law had largely displaced and limited the influence of seigniorial power in the running of the lord's court.[39]

The vast majority of the jurors determining what cases were heard in the manorial court and judging their outcome were villeins.[40] A recent comprehensive study by Spike Gibbs, drawing on thousands of named jurors on a variety of manors spread across England, concluded that they were the economically more prosperous peasants, most of whom were unfree and who served willingly and collaboratively, because they had a vested interest in so doing.[41] The judgments of the vast majority of manorial courts were said to be those of 'the whole body of the court', which conveyed that this was the collective verdict of the jurors and the lord's representatives. A handful of powerful ecclesiastical lords might claim the theoretical right to override decisions made in their courts, but they rarely exercised it; the vast majority of lords did not interfere with judgments and they complied with local customs.[42] The judgments of presentment juries relied less on an impartial scrutiny of the facts of the matter and more on insider knowledge of people and events: this distinguished their practice from the common law and from modern notions of principled adjudication.[43] Yet the jurors were heavily influenced in their decision-making by verbal testimonies, local customs, and the written precedents contained in court rolls and manorial custumals.[44] Cases brought by individuals as private plaints were usually determined either through witnesses stating on oath what happened; or through the production of tallies or recognisances; or by waging law; or, occasionally, by means of an inquest jury.[45]

The role of the manorial tenantry in general, and of villeins in particular, in the composition of presentment juries offered some protection from arbitrary seigniorial behaviour and the excesses of seigniorial officials. It helped to ensure that the lord and his officials met expectations, and managed to hold the latter to some sort of account.[46] Villein jurors were especially influential in the creation of detailed written records of the customs of the manor and contributed to the construction of written surveys and custumals recording the obligations of villeins.[47] The quantity of, and detail in, these records increased exponentially over the course of the thirteenth century, and while they documented the lords' rights over villeinage they also provided the villeins with an opportunity to resist new seigniorial demands, to record disagreements, to bargain and to negotiate solutions.[48] The ability of villeins to contribute to the creation of custumals, and to present and determine cases in manor courts, acted as a safety valve in lord–tenant relations, and, as Gibbs states, 'strongly refutes the notion of a largely conflictual relationship before 1349'.[49]

Gibbs has also conducted the most recent and holistic assessment of villein tenants in their roles as elected manorial officials (such as reeves and jurors), including of how successful they were in mediating the conflict between helping their lord to receive all the due profits of lordship and retaining good relations with their fellow serfs. He concluded that the tenant-office system allowed villeins 'to defend themselves against aspects of seigniorial administration'.[50] An excellent example is the way in which villein tenants dominated the office of affeerer, an elected court official who helped to determine the monetary value of fines (meaning fees and licences) and amercements (meaning punishments for misdemeanours) imposed by the court. The affeerer was there to ensure that the size of payments was referenced against a customary and accepted scale for the relevant licence or offence, and to ensure that the defendant's ability to pay was considered, all of which tempered the lord's notion of what should be rendered.[51] Most manor courts elected affeerers, so the practice was widespread and commonplace.[52] Their influence, alongside the influence of custom, explains the persistence of common patterns in the level of fines documented in Chapter 3. Of course, the lord might exert pressure for higher payments in specific cases, which affeerers might find difficult to resist, but the consistency of servile payments and their referencing against customary norms indicates that such pressures were unusual. After all, a thirteenth-century estate treatise advised lords to allow the peasantry to set the level of amercements themselves and even encouraged lords to intervene if they thought that the level of amercement was too high.[53]

By c. 1300 the role of villein jurors in presenting cases and resolving disputes, the presence of affeerers in regulating the size of fines and servile dues, and the use of common procedures and processes in almost every manorial court across the country serve as the most powerful testimony of the extent to which the mechanics of these 'private' courts had been standardised during the second half of the thirteenth century. We explore the reasons for this in Chapter 5, but one element was the importation of some basic procedures from the common law.[54] This is evident in the way in which courts handled the transfer of villein land from one tenant to another, which by the end of the thirteenth century was standardised and formulaic, and resembled the forms of action in royal courts.[55] As a result, to all intents and purposes, the transfer of customary land seems to 'have become all but indistinguishable from free land'.[56] Crucially, disputes over the title to servile land were not resolved through the arbitrary decision-making of the lord, but instead followed many of the basic principles involving free tenure in the common law. Hence, villein tenants routinely paid to have earlier court rolls searched for written evidence of their title to land or they produced their own written copies of the court record of their land transfer. These adaptations underpinned the de facto security of villein tenure, as described in Chapter 3. As a consequence, as Briggs writes, the manor courts 'extended to customary tenants the same security of tenure which the royal courts had earlier given to free tenants'.[57] The only difference was that a freeholder could access the royal courts, effectively a court of appeal, to defend the title to the land, whereas a villein could not.

Another major area where, by the end of the thirteenth century, common law processes had become embedded and standardised in manorial courts was the adoption of the staged process of summons, attachment and distraint to enforce compliance with the court's directives and decisions, rather than the immediate seizure of land or chattels by force. Thus, any villein who did not comply with a court order or decision would have to pass through each stage of the process before officials would order the seizure of either their land, their goods or their body (by being physically brought to the court), which were then held until the villein settled the issue. The distraint process was deployed whenever villeins breached the terms of villeinage – whether transferring their servile land illegally, or wasting the villein-holding, or leaving the manor without licence – and also in private litigation (see pp. 149–51).[58] The use of distraint in manor courts was also informed by an unstated but shared understanding about what constituted good reason for the seizure, what could be seized, and when any detained chattels could be returned or sold.[59]

The final example of the growing standardisation of procedures in manor courts along the lines of the common law is the growth of personal litigation between peasants, both free and unfree, which closely resembled the recommended legal procedure for plaints initiated without writs in the lower royal courts: indeed, they were progressed and enforced through the mechanisms of summons, attachment and distraint described above.[60] Briggs and Schofield have demonstrated a growing 'convergence' of the practice, understanding, procedures and recording of private litigation in manor courts across England, based on a large sample derived from over 100 court series in ten counties. Although there existed some local variations in the handling of private plaints, especially in western areas of England, by the early fourteenth century most manorial courts worked from the same basic procedural menu.[61] Once again, detailed technical knowledge and a pedantic insistence on procedural regularity is widely evident. For example, in 1332 Robert Hood of Newton (Yorkshire) lost a private plaint in his lord's manor court 'because he does not state his case in the words of the court'.[62] Briggs and Schofield have recently confirmed the broad uniformity of the format of this litigation across different manors, lordships and regions.[63] Private litigation in manor courts provides another example of the deployment of standardised processes and means of decision-making that did not directly involve the lord whose court it was.

Thus, by the end of the thirteenth century, many procedures in manor courts throughout England had become standardised along common law lines to an extraordinary degree (the reasons are considered in Chapter 5). The important point here is its effects on the business of manor courts, the status of written precedents in court rolls, and the process of dispute resolution. It provided villein tenants with de facto security of tenure. It transformed servile dues and local custom from an oral and malleable tradition into a written statement of the terms of villeinage and reinforced the importance of written precedents in determining its management. This in turn provided villeins with greater protection against arbitrary treatment and promoted a commitment to the rights and duties of each party.[64] Written records of villein obligations thus bound lords as well as peasants.[65] The 'common law effect' also reinforced the underlying principle that disputes should be resolved through a consistent and due process, the careful consideration of precedent and relevant details, and with at least a nod to impartiality.[66] Applying these practices to the management of villeinage accelerated a shift away from justice determined at the personal discretion of the lord towards justice determined according to standardised practices and procedures founded on some basic legal principles.[67] Finally, the development of inter-peasant personal litigation increased the proportion of non-seigniorial business in the manor court.

The existence everywhere of a framework of standardised curial procedures did not, of course, eradicate all local variations in the ways courts operated.[68] Nor did it remove all scope for seigniorial arbitrary action, because the lord's extensive rights in legal theory enabled the powerful, the mighty or the haughty to behave in this way if they chose to do so, in which case the villein had limited recourse elsewhere in medieval law. The written record of the court was not infallible.[69] Even some of the imported common law procedures presented scope for the unscrupulous lord to manipulate or contravene accepted norms, for example by taking goods that were exempt from seizure, by seizing goods of a higher value than the money owed in a debt case, or by careless storage of the chattels seized as distraint.[70] Similarly, lords who abused the process of distraint in their dealings with freemen were liable to a counter action in a royal court, whereas their villein tenants possessed no such redress. Of course, villeins could abuse the distraint process themselves, through either non-cooperation or threatening behaviour to lordly officials attempting to distrain their goods.[71] Overall, however, the general cultural and procedural developments described above rendered such arbitrary or flagrant behaviour less likely and less frequent, which is evident in how servile dues were actually managed (Chapters 2 and 3) and how manor courts actually operated (exemplified in Chapters 8–10). This did not mean that justice was either equitable or impartial, or affordable across all ranks and estates, but it did curb arbitrary seigniorial power and it vested a good deal of social control in the hands of the village elites, many of whom were villeins.[72]

Business

As the manor court was unquestionably the lord's court, and as it remained the principal forum for maintaining seigniorial rights and jurisdiction, it follows that the lord's economic and social rights did indeed constitute a core element of its business.[73] Yet the role of villein-dominated presentment juries in directing its business and judgments, and the facility for individuals to bring private plaints, meant that it also processed a much wider range of community and private – i.e. non-seigniorial – business. This included by-laws created and enacted by the local community for the purposes of public order and resource management, which also applied to those residents and visitors who were not under the jurisdiction of the lord.[74] Hence, manor courts dealt to varying degrees with private law suits between peasants; the regulation of agriculture and communal resources, such as protecting crops from wandering animals; and the maintenance of peace and order within the community, such as disciplining quarrelsome and vexatious peasants.[75] The exact range and volume of this additional business varied according to the structure of the manor and the agricultural resources under its control, but its effect was to broaden the function of the manor court far beyond the narrow interests of the lord.[76]

The tendency to portray the relationship between lord and villein as inherently conflictual in the academic literature encourages the sense that their interests were incompatible, whereas in reality the relationship was much more nuanced. For example, a recent study by Jordan Claridge and Gibbs reveals how villeins cooperated with the lord's officials to enforce the seigniorial privilege of waifs and strays (the right to manage and profit from stray livestock) on manor after manor. Few lords made any profit from this privilege, but by administering the system through the manor court the nuisance threat of strays to crops and pastures within the village was controlled to mutual benefit. Claridge and Gibbs argue that, in this way, the manor court was providing a public good for the community rather than deploying a seigniorial privilege to exploit the peasantry.[77]

Quantifying the relative importance of the types of business handled in manorial courts is challenging, however, because it is not always possible to categorise individual items tidily. For example, do we regard the supervision of stray animals as a seigniorial interest, because strays were forfeit to the lord if unclaimed, or as a community interest, because the system also reduced the nuisance threat of strays and returned them to their owners?[78] Likewise, should we count initiated cases or only those completed?[79] Such reservations aside, we can state with reasonable confidence that, in most places, less than half of all curial business was 'seigniorial'. In the pre-plague era seigniorial court business accounted for around 30 per cent of that at Sutton, 40 per cent at Redgrave, and 55 per cent at Hinderclay (including land transfers).[80] These three courts belonged to powerful monastic lords with large numbers of villeins, whereas the courts of the typically 'small' English manor, where serfs were relatively unimportant and their low-status lords possessed limited powers, were unlikely to have much seigniorial business and operated more like communal courts.

A cogent illustration of the varied business of the manor court is the processing of interpersonal litigation between peasants, which grew in popularity in the later thirteenth century. This category of business represents the most overtly legal – as opposed to the political and administrative – function of the manorial court, because these cases did not involve the lord and had nothing to do with villeinage.[81] Interpersonal plaints largely comprised actions of debt-detinue, trespass and covenant, initiated by oral plaint (rather than by the writ needed to initiate pleas in the royal courts) in order to recover unpaid debts, withheld goods, damages for various wrongs or broken agreements.[82] The volume of these plaints peaked in the early fourteenth century and varied significantly from manor to manor: some courts did not handle cases of private litigation, while others were flush with them.[83] For example, five out of a sample of fourteen manors in Northamptonshire included hardly any private litigation in their business, and the number recorded in the court of Thorncroft (Surrey) was 'tiny'.[84] Yet the majority of those Northamptonshire manors did include plaints, and elsewhere they absorbed at least one-quarter of court business: for example, 27 per cent in 1308–19 at Sutton, 29 per cent at Lakenheath (Suffolk) in 1320–45, and 51 per cent at Wakefield.[85] In the mid-fourteenth century the manor court of Westhall (Suffolk) handled hardly any business relating to seigniorial prerogatives or villeinage and instead was almost entirely dominated by private pleas between peasants.[86]

Such differences in the proportion of private plaints between courts have a variety of explanations. Without doubt, some lords conceived of the function of their court narrowly, making little effort to attract private litigation and confining its business as far as possible to their own seigniorial and some communal interests.[87] In contrast, Briggs has shown how some lords actively sought to attract litigation to their manor courts by subtle changes in curial procedures designed to improve the efficiency, speed and quality of justice.[88] In particular, manors with markets or high levels of commercial activity were likely to generate more pleas than those without.[89] Although personal plaints seldom include any detail about the issue under dispute, they were clearly being used to protect private and, especially, commercial interests.[90] Across the country, plaints were dominated by debt cases, which reflect the demand for, the supply of, and the involvement of villeins in, rudimentary forms of credit and commerce.[91] The benefit to lords of allowing private plaints to be registered and resolved in their manor courts was financial, and could be reckoned in pounds received each year. For example, between 1289 and 1364 there were nearly 3,000 cases of interpersonal litigation in the court rolls of Redgrave and Hinderclay (Suffolk), which raised 38 per cent of all court income for the lord at Redgrave and 19 per cent at Hinderclay.[92]

Manor courts were competing for the business of personal litigation to some extent, because private plaints could also be heard in other local tribunals, such as market, borough, church and royal courts. Few cases in manor courts involved disputes valued at more than 40s., which were supposed to be heard in the royal courts. At some point in the early fourteenth century, however, the courts of common law ceased to handle pleas based on informal and oral contracts, which must have diverted even more litigants to manorial courts.[93] Indeed, the exclusion of such cases from the royal courts may even have reflected an acknowledgement that claims based on informal agreements were better resolved through local manor courts because of the greater speed and accessibility – and probably the lower costs – compared to royal courts.[94] The costs of the process to the litigants depended on the nature and length of the case, but were reckoned in pennies rather than shillings. Private litigation in manorial courts was relatively cheap and accessible.

The personal status of peasants involved in inter-peasant litigation is seldom recorded in manorial court rolls, which is a clear indication that it was deemed irrelevant.[95] There is no doubt, however, that many involved villeins, especially the wealthier tenants (i.e. those with landholdings in excess of 10 acres).[96] Indeed, villeins were central to the effectiveness and popularity of the entire system as litigants, jurors and curial officials, which also steeped them in the legal processes, versed them in technicalities, and taught them the legal ropes through observation and practice.[97] Canny villein lenders concerned about the security of a loan could even opt to pay the manor court to enrol recognisances of debt and so mobilise its machinery to chase debtors.[98] As Schofield and Briggs observe:

> a broadly shared set of practices concerning the conduct of manor court litigation emerged in this period ... with the full participation of ordinary laypeople acting as officials, litigants and suitors ... the success of the manor court jurisdiction over personal actions represents the successful building of legal institutions 'from below' by people – free and villein, male and female – who had extensive knowledge of law courts, including royal law courts, lying beyond the boundaries of their own manors.[99]

Much of our knowledge of manorial courts is derived from the active, well-run and income-generating courts of high-status landlords on classic manors. Yet, as we saw in Chapter 2, the vast majority of English lords were low-status and possessing small manors, whose manorial courts transacted much less business. These low-status manorial courts were mainly found in the south and east of England, but were uncommon in the north and in the Welsh Marches, where fewer courts covered larger territories.[100] They have left fewer records than the courts held on high-status manors, but those which have survived reveal the same processes, procedures and types of business as described above: the main differences are the lower volume of business and the relative unimportance of villeinage.[101]

Dispute resolution between lords and serfs

As we have seen, villeins serving as jurors were the principal decision-makers in manorial courts, following broadly standardised and technically precise procedures and using written records as precedents.[102] Did these general principles apply, however, in disputes over villeinage where the lord's rights were at stake and where all parties knew that the villeins had no legal recourse to a royal court as a court of appeal on the matter under contention? The answer to this question cuts to the heart of the relationship between lords and villeins and, indeed, the lord's willingness to abide by a due process when the outcome had a direct bearing on his interests. Martin states that 'the lord had the right to overturn villagers' assessments ... moreover, he often became the plaintiff against his tenants, though tenants were unable to bring an action against him: this produced a situation of considerable power over villeins'.[103] Slota concludes that villeins on the estate of the abbey of St Albans did not win direct disputes with their mighty landlord, a view based on the abbot's arbitrary decision on one occasion to alter the arrangements for licensing subleases of villein land.[104] How typical was this example and how accurate are these views?

Before answering this question, it is important to emphasise how the chances of a dispute arising in the first place between villeins and lord were reduced through the emergence of presentment juries and the growing reliance on written precedents. The presentment jury had a sworn responsibility for ensuring that all transgressions of seigniorial rights were presented to the court, thereby acting as guardians of the lord's interests tempered by custom and precedence. Indeed, the mighty abbot of Crowland once asked a manorial jury for its verdict on *his* customary rights.[105] These juries were equally capable of presenting breaches of custom or rights by the lord or his officials. In either scenario, the jury could support its case through reference to precedents written in the record of the court or a manorial custumal.[106] Manorial custumals carried authority, and serfs routinely appealed to them in response to unjust or increased seigniorial demands (as did lords when serfs tried to evade services; see p. 281).[107] In these ways, presentment juries possessed some mechanism for monitoring the behaviour of the lord and his officials, ensuring their actions complied with local custom and holding them to some sort of account.[108] Hence, there are examples of juries ordering their own lord to take remedial action relating to agricultural misdemeanours and even wrongful seizure of land.[109] The jurors of Malden (Surrey) presented their manorial lord (Merton College, Oxford) for failing to maintain Kingsford bridge, and directed the warden of the college to repair it: there is no suggestion that the lord disputed their finding.[110] Conversely, manorial officials could take action against jurors who had breached established procedures.[111] Of course, villein jurors would probably only present their lord for customary infractions when they were confident of their ground, and such examples are not commonplace (although historians have not systematically looked to record them): but the fact that they did and they could prosecute their lord confounds claims that manorial courts were crude instruments of oppression.

Hence, a combination of custom, due process and a rudimentary system of accountability served to head off and to resolve many disputes between villein tenants and their lords.[112] Consequently, confrontations between lords and villeins over serfdom and custom appear very infrequently in court rolls.[113] For example, in the pre-plague era there was just one dispute between the lord of Cuxham (Oxfordshire) and his villeins, which rumbled on between 1327 and 1329 over the nature of a specific labour service, and the outcome was eventually recorded in the court rolls to protect against a recurrence in the future.[114] If, however, a dispute between serfs and lord escalated, the manorial court was still capable of finding in favour of serfs. For example, in 1315 a manorial inquisition jury upheld the claims of the villeins of Cakeham (Surrey) not to have to cart the lord's dung as part of their labour services.[115] Ongoing disputes between Merton College and its villeins on the manors of Malden (over carrying services) and Thorncroft (Surrey, also carrying services) also appear to have been resolved in favour of the villeins.[116] Again, future research could helpfully be more alert to similar examples so they can be properly quantified and contextualised.

These general processes of dispute resolution between lords and villeins in manor courts can be illustrated by specific examples taken from the manor of Wakefield, where some excesses of seigniorial officials and of other lords were monitored and punished. In 1331 the jury ordered the attachment of one of the lord's officials, the forester of Sowerby, whose actions and demands had 'ruined' one Adam Nelleson, a bond tenant of the manor. Similarly, in 1340 the jury investigated and upheld a complaint about the behaviour of the lord's receiver of monies towards the tenants.[117] In 1316 the abbot of Roche paid the lord of Wakefield 6s. 8d. to make a concord with one of the latter's serfs, 'to whom one of the [abbot's] monks had done amiss'.[118] Most telling of all, judgments in favour of the lord could also be overturned: in June 1317 Thomas atte Wode of Fixby was accused of using a hand mill, and therefore avoiding mill suit as a servile tenant, but he argued otherwise, waged his law in the manor court and was acquitted.[119] The lord's officials and other suitors monitored those serving on presentment juries, for example by punishing those who had spoken to jurors without permission, had withdrawn from jury service, had provided false information or had made malicious allegations.[120] While this underlines that the quality of justice was sometimes poor, tainted by corruption and false testimony, it also illustrates some willingness to address such issues, and the operation of checks and balances within the system to address potential matters of contention between lord and villeins.

Resolution of more complex or entrenched disputes over servile incidents between lords and serfs, especially over labour services, was a lengthier process, usually involving a temporary postponement of the case while various written records, such as custumals, were searched and consulted.[121] For example, at Codicote in 1329 two brothers claimed in the manorial court that they were not obliged to carry the demesne corn from the harvest field as part of their labour services, whereupon the case was adjourned until officials had consulted the manorial custumal: which duly established that the brothers were wrong (see Chapter 8). In 1319 the villeins of Worlingworth (Suffolk) argued in the manor court that no male, and no woman who held customary land by succession, owed merchet according to the custom of the manor. The steward was not able to identify immediately where these customary exemptions were documented, but a subsequent scrutiny of the court's rolls revealed that heiresses had indeed rendered merchet in the past. At a subsequent court, the villeins were forced to recant and were amerced for this false claim.[122] The loss of these cases probably provided little consolation to these villeins, but for our purposes they illustrate an important point: manorial courts did not resolve disputes between lords and their villeins by simply asserting the lord's will, but through a due process involving written precedents.

In some cases, the escalation of a dispute between lord and villein is described in the court rolls, but its final resolution remains unknown to posterity. For example, in 1300 a disagreement arose between a specific category of villeins at Elton (Huntingdonshire), known as cotmen, and their lord, the abbot of Ramsey, over the precise terms of one their labour services, known locally as a 'hay lovebene'.[123] The cotmen requested that the steward of the manor court appoint an inquest jury, drawn from other suitors of the court, to resolve the issue, and one was duly convened. The jury determined that although the hay lovebene required the cotmen to stack the lord's hay in the meadow or the manor courtyard, 'they are not bound to load the carts in the meadows'.[124] The steward did not have the manorial custumal to hand to check this very specific point and so the matter was adjourned until he could undertake the necessary research in the muniments of the abbey. The outcome is not recorded, either because the relevant court session has not survived or because the villeins were correct. Irrespective of the outcome, however, the conduct of this case reveals once again how a dispute between a powerful monastic institution and its villeins was addressed through the due process of an inquisition jury, how the villeins were alert to a possible technical loophole, how the written record conditioned the lord's scope for action, and how the resolution probably rested on the information contained in manorial custumals.

Written evidence could not always provide a resolution to a dispute between lord and villeins, either because it was indecisive on the point or simply did not exist or was incorrect. Such occasions were exceptional, however, because the relentless process of codification and clarification of customs, dues and services over the course of the thirteenth century tended to cover most eventualities.[125] In these circumstances the lord could pronounce on the matter, either based on his personal opinion or having sought the advice of his council (if he had such a body), and it is most likely that such judgments would favour the lord.[126] Indeed, in 1338 the council of the abbey of St Albans claimed the authority to overturn written precedents recorded in the court rolls of the manor of Park (Hertfordshire).[127] Such behaviour was rare, however, and on one occasion the council of the lord of Great Horwood (Buckinghamshire) found against the lord in an inheritance dispute involving villein land.[128] Entrenched and prolonged disputes between lord and villeins were precisely those which resulted in acrimony, local protest and even law suits in the royal courts, such as those sketched in Chapter 2. Any case that reached the royal courts was exceptional, although the lord was the likely winner in such cases.

There were of course many other subtle and informal ways in which villeins could express disagreement and opposition to their lords. They might resist passively, individually or collectively, by non-cooperation, foot dragging and rent strikes; they might resort to reprisals, such as theft or illegal pasturing on the lord's lands; they might simply leave the manor; or they might resort to outright refusals and coordinated protest. The most powerful act of passive personal resistance was to leave the manor, never to return (see Chapter 5).[129]

A major area of potential disagreement between lords and their dependent peasantry was the personal status of a specific individual, i.e. whether they were free or unfree. This was one dispute that the lord might choose to pronounce upon himself, because it cut deep to the core of their relationship. According to Dimmock, some free peasants were depressed into villeinage and stripped of legal protection, and Fryde argued that powerful lords accused 'humble freemen' of being serfs, hauled them in front of their own manor court and subjected them to 'flagrant denials of justice'.[130] The implication in these statements is that such behaviour was commonplace, although empirical evidence supporting such claims is flimsy. Fryde's assertion is based primarily on one case, that of Adam le Bedel of Elmley Castle (Worcestershire), which Hilton and Dyer have also cited as a classic example of how lords could attempt to enserf freemen, and impose punitive fines on villeins, through their manorial courts.[131] Yet this case is complicated and not at all straightforward to interpret. Adam had claimed to be free, and an inquisition jury had declared him to be free in the manorial court, but the lord overturned both the claim and the jury's verdict, and for good measure fined the attendees at the court £20 for false testimony. Fryde, Hilton and Dyer presume that the lord was perverting justice, and his actions were both arbitrary and punitive, but it is equally possible that the jurors were perverting justice. Furthermore, it is unclear whether the enormous fine was actually collected, and perhaps the lord's intention was to send a powerful message to those whom he believed had colluded to return an improper verdict rather than to insist on payment. Finally, Fryde implies that this case was typical of a wider pattern of behaviour, when it was in fact exceptional: it was one of just three disputes over personal status recorded in dozens of Elmley courts between 1347 and 1499. In the other two cases, both in the 1350s, the jurors upheld the claims to freedom of the two men involved and the lord accepted the verdicts without question, which increases the suspicions about the jury's behaviour in the Bedel case.[132] Thus, the provision of the wider context casts this case in a very different light.

The rarity of disputes over personal status in manor courts is confirmed whenever historians have computed their numbers systematically.[133] For example, in hundreds of court sessions covering the fourteenth and fifteenth centuries there were no recorded disputes over status at Codicote, two at Winslow (both in the 1350s) and two at Norton (see Chapters 8–10). Between 1300 and 1500 there were a grand total of seven such disputes recorded in nearly 2,000 court sessions from fourteen manors in the south Midlands and East Anglia.[134] Furthermore, when disputes over personal status did occur, lords never dictated their outcome status personally, but instead they followed an established due process through their manor court. The first response was usually for officials to scrutinise earlier rolls for any precedents of servility relevant to the claim, and in most cases a jury of inquiry was then sworn in to consider the evidence and pronounce on the matter. Its verdict was based on a combination of local knowledge and written precedents from the manorial court, such as whether the individual or his close relatives had ever paid merchet. These inquisition juries sometimes found the defendant to be free and sometimes confirmed his servile status.[135] For example, when a dispute arose in 1340 in the court of Wakefield over the personal status of three women and thirteen men, a jury was assembled to resolve the matter: in the event, eight of the men were found to be legally free, all of whom paid for the verdicts to be formally enrolled in the record of the court to protect against any future doubt, and the remainder were confirmed as serfs.[136] Lords almost always accepted the verdict of the jury, although in exceptional circumstances – such as when they suspected collusion and false testimony – they did challenge the outcome.[137] In fact, lords had a vested interest in following a due process in their own courts, despite the possibility of defeat, because by so doing and recording the outcome they vastly reduced the chances of the case being elevated to the royal courts, with all the associated time, expense and difficulty of proving servile status there (Chapter 1).

Hence, most disputes over serfdom – whether individual or collective – were raised initially in the lord's own court and many of them were resolved through a due process involving either juries of inquisition or written precedents. At one level, this is illustrative of the occasional need for villeins to take direct action to defend their rights under villeinage, and of the protective cloak of custom. At another level, it illustrates how the act of codifying servile dues, and the consequential reliance on written precedent, had fundamentally changed relations between lord and villein. It had shifted the ground further from personal discretion to a form of legal process, and serfs had become cannily adept at playing the rules of the new game.[138] They displayed high levels of technical knowledge, readily raised legal challenges against their lord in his own court and understood arcane legal points when litigating.[139] So while seigniorial courts and manorial custom were to some degree instruments of seigniorial discipline, and the source of some tension between lords and peasants, they were not naked engines of oppression, and they offered opportunities for collaboration and pursuing communal and personal interests.[140] As Gibbs has shown, 'whatever their initial purpose as tools of lordship, manorial courts were significantly adapted through their usage by officials on the ground, being shaped to meet purposes beyond those of their manorial lord'.[141]

The leet court

The leet court (also known as the tourn in some places) was not originally or strictly a court of manorial jurisdiction, although by the end of the thirteenth century in much of eastern England and the Midlands it had always become attached to one manor in the vill (usually the largest and highest-status manor when, as was usually the case, the vill contained more than one manor), and for all practical purposes was administered as part of the manorial system.[142] The leet, which met once or twice a year, represented the lowest unit of jurisdiction of civil administration in England, which had effectively become privatised as the franchise of a manorial lord.[143] Consequently, its personnel and business were different from those of the manor court. The leet discharged the civil responsibilities of the vill through the tithing or frankpledge system, which bound all resident male adults – free and unfree – into a framework for collecting royal taxes, organising defence, upholding public order, maintaining roads and ditches, implementing the royal assizes relating to foodstuffs, and reporting more serious misdemeanours upwards to the hundred (or wapentake) court. The leet elected its own representatives from each tithing ('capital pledges') to present and determine cases, together with its own officials, such as ale tasters and constables, to help discharge its business. Since the profits of the leet accrued to the lord holding the franchise, it is certainly possible for lords to have manipulated its business and decisions to their own advantage.[144] But did this occur in practice? What were the implications of this system for villeins?

Adult male serfs of every manor in the vill were required to attend and participate in the business of the leet, which meant that serfs of one lord could be attending a leet court run by another. All adult male serfs, and their female and underage dependants, were subject to the authority of the leet in criminal and statute law, and in relation to its public responsibilities.[145] Furthermore, since the leet was responsible for reporting certain offences upwards to the hundred court, serfs could also appear there. In these areas of jurisdiction the serf was free as against everyone, which included a theoretical obligation to report his lord for any relevant infractions, such as a failure to maintain demesne ditches in a proper state. A serf who was elected as a constable possessed powers of enforcement over all adults – male and female, free and unfree – within the jurisdiction of the leet, while a serf who was elected to serve as a capital pledge possessed similar powers of presentment and judgment. There is no doubt that serfs dominated these important offices: for example, before the Black Death the 'capital pledges were in all cases customary tenants' on the Ramsey abbey estates, and no fewer than three-quarters of capital pledges serving at Birdbrook (Essex) were villeins.[146]

Hence, the participation of serfs in the business of the leet immersed them fully in statute law in general, and in the administration of the royal assizes of bread and ale in particular. Serfs could brew and sell ale; they could bake and retail bread; and they could process and sell other types of foodstuffs, especially meat and fish, without seigniorial interference, subject only to the provisions of statute law. R. M. Smith has documented how the wealthy villeins of Redgrave were fully engaged in brewing; baking; and, indeed, many other commercial activities in nearby Botesdale market.[147] Furthermore, serfs acted as officials on behalf of the court in enforcing the assizes within the jurisdiction of the leet. Indeed, this represented a major element of its business, occupying 20 per cent of all business at Lakenheath in the 1320s and 1330s and 30 per cent at Alrewas (Staffordshire).[148] In 1360–61 58 per cent of 349 recorded cases in the tourns of Wakefield related to the sale of ale, bread and meat.[149] Court roll after court roll on manor after manor exhibit no interest at all in recording the personal status of those involved in such trading activities or offences.[150] The most wide-ranging and comprehensive survey of commercial brewing on the eve of the Black Death in rural communities, featuring a detailed assessment of the implementation of the assize of ale in manorial courts, identifies some discrimination on the grounds of gender but none at all on the grounds of personal status.[151] Such indifference was also characteristic of the compilers of the Crown's formal records of purveyance, who did not identify the personal status of their suppliers even though many of them were villeins.[152] The direct implication is that villeins were commercially active and their legal status did not matter.

Access to other courts

Although historians such as Cheyney, Dimmock and others have suggested that villeins did not transact business in other jurisdictions, others – spurred on by Paul Hyams – have argued otherwise.[153] The difficulty has been in finding direct evidence either of villeins suing in other courts or of their manorial court prohibiting such actions rigorously. There also needs to be a distinction between those occasions when serfs were summoned to other courts to act as witnesses, or to answer for their actions under statute and canon law, and those occasions when they were appearing as litigants on their own initiative. Unfortunately, the personal status of litigants and their backgrounds is very seldom stated in court records, so we cannot easily identify the presence of villeins. An alternative is for us to trace a litigant in a foreign court back to his own manor court roll where his villein status could be securely ascertained (for example by paying merchet or holding customary land), but this is only possible in the unlikely circumstances that his place of origin is recorded in the foreign court and that relevant rolls are extant for his manor court.[154]

If lords were intent on prohibiting their villeins from litigating outside the manor court, then they would have enforced it through presentments and punishments within the manor court. Very occasionally, a manor court passed an ordinance explicitly prohibiting unfree tenants of the same manor from suing each other in another jurisdiction, as occurred at Cockerham (Lancashire) in 1326, although the ordinance did not prevent one villein suing a non-villein elsewhere.[155] Similarly, some manor courts amerced villeins retrospectively for transacting business in outside courts.[156] Such cases were, however, uncommon. For example, there are just four recorded cases of villeins being fined for suing in other jurisdictions in the hundreds of extant courts from fourteenth-century Walsham, with most of them involving the same person, Elyas Typtot, who was amerced for impleading other tenants at courts held in nearby Bury St Edmunds and other unnamed places.[157] Likewise, there were just seven cases at Sutton from its fourteenth-century court rolls.[158] Not a single serf was amerced for pleading in other jurisdictions in the eighty-five extant court sessions of Layham (Suffolk) between 1330 and 1375, or in the 228 courts extant from Newton Longville (Buckinghamshire) between 1327 and 1422.[159]

The challenge for the historian is what to make of this evidence. Does the scarcity of such amercements reflect the rarity of such behaviour, or was it in fact widespread but courts occasionally chose to fine a selected individual for some specific, but unstated, reason? On balance, it is highly likely that serfs did sue in other courts with some frequency and, for the most part, without challenge from the transacting court and without hindrance from their own lord. There are a number of reasons to support such a view. The first is that the indifference to recording the personal status of plaintiffs and defendants in the records of any medieval court is a clear indication that status was unimportant. Second, lords might reasonably expect litigation between their own villeins to take place in the home manor court rather than elsewhere, but there was nothing to prevent a villein suing a third party who was not a villein of the same lord in another tribunal.[160] Third, serfs were required to attend royal and church courts legitimately, for example as witnesses, which presented obvious opportunities for them to use the occasion to sue there for themselves.[161] Finally, the seigniorial decision to impose a (usually) small retrospective fine on serfs who did sue elsewhere often has some wider context or explanation, such as making a point to a serf who was proving troublesome in other ways.

Manor courts of other lords

Serfs could and did litigate in the manor courts of other lords. The rules of manor courts did not prevent people from outside the manor transacting business there and, conversely, 'lords rarely if ever sought to stop litigation outside the manor purely on the grounds that the party suing or being sued was a villein'.[162] Direct evidence of villeins suing in the manor courts of other lords requires painstaking reconstructions and cross-referencing of cases from multiple manors, plus intimate knowledge of the background of individual suitors: such reconstructions are rare because they are so difficult and time-consuming, but they do yield explicit confirmation of villeins of one lord litigating in the courts of others. For example, customary tenants of Warboys and Broughton (Huntingdonshire) were routinely involved in the business of the courts of neighbouring manors, without incurring amercements for such activity in their own manorial court.[163] Similarly, Richard le Eyr, a villein of Holywell (Huntingdonshire), also held free and customary land from other nearby manors, and as a tenant could therefore legitimately sue in those manor courts.[164]

Thus, manor courts regularly accepted and processed business from people who were not tenants or connected with the manor.[165] This was especially true in south-east England, where there was a high density of small manors and therefore seigniorial courts existed in close proximity to one another. For example, many of the people who appeared in the Gressenhall (Norfolk) manorial court did not hold land from the manor, but nevertheless chose to litigate there because the court was relatively efficient in dealing with defendants who failed to appear or to honour their obligations.[166] Outsiders routinely used the Warboys court to pursue and defend civil cases.[167] Outsiders represented at least 13 per cent of all litigants in a sample of twelve Northamptonshire manorial courts, some of whom had travelled considerable distances to litigate.[168] Three manors on the Breckland–Fenland edge in East Anglia, whose inhabitants were immersed in interregional trade, ran busy manorial courts that attracted litigants from 114 named settlements located all over eastern England.[169] Their personal status was not recorded, underlining its irrelevance to the court. Many of these outsiders would have been personally free, but many others would have been villeins pursuing personal pleas.

Royal courts

As discussed in Chapter 1, villeins were not able to plead on matters relating to servile tenure in the royal courts, or on most other matters regarding their own lord. Serfs could plead or defend certain types of cases in the courts of common law against third parties, such as trespass and debt, so it is likely that they did appear there.[170] Similarly, villeins were answerable for themselves in any royal court dealing with statute and criminal law, including occasional judicial commissions.[171] Explicit evidence of their presence in royal courts is, however, thin on the ground, partly because the court records of common law and manorial law have been studied in separate scholarly traditions, so linkages between the two are rare, but also because of the methodological difficulties in positively identifying villeins among those named as bringing cases in the court records.[172] For example, Peter Waryn of Drinkstone (Suffolk) is recorded as the plaintiff in a debt case in the Court of Common Pleas, but it required the chance survival of contemporary court rolls for the manor of Drinkstone and some careful cross-referencing to discover that Peter was a serf.[173] On the very rare occasions when litigants were explicitly identified as villeins in the records of the royal courts, it was usually because they were defendants who were invoking the status as a ploy to avoid answering a plea against them. For example, in 1309 John Bagge refused to defend himself in the Court of Common Pleas in a dispute over a substantial area of land in Nottingham on the grounds that he was a villein, and therefore had no standing in the common law, even though he had appeared there as a litigant in an earlier case without making any mention of his status.[174]

Putting aside these challenges, what other evidence is there of serfs appearing in royal courts? They routinely appeared in leet courts – the lowest, albeit privatised, civil courts in England – and sometimes in hundred courts. Serfs did appear as witnesses in the higher courts of the Crown, and they even featured in juries there or were willing to pay to avoid being required to serve.[175] For example, in 1298 John Parys, *villanus*, of South Witham (Lincolnshire) paid a royal sub-bailiff 4s. to avoid jury service at the royal assizes.[176] Some manor courts do contain occasional references to their villeins litigating in royal courts. In 1333 Thomas, son of Richard Clericus, a bond tenant of Wakefield manor, was distrained for impleading other tenants of the manor in the king's courts rather than in the manor court.[177] In 1333 the lord of Walsham actively encouraged two serfs to appear in a royal court on behalf of the reeve.[178] So serfs were present in the royal courts and were active litigators there, although we can never know the scale. In reality, serfs were surely pragmatic about where to litigate, and were indifferent to accessing royal courts if they could achieve the same ends in more accessible, local, courts.[179]

Canon law courts

Canon law existed alongside common law and customary law, sometimes competing and sometimes overlapping with them.[180] It possessed its own legal machinery and tribunals, from the lowly rural archdeaconry courts to episcopal and provincial courts.[181] Levels of proof here appear to have been lower than in royal courts.[182] Cases were usually brought by the court itself, but some were initiated by individuals in a manner roughly analogous to civil litigation.[183] Cases relating to wills and probate dominated this 'private' litigation, but debt cases, breach of contract, and other general aspects of dispute resolution and arbitration could also feature.[184] The latter were permitted because many commercial agreements between individuals were sealed with oaths, the breach of which constituted a moral offence that provided a pretext for pursuing the wrong through the church courts.[185] Defamation cases also featured in lower church courts, because medieval people were keen to protect and maintain their good reputation, upon which their commercial standing might depend.[186] Hence, some business usually found in secular courts could sometimes find its way into church courts, presumably because plaintiffs perceived advantages in pursuing particular cases there rather than elsewhere.[187]

The strict theory of common law villeinage prevented villeins from pursuing cases in church courts, because the villein was the lord's chattel and therefore did not possess any goods or hold any property that could be devised to an heir or alienated to a third party. Once again, however, the theory was not consistent with practice, because, as we have seen, villeins did inherit land and goods, and they could and did make wills. Canon law recognised these realities and therefore handled cases relating to servile wills, which during the early thirteenth century had caused some friction between royal and ecclesiastical courts. However, the stance of common law courts eventually softened, and by the middle of the fourteenth century secular lawyers were reconciling legal theory with everyday reality by conceding that villeins had obtained '*de facto* power of testamentary disposition, subject to the lord's right to enter the land at any time before probate of the will and seize the goods on it'.[188] In most places, villeins enjoyed customary rights to make their own arrangements over wills.[189] On some estates, such as the cellarer of St Albans abbey, villeins were permitted to make wills as long as they were registered with the cellarer (Chapter 10).

Serfs routinely attended the lower tier of ecclesiastical courts to prove their wills and for other legitimate reasons, such as matrimonial disputes (excluding cases involving merchet) and moral offences.[190] Likewise, serfs attended church courts as witnesses.[191] So they had ample opportunities to pursue their own business there, although, once again, direct and explicit evidence of their presence in the records of church courts is scarce, because very few have survived from the lower levels of ecclesiastical jurisdiction and, even where they have, the personal status of plaintiffs and defendants is seldom recorded.[192] Although there was no ecclesiastical prohibition on serfs using church courts, a few lords reprimanded some of those who did pursue defamation and debt cases there rather than in the manor court.[193] For example, in 1318 some villeins of Littleport (Cambridgeshire) were amerced for suing for defamation in local church courts.[194] In 1332 the Wakefield manor court amerced two men a total of 9d. for impleading another man in an ecclesiastical court when the matter could have been settled in the lord's own court, and the following year it tenaciously pursued another tenant who failed to appear to answer the charge of taking a defamation case to an ecclesiastical court.[195] The frequency of such cases is low, however, with just six presentments and three amercements for such offences in around 550 published courts of Wakefield between

1274 and 1348. The three amercements averaged 5d., so the court was effectively charging a retrospective licence for taking a case elsewhere.[196]

The rarity of amercements in manorial courts for serfs pleading cases in canon law courts is underlined by the example of the three well-documented manors of Walsham, Walsham High Hall and Walsham Church House, held by a succession of middling status lords, where just a single reference to a villein pleading a case in an ecclesiastical court (in this case, a tenant of villein land in the diocesan court of Norwich in 1467) is recorded in 410 manorial and leet courts held between 1316 and 1500.[197] The vast majority of manors rarely amerced serfs for litigating in church courts. The few to do so were usually those of high-status landlords, such as the earls of Surrey at Wakefield and the bishop of Ely at Littleport, and they were effectively charging small retrospective licences to do so in very specific circumstances.

The rarity of reprimands in manor courts indicates either that villeins were completely avoiding church courts, which seems unlikely given their attendance for other matters, or that most lords tolerated some litigation.[198] The most obvious place for serfs to litigate would have been in archdeaconry courts, which were geographically the most accessible to rural inhabitants.[199] Indeed, there is some evidence in the few surviving records of archdeaconry courts of villeins opting to litigate there, such as when in the 1290s Nicholas Woodward, a leading villein of Hinderclay, was embroiled in a scandalous affair.[200] Extramarital sexual relations were likely to be heard in church courts.[201] Occasionally, incidental references to villeins using church courts appear in manor courts.[202] For example, in 1276 Nicholas the Dyer was amerced in the manor court of Hadleigh (Suffolk) for attacking one of the lord's villein tenants (*custumarius*) 'in the court Christian', but here the punishment was for the attack, not for its location.[203] Defamation and debt cases could be heard in either manorial or church courts, but lords were likely to insist that cases between two villeins belonged in the former.

In general, serfs handled matters relating to wills, marriage and sexual misconduct in church courts. Some also pursued private defamation, debt and breach-of-contract cases there, although these were more likely to attract some retrospective licensing from their lord. How frequently serfs litigated on the lower rungs of church courts is impossible to know, given the rarity of surviving documents from such tribunals.

Merchant law courts

The volume of commercial activity and petty trading increased exponentially during the course of the thirteenth century, and it was regulated by a multitude of laws and regulations designed to ensure just prices, standardised weights and measures, good quality produce and redress for trading infractions, and to discourage fraud and malpractice. The regulatory framework for commercial activity comprised a combination of royal statutes, town ordinances, manorial by-laws and merchant law, and, despite the resulting complexity, was closely adapted to the needs of market goers.[204] Day-to-day trade in essential foodstuffs – bread, ale, meat and fish – was covered by statutory assizes enforced in borough courts and manorial leets.[205] Other trade was channelled through weekly markets and seasonal fairs, most of them granted by the Crown to local lords and operating in rural settings. By 1350 more than 4,000 charters for weekly markets and seasonal fairs had been granted, as a result of which few residents of south-east England were further than 5 miles from one of these formal trading outlets. None of these charters specifies what exactly the franchise entailed beyond the day(s) on which it was to be held, but Masschaele has argued persuasively that it conferred upon the holder a number of 'inherent' rights, including jurisdiction over trading disputes.[206]

Commercial transactions in markets and fairs were mainly subject to *lex mercatoria* (merchant or market law), which existed alongside common, statute and customary law.[207] It comprised the 'rules and legal doctrines for merchants and mercantile transactions that were regarded alike by merchants and by jurists, as distinct from the common law of the land'.[208] It was an amorphous body of law, customary in origin and therefore varying locally throughout Europe, dedicated to addressing the requirements of traders for the speedy resolution of commercial disputes. In thirteenth-century England it became increasingly standardised in its processes for enforcing credit and contractual agreements, and incorporated many elements of the common law.[209] The formal creation of a market franchise implied a requirement to delineate where and when merchant law operated, because it applied only to transactions that occurred in open trade: hence the creation of delimited market 'places' and fair 'grounds'.[210] In the largest markets and fairs, merchant law was applied through the mechanism of dedicated courts. The evidence of the few court proceedings to have survived from them reveals the adoption of the basic forms of pleading and action used in common law, so the business of the court of a great fair, such as St Ives (Huntingdonshire), was dominated by familiar actions of debt; trespass; contract; and, to a lesser extent, breaches of the assizes of bread and ale.[211] The costs of initiating a plea were low, usually 3d. These courts provided cheap; relatively speedy; and, presumably, effective justice for local traders.[212]

In contrast to the great markets and fairs, it is unclear how merchant law was administered within the thousands of smaller franchises of weekly markets and seasonal fairs, where most villeins would have traded. The most obvious mechanism was for the lord's officials to hold a special court, a smaller version of those held at the great fairs and larger boroughs, but few of these lesser markets and fairs bothered to do so.[213] How, then was merchant law applied, and how were disputes resolved in such places? Most petty trading contracts were oral and informal, sealed through a handshake, a drink, the payment of God's penny or earnest money, proof of which was obtained either through witnesses to the deal or by wooden tallies.[214] Market and fair officials must have resolved trading disputes on the spot through summary judgments or arbitration, without any formal written record, and any outstanding or more complex disputes must have been channelled through the manor court.[215] This probably explains why interpersonal disputes were more common in the Redgrave court than at nearby Hinderclay, because the former had a weekly market and the latter did not.[216] Wealthier merchants sometimes made use of manor courts to pursue their trading disputes.

As merchant law was focused upon the practical needs of traders, its judgments were quicker, its standards of evidence and proof were lower, and its spirit of equity was greater than in the common law.[217] Cases were determined not by the lords who held the commercial franchises, but by the body of burgesses (in borough courts) or representatives of the active traders (in market and fair courts) acting as jurors.[218] The fair court of St Ives, for example, refers repeatedly to juries 'of neighbours and merchants', and to 'the merchants and all others of the court', who determined cases.[219] Of course, traders could always exercise choice and access other courts, including common law courts, to resolve a dispute if they rated their chances of success higher there.[220] There were, however, some limitations as to choice, since actions involving certain types of written agreement, and any debt claim over 40s., were supposed to be sued in the royal courts.[221]

Could serfs access merchant law freely? The charters of some continental towns stated unequivocally that traders were to be judged according to market law irrespective of their legal status.[222] Similarly, although there is nothing in English legal sources that explicitly confirms or denies that villeins could operate freely within market law, all the available direct and indirect evidence confirms that they could and did do so. Charles Gross's edited volume of scores of cases relating to merchant law in England, mainly taken from late-thirteenth- and early-fourteenth-century fair courts, contains not a single case in which the personal status (i.e. whether free or unfree) of either plaintiff or defendant was specified. Rather, the primary concern of the courts was to identify the place of origin of the disputants and, of course, to record the basic details of the dispute.[223] Hence, they distinguished between 'indigenous' and 'foreign' merchants, i.e. between locals and visitors, but not between the free and unfree.[224] Market courts exhibit the same indifference to personal status, and instead describe the vast majority of plaintiffs and defendants simply as '*mercator*'.[225] In this context, the word 'merchant' includes petty dealers trading in the prescribed manner in a market or fair and whose activities were therefore subject to merchant law.[226] Indeed, no less a legal authority than Bracton noted that villeins travelling away from their home manor for long periods were likely to be either commercial *mercatorii* or fighting *mercenarii*.[227] Hence, the fair court of St Ives recorded Richard May's involvement in a plea of broken contract over the sale of livestock and simply noted his residence in Needingworth (Huntingdonshire). For evidence of his personal status we have to turn to the manorial court rolls of Needingworth, which reveal that the Mays were a prominent family of customary tenants and hereditary serfs.[228] Serfs such as Richard used these private plaints to reduce the risk and the transaction costs of their personal commercial relationships.

An episode recorded in the manor court of Walsham High Hall in December 1321 captures the fluidity of business, the variety of legal codes and the range of people involved in commercial cases heard in the lesser courts of pre-plague England. The facts of the case are clear enough. John Bonde of Ipswich sued a Walsham villein, William Wodebite, for a debt of £8 in silver coins. John had provided this sizeable sum of money for William 'to trade and profit for John's benefit', presumably wheeling and dealing in the vicinity of Walsham, which is some 25 miles from Ipswich. As part of the deal, 'William was required to render faithfully a true account thereof quarterly in accordance with the Law Merchant and by a certain written agreement.'[229] So Bonde, who was probably a burgess of Ipswich, had entered into a trading agreement with Wodebite, a rural serf residing in a manor far beyond Ipswich's usual hinterland, in which Wodebite was to obtain a considerable quantity of unspecified goods on his behalf, and the agreement was formally and explicitly sealed according to merchant law. The size of the debt is unusual, because it comfortably exceeded the 40s. limit for pleas in local courts: evidence for such high-value pleas outside the royal courts is unusual, but not unknown.[230] Bonde may have been seeking additional supplies of food from sources far beyond his town's normal hinterland, because poor weather in the summer of 1321 had created severe local shortages of food during the ensuing winter.[231] He could have pursued the case in the borough court of Ipswich or in one of the royal courts, but opted instead to travel to William's home manorial court to pursue the debt, presumably because he reckoned this offered the best chance of help in enforcing any decision: John was successful, too, because William acknowledged the debt and was ordered to repay it. Clearly, then, serfs could trade with wealthy urban residents under merchant law, and the serf's own manor court was willing to uphold such contracts.

One final, and very powerful, indicator of the extent of the immersion of villeins in markets, fairs and merchant law is their involvement as officials in the running of these franchises. For example, soon after its charter was renewed in 1318 the market at Balsham (Cambridgeshire) was supervised by a bailiff of the market supported by 'wardens of market attachments', 'wardens of receivers of tolls' and other dedicated officials. As Briggs notes, 'virtually all the various officials who ran the market on behalf of the landlord were customary tenants of Balsham manor'.[232] Furthermore, some villeins played a direct role in running market franchises for themselves. From the early fourteenth century many lords began to lease their weekly market and seasonal fair franchises to third parties (either individuals or groups) for a set sum, rather than collecting the rents and tolls or holding the associated court, directly through their own officials. Serfs featured among such lessees, who were therefore fully responsible for administering the market, including holding the market court, monitoring weights and measures, and resolving disputes between traders. In other words, serfs could run courts themselves, enforcing aspects of mercantile, statute and common law. For example, in the 1340s the abbey of Bury St Edmunds had opted to lease its weekly market of Botesdale, and the assize of bread and ale there, to a succession of hereditary serfs in return for an annual rental income of around £5 per annum, with the serfs therefore taking responsibility for ensuring the effective operation of the commercial franchises – including any market court – of this small town.[233] Similarly, John del Fery, a villein tenant, leased the 'tolls' of Kirkburton and of Halifax (Yorkshire) for 26s. 8d. each for one year from the manor of Wakefield. In 1351 the Kirkburton tolls were explicitly described as market tolls, at which date the Halifax tolls were leased by another servile tenant, Thomas Culpon.[234] As lessees of the tolls of two small markets, John and Thomas must have had some powers to uphold aspects of merchant law and to sanction offenders, including freemen and women, merchants and other urban dwellers, who came to the market to trade.

Conclusion

As we have seen, historians have adopted two very different viewpoints about how the manor court operated, arising from two fundamentally different assumptions about medieval lordship. One emphasises the pervasive and inherently exploitative nature of lordship, following the theory of the common law of villeinage, and therefore presents the manor court as an instrument of seigniorial control and extraction, and the only legal tribunal available to serfs. The other perspective emphasises seigniorial respect for custom and due process, and the emergence of a legal culture deep within society, and therefore points to the manor court's communal function, its wide range of business and the serf's access to tribunals in other legal jurisdictions. Here we have tested these contradictory views against the large corpus of research into the operation of manorial and other petty courts, which shows that the direct interests of the lord represented a sizeable minority of the business of most manor courts, reinforcing its role as the principal medium for regulating the relationship between lord and villeins. The court manifestly managed and protected seigniorial interests. Yet the pursuit and defence of seigniorial privileges were not necessarily at the expense of the villeins, who were deeply immersed in the court's decision-making as jurors and officials. The example of the management of waifs and strays as a seigniorial right illustrates effectively how the court could also serve as a public good.

Communal and private business involving the peasantry were the main business of the manor court. Most of the communal business was generated through sworn presentments by juries assembled from the leading villeins, who also determined the outcome of many cases. Villeins also dominated the juries of inquiry sworn in to pronounce judgment on a particular dispute. They also dominated the ranks of capital pledges who presented cases to the leet courts. Villeins serving as jurors were to some extent enforcing the incidents of serfdom on their lord's behalf, but for the most part the system worked and endured because it provided a check on seigniorial power and because it created a collaborative mechanism capable of serving a wide range of interests and purposes, from communal control to dispute resolution.[235] The ubiquity of juries of presentment and inquiry in manorial and leet courts of different lords testifies to the exceptional degree of standardisation in curial procedures in pre-plague England. Standardisation of court procedures is also clearly apparent in the widespread adoption in manorial courts of certain key processes from the courts of common law, such as the use of written records as precedents, the regularisation of the procedure for and language in customary land transfers, and the routine use of summons and distraint to ensure compliance with the court's decisions.[236] Of course, there existed local differences in processes and efficiency within this general framework, but, overall, the cumulative impact of these innovations and adaptations was to curtail considerably the scope for seigniorial command and control over the business and decision-making of the manorial court. Furthermore, most English lords were low-status, their courts generating very modest incomes. Disputes between villein and lord followed due process, and courts could and did resolve them in favour of the former. While none of this eradicated conflict between lords and villeins, or prevented a lord from acting arbitrarily, it significantly reduced its frequency and scale, and provided serfs with some protection.[237]

Many of the largest manorial courts handled a sizeable volume of private civil actions relating to debt, trespass and covenant, which followed procedures very similar to those in the royal courts. A complex range of forces lay behind this development, but peasants – many of them villeins – brought these cases to court.[238] A variety of other local tribunals also processed such plaints, including market, fair and lesser church courts, so villeins enjoyed some choice over where to litigate. Extant records do not provide sufficient evidence to assess the scale of activity by serfs outside their own manor court, but all the indications are that it was widespread.[239] The decision about where to take such business was largely a matter of personal choice determined by cost, distance and a reckoning on the chances of success.[240] Justice was relatively cheap, but also required a tactical judgement about where to litigate.[241] Very occasionally, some lords looked to sanction serfs who litigated elsewhere when the same case could have been handled in their home manor, which had the effect of raising the inconvenience and costs of conducting business for the serfs concerned. This type of restrictive behaviour was not exclusive to villeinage, however, because boroughs were just as likely to fine their own burgesses who pursued cases in other tribunals.[242]

Private litigation enabled serfs to make enforceable contracts cheaply and efficiently, and provided them with an effective means of dispute resolution thereby reducing the risks of their participation in labour and commodity markets.[243] They did so through an interlocking system of local courts whose jurisdictional boundaries were hard and separate in theory, but soft and overlapping in practice. Villeins were able to access the labour and commodity markets without any discrimination and scarcely any prohibition on the basis of their status, thus allowing them to trade on equal terms with freemen in merchant and statute law. Serfs even ran market franchises. In all of this, the substantive difference between the villein and the freeman was that the latter could always take a private action to the royal courts if dissatisfied with the quality of justice obtained in another court, or if the claim was valued above 40s., whereas this course of action was riskier for villeins, given the theoretical impediments they faced in accessing the royal courts.[244] The last point serves as an important reminder that villeinage created constraints and obstacles. If a lord chose to deploy violence and coercion, or if a lord had local officials in his pocket or resorted to extortion, the villein's position was weak for want of the right of appeal to the royal courts. Not only did this exclusion of villeins from the royal courts create some vulnerability in law, its dishonour was also socially stigmatising and must have been keenly felt.

Yet the proliferation of a culture of law, and of a concept of equity about what was fair and just, did bring villeins some inadvertent benefits, because it had the consequence of weakening and limiting the potential for arbitrary seigniorial behaviour.[245] The broader influence of this culture of law reduced the risks of participation in land, labour and commodity markets; it diminished the likelihood of the use of force in dispute resolution; it promoted a general ethos that was more hostile to lordly discretion and friendlier to rule-based behaviour; and, by extension, it encouraged a respect for contracts and for due process.[246] None of this means that villeins were sanguine about their exclusion from the courts of common law: on the contrary, it probably sharpened their desire to gain access to it when it might best serve their purposes and fuelled resentment at their exclusion. Nor does it mean that they invariably received high-quality justice, or that they were equal in law to freemen. But it does mean that villeins had gained a range of collateral benefits from the common law, even though they did not have access to its courts in cases of tenure. The common law reforms were not intended to affect other jurisdictions, but they influenced the lives of villeins inadvertently and indirectly in ways that helped to reduce the constraints and to increase the choices that they faced under serfdom.[247]

Notes

1 Domar, 'The causes of slavery'; North and Thomas, 'The rise and fall', p. 778.
2 P. Coss, *The Foundations of Gentry Life: The Multons of Frampton and Their World, 1270–1370* (Oxford: Oxford University Press, 2010), p. 115; Campbell, 'The agrarian problem', p. 42; C. Briggs and P. R. Schofield, 'The evolution of manor courts in medieval England, c. 1250–1350: The evidence of the personal actions', *The Journal of Legal History*, 41 (2020): 1–28 (p. 2).
3 For a useful summary of the arguments supporting this viewpoint, see S. Gibbs, 'Lords, tenants and attitudes to manorial office holding, c. 1300–c. 1600', *Agricultural History Review*, 62 (2019): 155–74 (pp. 155–6).
4 Cheyney, 'The disappearance', p. 22; Dimmock, *The Origin of Capitalism*, p. 65.
5 See, for example, Hilton, *Class Conflict*, p. 123; Hilton, *A Medieval Society*, pp. 218–19, 240–1; Brenner, 'The rises and declines', pp. 260–1; and Rigby, *Marxism and History*, pp. 251–4.
6 Kosminsky, *Studies*, pp. 336–7.
7 Brenner, 'The rises and declines', p. 259; see also Brenner, 'Property and progress', pp. 262, 265.
8 Martin, *Feudalism to Capitalism*, pp. 37–8.
9 Dimmock, *The Origin of Capitalism*, pp. 67, 70.
10 Dyer, 'Memories of freedom', p. 277; Dyer, *Everyday Life*, p. 207. See also Dyer, *Standards of Living*, pp. 136–8; Dyer, *Lords and Peasants*, p. 265; Hilton, *Class Conflict*, p. 52; and Kitsikopoulos, 'England', pp. 46–7.
11 Evans, 'Whose was the manorial court?', pp. 155–6, 158; Evans, 'Merton College's control', pp. 226, 254. Despite these strident statements, Evans's evaluation of how courts functioned in practice was more nuanced.
12 Slota, 'Law, land transfer', pp. 119, 125; see also Evans, 'Whose was the manorial court?', pp. 156–8.
13 Fryde, *Peasants and Landlords*, p. 33.
14 Campbell and Bartley, *England on the Eve*, pp. 249–70.
15 Hyams, 'What did Edwardian villagers mean?', pp. 71, 74.
16 Vinogradoff, *Villeinage*, p. 357; F. W. Maitland, *The Court Baron*, Publications of the Selden Society, 4 (London: B. Quaritch, 1889), p. lx. See also Titow, *English Rural Society*, pp. 58–9.
17 Campbell and Bartley, *England on the Eve*, p. 80.

18 Olson, *A Mute Gospel*, pp. 10–19, 125–42; Olson, *A Chronicle*, pp. 23–5, 232.
19 Olson, *A Chronicle*, p. 35. See also the analysis in Bailey, *After the Black Death*, pp. 45–7; and J. Claridge and S. Gibbs, 'Waifs and strays: Property rights in late medieval England', *Journal of British Studies*, 61 (2022): 50–82 (pp. 54–5).
20 Vinogradoff, *Villeinage*, 387–90; Eldridge, *Law and the Medieval Village Community*, 203–4.
21 P. Brand, *Kings, Barons and Justices: The Making and Enforcement of Legislation in Thirteenth-Century England* (Cambridge: Cambridge University Press, 2003), pp. 42–51.
22 Bennett, *Life on the English Manor*, pp. 201–2.
23 Eldridge, *Law and the Medieval Village Community*, pp. 203–4.
24 See, for example, the explicit record of expectations for attendance at court in the Hundred Rolls of the late 1270s, in T. John, ed., *The Warwickshire Hundred Rolls of 1279–80: Stoneleigh and Kineton Hundreds* (Oxford: British Academy, 1992), pp. 46, 62, 76–7, 79, 87, 89, 105, 107, 108, 127. For a detailed study, see Evans, 'Merton College's control', pp. 228–35.
25 Phillips, 'Collaboration and litigation', p. 50.
26 Thompson, *Hundreds, Manors*, pp. 190–203; see also Evans, 'Merton College's control', pp. 228–35.
27 Briggs, *Credit and Village Society*, pp. 12–13.
28 J. S. Beckerman, 'Procedural innovation and institutional change in medieval English manorial courts', *Law and History Review*, 10 (1992): 197–252 (p. 201); S. Olson, 'Jurors of the village court: Local leadership before and after the plague in Ellington, Huntingdonshire', *Journal of British Studies*, 30 (1991): 237–56; Gibbs, 'Lords, tenants'.
29 Phillips, 'Collaboration and litigation', pp. 64–5, Table 2.12.
30 L. Bonfield, 'The role of seigneurial jurisdiction after the Norman Conquest, and the nature of customary law, in England', in L. Bonfield, ed., *Seigneurial Jurisdiction* (Berlin: Duncker & Humblot, 2000), pp. 177–94 (p. 183).
31 Slota, 'Law, land transfer', pp. 121–3; Razi and Smith, 'The origins', pp. 36–63; Beckerman, 'Procedural innovation', pp. 213–19; L. R. Poos, 'Medieval English manorial courts: Their records and their jurisdiction', in Bonfield, *Seigneurial Jurisdiction*, pp. 195–214 (pp. 199–203).
32 Bonfield, 'The nature of customary law', pp. 517–33; Beckerman, 'Toward a theory'; Hyams, *King, Lords*, pp. 69–102; Hyams, 'What did Edwardian villagers mean?', pp. 101–2; L. Bonfield, 'What did Edwardian villagers mean by customary law?', in Razi and Smith,

Medieval Society, pp. 102–16; Poos and Bonfield, *Select Cases*, pp. xxxii–xlix; P. R. Schofield, 'Peasants and the manor court: Gossip and litigation in a Suffolk village at the close of the thirteenth century', *Past & Present*, 159 (1998): 3–42 (pp. 3–10); Poos, 'Medieval English manorial courts'; Bonfield, 'The role of seigneurial jurisdiction'; R. H. Helmholz, 'Independence and uniformity in England's manorial courts', in Bonfield, *Seigneurial Jurisdiction*, pp. 215–36; C. Briggs, 'Manor court procedures, debt litigation levels, and rural credit provision in England, c. 1290–c. 1380', *Law and History Review*, 24 (2006): 519–58 (pp. 519–22, 526–7); Eldridge, *Law and the Medieval Village Community*, pp. 1–13, 92–122, 215–18.

33 Evans, 'Merton College's control', pp. 206–11.

34 Smith, 'The English peasantry', p. 351.

35 Evans, 'Whose was the manorial court?', pp. 156–7, 164.

36 Hyams, 'What did Edwardian villagers mean?', pp. 83–5; Poos and Bonfield, *Select Cases*, pp. xxxvi–xxxviii; Eldridge, *Law and the Medieval Village Community*, pp. 199–203.

37 The differences between presentment and inquisition juries could be obscure; see Briggs, 'Manor court procedures', pp. 543–8.

38 For a comprehensive introduction to the role and background of presentment juries in manorial and leet courts, see S. Gibbs, '"Open" or "closed"? Participation in English manorial presentment juries, c. 1310–c. 1600: A quantitative approach', *English Historical Review*, 137:587 (2022): 1003–51 (pp. 1004–16). See also Gibbs, *Lordship, State Formation*, pp. 37–41.

39 Bonfield, 'The nature of customary law', pp. 519–20.

40 Beckerman, 'Procedural innovation', pp. 228–9, 232–4; Bonfield, 'The role of seigneurial jurisdiction', pp. 182–3; Dyer, 'Memories of freedom', pp. 282–3; Larson, *Conflict and Compromise*, pp. 60–1; Eldridge, *Law and the Medieval Community*, pp. 203–4. The same holds for the case studies below: see, for example, Noy, *The Winslow Manor Court Books, 1322–1377*, p. xiv.

41 Gibbs, *Lordship, State Formation*, pp. 122–5; see also DeWindt, *Land and People*, pp. 196–9.

42 Levett, *Studies*, pp. 147–8, 161; Bonfield, 'The role of seigneurial jurisdiction', pp. 182–4; Eldridge, *Law and the Medieval Village Community*, pp. 183–4.

43 See the contrasting views of Bonfield, 'The nature of customary law', pp. 521–3, 531–2; and Beckerman, 'Toward a theory', pp. 3–22.

44 Beckerman, 'Procedural innovation', pp. 222–4.

45 Waging law was a particular procedure used in the courts for settling disputes.

46 Gibbs, 'Lords, tenants', pp. 165–7.
47 Beckerman, 'Procedural innovation', p. 229; Birrell, 'Manorial custumals', p. 10.
48 Evans, 'Whose was the manorial court?', 165–7; Birrell, 'Manorial custumals', pp. 15–24, 28.
49 Gibbs, 'Lords, tenants', p. 174.
50 Ibid., pp. 161, 165–7.
51 Page, *The Estates*, pp. 41, 74, 68; Homans, *English Villagers*, pp. 313, 319; Evans, 'Merton College's control', p. 209; H. S. A. Fox, 'Exploitation of the landless by lords and tenants in early medieval England', in Razi and Smith, *Medieval Society*, pp. 518–68 (p. 522); Bailey, *The English Manor*, pp. 171, 176–7; Evans, 'Whose was the manorial court?', p. 165; Woods, *Medieval Hadleigh*, pp. 202–3; Davis and Sear, *Records of Medieval Newmarket*, p. xxxvi; Aldous, *Monks Eleigh*, p. xlvi; Eldridge, *Law and the Medieval Village Community*, p. 190.
52 See, for example, Harvey, *A Medieval Oxfordshire Village*, pp. 146–7; Lock, *The Court Rolls 1303–1350*, p. 364; Gibbs, *Lordship, State Formation*, Table 3.2; Davis and Sear, *Records of Medieval Newmarket*, p. 313; and Aldous, *Monks Eleigh*, p. 367.
53 D. Oschinsky, ed., *Walter of Henley and Other Treatises on Estate Management and Accounting* (Oxford: Clarendon Press, 1971), p. 311.
54 Hyams, 'What did Edwardian villagers mean?', pp. 80–5.
55 Hyams, *King, Lords*, pp. 68–9; Harvey, *Westminster Abbey*, p. 279; Beckerman, 'Toward a theory', p. 12; Hyams, 'What did Edwardian villagers mean?', pp. 81–2; Poos and Bonfield, *Select Cases*, pp. lxxiii–cviii; Schofield, *Peasants and Historians*, pp. 210–20; McGibbon Smith, 'Reflections', pp. 73–9; Phillips, 'Collaboration and litigation', p. 100; Slota, 'Law, land transfer', p. 131.
56 Schofield, *Peasants and Historians*, p. 219.
57 Briggs, 'English serfdom', p. 24.
58 Hyams, 'What did Edwardian villagers mean?', pp. 84–6; Slota, 'Law, land transfer', pp. 125–6; Beckerman, 'Toward a theory', pp. 15–16; Briggs, 'Manor court procedures', pp. 537–42.
59 Pollock and Maitland, *The History of English Law*, Vol. I, pp. 353–5.
60 Ibid., p. 377; Briggs, 'Manor court procedures', pp. 537–9; Beckerman, 'Toward a theory', p. 16; Poos and Bonfield, *Select Cases*, pp. xxxix–lvi. The format of private litigation in the manor courts of Redgrave and Hinderclay (Suffolk) is 'recognisable from the common law courts'; Phillips, 'Collaboration and litigation', p. 69.
61 Briggs and Schofield, 'The evolution', pp. 6–20.

62 Walker, *The Court Rolls 1331–3*, p. 34. See also Briggs and Schofield, 'The evolution', p. 21.
63 Briggs and Schofield, 'The evolution', p. 23.
64 Hyams, *King, Lords*, pp. 198, 240–1; Smith, 'Some thoughts', p. 110; Campbell, 'The land', pp. 210–12, 228–30.
65 Campbell, 'The agrarian problem', p. 66.
66 Hyams, 'What did Edwardian villagers mean?', p. 100; Bonfield, 'The nature of customary law', p. 521; Beckerman, 'Toward a theory', pp. 15–17.
67 Palmer, 'The origins', p. 8; Poos, 'Medieval English manorial courts', p. 203.
68 Briggs, 'Manor court procedures', p. 557.
69 Poos, 'Medieval English manorial courts', pp. 212–13.
70 M. S. Arnold, ed., *Select Cases of Trespass from the King's Courts*, Vol. I, Selden Society, 100 (London: Selden Society, 1987), pp. lv–lx.; Dyer, 'Memories of freedom', p. 291.
71 E. Powell, *The Rising in East Anglia in 1381* (Cambridge: Cambridge University Press, 1896), p. 65.
72 Briggs and Scholfield, 'The evolution', p. 24.
73 Oschinsky, *Walter of Henley*, p. 265; Evans, 'Whose was the manorial court?', pp. 155–8, 168.
74 Eldridge, *Law and the Medieval Village Community*, p. 89.
75 Razi, *Life, Marriage*, pp. 2–3; M. K. McIntosh, *Controlling Misbehavior in England, 1370–1600* (Cambridge: Cambridge University Press, 1998), pp. 34–5; Bonfield, 'What did Edwardian villagers mean?', pp. 105–6; Bailey, *The English Manor*, pp. 167–71, 193; Eldridge, *Law and the Medieval Village Community*, p. 98; Gibbs, *Lordship, State Formation*, pp. 41–63.
76 Bonfield, 'The nature of customary law', p. 518; Poos, 'Medieval English manorial courts', pp. 195–6, 203; Bonfield, 'The role of seigneurial jurisdiction', pp. 182–3; Evans, 'Whose was the manorial court?', pp. 158–68.
77 Claridge and Gibbs, 'Waifs and strays', pp. 50–82.
78 Ibid., p. 52.
79 McGibbon Smith, 'Reflections', pp. 22–9.
80 Ibid., Appendix 1; Phillips, 'Collaboration and litigation', Figs 2.4, 2.6 and Table 2.2.
81 Briggs and Schofield, 'The evolution', pp. 1–5.
82 Ibid., p. 4. Debt was used to return money; detinue to return goods; trespass for other wrongs; covenant to recover damages for wrongful breach of agreement. The phrases interpersonal plaints/civil law suits/private litigation are all taken to mean the same thing and are here

used interchangeably, as are the words actions/suits/cases/plaints/pleas; Briggs, 'Manor court procedures', p. 522.

83 Briggs and Schofield, 'The evolution', p. 5.

84 M. J. Thornton, 'Rural society in the manor courts of Northamptonshire, 1350–1500' (PhD thesis, University of Leicester, 2004), pp. 36–9. Briggs, 'Manor court procedures', p. 524.

85 J. Williamson, 'Dispute in the manorial court: Lakenheath in the early fourteenth century', *Reading Medieval Studies*, 11 (1985): 133–41 (p. 136); McGibbon Smith, 'Reflections', p. 43; Watson, *The Court Rolls*, pp. 6–8.

86 SA, HA32/50/22/20.9 (1).

87 Phillips, 'Collaboration and litigation', pp. 67–79, 90–2; Briggs, 'Manor court procedures', p. 525.

88 Briggs, 'Manor court procedures', pp. 521–2, 524–7, 530–1, 540–1, 550–6. The speed of the Redgrave court in resolving personal pleas, for example, declined sharply after 1330; Phillips, 'Collaboration and litigation', pp. 75–9.

89 Phillips, 'Collaboration and litigation', pp. 67–79, 90–2; Briggs, 'Manor court procedures', pp. 525–6.

90 Phillips, 'Collaboration and litigation', p. 54; Briggs, *Credit and Village Society*, p. 13.

91 E. Clark, 'Debt litigation in a late medieval English vill', in Raftis, *Pathways*, pp. 247–79.

92 Phillips, 'Collaboration and litigation', p. 58.

93 For a recent statement on the debate among legal historians over this point, see J. H. Baker, *Collected Papers on English Legal History*, Vol. I (Cambridge: Cambridge University Press, 2013), pp. 1127–48.

94 Razi and Smith, 'The origins', pp. 46–9; Hyams, 'What did Edwardian villagers mean?', p. 82; Dyer, *Lords and Peasants*, p. 266; Britnell, *The Commercialisation,* pp. 142–3; Schofield, 'Peasants and the manor court', p. 17; Bennett, *Women*, p. 31. Royal courts were better suited to handling land disputes; Briggs and Schofield, 'The evolution', pp. 5–6.

95 Phillips, 'Collaboration and litigation', pp. 164–5; McGibbon Smith, 'Reflections', p. 45.

96 Schofield, 'Peasants and the manor court', pp. 3–42; C. Briggs, 'Seigniorial control of villagers' litigation beyond the manor in later medieval England', *Historical Research*, 81:213 (2008): 399–400; McGibbon Smith, 'Reflections', p. 44; Briggs, *Credit and Village Society*, pp. 13, 23–4, 26.

97 Briggs and Schofield, 'The evolution', pp. 2, 20–2.

98 Lister, *Court Rolls 1315–1317*, pp. 98, 130, 148, 158, 201.

99 Briggs and Schofield, 'The evolution', pp. 22, 24.
100 Campbell and Bartlett, *England on the Eve*, pp. 269–73.
101 See, for example, the records from Walsham High Hall in Lock, *The Court Rolls 1303–1350*. I am currently researching low-status, lay courts from Eling (Hampshire) and Easton Bavents (Suffolk).
102 Hyams, 'What did Edwardian villagers mean?', pp. 79–81, 84; Slota, 'Law, land transfer', p. 125.
103 Martin, *Feudalism to Capitalism*, p. 38.
104 Slota, 'Law, land transfer', p. 131. This issue is addressed in the case studies in Chapters 8–10).
105 Page, *The Estates*, p. 69.
106 Gibbs, 'Lords, tenants', pp. 167–8; Eldridge, *Law and the Medieval Village Community*, pp. 164–5.
107 Dyer, 'The language of oppression', pp. 74–5.
108 Page, *The Estates*, pp. 68–9; Harvey, *A Medieval Oxfordshire Village*, pp. 65–6, 69–70; Evans, 'Whose was the manorial court?', pp. 157–8; Gibbs, 'Lords, tenants', pp. 161–5; Eldridge, *Law and the Medieval Village Community*, p. 184.
109 Eldridge, *Law and the Medieval Village Community*, pp. 184–5.
110 Evans, 'Whose was the manorial court?', p. 161.
111 Beckerman, 'Procedural innovation', pp. 222, 228; Dyer, *Peasants Making History*, pp. 165–7; Eldridge, *Law and the Medieval Village Community*, pp. 209–10.
112 Eldridge, *Law and the Medieval Village Community*, p. 186.
113 Poos, 'Medieval English manorial courts', p. 207.
114 Harvey, *A Medieval Oxfordshire Village*, pp. 129–30.
115 Eldridge, *Law and the Medieval Village Community*, p. 185.
116 Evans, 'Merton College's control', pp. 250–1; Evans, 'Whose was the manorial court?', pp. 167–8.
117 Walker, *The Court Rolls 1331–3*, pp. xiv, 29, 37, 134, 161, 199; Troup, *The Court Rolls*, p. 224.
118 Lister, *Court Rolls 1315–1317*, p. 59.
119 Ibid., p. 192.
120 W. P. Baildon, ed., *Court Rolls of the Manor of Wakefield*, Vol. II, *1297–1309*, Yorkshire Archaeological Society Record Series, 36 ([Leeds]: Yorkshire Archaeological Society, 1906), pp. 70–1, 78–9, 100–1; Watson, *The Court Rolls*, p. 84; Lister, *Court Rolls 1315–1317*, pp. 30–1. See also Lock, *The Court Rolls 1303–1350*, pp. 79, 108, 129, 158, 259.
121 Birrell, 'Manorial custumals', p. 28.
122 Poos, 'Medieval English manorial courts', pp. 204–5; Eldridge, *Law and the Medieval Village Community*, pp. 185–6.

123 Homans, *English Villagers*, p. 263.
124 Ibid.
125 Bonfield, 'The role of seigniorial jurisdiction', p. 183.
126 Evans, 'Merton College's control', p. 254.
127 Eldridge, *Law and the Medieval Village Community*, p. 165.
128 Ibid., p. 212.
129 Evans, 'Merton College's control', pp. 246–51; Bush, 'Introduction', p. 11; S. H. Rigby, 'Justifying inequality: Peasants in medieval ideology', in Kowaleski et al., *Peasants and Lords*, pp. 173–200 (pp. 190–1).
130 Dimmock, *The Origin of Capitalism*, pp. 65, 68, 70; Fryde, *Peasants and Landlords*, pp. 25–6. Neither points out that even if a freeman were wrongly pronounced a serf in a manor court, he would be able to defend his status in the royal courts. See, for example, a case from 1305 where John Royes defended himself in the royal courts against a charge of servility; P. Brand, 'Stewards, bailiffs and the emerging legal profession', in Evans, *Lordship and Learning*, pp. 138–53 (pp. 138–40).
131 Fryde, *Peasants and Landlords*, pp. 25–6; Hilton, *The Decline of Serfdom*, p. 42; Dyer, *Peasants Making History*, p. 79.
132 R. K. Field, ed., *Court Rolls of Elmley Castle, Worcestershire 1347–1564*, Worcestershire Historical Society, 20 (n.p.: Worcestershire Historical Society, 2004), pp. 9, 13.
133 Bailey, *The Decline of Serfdom*, pp. 274–5.
134 Ibid., pp. 104–239.
135 For some later examples, see ibid., pp. 144, 274–5.
136 Troup, *The Court Rolls*, pp. 183–5, 254.
137 Such as at Elmley Castle, as noted above, n. 132.
138 Birrell, 'Manorial custumals', pp. 29–35.
139 Dyer, 'Memories of freedom', pp. 282–3.
140 Beckerman, 'Procedural innovation', p. 251; Gibbs, *Lordship, State Formation*, pp. 66–7, 142–3.
141 Gibbs, *Lordship, State Formation*, p. 66.
142 Campbell and Bartley, *England on the Eve*, pp. 273–4, Map 15.3.
143 For an introduction to the running and business of the leet, and for references to its historiography, see Bailey, *The English Manor*, pp. 178–84, 221–33; for an assessment of the unfree in the business of the leet, Gibbs, *Lordship, State Formation*, Chapter 3.
144 Gibbs, 'Lords, tenants', p. 156.
145 Vinogradoff, *Villeinage*, pp. 66–9.
146 Raftis, *Peasant Economic Development*, pp. 36–40; Gibbs, *Lordship, State Formation*, pp. 83–7, Table 3.2; P. R. Schofield, 'The late

medieval view of frankpledge and the tithing system: An Essex case study', in Razi and Smith, *Medieval Society*, pp. 408–49, pp. 427–9.
147 Smith, 'Some thoughts', p. 121; see also DeWindt, *Land and People*, pp. 235–9.
148 Williamson, 'Dispute in the manorial court', pp. 136–7.
149 Watson, *The Court Rolls*, pp. 6–8.
150 McGibbon Smith, 'Reflections', pp. 79–85.
151 J. M. Bennett, *Ale, Beer and Brewsters in England: Women's Work in a Changing World, 1300–1600* (Oxford: Oxford University Press, 1996), pp. 16–36, 98–106, 170–82.
152 Masschaele, *Peasants, Merchants*, pp. 36–41.
153 Hyams, 'What did Edwardian villagers mean?', pp. 71–2; C. Briggs and P. R. Schofield, 'Understanding Edwardian villagers' use of law: Some manor court litigation evidence', *Reading Medieval Studies*, 40 (2014): 117–39.
154 Briggs, 'English serfdom', 21.
155 Briggs, 'Seigniorial control', pp. 399–401, 412–13; Bailey, *The English Manor*, pp. 62–3; Briggs, 'English serfdom', p. 21.
156 Hyams, 'What did Edwardian villagers mean?', p. 73; Helmholz, 'Independence and uniformity', p. 232; Briggs, 'Seigniorial control', pp. 412–13.
157 R. Lock, ed., *The Court Rolls of Walsham le Willows 1351–1399*, Suffolk Records Society, 45 (Woodbridge: Boydell Press, 2002), pp. 120, 147.
158 McGibbon Smith, 'Reflections', pp. 18, 44.
159 Layham: SA, E3/1/2.1–2.7 and HD526/92/1; thanks to Margaret Woods for this information. Newton Longville: Oxford, New College, MSS 3872–76.
160 Briggs, 'English serfdom', pp. 21–2; Eldridge, *Law and the Medieval Village Community*, p. 179.
161 Hyams, 'What did Edwardian villagers mean?', p. 75.
162 Briggs, 'English serfdom', p. 21.
163 J. A. Raftis, *Warboys: Two Hundred Years in the Life of an English Medieval* Village (Toronto: Pontifical Institute of Mediaeval Studies, 1974), pp. 137–40; Britton, *The Community of the Vill*, p. 182.
164 DeWindt, *Land and People*, pp. 48–50.
165 Briggs, 'Manor court procedures', pp. 535–7.
166 Z. Razi, 'Manorial court rolls and local population: An East Anglian case study', *Economic History Review*, 49 (1996): 758–63 (pp. 761–2).
167 Raftis, *Warboys*, pp. 137–40.
168 Thornton, 'Rural society', pp. 23–4, 85–8, 93–9.

169 Bailey, *A Marginal Economy?*, pp. 147–8, 323.
170 Pollock and Maitland, *The History of English Law*, Vol. I, pp. 420–1; Hyams, *King, Lords*, pp. 132–3; Hyams, 'What did Edwardian villagers mean?', pp. 71, 87; Helmholz, 'Independence and uniformity', pp. 231–22; Eldridge, *Law and the Medieval Village Community*, pp. 180–1.
171 Vinogradoff, *Villeinage*, pp. 66–7.
172 Briggs, 'English serfdom', p. 21; Briggs and Schofield, 'Understanding', pp. 123–4.
173 Bailey, *After the Black Death*, p. 110.
174 Pollock and Maitland, *The History of English Law*, Vol. I, pp. 420–1; F. W. Maitland, ed., *Year Book of Edward II 2 and 3*, Vol. II (London: Selden Society, 1904), pp. 99–100; TNA, CP40/149r 331d; I am grateful to Dustin Neighly for the reference. The legal point here is, of course, that the royal courts could not hear a plea involving unfree tenure, which could only be heard in the manor court.
175 Masschaele, *Jury, State*, pp. 132–40. Schofield, 'Peasants and the manor court', pp. 4, 14, details a villein attending various sessions of the royal justices.
176 W. S. Thomson, ed., *A Lincolnshire Assize Roll*, p. 74.
177 Walker, *The Court Rolls 1331–3*, p. 179; Habberjam et al., *The Court Rolls*, p. 29. For other examples, see Briggs and Schofield, 'Understanding', pp. 124–5.
178 Eldridge, *Law and the Medieval Village Community*, p. 181.
179 Briggs, 'English serfdom', pp. 22–3.
180 R. H. Helmholz, 'Crime, compurgation and the courts of the medieval church', *Law and History Review*, 1 (1983): 1–26 (pp. 3–8); R. N. Swanson, *Church and Society in Late-Medieval England* (Oxford: Basil Blackwell, 1989), pp. 140–58; A. J. Musson, *Medieval Law in Context: The Growth of Legal Consciousness from Magna Carta to the Peasants' Revolt* (Manchester: Manchester University Press, 2001), p. 9.
181 Swanson, *Church and Society*, pp. 158–66.
182 Helmholz, 'Crime, compurgation', pp. 18–21; Swanson, *Church and Society*, pp. 174–8.
183 L. R. Poos, ed., *Lower Ecclesiastical Jurisdiction in Late-Medieval England*, Records of Economic and Social History, new series, 32 (Oxford: British Academy, 2001), p. xlv.
184 Swanson, *Church and Society*, pp. 173–4; Poos, *Lower Ecclesiastical Jurisdiction*, pp. l–lvii; S. Walker, 'Order and law', in Horrox and Ormrod, *Social History of England*, pp. 91–112 (pp. 95–6); Thornton, 'Rural society', p. 107; S. F. C. Milsom, *Historical Foundations of the*

Common Law, 2nd edn (Oxford: Oxford University Press, 1981), pp. 90–1.

185 Dyer, *An Age of Transition?*, pp. 184–5.

186 R. H. Helmholz, *Canon Law and the Law of England* (London: Hambledon Press, 1987), p. 126; D. J. Ibbetson, *A Historical Introduction to the Law of Obligations* (Oxford: Oxford University Press, 1999), p. 42; Dyer, *An Age of Transition?*, p. 185.

187 Poos, *Lower Ecclesiastical Jurisdiction*, pp. l, lxiii; Helmholz, 'Independence and uniformity', pp. 233–5.

188 Hyams, *King, Lords*, pp. 25, 66–77 (quotation p. 74); Poos and Bonfield, *Select Cases*, pp. cxlv–cliii.

189 Hyams, *King, Lords*, p. 71.

190 Dyer, *Peasants Making History*, p. 135.

191 Hyams, 'What did Edwardian villagers mean?', p. 78.

192 Poos, *Lower Ecclesiastical Jurisdiction*, p. xi.

193 Schofield, 'Peasants and the manor court', p. 21. For example, a chaplain was amerced for summoning some villein tenants of Wakefield to an ecclesiastical court for matters not relating to wills or marriages; Habberjam et al., *The Court Rolls*, p. 96.

194 F. W. Maitland and W. P. Baildon, eds, *The Court Baron* (London: Selden Society, 1891), p. 125.

195 Walker, *The Court Rolls 1331–3*, pp. 149, 194, 206, 211, 218.

196 Ibid., pp. 149, 194.

197 Lock, *The Court Rolls 1303–1350*; Lock, *The Court Rolls 1351–1399*; plus scores of unpublished fifteenth-century courts. The reference occurs in the January 1467 court; SA/B, HA504/1/14.8.

198 Hyams, 'What did Edwardian villagers mean?', pp. 77–9; Briggs, 'Manor court procedures', p. 555.

199 Swanson, *Church and Society*, pp. 160–3, 174; Hyams, 'What did Edwardian villagers mean?', pp. 77–9; Briggs, 'Seigniorial control', pp. 417–18.

200 Schofield, 'Peasants and the manor court', pp. 4–5, 14, 20–1, 29–30.

201 Helmholz, *Canon Law*, pp. 144–8.

202 Maitland and Baildon, *The Court Baron*, p. 125; see also McGibbon Smith, 'Reflections', p. 18.

203 Canterbury Cathedral Archives, U15/16/2. I am grateful to Margaret Woods for this reference.

204 The best recent summary is J. Davis, *Medieval Market Morality: Life, Law and Ethics in the English Marketplace, 1200–1500* (Cambridge: Cambridge University Press, 2011), pp. 137–273.

205 Britnell, *The Commercialisation*, pp. 90–7; Davis, *Medieval Market Morality*, pp. 231–409.

206 Masschaele, *Peasants, Merchants*, pp. 60–1; Davis, *Medieval Market Morality*, pp. 176–84.
207 The best introductions to merchant law are W. Mitchell, *An Essay in the Early History of the Law Merchant* (Cambridge: Cambridge University Press, 1904); J. H. Baker, 'The law merchant and the common law before 1700', *Cambridge Law Journal*, 38 (1979): 295–322; Davis, *Medieval Market Morality*, pp. 207–13; and J. Davis, 'Market courts and *lex mercatoria* in late medieval England', in M. Allen and M. Davies, eds, *Medieval Merchants and Money: Essays in Honour of James L. Bolton* (London: Institute of Historical Research, 2017), pp. 271–90.
208 Mitchell, *An Essay*, p. 9.
209 Ibid., pp. 10–11, 113–18, 156; Davis, 'Market courts', pp. 277, 281.
210 C. Gross, ed., *Select Cases Concerning the Law Merchant, 1293–1633*, Vol. I, Publications of the Selden Society, 23 (London: B. Quaritch, 1908), p. xxv.
211 Ibid., pp. xvii, xxiv.
212 Bailey, *Medieval Suffolk*, pp. 142–4; Davis, 'Market courts', pp. 278–83.
213 Davis, 'Market courts', pp. 271, 274, 279; Davis and Sear, *Records of Medieval Newmarket*, pp. 31–119.
214 Ibbetson, *A Historical Introduction*, p. 74; R. L. Henry, *Contracts in the Local Courts of Medieval England* (London: Longmans, 1926), pp. 21, 49–50, 70–80; A. W. B. Simpson, *A History of the Common Law of Contract: The Rise of the Action of Assumpsit* (Oxford: Oxford University Press, 1987), pp. 45–7, 161–2.
215 Davis, 'Market courts', pp. 271, 274–5; Briggs, 'Peasants, lords; J. Davis, 'Reassessment of village markets in late medieval England', in Kowaleski et al., *Peasants and Lords*, pp. 272–96.
216 Redgrave: 16 per cent (range 1–35 per cent); Hinderclay: 11 per cent (1–23 per cent). Phillips, 'Collaboration and litigation', p. 61.
217 Mitchell, *An Essay*, pp. 10–16; Baker, 'The law merchant', pp. 299–302.
218 Gross, *Select Cases*, pp. xxii–xxiii.
219 Ibid., pp. 29, 35, 88; Henry, *Contracts*, pp. 70–1.
220 Baker, 'The law merchant', pp. 302–3.
221 Briggs, 'Seigniorial control', pp. 416–17.
222 In Gandersheim (Lower Saxony) in 1188 'in market business a person was not to be treated according to his legal status but was subjected to the law of the market, *lex forensis*'; see P. Johanek, 'Seigneurial power and the development of towns in the Holy Roman Empire', in A. Simms and H. B. Clarke, eds, *Lords and Towns in Medieval Europe:*

The European Historic Towns Atlas Project (London: Routledge, 2015), pp. 117–54 (pp. 132–3).

223 Gross, *Select Cases*, pp. 1–107.

224 Ibid., p. 90.

225 Davis, 'Market courts', p. 277.

226 Miller and Hatcher, *Medieval England: Rural Society*, p. 162; Davis, 'Market courts', p. 285.

227 Hyams, *King, Lords*, p. 34 n. 48.

228 Gross, *Select Cases*, p. 80; DeWindt, *Land and People*, pp. 91, 181n, 249n.

229 Lock, *The Court Rolls 1303–1350*, p. 92.

230 When in 1310 one defendant tried to argue that the borough court of Colchester could not hear the debt plea against him because it exceeded 40s., and that such pleas could only be heard in royal courts, the bailiffs dismissed the ruse: they pointed out that the court had heard many pleas for debts over 40s., including one of £10. I. H. Jeayes, trans., *Court Rolls of the Borough of Colchester*, Vol. I, *1310–1352* (Colchester: Colchester Town Council, 1921), p. 33.

231 K. Pribyl, *Farming, Famine and Plague: The Impact of Climate in Late Medieval England* (Berlin: Springer, 2017), pp. 118–30.

232 Briggs, 'Peasants, lords', pp. 259–63.

233 Bailey, *After the Black Death*, pp. 48–50.

234 Watson, *The Court Rolls*, pp. 38, 67, 69–70, 124; Habberjam et al., *The Court Rolls*, pp. 34, 36, 56, 101.

235 Gibbs, 'Lords, tenants', pp. 173–4; Gibbs, *Lordship, State Formation*, pp. 66–7, 142–3.

236 Slota, 'Law, land transfer', pp. 119–20; Beckerman, 'Toward a theory', p. 17.

237 Slota, 'Law, land transfer', pp. 119–20, 129–31.

238 Briggs and Schofield, 'The evolution', pp. 1–28.

239 Hyams, 'What did Edwardian villagers mean?', p. 71; Briggs, 'Seigniorial control', pp. 399–422; Eldridge, *Law and the Medieval Village Community*, p. 180.

240 Hyams, 'What did Edwardian villagers mean?', p. 79; Briggs, 'Seigniorial control', p. 422. The expense of time and travel to litigate in, say, the nearest church court and the requirement to pay a fine to their own lord for using another curial jurisdiction probably increased the costs of using other courts, but villeins were at least exercising their own choice in the matter; Helmholz, 'Independence and uniformity', pp. 233–5.

241 Hyams, 'What did Edwardian villagers mean?', pp. 76–7.

242 S. H. Rigby, *Medieval Grimsby: Growth and Decline* (Hull: Hull University Press, 1993), pp. 80–1; Jeayes, *Court Rolls*, Vol. I, p. 136; I. H. Jeayes, trans., *Court Rolls of the Borough of Colchester*, Vol. II, *1353–1367* (Colchester: Colchester Town Council, 1938), p. 49.
243 E. Clark, 'Medieval labor law and English local courts', *American Journal of Legal History*, 27 (1983): 330–48 (pp. 335–6, 347–8); Briggs, 'English serfdom', p. 23.
244 Gross, *Select Cases*, p. xxv; Hyams, 'What did Edwardian villagers mean?', p. 87.
245 Hyams, 'What did Edwardian villagers mean?', pp. 92–9; Bonfield, 'The nature of customary law', p. 520.
246 Palmer, 'The economic and cultural impact', pp. 394–6; Hyams, *King, Lords*, p. 257; Bailey, *After the Black Death*, pp. 44–5.
247 Hyams, 'What did Edwardian villagers mean?', p. 87; Bailey, *After the Black Death*, pp. 44–50, 196–200, 334–7.

Part II

Serfdom in England: Causes and consequences

5

Causes: Explaining the weakness of serfdom

Given the evidence compiled in the previous three chapters, there is no doubt that on the eve of the Black Death serfdom in England was less prominent than some historians would have us believe and, furthermore, that its practice was much weaker than its legal theory. So, despite their favourable legal powers and despite the shortages of land, English lords, as Dyer put it, treated 'their tenants gingerly'.[1] The purpose of this chapter is to explore why. Indeed, Hatcher recently observed that:

> a full and convincing explanation of why lordship was so weak in the long thirteenth century when the legal and economic environments were so favourable is still awaited, and its construction will require a deeper and wider understanding of the social and cultural mentalities of the age than has so far featured in the narratives of most economic and social historians.[2]

Although a number of reasons for this have already been suggested in the previous chapters, here I bring the strands together to explain why.

I begin with a comparison between the structural underpinnings of the highly onerous forms of serfdom in early modern central and eastern Europe and those of medieval England, which provides some clues as to the weakness of the latter. The rest of the chapter attempts to provide a fuller explanation by exploring the key elements in turn: the power of custom; the codification of servile dues and the reliance on written precedents to resolve disputes; the inadvertent consequences of the common law; the unevenness of serfdom from one manor and one region to the next; the capacity of the peasantry to resist seigniorial demands, including migration; and contemporary moral frameworks.

Eastern European serfdom compared

The development of highly onerous systems of serfdom in many parts of central and eastern Europe during the late medieval and early modern periods is well documented. During the course of the fifteenth and sixteenth centuries peasants in lands east of the River Elbe were subject to an intensification of forms of serfdom, characterised principally by increased demands for labour rent and tighter restrictions on their movement.[3] This development has often been labelled as a 'second serfdom', although recent studies have shied away from using this phrase, because serfdom had not always existed in the first place in some of these regions, such as Saxony.[4] Furthermore, the blanket use of 'second serfdom' implies the existence of a heavy, monolithic system across swathes of the continent, when in fact there was much local variation in its exact operation and weight.[5] Nevertheless, a comparison between the strongest elements of East Elbian serfdom and the weaker medieval English version exposes some key structural differences between them.[6]

The most onerous forms of serfdom in central and eastern Europe have a number of common characteristics. First, they were invariably a feature of regions where seigniorial lands occupied a high proportion of the overall area of arable land. For example, demesne land made up less than 10 per cent in southwest Germany, Denmark and Scandinavia, where serfdom gradually disappeared, whereas it represented up to 40 per cent in heavily enserfed regions such as Bohemia, Hungary and Russia, and more than 50 per cent in Poland, Schleswig-Holstein and Pomerania.[7] Often the demesnes were located on vast estates held by nobles and princes.[8] In some places, such as Schleswig-Holstein, this seigniorial dominance was a function of the aggressive acquisition of lands deserted in the century or so following the Black Death, including some seizures of peasant land, while in others, such as Poland and Mecklenburg, large demesnes held by noble and aristocratic landlords had always dominated.[9] Second, the presence of vast arable demesnes was directly linked to the imposition of labour services on the peasantry, thereby guaranteeing a workforce to cultivate the land. During the sixteenth century labour services increased from around one day a week to at least three days on noble estates in many areas of north-east Germany, Pomerania and Poland.[10]

The third general characteristic of strong systems of serfdom was the consolidation of the territorial powers of lordship, whether through enhanced jurisdictional rights, privileges and monopolies, or greater restrictions on the ability of peasants to dispose of their landholdings. Thus, enserfment was achieved through an intensification of authority over tracts of territory rather than through the type of personal bondage that bound English serfs to their lords.[11] Labour coercion and mobility restrictions were often imposed through government decree, effectively through forms of civil or statute law, with a wide range of powers and enforcement capability. For example, during the fifteenth century monarchs granted expanded rights to dispense justice to local lords in Hungary, who subsequently tightened their grip on the peasantry and exercised 'ruthless arbitrary justice'.[12] From the sixteenth century onwards lords in Bohemia increased money rents, labour services and market monopolies, and also indirectly constrained peasant migration and their access to the land market and non-agricultural activities.[13] Royal and episcopal decrees drove similar developments in the Tyrol and Poland.[14] The use of civil law explains why in the nineteenth century serfdom had to be formally abolished in many regions of eastern Europe.[15] Peters argues that monarchs passed such coercive laws as a concession to the nobility in those states where sovereigns needed the nobility to finance the government: in contrast, in states such as France and England, where monarchs had alternative sources of government finance based on an established system of taxation that reached far down the social scale, they had no need to curry the nobility's favour. According to Peters, 'sovereigns imposed serfdom when they needed the nobility to finance the government. When they had other sources of financing, peasants gained or maintained their freedom.'[16]

The fourth trait of strong systems of East Elbian serfdom is the presence in some areas of a commune system of organisation at village level, which helped to institutionalise and incentivise the coercive aspects of serfdom. In Russia the village commune was a formal corporate entity with collective responsibility for allocating servile dues to individual households within the community and for ensuring that those dues were rendered. Thus, the village elites exercised considerable social control and power over other members of the community, and they had a stake in ensuring servile dues were performed, because the community as a collective had to make good any shortfall in contributions. The elites were prone to exercising their powers in arbitrary and overbearing ways, which sometimes elicited complaints from other villagers, although serfs had few avenues to seek redress.[17]

Finally, the relative absence of 'outside options' for peasants in eastern Europe to obtain land or work away from the lord's demesne enhanced the cost-effectiveness of imposing serfdom. For Daron Acemoglu and Alexander Wolitzky, the relative absence of towns reduced the opportunities for rural serfs to find alternative employment, while the seigniorial demesnes were thirsty for workers to meet the demand in western Europe for eastern European grain and livestock production.[18] Indeed, estimates of medieval urbanisation ratios – the proportion of the population living in towns – place central and eastern Europe at the lower end of the European scale.[19] Consequently, decrees restricting migration and imposing labour services on the peasantry were more readily enforceable.

At first glance, some of the principal features of the most onerous systems of eastern European serfdom are consistent with those of English serfdom in the pre-plague era. The most obvious is that English demesnes represented a large proportion – around 30 per cent – of the country's arable land. As much of this demesne land was being exploited directly, it might be expected that lords were heavily dependent on labour services and also were seeking to squeeze more revenue from their villeins through hands-on management, especially when land was becoming scarce and labour abundant. Another common characteristic is the state-backed common law of villeinage, which ostensibly equipped English lords with extensive legal powers over serfs, including the theoretical right to appropriate labour at will. These two traits largely explain why, for example, Brenner portrayed English serfdom as a highly extractive system that placed a premium on labour services, and why Carocci characterised the legal powers of English lordship over serfs as 'pervasive' by European standards.[20] Indeed, they also explain why various English historians have characterised serfdom as being at the height of its extractive powers in exactly this period.[21]

The similarities cease at this point, however. English demesnes may have occupied a relatively high proportion of total arable land, but they were organised into relatively fragmented and dispersed estates. On the eve of the Black Death, even those belonging to the greatest aristocratic and ecclesiastical lords had become 'dispersed, heterogeneous in their tenemental and economic structure, more mobile and fluid in their boundaries'.[22] Thus, hardly any English lords held unbroken, consolidated blocks of land extending over many miles, but instead lordship and demesne land were dispersed and scattered (Chapter 2). Where large, consolidated estates did exist – as on monastic and aristocratic estates in northern England – labour services and the personal dues of serfdom remained relatively light, and so the seigniorial grip over the peasantry was slight.[23] In any event, most English estates were small, held by low-status gentry lords who were scarcely distinguishable from wealthier freeholders. Furthermore, a handful of English lords possessed jurisdictional rights over wider territories than their own estates – such as the three northern Palatine counties and monastic liberties – but nothing to compare with the scale of the territorialisation of authority, or the range of powers, enjoyed by the nobility in eastern Europe. Finally, labour services were relatively unimportant in England, even though demesne land was being directly exploited, because of the availability of cheap wage labour and the monetarisation of the economy. Thus, the powerful link that existed in East Elbian systems of serfdom among extensive consolidated demesnes, high dependence on corvée labour and high-status lordship wielding extensive jurisdictional rights simply did not exist in England.

Moreover, although the emergence of common law villeinage has the superficial appearance of state-backed serfdom, in reality it was riddled with complex loopholes and it offered no effective means of enforcing the legal powers of landlords, as demonstrated in Chapter 1. As such, English common law was nowhere near as effective at imposing or maintaining serfdom as was civil law in Europe.[24] Indeed, the common law extended some protection to villeins, whereas in parts of eastern Europe local legal frameworks provided no formal checks on landlords and left serfs more vulnerable to abuses.[25] Furthermore, during the thirteenth century the

English state had developed a system of direct and indirect taxation to finance its military ambitions, and so did not have to introduce far-reaching new civil laws that enhanced the nobility's powers over labour. As Peters writes, 'the English Crown did not have to beg the nobility for taxes the way the monarchs of Eastern Europe did and allowed serfdom to wither away'.[26] Indeed, wealthier villeins paid taxes to the state and were heavily involved in its assessment and collection within their own communities. In this and in other ways, English village communities possessed and exercised a range of collective powers, and therefore a capacity for independent leadership and economic decision-making.[27] Crucially, this did not extend to a collective responsibility for servile dues or to being held accountable for any shortfall, in contrast to the Russian communes.

English serfs also enjoyed a wide range of outside options for obtaining alternative employment and land, which made serfdom more difficult for landlords to enforce. In part, this was due to the presence of towns: in 1300, and again in 1500, England was more urbanised (perhaps 20 per cent of the population) than most areas of east central Europe and Russia (closer to 10 per cent).[28] However, opportunities for *rural* employment were also greater in medieval England.[29] The waged labour market was relatively large, occupying perhaps one-third of all productive labour, and it was also unregulated: indeed, the ready availability of cheap labour and the challenges of motivating a coerced workforce explain why in c. 1300 English demesnes were overwhelmingly reliant on hired workers.[30] The existence of half-a-dozen markets and fairs within a couple of hours' travel from their home, and the presence of rural industries, further increased the opportunities for alternative employment.[31] The close co-existence of small manors, the interspersal of multiple lordships and their lands, and the capacity of serfs to sublet or even to buy land on other manors further augmented the outside options and choices available to them, whereas the much narrower range of outside options in both urban and rural settings rendered serfdom more cost-effective to impose in central and eastern Europe.

Thus, although the systems of serfdom in early modern eastern Europe and pre-plague England share two superficial similarities – large demesne systems in direct management, and state-backed legal codes – on closer inspection the differences are significant.

In England large demesnes did not depend on corvée labour, and the common law of villeinage did not provide an effective framework for imposing serfdom. English lords possessed few jurisdictional powers over large, consolidated territories and the cost-effectiveness of enforcing serfdom was undermined by the varied options available to serfs to acquire land and employment away from the manor.

Explaining the weakness of English serfdom

Although the foregoing comparison affirms some of the reasons for the weakness of medieval English serfdom, it does not explain why, for example, stated-backed villeinage was ineffective. Nor does it explain why English lords did not demand more labour services from their villeins when the economic conditions – rising land values and surpluses of labour – were so favourable. For such explanations, we must explore other forces at play in pre-plague England.

The power of custom

Manorial custom was influential in mediating the relationship between lords and serfs and in diluting the full legal powers of English serfdom.[32] It comprised an array of local and regional by-laws, inheritance rules, rights, values and social practices 'commended by convenience and sanctioned by *de facto* conduct and repetition, gradually ripening into customary usage'.[33] Its influence is evidenced by, for example, the fact that manor courts were to some extent customary courts, not just seigniorial courts, and we have also seen how servile land was sometimes described in contemporary sources as 'customary' or as being 'held according to the custom of the manor', as well as 'at the will of the lord'. Consequently, medieval historians do not dispute that custom mattered: they do, however, contest the extent to which it was capable of tempering the legal theory of villeinage and the arbitrary powers of lords.[34]

Early historians, such as Vinogradoff, tended to present custom as a cogent ameliorating influence on the behaviour of lords, which is captured in Frances Page's statement that 'for all practical purposes, [the villein's] everyday rights were amply protected by the custom of the manor'.[35] Yet historians writing in the middle of the twentieth century challenged this view, arguing instead that custom was largely ineffective in protecting serfs. For example, for Kosminsky 'manorial custom ... established a regulated and ordered form of exploitation', and Dobb; Hilton; Postan; and, initially at least, Miller, endorsed his views.[36] From the 1980s, however, scholastic opinion shifted back again, as a 'formidable body' of research into manorial documents reinforced the impact of custom in maintaining, in Hatcher's words, 'a prodigious gap between the common law and the common practice of villeinage'.[37] In this view, the 'will of the lord' was not literally a free will, but subject to customary observances.[38]

So to what extent did the power of custom weaken serfdom? Dyer has recently reminded us that custom was neither 'a fixed legal code enforced by fair-minded judges' nor immutable, because it could be manipulated, contested and changed by lords, or indeed peasants.[39] Furthermore, manorial surveys and custumals – which recorded the customs of the manor – never stipulated the frequency or the sums due from the key servile incidents of tallage, chevage, merchet, entry fines and heriot, unlike labour services and other rents, which were recorded in great detail and were fixed as a consequence. Dyer deduced that if some servile dues 'were not fixed by custom' then they were 'much more controversial' and could be manipulated at the lord's will.[40] Dyer is correct in some of these assessments: custom was malleable, it did not cover every eventuality, and it did not have a dedicated judiciary to enforce it. Custumals did not stipulate 'fixed' fines for some servile dues. Some lords did occasionally ride roughshod over custom to enforce their will, and, conversely, juries of villeins also invented 'custom' to suit their needs.[41]

Nevertheless, the inability of custom to provide comprehensive and inviolable protection for serfs in all cases did not diminish its protective powers most of the time. In Hatcher's words, 'it is not the breaching of custom which is most striking but the observing of it'.[42] Seigniorial breaches of custom were rare, partly because manorial courts were capable of ruling on any such breach and partly because they incurred social and economic costs, including provoking direct or indirect resistance from villeins.[43] Custom may have lacked its own fair-minded judges, but contemporary legal opinion did acknowledge its authority.[44] Eldridge states that 'the common law position was that, in principle, custom was a special law which took precedence and could be used to establish legal title to a right'.[45] Finally, it does not follow that the omission of some servile dues from manorial custumals therefore removed them from the protective cloak of custom and left serfs exposed to the arbitrary will of the lord, because in practice they were still located within a customary framework and their level was moderated by affeerers elected from among the villein tenants. This is demonstrated by the ubiquitous 6d. fine for leyrwite discussed in Chapter 3, and the fixed fine of 2s. 8d. for childwite on manors held by different lords throughout East Anglia.[46] Overwhelmingly, custom was observed and applied with reasonable consistency to all relations between lord and villeins for which there were precedents, and customary precedent covered and regulated dues such as tallage and entry fines. Indeed, villein juries used the manor court to address any breaches of custom.[47] As a result, disputes between lords and villeins over custom were the exception, not the norm.[48]

The binding power of custom is most obviously revealed in the operation of the customary land market, where in practice villeins enjoyed a relative security of tenure, despite their precariousness in legal theory, and where custom determined rights of inheritance and the operation of heriot.[49] Custom must also explain why lords persistently eschewed opportunities to charge the market rate for villein land through entry fines and licences to sublet. It must explain too why lords persisted in granting heritable tenures with fixed head rents, rather than opting for shorter-term leaseholds where the head rent could be renegotiated in line with rising land and grain prices. In all these cases, it was the tenant, not the lord, who obtained the benefit of rising land values. Lords routinely used leasehold when granting out their demesne resources, and so were certainly familiar and comfortable with this form of tenure. Yet, before the mid-fourteenth century, they seldom granted new lands to their peasantry on leases, or converted villein land to leasehold, when the opportunity presented itself, even though they were legally entitled to impose competitive head rents, and to renegotiate them regularly in line with market fluctuations. The fact that few did so is a powerful indication of their observance of custom.[50]

The codification of custom

During the course of the thirteenth century two interrelated developments greatly strengthened the power of custom in mediating relations between lords and serfs on the ground. The first was its codification in various written formats and the second was the burgeoning culture of providing justice based on written precedents.[51] From the late twelfth century the growing tendency to create written records of servile dues and incidents 'eroded the arbitrary principle that they were at the will of the lord', while also enabling tenants to anticipate the demands upon them.[52] Such codification of rents, services and dues was a key factor in giving them fixity, and reducing the scope for either lords or villeins to manipulate custom in their favour.[53] The prospect of increasing the volume of services and the levels of rent attached to a villein-holding became 'hard or impossible' once they had been written down, while fortifying the binding force of custom.[54] The codification of tenurial terms offered protection to landlords on a day-to-day basis, by injecting certainty and stability into their relationship with villeins and also by delimiting the administrative authority, and specifying the accountability, of their own estate officials.[55] However, this became more problematic in the longer term as the fixity prevented them from taking full advantage of rising land values by applying market rates.

The fortification of custom through codification is exemplified by the proliferation of written manorial custumals, whose purpose was to specify and clarify the exact nature of the customs and services owed to the landlord, which from the mid-thirteenth century became increasingly common, sophisticated, lengthy and detailed.[56] Custumals reduced uncertainty by spelling out the nature of the rent package in considerable detail. Hence, as George Homans observed, 'when lawyers spoke of the uncertainty of services, manorial documents speak of them as customary'.[57] For example, the extensive custumal drawn up for the manor of Hartest (Suffolk) in 1251 displays careful, bureaucratic attention to the listing of dues and rents from each villein-holding and, especially, to the discharging of week works.[58] In essence, the custumal articulated for the first time the small print in the 'contract' between lord and villein: what exactly constituted one unit of labour service (a 'work'); which religious feast days carried exemption from works; which works required the lord to provide lunch, and what food was to be provided; the arrangements in case of illness; exactly how many bundles of wood were to be prepared (and where to take them) in order to discharge a single work; how deep and wide a trench must be dug (including differentiating between old and new ditches); and so on. Sentence after sentence of close definition and clarification chased away shadows of uncertainty within the obligations. If either lord or villein attempted to dispute what was owed, or how it was to be discharged, the custumal contained the authoritative written precedent with which to resolve the conflict.

This production of increasingly detailed and prolix custumals during the course of the thirteenth century was symptomatic of a wider contemporary movement, which 'saw the increasing reliance on and deference to the authority of written documents'.[59] This movement benefited both parties by reducing the risk and uncertainty around their mutual expectations and obligations.[60] Both lord and serf had some shared interest in reducing uncertainty in their everyday dealings, to know in advance what was required, because cooperation was cheaper for both and involved less wear and tear.[61] The timing and nature of these developments are usually attributed to a decisive change in the management of manorial demesnes, which after c. 1200 shifted by degrees from leasing to direct exploitation, and which peaked in the late thirteenth century.[62] Thus, manorial accounts first appeared in mid-century then rapidly proliferated as a means of managing manorial assets and protecting the lord against fraud by local officials. Landlords managing their demesnes directly wanted to know exactly what services and incidents were available, they wanted to record obligations with increasing precision so as to minimise disputes and disagreements with their tenants, and they required a detailed written account of how these works had been used each year.

The high degree of standardisation of the layout and format of these documents from all types of estate across all parts of England confirms the premium placed on consistency, precision and accountability during a period when landlords were exploiting many of their manors directly. Treatises on estate management proliferated, and the emergence of a group of semi-professional administrators may have been aided by management training.[63] The spread of good accounting practices helped protect the lord's financial interests. Yet the financial motive in an era of direct estate management does not provide a full explanation for the spread of written records: for example, it cannot explain why the format of manorial custumals and court rolls became standardised.[64] As Richard Britnell observes, any 'piecemeal explaining misses the full force of the phenomenon, which seems to represent rather a broad culture shift in favour of recording and preserving detailed information of a legal and financial nature … record keeping, like monetized trade, was a large cluster of innovations interrelated in complex ways'.[65]

Among the complex forces behind this cluster of innovations, Britnell pointed to the link between the multiplication of written records and the commercialisation of the English economy.[66] Record keeping started earlier and developed further in southern and eastern England, where there were higher levels of urbanisation, population density and commercialisation. Commerce generated revenues, which needed tracking; it changed social relationships from their customary frameworks, which needed recording; and it was increasingly regulated by legal processes, which implied the rise of administrative records.[67] Estate documentation also enabled lords to exercise social control, because 'literacy was an instrument used by lords in the process of establishing, contesting, and renegotiating their relations with their tenants and servants'.[68] The production of detailed written custumals must reflect the outcome of a two-way process, involving input from villeins from below and loophole closure by the lord's officials from above. More generally, the spread of custumals, and the standardisation of manor court records, were connected to contemporary developments in royal law and the associated cultural shift to providing justice according to precedent.[69] It is to this issue that I now turn.

The common law

Direct estate management, commerce and social control all contributed to the multiplication of written records. None of these forces, however, was an exclusively English phenomenon, whereas the shift from an oral to a written culture during the thirteenth century was peculiarly English.[70] There are no continental parallels at this date to either the scale of production of English government and estate records or to their standardised format.[71] For example, it was not until the fifteenth century that estate management in southern Germany generated written documents on the scale of thirteenth-century England, including routinely recording the business and decisions of local courts, and, even then, the formats of court records and accounts were not standardised.[72] The obvious English peculiarity that explains the spread of practical literacy and standardisation, and its timing, is the emergence of the common law. A body of law that emerged and evolved on the basis of precedent and case law, and which sought to provide consistency of practice throughout its courts, is by its very nature heavily dependent upon written records and judgments, because literacy supports procedural formalisation and bureaucratic centralisation.[73] The growing reliance upon documentary proof and the written word to establish precedent in common law courts, and its evident success in dispute resolution, spread rapidly to other local courts, whose procedures depended increasingly on the evidence of the court record and other documents.[74] This development encouraged manorial lords to create their own documentary proof of villeinage to strengthen their position against any attempt by their villeins to claim free status in the royal courts.[75]

The exclusion of villeins from the royal courts was the fundamental point of difference with freemen, and the most explicit and humiliating manifestation of their inferior status. Likewise, the common law of villeinage rendered the serf rightless with regard to his lord. Yet the legal processes, systems and habits set in motion by the common law eventually had the unintended effect of promoting relationships between lords and serfs based more on rules and precedents than on arbitrary action.[76] Lords increasingly utilised written records and borrowed formal and set procedures from the common law in order to manage villeinage, and sought to resolve disputes using written precedent. The seigniorial desire for written proof spread to peasants themselves: 'illiterate peasants felt that possession of a written document must carry with it some power or advantage'.[77] Documents provided some protection in case of dispute, and official records kept by the lord were regarded as the best form of proof.[78] The growing use of private land charters in the thirteenth century reflected the commoditisation of the land market and the growing sense of trust and security in the rule of law, and also provided a good layer of protection in disputes over ownership.[79] As a result, villeins, including women, acquired relatively secure de facto rights in property, and their relationship with their lord became more contractual and less personal.[80]

The expansion of royal justice generated a growing appetite throughout society for dispute resolution and contract enforcement through legal means, and it spawned manifold local courts – manorial, ecclesiastical and commercial – emulating many of the same procedures and some of its business.[81] The introduction into manorial and other local courts of civil actions very similar to those used in the royal courts relating to debt, trespass and covenant provided villeins with a cheap and effective means of private dispute resolution, reducing risk in their contractual and commercial affairs, without requiring access to the royal courts.[82] Cheap access to legal redress reduced the risks involved when participating in labour and commodity markets, and so promoted the development of those markets within rural society.[83] As a consequence, villeins enjoyed substantial rights in moveable property and made enforceable contracts relating to debts and sales of goods, land and labour in a variety of courts.[84]

The proliferation of a network of local courts deploying, to varying degrees, standardised processes and practices imported from the common law represents an institutional change of great significance, and, furthermore, is a trend with no direct continental parallels.[85] At the most obvious and observable level, it increased access to a system of justice that was – to some degree at least – reliable, but it also had an impact on behaviour and expectations. The spread of procedures and practices from the common law altered social perceptions of justice, whereby dispute resolution became embedded within a centralised and standardised system of law, within which decision-making was based increasingly but decisively on written precedents and set procedures. It engendered trust in legal processes, reduced risks and costs in commercial transactions, promoted decision-making relying less on discretion than on due process and contracts, weakened the potential for arbitrary seigniorial behaviour, and diminished the likelihood of the use of force in dispute resolution.[86] None of this eroded the lord's fundamental legal right to direct the business of the manor court personally, or to behave arbitrarily if he so wished: serfs were vulnerable in such circumstances and, unlike the freeholder, had few formal options for recourse against their lord. It did, however, reinforce the influence of codified custom in rendering such behaviour much less likely in c. 1300 than it had been a century or so earlier.

Over the course of the thirteenth century the multiplication of local tribunals utilising some aspects of common law procedure and replicating some of its business, and the spread of an associated legal culture, were a juristic accident rather than an intended or predicted consequence of the growth of the common law. They were probably driven by competition between courts for business, especially private pleas.[87] The irony is striking. The common law directly excluded villeins, and thereby demeaned and weakened them, but eventually it offered them indirect, inadvertent but tangible benefits: they were able to access and utilise many common law processes, even though they lacked direct access to the royal courts, and those processes promoted a legal culture that reinforced respect for written precedents, contracts and custom. The extraordinary aspect of this whole process is the extent to which virtually every English lord had opted into this emerging legal and literate culture, as indicated by the highly standardised format of manorial tribunals and records across the length and breadth of England by c. 1300.

Why did lords all over England allow their manor courts to adopt some of the basic practices, procedures and innovations from the royal courts? One reason was the powerful momentum generated during the course of the thirteenth century within rural society through exposure to the royal courts and the spread of a shared legal knowledge, and the prospect of some profit from the provision of justice.[88] The ubiquity of freemen in rural communities who could access royal justice must have encouraged landlords to extend the range of business within their 'private' manorial courts and to import common law procedures, especially after the 1260s, when the compulsion for freemen to attend manorial courts was eased following the Provisions of Westminster (1259) and the Statute of Marlborough (1267).[89] Thereafter, lords had to find ways of actively attracting their freemen to the manor court, and one obvious way was to offer the facility to register and resolve interpersonal plaints there, and to handle them more quickly and cheaply than in the royal courts.[90] By offering the same service to their own villeins, lords were responding to a prevailing enthusiasm for legal services while also generating revenue for good measure.[91]

Another reason for the spread of common law practices was the formal teaching of law and estate administration in Westminster in the second half of the thirteenth century, and the associated emergence of a 'professional corps of administrators and lawyers familiar with the procedures and doctrines of the common law' who applied their training to estate management.[92] The stewards who ran the manorial courts on behalf of the lord often had a legal background, and this training and experience shaped the courts' conduct and business.[93] For example, successive stewards of the manor of Wakefield were trained lawyers who were familiar with the operation of the royal courts and who consequently followed many of their procedures in the manor court.[94] As a result, some aspects of cases heard in the manorial court took 'the shape of the contentions before the royal judges'.[95] Most rural communities had ready access to scribes – how else were the millions of land charters produced? – who must also have possessed a good deal of practical legal knowledge.[96] The leading villagers, including the wealthier villeins, were themselves a repository of legal know-how, who were an essential component in sustaining the culture of law.[97]

The unevenness of villeinage

Another explanation for the relative weakness of serfdom is its uneven character and weight from one manor to another, which is evident in various ways. First, the proportion of customary land varied from manor to manor: customary land was absent on some manors, whereas it dominated others. Second, customary land was held on different types of tenures, even within the same manor. Most was held on hereditary service tenancies, where the rent package was a mixture of cash and kind, labour services and servile dues, and the total customary value of the rent was below the commercial rate for land.[98] However, a small but growing proportion of customary land was being held as a heritable or life monetary tenure – for a fixed annual cash rent, with an entry fine, heriot and suit of court – or, less commonly, on non-heritable cash leases fixed for short terms at commercial rates.[99] Such variety created an element of choice and a hierarchy of preference in a world where serfs were able to migrate with few restrictions and where a market in villein land existed. Third, the composition and weight of the rent package on hereditary service tenancies, such as the quantity and format of labour services, varied markedly both within and between manors.[100] Similarly, the weight of other servile dues varied markedly from one manor to another.[101] For instance, in Chapter 2 I explored how mill suit was most prevalent in northern England and on the estates of 'the more authoritarian forms of lordship', but was uncommon elsewhere, with many small manors not possessing demesne mills.[102] Similarly, tallage was levied annually on some manors, but was light or entirely absent on most others, and its form was not even standardised within the estates of individual lords.[103] Finally, this variety in the composition and weight of tenurial villeinage was exacerbated by wide variations in the managerial rigour of its enforcement.[104] Some lords were administratively careless; others were fastidious and pedantic. The same estate might be lax about villeinage for extended periods, but then begin to manage it tightly.[105] Even the most powerful landlords did not enforce all aspects of villeinage rigorously or evenly (see the case studies in Chapters 8–10).

Thus, the experience of being a villein differed widely from one manor to another, and even within individual manors. Both the unevenness of villeinage and the fragmentation of lordship increased the volume, range and accessibility of alternative options to serfs, thereby increasing the range of outside options available to them. The scale of such options was greatest in those areas of the country where the villein land market was most active, i.e. in eastern England and the area around London. An active land market meant that the serf of one lord could acquire land – sublet or purchased – from another, thereby becoming the villein tenant, though not the personal serf, of another lord. The leading villein families on the estate of the bishop of Winchester routinely bought and sold land in more than one manor, and William de Cranmer was both a serf of Walsham manor and a free tenant of High Hall manor.[106] The outside options available to serfs were extended further through the market in waged labour, which existed in part because labour services absorbed so little of their time. Controls over the waged labour market were minimal before the Black Death, so serfs could access it with little direct interference.[107] Few lords bothered to track or control serf emigration, because of the costs and bother of doing so in an era when hired labour was relatively abundant and cheap.[108] The problem for serfs around 1300 was not whether they had sufficient freedom of time and action to participate in the waged labour market, but rather whether they could secure all the work they sought at a time when wages had low purchasing power.

If villeinage had been much more homogeneous and undifferentiated from manor to manor, then landlords would have competed less with each other, and their ability to assert their will over servile land and labour would have been greater. The highly heterogeneous nature of English serfdom in both form and imposition increased its comparative advantage on certain manors over others, which in turn fuelled competition between landlords and increased the costs and challenges to lords of enforcing serfdom. The absence of any effective means for lords to prevent their serfs from migrating to take advantage of opportunities elsewhere also weakened serfdom.

The strength of the peasantry

The power of custom was buttressed by the ability of the English peasantry to deploy a range of tactics against those lords who did attempt to ignore customary expectations or to behave in an arbitrary and rapacious fashion. The role of villeins as seigniorial officials, such as manorial reeves, and in discharging other responsibilities, such as jurors in manorial courts, provided legitimate grounds for challenging unreasonable seigniorial policies and for holding the lord and his representatives to account. The 'private' seigniorial court performed an important 'communal' function and became a medium for promoting mutual interests, and for encouraging social and economic independence among peasants, instead of operating more narrowly as a seigniorial tool for exploitation.[109]

The creation and maintenance of written records of servile dues, rents and customs worked both ways. On the one hand, the written record of servility cemented the seigniorial ability of landlords to impose those dues, to refute claims to freedom effectively, and to assert and protect their rights within the manor.[110] On the other hand, written records created limits to what lords could demand of villeins and clarified exactly what, for example, a single labour service would entail. Both parties recognised the significance of the written record in framing the relations between them. Lords involved their leading villeins in the compilation of those records.[111] Villeins would have regarded the precise factual matters contained within the written record as important, because it offered an authoritative reference point in the event of subsequent challenge or dispute.[112] Birrell argues that the codification of services also reflects the outcomes of the 'struggle' and 'battle' between peasants and lords over rent. Certainly, the production of countless written custumals during the course of the thirteenth century must have involved disagreements and compromises, which occasionally required prickliness and organised action among villeins in order to obtain a position as advantageous to them as possible.[113] The document that was eventually produced thus preserved and protected the results of bargaining, negotiations and compromises between what Birrell describes as 'vigilant' peasants and 'aggressive' and 'exasperated' estate officials.[114]

Serfs also found a variety of low-key and low-risk ways to resist the demands of their lords in everyday situations – actions that James Scott has characterised as the 'weapons of the weak'.[115] For example, serfs might fail to attend the manorial court when required to do so, or shirk labour services by working slowly or performing the task badly. David Stone has shown how corvée labour was less productive than hired labour on English demesnes, and manor courts contain many petty amercements for shoddy work.[116] Other tactics included the failure to report the names of emigrant serfs to the manorial court unless explicitly instructed to do so, or ignoring court orders to repair buildings on villein-holdings. These low-level acts of resistance were occasionally supplemented by coordinated collective action, such as challenges to a seigniorial obligation, rent strikes or even targeted violence against a manorial official. It is not always clear what triggered such active collective resistance in specific cases, but it was often a response to heavy-handed officialdom or seigniorial attempts to pervert custom or to impose new obligations.[117]

Migration from the manor was sometimes an act of individual resistance, although we can never know how far a dislike of serfdom influenced the decision of serfs to migrate. Indeed, it was not uncommon for serfs to move to another manor held by the same lord, which would be the last destination of a migrant seeking riddance of their personal status.[118] A complex mixture of push factors from the manor and of pull factors from other locations drove individual migration, making it impossible for the historian to be certain of the driving motives. In many ways, the motives are less important than the impact of migration, because the ability of serfs to migrate with limited or no seigniorial interference diminished serfdom's force.[119] Brenner was undoubtedly correct to stress how high levels of seigniorial coercion depended mainly on having effective controls over migration: if a serf could easily leave the manor with little interference, hassle or cost, then the lord would find enforcing serfdom difficult.[120] The availability of alternative employment and the prospect of easier tenures elsewhere, the reluctance of lords to return serfs to their own manors and the widespread indifference to licensing departures all encouraged migration and weakened serfdom in the pre-plague era: the same forces were to act as its solvent in the post plague era.

The frequency of low-level actions of various kinds testifies to the preparedness of villeins to resist the demands of serfdom in ways that could be subtle or confrontational as the circumstances dictated, and they are exemplified in the case studies in Chapters 8–10). They often resulted in concessions through compromise or negotiation. When such tactics failed, and in exceptional circumstances, villeins might pool funds to obtain legal advice and mount a direct and formal challenge to their status in the royal courts, such as on the manors of Darnhall and Mickleover documented in Chapter 1. The most common tactic was for villeins to claim their manor was part of the Ancient Demesne of the Crown, which, if correct, would entitle them to petition the king's justices to hear their case.[121] Taking cases to the royal courts represented the most extreme, rarest and riskiest form of direct action by serfs against their lord, and they were unlikely to succeed.

Another source of strength for villeins was their role as jurors and affeerers in the manorial court, which offered opportunities to protect their fellows against overbearing seigniorial behaviour and to head off confrontation with their lord. As we have seen, villeins on presentment juries were directly involved in the provision of remedies in a public forum based on custom and precedent, which promoted continuity and stability. Likewise, the selective granting of rights and responsibilities to serfs encouraged collaboration and, to some extent, mutual interests:[122] serfs leased demesne mills as going concerns; they leased the lord's demesne land; and they even ran their lord's commercial franchises and market courts, either individually or collectively.[123] All these developments embedded villeins within a shared literate and administrative culture, which enabled them to use its apparatus and documents for their own ends.[124] Confrontational behaviour by lords was ultimately time-consuming and counterproductive, and in the long run both lords and their villeins gained something from mutual cooperation.[125] None of this eradicated conflict, but it created safety valves and alternative avenues for resolving disputes.

Moral frameworks

During the thirteenth century a growing body of moral literature encouraged lords to act with restraint and to respect customary practices.[126] This literature was socially conservative, because it was promoting the longstanding social ideal of the three estates – which was divinely ordained – and the pursuit of the common good. In essence, it emphasised the types of exemplary and virtuous behaviour necessary to reinforce the inequality but interdependence of each estate for common profit, as well as discouraging and condemning as immoral any behaviour that might undermine or be detrimental to that interdependence.[127] Sermon books, such as the *Memoriale presbiterorum* (1344), repeatedly reminded lords that merciful and charitable behaviour carried rewards, whereas oppressive and aggressive behaviour 'provoked God to anger and contemporaries to condemnation'.[128] The thirteenth-century theologian John of Freiburg argued that the specified terms and dues of an agreement were to be observed, and where dues were not specified then any levy had to be exceptional, for the common good and within the capacity of the tenant to pay.[129]

Thus, contemporary moral frameworks promoted respect for customary norms and contractual frameworks. Landed estates, wealth and lordship may have been God-given, but landlords carried a responsibility to exercise 'good lordship', whereby relations with their tenants were based on wisdom, restraint, moderation and justice, and they should pay fair wages for work and fair prices for goods.[130] Of course, serfs were expected to pay their rents and dues, but natural and canon law forbade excessive exactions, and so contemporary moralisers condemned lords who demanded 'unjust', 'unreasonable', 'arbitrary' or 'unrestrained' tallages (taxes) and rents as extortionate, oppressive and avaricious. For example, Nicholas Bozon condemned the financial benefits gained by the rich at the expense of the poor. John Bromyard regarded anyone who took more than was owed to them by right or custom as ravine, and the *Memoriale presbiterorum* argued that exactions were unjust if they were to support a frivolous and extravagant lifestyle.[131] The latter also instructed that lords who abrogated custom were 'robbers and men of bad faith ... no temporal lord ought by natural law to exact anything from his tenant beyond what is owed to him by the same by custom or by contract made'.[132] Hence, contemporary theologians possessed a strong sense that charging serfs excessive sums of money for rents and dues was immoral.

Lay literature also reminded lords of their quasi-paternalistic role to their peasantry and of their responsibility for the actions of their officials.[133] Since true nobility lay in one's deeds rather than one's birth, magnates were encouraged to act in the interests of the 'common good' of society to justify their social and economic dominance. The common law was man-made and therefore to be pursued with restraint, flexibility and mercy, not deployed as an instrument of naked exploitation.[134] Legal actions that impoverished villeins below the level of subsistence were condemned: excessive tallages and services, and extortion of excessive fines and amercements, were actively discouraged.[135] Thus, lords were not supposed to take unreasonable distresses or distraints from their tenants.[136] Walter of Milemete (1320s) advised the king and the nobility not to 'destroy their tenants nor extort their goods through unjust lordship'.[137]

Thirteenth-century training manuals for estate administrators contained similar advice. According to Walter of Henley, lords would naturally be wealthy and powerful but should nevertheless avoid committing wrongs and trespasses. Thus, a lord should take nothing wrongfully from any person; he should allow his free and unfree tenants to be amerced by their peers, should moderate the amercements if his conscience told him they were too high, and should look after the poor. The author of the *Seneschaucy* advised that a lord should command his auditors to hear any complaints against his steward, bailiff and reeve 'so that full justice be done to free and customary tenants'.[138] Robert Grosseteste (1240s) similarly advised that stewards and bailiffs were not to molest, hurt or ruin their lord's tenants through tyrannical demands, and the lord should provide redress for any such behaviour.[139]

This legal, theological and moral framework was firmly grounded in the idea that while inequality in society was natural and divinely ordained, the actions of those who enjoyed wealth, status and power should promote the common good of all within society. Hole has attempted to assess whether the treatment of English peasants by their lords did in fact conform to such idealistic notions of virtue and reason or whether it was mostly rapacious.[140] She recognises the difficulties involved in any attempt to judge whether the resulting evidence should be interpreted as either 'reasonable', 'rapacious' or 'exploitative' seigniorial behaviour, because such judgements reveal more about the attitudes of historians than they do about the past, although her own conclusions do not always avoid such value judgements. Hole offers a credible case for the importance medieval society placed on moral instruction, although her narrow evidentiary base permits only a tentative conclusion about the extent to which 'economic ethics and moral concepts more generally were thoroughly embedded'.[141]

The extent to which individual lords responded to such moral exhortation is a moot point, although there are scattered examples of even powerful monastic lords following these precepts. For instance, in 1290 the tenants of servile 40-acre virgates in Shapwick (Somerset) met with their lord, the abbot of Glastonbury, to plead their poverty, as a result of which their ploughing services on the demesne were reduced permanently.[142] Likewise, Merton College occasionally reduced levels of amercements, rents and fines to help those villeins suffering from adversity, such as the remissions granted in 1313 to Joan Bovecheriche of Cuxham following the destruction of her house in a fire, and Crowland abbey provided support to destitute tenants after the famine of 1322.[143] Raban noted the cautious management of rents by ecclesiastical landlords in parts of the east Midlands and suggested that religious and social values discouraged them from pursuing rent-maximising policies towards their hard-pressed peasantry.[144] Thus, the contemporary moral framework did promote some seigniorial restraint and moderation when dealing with peasants, and some lords did respond favourably to such exhortation. As such, it created a broad culture and a set of attitudes that regarded riding roughshod over customary rights or ignoring written precedents as wrong. Its general effects contributed to the broad flow of forces diluting the full legal force of common law villeinage and discouraging arbitrary seigniorial behaviour.

Conclusion

The combination of common law villeinage; large, directly managed demesnes; and economic conditions advantageous to landlords were all favourable to the imposition of a strong system of serfdom in pre-plague England, but this did not happen in practice, as documented in Chapters 2–4. The comparison of the structure of English serfdom with those of systems in central and eastern Europe, where serfdom was imposed strongly in the early modern period, has highlighted the importance of the latter's enforcement capability. Large demesnes were consolidated in central Europe, and statute law applied over sizeable tracts of territory under the control of high-status nobles, in contrast to the fragmented demesnes, diffuse power structures and weaker enforcement powers of English common law. The framework of serfdom in central Europe tended to provide more effective controls over servile migration than in England, a key element in the cost-effectiveness of serfdom.

Against this backdrop, the second part of this chapter has responded to Hatcher's call for 'a full and convincing explanation of why lordship was so weak when the legal and economic environments were so favourable' in England.[145] One factor was the power of custom. Much credence has been given previously to its role in tempering common law villeinage, but here I have emphasised how the power of custom was fortified by its widespread *codification* during the thirteenth century. The production of written records of local customs and the rendering of servile dues bestowed even greater fixity on the rents, services and incidents of villeinage. The creation of a formal record not only eroded the principle that they were determined by, and changeable at, the will of the lord, but also enhanced the obligatory sanction of custom, thus making annual head rents on customary land difficult to alter and, especially, to increase, even when market conditions became favourable to such increases. Additionally, once in existence a written precedent became the starting point for resolving disputes between lords and villeins following an established procedure in manorial courts: and, in doing so, reduced the scope for lords (or villeins) to manipulate custom to their advantage.

The explosion in the quantity of written manorial documents during the thirteenth century is often attributed to the professionalisation of direct estate management and the spread of lay literacy. As Birrell has shown, it also involved resistance, bargaining and negotiation by the villeins who helped compile those documents, especially detailed custumals.[146] Yet these forces do not provide a sufficient explanation for the degree to which the format of manorial documents became standardised across the manors and estates of very different landlords. This is especially true of manor courts, where lords were technically at liberty to determine and adopt whatever procedures they chose in what was their own private court. The missing link here is the spread of common law culture and procedures into English society, which reinforced the practice of dispensing justice according to written precedent and discouraged arbitrary seigniorial action. The infusion of various common law procedures into relations between lord and serfs inadvertently eroded the former's legal powers over the latter. The common law reforms were not intended to affect other jurisdictions – whether manorial, commercial or ecclesiastical – but they did so in ways that rendered the lives of villeins more predictable and, in some respects, more advantageous than their formal, debased legal standing would indicate.[147]

The impact of the common law on villeins was therefore complex and, in some ways, contradictory. On the one hand, it directly excluded them from the royal courts and subjected them entirely to their lord's will. On the other hand, it triggered a raft of legal, cultural and social reforms that indirectly altered the behaviour of lords and benefited villeins. As a result, the influence of common law on the operation of English serfdom was far less effective than was the influence of civil law on its operation across many eastern European lands in the early modern period. This reinforces the point that serfdom always operated within different institutional contexts, and reconstructing such contexts is essential to understanding the different degrees of peasant agency that could be found under serfdom. It also illustrates the potential for legal reform to carry inadvertent consequences: the general processes and procedures of the common law seeped into society in ways that ultimately helped to undermine the full force of common law villeinage.

Assessing objectively the relative weight of the various forces ameliorating the power of lordship is almost impossible. It is one thing, for example, to acknowledge the presence of a moral framework hostile to greedy and exploitative lordship, and another thing entirely to assess how far it really did temper the actions of lords on the ground. We can be confident, however, that three forces had a ubiquitous influence throughout England: custom existed everywhere, by the end of the thirteenth century custom had been codified almost everywhere, and serfs would resist seigniorial pressure in manifold ways. The extent and the pervasiveness of these developments, reinforced by the seeping of a common law culture throughout society, elevates them to the first rank of explanations for the weakness of English lordship.

There remains one fundamental and outstanding problem with the conclusion that English serfdom was weak. A prominent line of argument in the scholarship attributes the slowing of economic growth in the late thirteenth century and the mounting crisis in the early fourteenth century to the highly extractive and exploitative nature of English serfdom. Hence, the discovery that serfdom was weak not only overturns a major theme in the scholarship, but also prompts an even bigger question: was serfdom irrelevant to economic development and, if so, what did cause the slowdown and crisis? Chapter 6 considers these issues.

Notes

1 Dyer, 'Ineffectiveness of lordship', p. 79.
2 Hatcher, 'Lordship', p. 138.
3 J. Blum, 'The rise of serfdom in eastern Europe', *American Historical Review*, 62:4 (1957): 807– 36; M. North, *The Expansion of Europe, 1250–1500* (Manchester: Manchester University Press, 2012), pp. 256–8; J. Mysliwski, 'Central Europe', in Kitsikopoulos, *Agrarian Change*, pp. 268–71; Peters, 'Government finance', pp. 149–73.
4 Melton, 'The agrarian East', pp. 428–32; Cerman, 'Demesne lordship', pp. 243–4; M. Cerman, 'Social structure and land markets

in late medieval central and east-central Europe', *Continuity and Change*, 23:1 (2008): 55–100 (p. 78); M. North, 'Serfdom and corvée labour in the Baltic area, sixteenth to eighteenth centuries', in Cavaciocchi, *Serfdom and Slavery*, pp. 139–54 (p. 141); P. Malanima, 'Serfdom in eastern Europe after the revisions', in Cavaciocchi, *Serfdom and Slavery*, pp. 677–88 (pp. 677–8); S. Brakensiek, 'North-west Germany, 1000–1750', in B. J. P. van Bavel and R. W. Hoyle, eds, *Rural Economy and Society in North-Western Europe, 500–2000: Social Relations, Property and Power* (Turnhout: Brepols, 2010), pp. 227–52 (pp. 246–7).

5 T. Scott, *Society and Economy in Germany 1300 to 1600* (Basingstoke: Macmillan, 2002), pp. 155, 171–5, 195–6; Ogilvie, 'Serfdom and the institutional system', pp. 37–40; Cerman, 'Demesne lordship', pp. 249–54; T. Ertl, T. Frank and S. Nussbaum, 'Introduction', in T. Ertl, T. Frank and S. Nussbaum, eds, *Busy Tenants: Peasant Land Markets in Central Europe (15th to 16th Centuries)* (Stuttgart: Franz Steiner Verlag, 2021), pp. 7–13.

6 See also M. Bailey, 'Comparing serfdom in England to southern Germany in the century before the Black Death: Possibilities and pitfalls', in J. Peltzer and N. Vincent, eds, *Thirteenth-Century England 20: Proceedings of the Heidelberg Conference, 2023* (Woodbridge: Boydell and Brewer, [forthcoming, 2026]).

7 Malanima, 'Serfdom in eastern Europe', p. 680; Ogilvie, 'Serfdom and the institutional system', pp. 39–40; North, 'Serfdom and corvée labour', pp. 144–6.

8 M. Cerman, 'Seigniorial systems in east-central and eastern Europe 1300–1800: Regional realities', in Cavaciocchi, *Serfdom and Slavery*, pp. 188–211 (pp. 204–5, Table 1); Bush, 'Serfdom', pp. 213–15.

9 W. Rosener, *The Peasantry of Europe* (Oxford: Basil Blackwell, 1994), pp. 106–10; Scott, *Society and Economy*, p. 186; North, 'Serfdom and corvée labour', pp. 142–4; Cerman, 'Social structure', pp. 76–9; J. R. Myking and C. P. Rasmussen, 'Scandinavia 1000–1750', in Van Bavel and Hoyle, *Rural Economy and Society*, pp. 287–314 (pp. 294–5); J. Martin, 'Russia', in Kitsikopoulos, *Agrarian Change*, pp. 292–329 (pp. 303–4).

10 Cerman, *Villagers and Lords*, 75–84; W. Hagan, 'Subject farmers in Brandenburg-Prussia and Poland: Village life and fortunes under manorialism in early modern central Europe', in Bush, *Serfdom and Slavery*, pp. 296–310 (pp. 302–6); Rosener, *The Peasantry*, p. 77; Malanima, 'Serfdom in eastern Europe', p. 679.

11 W. Rosener, *Peasants in the Middle Ages* (Cambridge: Cambridge University Press, 1992), pp. 270–5; Scott, *Society and Economy*, pp.

171–4, 182–8; Rosener, *The Peasantry*, pp. 104–10; Cerman, 'Social structure', pp. 77–8; Ogilvie, 'Serfdom and the institutional system', p. 42; Bush, 'Serfdom', p. 205; Brakensiek, 'North-west Germany', p. 236; K. Andermann, 'Leibeigenschaft in der Markgrafschaft Baden an der Wende vom Mittelalter zur Neuzeit', in Freedman and Bourin, *Forms of Servitude*, pp. 197–212 (p. 197).

12 J. M. Bak, 'Servitude in the medieval kingdom of Hungary (a sketchy outline)', in Freedman and Bourin, *Forms of Servitude*, pp. 387–400 (pp. 394, 398).

13 A. Klima, 'Agrarian class structure and economic development in pre-industrial Bohemia', in Aston and Philpin, *The Brenner Debate*, pp. 192–212; Klein and Ogilvie, 'Occupational structure', pp. 494–5, 509–17.

14 H. Dopsch, 'Neue Leibeigenschaft oder alte Hörigkeit? Zu den Beschwerden und Forderungen aufständischer Bauern im Ostalpenraum an der Wende zur Neuzeit', in Freedman and Bourin, *Forms of Servitude*, pp. 313–42 (pp. 314–16). M. Dygo, 'Zur Genese der sog. "zweiten Leibeigenschaft" in Polen 15–16 Jahrhundert', in Freedman and Bourin, *Forms of Servitude*, pp. 401–18 (pp. 401–2).

15 W. Kula, *An Economic Theory of the Feudal System* (London: Humanities Press, 1976), pp. 196–201; Klima, 'Agrarian class structure', p. 196; Cerman, *Villagers and Lords*, pp. 75–84; Melton, 'The agrarian East', pp. 436–43; Ghosh, 'Rural economies', pp. 266–7; Myking and Rasmussen, 'Scandinavia 1000–1750', p. 301; S. Schmitt, 'Wildfange, Ausleute und rechte Untertanen: Die Herausbildung der Territorialleibherrschaft im Mittelrheingebiet (15.–16. Jahrhundert)', in Freedman and Bourin, *Forms of Servitude*, pp. 213–27; Martin, 'Russia', pp. 318–19; Hyams, *King, Lords*, p. 266.

16 Peters, 'Government finance', p. 170.

17 Dennison, 'The institutional context', pp. 254–62; Ogilvie, 'Choices and constraints', pp. 289–95.

18 D. Acemoglu and A. Wolitzky, 'The economics of labour coercion', *Econometrica*, 79 (2011): 555–600 (pp. 577–8); Peters, 'Government finance', pp. 153–4.

19 Campbell, *The Great Transition*, pp. 121–5.

20 Brenner, 'The rises and declines', pp. 263–6, 268; Carocci, 'The pervasiveness of lordship', pp. 45–6.

21 For example, Maddicott, *The English Peasantry*, pp. 73–4.

22 M. A. Barg, 'The social structure of manorial freeholders: An analysis of the Hundred Rolls of 1279', *Agricultural History Review*, 39 (1991): 108–15 (p. 115).

23 See Map 2.1; Larson, *Conflict and Compromise*, pp. 62–7.

24 Ogilvie, 'Choices and constraints', pp. 295–302.
25 T. Dennison, 'Contract enforcement in Russian serf society', *Economic History Review*, 66 (2013): 715–32 (pp. 728–30); Dennison, 'The institutional context', pp. 258–9, 264–6.
26 Peters, 'Government finance', pp. 159–60.
27 Raftis, *Peasant Economic Development*, pp. 118–31; C. Dyer, 'The English medieval village community and its decline', *Journal of British Studies*, 33 (1994): 407–29.
28 Campbell, *The Great Transition*, pp. 121–5, Table 5.1.
29 Compare, for example, Bailey, 'Servile and gender migration', pp. 66–75, with T. K. Dennison, *The Institutional Framework of Russian Serfdom* (Cambridge: Cambridge University Press, 2011), p. 172.
30 Rigby, *English Society*, p. 75; B. M. S. Campbell, *English Seigniorial Agriculture, 1250–1450* (Cambridge: Cambridge University Press, 2000), pp. 55–6, 357, 420–1; Bailey, 'The regulation', pp. 140–4.
31 Britnell, *Britain and Ireland*, pp. 138–57; Farmer, 'Marketing the produce', pp. 330–1; Briggs, 'Peasants, lords', pp. 268–9; Davis, 'Reassessment', pp. 277–91.
32 Bonfield, 'The role of seigniorial jurisdiction', pp. 182–93.
33 Beckerman, 'Toward a theory', p. 9; Dyer, 'The ineffectiveness of lordship', p. 78. See the discussion in Faith, *The Moral Economy*, pp. 171–83.
34 See, for example, the survey in Hole, *Economic Ethics*, pp. 191–7.
35 Vinogradoff, *Villeinage*, p. 177; Page, *The Estates*, p. 134.
36 Kosminsky, *Studies*, p. 334; for a synthesis of these early views, see Hatcher, 'Lordship', pp. 119–25.
37 Hatcher, 'Lordship', pp. 126–35 (quotations p. 127).
38 Hatcher, 'English serfdom', pp. 3–39; Poos and Bonfield, *Select Cases*, p. lxxiv; Beckerman, 'Procedural innovation', p. 250; Hatcher, 'Lordship', pp. 119–25; and, for an authoritative recent analysis, Eldridge, *Law and the Medieval Village Community*, pp. 159–214.
39 Dyer, 'Villeins, bondsmen', pp. 424–8 (quotation p. 427). See also Britnell, *The Commercialisation*, pp. 60–1; and Birrell, 'Manorial Custumals', p. 31.
40 Dyer, 'The language of oppression', pp. 82–3.
41 Bonfield, 'The role of seigniorial jurisdiction', p. 191.
42 Hatcher, 'English serfdom', p. 22.
43 Vinogradoff, *Villeinage*, p. 361; Hyams, *King, Lords*, p. 198; Beckerman, 'Procedural innovation', p. 251; Dyer, 'Memories of freedom', p. 290.
44 Poos and Bonfield, *Select Cases*, pp. xxvii–xxxv.
45 Eldridge, *Law and the Medieval Village Community*, pp. 166–7; Poos and Bonfield, *Select Cases*, pp. xxviii–xxix.

46 Bonfield, 'The role of seigniorial jurisdiction', p. 186.
47 Ibid., p. 190.
48 Poos, 'Medieval English manorial courts', pp. 205–7.
49 Poos and Bonfield, *Select Cases*, pp. lxxii–cviii.
50 Campbell, 'The land', pp. 210–12, 228–9.
51 Smith, 'Some thoughts', p. 102; Hyams, *King, Lords*, p. 257; Hatcher, 'English serfdom', p. 23; Bonfield, 'The role of seigniorial jurisdiction', pp. 182–93.
52 Birrell, 'Manorial custumals', p. 29.
53 Miller, *The Abbey and Bishopric*, p. 103; Harvey, *Westminster Abbey*, p. 223; Searle, *Lordship and Community*, p. 169; Birrell, 'Manorial custumals', pp. 32–5; Bonfield, 'The nature of customary law', pp. 519–20; Poos and Bonfield, *Select Cases*, p. xxi.
54 Hyams, *King, Lords*, p. 185; Dyer, 'Memories of freedom', p. 290.
55 Beckerman, 'Procedural innovation', pp. 250–1; Wells-Furby, *The Berkeley Estate*, pp. 116–18; D. Wood, *Medieval Economic Thought* (Cambridge: Cambridge University Press, 2012), pp. 50–2.
56 Homans, *English Villagers*, pp. 260–72; DeWindt, *Land and People*, pp. 79–85; Birrell, 'Manorial custumals', pp. 9, 16–17.
57 Homans, *English Villagers*, p. 271.
58 Bailey, *The English Manor*, pp. 48–57.
59 Beckerman, 'Procedural innovation', p. 224. See M. T. Clanchy, *From Memory to Written Record: England 1066–1307*, 3rd edn (London: Wiley Blackwell, 2012); R. H. Britnell, ed., *Pragmatic Literacy, East and West 1200–1330* (Woodbridge: Boydell and Brewer, 1997); and K. Heidecker, ed., *Charters and the Use of the Written Word in Medieval Society* (Turnhout: Brepols, 2000).
60 Slota, 'Law, land transfer', pp. 119–20, 129–31.
61 Campbell, 'The land', p. 226.
62 Oschinsky, *Walter of Henley*, pp. 213–14; Smith, 'Some thoughts', p. 98; Bailey, *The English Manor*, pp. 19–20, 24, 98–9, 167–8; Birrell, 'Manorial custumals', pp. 14–15.
63 Beckerman, 'Toward a theory', pp. 11, 15; Poos, 'English manorial courts', pp. 202–3.
64 Poos, 'Medieval English manorial courts', pp. 201–2.
65 Britnell, *Britain and Ireland*, p. 275.
66 Ibid., pp. 277–8.
67 Ibid., pp. 278–80.
68 Ibid., p. 279.
69 Smith, 'Some thoughts', pp. 100, 126; Hyams, 'What did Edwardian villagers mean?', p. 82; Poos, 'Medieval English manorial courts', pp. 201–3.

70 Razi and Smith, 'The origins', p. 36.

71 P. D. A. Harvey, 'English estate records', in Britnell, *Pragmatic Literacy*, pp. 107–18 (p. 118).

72 Cerman, 'Seigniorial systems', p. 211; S. Ghosh, 'Rural commercialisation in southern Germany, c. 1200–c. 1500: Sources, problems, and potential', *Mediaeval Studies*, 82 (2020): 207–74 (pp. 215, 222, 229, 266); R. Schafer, 'Inheritance disputes from Ingelheim court records on the threshold of the early modern period (fourteenth to fifteenth centuries)', in M. Lanzinger, J. Maegraith, S. Clementi, E. Forster, and C. Hagen, eds, *Negotiations of Gender and Property through Legal Regimes (14th–19th Century): Stipulating, Litigating, Mediating* (Leiden: Brill, 2021), pp. 52–83.

73 Palmer, 'England', pp. 245–7.

74 Beckerman, 'Procedural innovation', pp. 222–4; J. Hudson, *The Formation of the English Common Law: Law and Society in England from the Norman Conquest to Magna Carta* (London: Longman, 1996), pp. 142–4.

75 Razi and Smith, 'Origins', p. 45; Hyams, 'What did Edwardian villagers mean?', p. 82; Smith, 'The English peasantry', pp. 347–60; Poos, 'Medieval English manorial courts', p. 200.

76 Bailey, *After the Black Death*, pp. 44–50.

77 Hyams, *King, Lords*, p. 46. See also Beckerman, 'Procedural innovation', p. 225; and Poos and Bonfield, *Select Cases*, pp. xxi–xxii.

78 Beckerman, 'Procedural innovation', p. 224.

79 J. Masschaele, 'The public life of the private charter in thirteenth-century England', in B. Dodds and C. D. Liddy, eds, *Commercial Activity, Markets and Entrepreneurs in the Middle Ages: Essays in Honour of Richard Britnell* (Woodbridge: Boydell and Brewer, 2011), pp. 199–216 (pp. 199–200, 215–16).

80 Briggs, 'English serfdom', p. 28; Campbell, *The Great Transition*, pp. 77–80.

81 Vinogradoff, *Villeinage*, pp. 369–70; Hyams, 'What did Edward villagers mean?', pp. 79–80; Briggs, 'Manor court procedures', pp. 519–21.

82 Hyams, 'What did Edwardian villagers mean?', pp. 71–2; Schofield, 'Peasants and the manor court', pp. 20–6; McGibbon Smith, 'Reflections', pp. 17–19.

83 Clark, 'Medieval labor law', pp. 335–6, 347–8.

84 Briggs, 'English serfdom', pp. 20–3.

85 Faith, *The English Peasantry*, p. 252; Dennison, 'Contract enforcement'; Dennison, 'The institutional context', pp. 259–65, 268; Ogilvie, 'Choices and constraints', pp. 295–7; T. Buhler, 'Seigniorial

jurisdictions in the territories of the diocese of Basle according to sources of the thirteenth to fifteenth centuries', in Bonfield, *Seigniorial Jurisdiction*, pp. 77–102.

86 Hyams, 'What did Edwardian villagers mean?', p. 102.

87 Smith, 'The English peasantry', p. 350.

88 Smith, 'Some thoughts', p. 128; Razi and Smith, 'The origins', pp. 36–7; Phillips, 'Collaboration and litigation', pp. 67–8.

89 Brand, *Kings, Barons*, pp. 42–51; Dyer, 'The ineffectiveness of lordship', p. 82.

90 Vinogradoff, *Villeinage*, pp. 369–70; Razi and Smith, 'The origins', pp. 46–9; Hyams, 'What did Edwardian villagers mean?', pp. 79–82, 84; Dyer, *Lords and Peasants*, p. 266; Britnell, *The Commercialisation*, pp. 142–4; Schofield, 'Peasants and the manor court', p. 17; Briggs, 'Manor court procedures', pp. 536–57.

91 Raftis, *Warboys*, pp. 137–40; Schofield, 'Peasants and the manor court', pp. 3–42; Briggs, 'Seigniorial control', pp. 399–400, 412–13; McGibbon Smith, 'Reflections', p. 44; Briggs, *Credit and Village Society*, pp. 13, 23–4, 26.

92 Beckerman, 'Toward a theory', pp. 11, 15; J. S. Beckerman, 'Law writing and law teaching: Treatise evidence of the formal teaching of English law in the late thirteenth century', in J. A. Bush and A. Wijffels, eds, *Learning the Law: Teaching and the Transmission of Law in England 1150–1900* (London: Hambledon Press, 1999), pp. 33–50; P. Brand, 'Legal education in England before the Inns of Court', in Bush and Wijffels, *Learning the Law*, pp. 51–84 (pp. 82–4); Briggs, 'Manor court procedures', p. 527.

93 Poos, 'Medieval English manorial courts', pp. 201–3; Briggs and Schofield, 'The evolution', pp. 16–17.

94 Walker, *The Court Rolls 1331–3*, pp. xi–xii.

95 Vinogradoff, *Villeinage*, pp. 369–70.

96 M. Bailey, 'Historiographical essay: The commercialisation of English society 1086–1350', *Journal of Medieval History*, 24 (1998): 297–321 (p. 301).

97 I. Forrest, *Trustworthy Men: How Inequality and Faith Made the Medieval Church* (Princeton: Princeton University Press, 2018), pp. 129–60.

98 Hatcher, 'English serfdom', pp. 18–23; Campbell, 'The agrarian problem', pp. 52–3; Campbell, 'The land', pp. 228–30.

99 For example, Fryde, *Peasants and Lords*, pp. 26–8; Wells-Furby, *The Berkeley Estate*, pp. 89–139.

100 Campbell, 'The agrarian problem', pp. 36–40; Campbell and Bartley, *England on the Eve*, pp. 264–5.

101 Bailey, *The Decline of Serfdom*, pp. 39, 41–3, 46, 56.
102 Lucas, *Ecclesiastical Lordship*, pp. 285–6, 313–14; Bailey, *Medieval Suffolk*, p. 57.
103 Bailey, 'Tallage-at-will', pp. 26–44.
104 Hilton, *A Medieval Society*, pp. 147–8; Dyer, 'The ineffectiveness of lordship', pp. 79–81; Bailey, 'Villeinage in England', pp. 430–57.
105 Bailey, *The Decline of Serfdom*, p. 43.
106 Mullan and Britnell, *Land and Family*, p. 121; Lock, *The Court Rolls 1303–1350*, pp. 319, 321.
107 Bailey, *After the Black Death*, pp. 32–8.
108 Briggs, 'English serfdom', pp. 28–31.
109 Olson, *A Chronicle*, pp. 23–5, 232; Raftis, *Peasant Economic Development*, pp. 118–31; Olson, *A Mute Gospel*, pp. 139–42.
110 Razi and Smith, 'The origins', p. 45.
111 Birrell, 'Manorial custumals', p. 19.
112 Poos, 'Medieval English manorial courts, p. 203.
113 Dyer, 'Villeins, bondsmen', pp. 426–7; Birrell, 'Manorial custumals', pp. 19, 34–6.
114 Birrell, 'Manorial custumals', pp. 10, 14–18, 36.
115 J. C. Scott, *Weapons of the Weak: Everyday Forms of Peasant Resistance* (New Haven: Yale University Press, 2008), pp. 304–32.
116 Stone, 'The productivity'.
117 Hilton, *A Medieval Society*, pp. 156–61; Hatcher, 'English serfdom', pp. 34–5; Rigby, *English Society*, pp. 105–7, 110; Crook, 'Freedom, villeinage'; Wells-Furby, *The Berkeley Estate*, pp. 114–16; Dyer, 'From slavery to freedom', pp. 40–4.
118 Bailey, 'Servile and gender migration', pp. 62–6.
119 Dyer, 'From slavery to freedom', pp. 38–40.
120 Brenner, 'The rises and declines', pp. 248, 263; Brenner, 'Property and progress', p. 64.
121 Dyer, 'Memories of freedom', pp. 277–95.
122 Rio, *Slavery*, p. 239; Rigby, *English Society*, pp. 25–34, 46–9.
123 Bailey, *After the Black Death*, pp. 48–50.
124 Olson, *A Chronicle*, pp. 3–12, 44–55, 230–2; Olson, *A Mute Gospel*, pp. 124–42; Wood, *Medieval Economic Thought*, pp. 50–2; Cerman, *Villagers and Lords*, pp. 36–7.
125 Campbell, 'The agrarian problem', p. 40.
126 J. Gibbs, 'Restraints on landlords in the moral literature of late-medieval England' (BA dissertation, University of Cambridge, 2008), pp. 2–4.
127 Ibid., pp. 17–29; Hole, *Economic Ethics*, pp. 99–125.
128 Hatcher, 'Lordship', p. 139; Rigby, *English Society*, p. 313; S. H. Rigby, 'England', in Rigby, *A Companion*, pp. 497–520 (pp. 510–12).

129 M. Haren, *Sin and Society in Fourteenth-Century England: A Study of the 'Memoriale presbiterorum'* (Oxford: Oxford University Press, 2000), pp. 114–15.
130 Hole, *Economic Ethics*, pp. 90–4.
131 Rigby, *English Society*, pp. 313–14; Hole, *Economic Ethics*, pp. 73–5, 154, 160.
132 Haren, *Sin and Society*, p. 113.
133 Gibbs, 'Restraints', pp. 25–7; Hatcher, 'Lordship', p. 140; Hole, *Economic Ethics*, pp. 93–4, 97.
134 Richardson and Sayles, *Law and Legislation*, p. 143; Gibbs, 'Restraints', pp. 37–41.
135 Hyams, *King, Lords*, pp. 27–9; Hole, *Economic Ethics*, pp. 90–4.
136 Beckerman, 'Toward a theory', p. 17.
137 Hole, *Economic Ethics*, p. 86.
138 Oschinsky, *Walter of Henley*, pp. 291–5, 310–11.
139 Ibid., p. 391.
140 Hole, *Economic Ethics*, pp. 177–204, 246.
141 For example, Hole emphasises the potential arbitrariness of tallage, but her discussion of its operation extends to just two pages and is inconclusive; *Economic Ethics*, pp. 191–2, 247, 250–1.
142 Thompson, 'The Polden Hill manors', p. 110.
143 Harvey, *A Medieval Oxfordshire Village*, pp. 128–30, 133; Ravensdale, 'Population changes', p. 207.
144 Raban, 'Landlord returns', p. 27.
145 Hatcher, 'Lordship', p. 138.
146 Birrell, 'Manorial custumals', pp. 9–24.
147 Hyams, 'What did Edwardian villagers mean?', p. 87.

6

Consequences: Serfdom and the crisis of the early fourteenth century

From the tenth century, England, no less than the rest of Europe, experienced sustained economic expansion in both absolute and per capita terms. In the second half of the thirteenth century this expansion began to falter, and by the early fourteenth century it had even begun to reverse in places. For many historians, the signs of mounting immiseration and sensitivity to calamity, notably a string of harvest failures and food shortages between the 1290s and 1340s, constituted a widespread and profound socio-economic crisis.[1] According to one powerful and influential narrative, the two central elements in this crisis were the ability of landlords to extract a sizeable surplus from their villeins and their appetite for conspicuous consumption rather than productive investment, a combination that was wasteful and ultimately deleterious to general economic and social wellbeing.[2] This explanatory framework is constructed on the twin assumptions that villeinage was the dominant condition of most of the population and that it was a highly effective means of extracting peasant surpluses. Yet, as we have seen, these assumptions are incorrect: villeinage affected at most 40 per cent of the total populace and one-third of the area under cultivation, and its operation was weak. So, what *does* explain the socio-economic malaise of this period, and did serfdom have any role to play in it? This chapter sketches the chronology and symptoms of the economic downturn of the late thirteenth and the ensuing crisis of the early fourteenth century before assessing the role of serfdom in arresting economic development.

Economic trends, 1270–1348

After the tenth century England experienced a long phase of economic, social and cultural efflorescence, which peaked around the middle decades of the thirteenth century. Among the achievements of this period were the colonisation of new lands; the foundation of new settlements; an estimated tripling of the size of the economy with increased wealth per head; the creation of an extended commercial infrastructure of towns, ports and bridges; the expansion of the coinage with smaller denominations to lubricate exchange; and the proliferation of new institutions for trade, such as markets, fairs and courts.[3] The population of England had at least doubled since the Domesday survey of 1086, and continued to grow until the first decade of the fourteenth century. Estimates of population at its peak in c. 1300 vary from around 4.75 million to 6.2 million people.[4]

Although the population continued to grow until the 1310s, from the 1270s signs of an economic slowdown become increasingly apparent. Langdon and Masschaele have shown how the middle decades of the thirteenth century represented the optimal period of employment and prosperity, but thereafter profit margins and the viability of new ventures declined.[5] The best locations and sites for trade and industry had already been developed and few opportunities for new investment were available.[6] The growth of urban centres, which had been such a prominent feature of the twelfth century, slowed from the middle of the thirteenth century and slipped into recession thereafter. From the 1270s the foundation of new boroughs, fairs and markets was well past its peak.[7] Wool exports became highly volatile, plummeting in the late 1270s, recovering to a peak by the 1310s, then tumbling again in the 1330s.[8] Increased warfare across the continent disrupted trading routes, raising the risks and therefore the costs of commerce, and sapping aggregate demand, with rising transaction costs undermining the viability of the English textile trade. Long-distance international trade in luxury goods was also severely disrupted, which had an adverse trickle-down effect on wealth generation. The revenues of English fairs almost halved between the 1250s and 1270s, then those of Champagne (France) fell 70 per cent between the 1290s and 1310s.[9]

Another indicator of the mounting pressures within English society is the direction of real wage rates, which compute the purchasing power of a day's pay for skilled and unskilled workers. These peaked in the 1260s, then began on a clear downward path, 'declining on average by 15 per cent over the next forty years' until they reached a historic low point in the mid-1310s.[10] Low real wages reflect the harsh reality of too many people chasing too little employment and the relative scarcity of commercial food supplies. Another way of assessing welfare is to estimate the income of a representative peasant family measured against the known cost of its basic consumption requirements, which projects that between the 1280s and 1340s such families were just managing to cope at a bare-bones level of subsistence, the lowest reconstructed level of family welfare in the last millennium.[11] In essence, the combination of a rising population, low disposable incomes and stalled economic growth had resulted in rapidly diminishing marginal returns to labour. Those historians who have offered estimates of gross domestic product (GDP) per head all agree that it began to fall from the 1260s, although estimates of its degree vary from Clark's pessimistic calculation of a 31 per cent decline by the 1300s to Stephen Broadberry et al.'s 14 per cent.[12]

The cumulative effects of this faltering economic performance meant that, as Campbell has argued, 'by the 1290s a turning point had been reached and the European economy was in recession. Transaction costs in international trade were rising and market generated growth had ceased. Everywhere financial and credit arrangements were under strain.'[13] By the early fourteenth century many sectors of the economy had reached saturation point or were even contracting, and the existing level of infrastructure could no longer sustain economic growth.[14] Some towns were suffering a downturn in industrial activity and declining rent rolls.[15] Even in Cheapside, London's main market, rents began to fall.[16] The most recently founded markets and fairs were transacting little business, and some folded.[17] The number of grain mills in England ceased to grow after 1300 and declined slightly from the 1310s, and any new constructions tended to be small and speculative, often replacing damaged existing structures.[18] Likewise, the value of mills ceased rising after the 1270s and declined in the early fourteenth century, especially in the counties surrounding London.[19] Major building projects in cathedrals and large monasteries peaked in the 1270s and by the 1320s were in pronounced decline.[20]

The economic slowdown was accompanied by a sequence of exceptional climatic and pathogenic events, and by a sudden upturn in the scale and frequency of warfare. From the 1260s reduced solar and increased volcanic activity caused major changes to weather systems across the globe. Although the precise effects varied from one region of the planet to another, the general effect was a heightened volatility in temperature and levels of precipitation from one year to the next, especially in the second quarter of the fourteenth century. The frequency and severity of extreme weather events increased, from storm surges in the North Sea region to extended bouts of wet weather, whilst after the 1270s north-west Europe became generally colder and wetter.[21] The most extreme single weather event resulted in the biblical quantities of rain and flooding between 1315 and 1317.[22] The deluge triggered the greatest famine in documented history in northern Europe, propelling grain prices to unprecedented heights and claiming the lives of at least one-tenth of the English population.[23] This was then followed by two of the worst droughts of the last millennium in 1325 and 1326, and further episodes of drought into the early 1330s in some areas of southern England, further illustrating the profound instability and unpredictability of the weather in these three decades.[24] Such extreme events brought about devastating harvest failure and triggered outbreaks of disease, causing mortality to surge and population levels to fall in many communities in the worst-affected regions.

The Great Famine of 1315–17 was the most dramatic instance of extreme weather combining with the widespread failure of food supplies, but this period also witnessed a number of other serious harvest failures in 1290–94, 1304–5, 1321–23, 1325–26, the early 1330s and the mid-1340s, which imposed misery and hardship on local populations and caused sharp rises in levels of mortality locally.[25] The variable and extreme weather of this period is also evident in the volatility of grain prices, which were high and fluctuating from year to year. While this benefited those with surplus grain to sell, most peasant households struggled to produce enough to meet their own subsistence needs, which forced them to buy grain, bread or ale on the open market on unfavourable terms and when their wages were failing to keep pace.[26] In those regions most vulnerable to the extreme weather, such as upland areas or low-lying coasts, agricultural output fell, arable land was lost or abandoned, and communities faced additional costs to replace damaged infrastructure, such as buildings and seawalls.[27] For example, the average cost of maintaining seawalls at Barksore (Kent) had seldom exceeded a couple of pounds per annum in the 1290s and 1300s, but over £36 was expended in 1334–35 following one disastrous inundation.[28]

The difficulties faced by peasants in this period were made worse through heightened disease among their livestock, which devastated the ovine and bovine population in particular, most notably through an outbreak of scab in the late 1270s, killing around 40 per cent of all sheep in England, and the great cattle panzootic of 1319–20, which killed around two-thirds of all oxen and cows. Lost livestock could only be replenished through natural replacement, a slow process that amplified and extended the consequences of these two great panzootics. According to Slavin, the sheep population did not recover its pre-scab population until the 1330s and, furthermore, recurrent outbreaks of ovine disease reduced the weight and quality of wool during this period, triggering 'a serious reduction in the total productive capacity of the English wool industry'.[29] Only in the 1340s did the bovine population recover its pre-panzootic population and the ramifications of the losses during the 1320s and 1330s were profound, because oxen were a major source of traction and because cows' milk was the main source of calcium and of vitamins A and B12 for the human population. Furthermore, livestock in general were a repository for peasant wealth in the absence of a banking system, and their loss through disease eroded the financial reserves of households. The scale and frequency of livestock panzootics from the end of the thirteenth century were unprecedented, although what caused the sudden rise in the epidemiological burden is uncertain: probably a combination of pathogenic mutation and low levels of animal immunity and resistance. The latter was perhaps weakened by the prevalence of wet summers and cold winters, which deprived livestock of feed and increased their exposure to malnutrition. Whatever the reasons, these outbreaks represented major biological disasters with far-reaching consequences.[30]

Finally, the frequency and scale of warfare increased, generating further economic disruption and strain. Parts of northern England became war zones sporadically from the 1290s, and especially between 1311 and 1328, as English renegades and Scottish armies pursued a brutal scorched-earth policy, looted rural settlements and besieged towns. Fields and crops were devastated, woodland destroyed, and livestock – especially cattle – rustled where communities were directly exposed to the marauding armies. County Durham and towns such as Carlisle (Cumberland) and Ripon (Yorkshire) paid tribute money to the Scots to be spared such destruction, which cumulatively amounted to tens of thousands of pounds, far more than the English king could raise in taxes from the same places. Towns on the south coast, notably Southampton and Portsmouth (Hampshire), suffered burning and looting through French naval attacks: the effects of an attack in 1338 were felt for years.[31] Indeed, a combination of weather and war meant that peasant arable production collapsed in the Tyne Tees region in the 1310s and 1320s, and did not recover its pre-1312 level at any stage in the late medieval period.[32]

It was not, however, just those places directly hit by warfare that suffered, because the increase in military activity also carried significant consequences for communities outside the war zones. War was continuous and increasingly expensive, so the English Crown could only sustain its ambitions through an onerous repetition of direct lay and religious taxation, together with inflated duties on exports of the key commodity of wool. Between 1290 and 1346 twenty-two lay subsidies levied taxes amounting to £1.1 million on the English people, which meant that on average the Crown raised around £50,000 each year through taxation, equivalent to perhaps 5 per cent of all the coinage then in circulation, or around 1 per cent of GDP. While some of this money was recycled back into the economy, for example through the construction of fortresses or the production of military hardware, much of the expenditure was a net economic drain. Peasant resources were eroded yet further by the Crown's more frequent exercise of its right of purveyance, the compulsory purchase of grain and livestock at artificially low prices to supply the royal household and its armies. These demands were unpredictable, but, when added to the impact of direct taxation, their cumulative effects cut deep into peasant resources: in the early 1340s, royal tax assessors attributed a recent contraction in both the area under cultivation and the numbers of livestock to heavy taxation in places as far apart as Shropshire and the east Midlands.[33] By one estimate the area under cultivation in 1341 was a bare minimum of five per cent lower than it had been in 1291.[34]

Underlying and intertwined with these heightened, recurrent and devastating socio-economic shocks was a mounting structural poverty among the population, partly reflected in the fall in real wages but also in the extreme morcellation of landholdings. For example, by the end of the thirteenth century one-third of the land-holding population on a sample of estates scattered from Sussex to Northumberland held fewer than 5 acres of arable, whilst on various manors in Norfolk the median holding size was 1 acre.[35] The commonplace view in the academic literature is that anything between 12 and 18 acres of land were required to feed a household of five people.[36] By one estimate, in 1280 half the unfree, and four-fifths of the free, population of England were either landless or smallholders, and therefore fell below this threshold; by another estimate, in the 1290s one-third of the population were already surviving at the most basic level of subsistence.[37] To varying degrees these people were locked into a 'vicious cycle of poverty with remarkably few escape routes' and faced a 'liquidity problem on a quasi-permanent basis'.[38] At moments of greatest need, they were failed by the shrinkage of credit and the inadequacy of institutionalised charitable relief.[39] As Schofield states, 'institutions of various kinds and scale were both aware of the reality of food insecurity but unwilling and often unable to confront the challenge posed by an insecure food supply'.[40]

Left to their own resources and reserves, families had no option but to sell livestock or land, or to beg, to survive the immediate crisis. Such strategies are suggested by the strong correlation between harvest failures and spikes in the sales of small parcels of free land between 1290 and 1340 across some regions of England.[41] A growing tail of poorer peasants perforce sold off parcels of their most vital asset, usually to a small group of wealthier peasants in the community or to outsiders, in order to acquire sufficient liquidity to survive the immediate crisis confronting them. Freeholders were especially 'vulnerable to distress land sales as they worked ever-smaller holdings', creating a sequence of mounting poverty and a growing dependence on wage labour at a time when real wages were themselves in decline.[42] For example, in four east Midland counties surveyed in the Hundred Rolls of 1279, 59 per cent of freeholders held under 7 acres of land, compared with 38 per cent of the unfree.[43] However, the same hypersensitivity to external shocks is also evident among villein tenants in those areas where a highly active market in servile land existed.[44] Schofield has demonstrated how spikes in servile land sales occurred in 1282–84, 1294–95 and 1296–99 at Hinderclay in response to either bad harvests or high taxation, and as credit dried up.[45] Yet the desperate strategy of offloading land – the chief means of livelihood – to survive the immediate subsistence crisis was likely to heighten vulnerability to the next.[46] Distress sales were less evident, however, in places where standardised villein-holdings remained largely intact (see Chapters 8–10).

The stresses on the population were greatest between the 1310s and 1330s because of the dire sequence of terrible famine in 1315–17, the loss of sheep and cattle in 1316–20, harvest failures in 1321–23, the effects of severe drought in 1325–33, and the mounting weight of lay taxation and purveyancing from the later 1320s, the cumulative effects of which seriously impaired economic recovery. The ravages of the 1310s and 1320s induced malnutrition and physiological stresses among the population, and perhaps reduced their resilience to disease.[47] Grain production on one half of all English demesnes took until the early 1330s to recover its pre-1315 level of output, although one-quarter never recovered.[48] The consensus is that in the 1340s the total output of grain and the area under cultivation in England were decisively lower than they had been in the 1290s.[49] As Jean-Paul Chavas and Daniel Bromley state, 'large shocks or structural changes negatively affected productive efficiency. The adjustments of the economy to such changes were slow and costly.'[50]

Serfdom and the extraction of peasant resources

Thus, from the 1290s the English economy faced mounting challenges of heightening severity. In part, these were systemic: falling mean landholding size and real wages, and creeping immiseration and poverty. They were compounded by a series of contingent shocks, in part due to warfare but also to highly variable and extreme weather as the global climate changed, and to increased pathogenic activity among livestock. The key question for us is the role of serfdom in bringing about first the slowdown, then the crisis of this period. This has generated much scholarly debate, in which some historians portray serfdom as the primary cause and some regard it as simply one of a number of contributing factors, whereas others dismiss it as an irrelevance.

For those historians who portray English serfdom as a powerful, pervasive and intrusive institution in the pre-plague era, the scale of its demands played a decisive role both in the economic slowdown and in the ensuing crisis of productivity. In this perspective, it is the increasing rate of seigniorial exploitation of serfs over the course of the thirteenth century that explains the peasantry's mounting poverty and their amplified vulnerability and sensitivity to external shocks. For example, Kitsikopoulos argues that social relations were the one consistent and unifying experience across England, in contrast to the effects of warfare and weather, which were highly variable from place to place. Consequently it was the nature and strength of feudal property rights that 'functioned as the primary conditioning factor of economic growth in the pre-plague period', with the 'exploitative extractive mechanism' of villeinage inexorably draining the resources of serfs and triggering the crisis of productivity.[51] Dimmock adopts a similar position, arguing that the institutional framework of seigniorial rent extraction and private jurisdiction, when added to the impact of paying ecclesiastical tithes and royal taxation, created a stifling system of extra-economic coercion whose powers peaked in the early fourteenth century. The extraction of peasant surpluses on a grand scale reduced their productive capacity, promoted poverty and increased their vulnerability to external shocks. Meanwhile, landlords spent their swollen revenues on conspicuous consumption and 'political accumulation' rather than on productive investment: the result was 'the growing weight of non-productive production' on society, which ultimately bled the populace of its ability to feed itself.[52]

By contrast, whilst recognising the extractive capacity of serfdom as an important element in the crisis of this period, other historians have rejected the notion that it played a primary causal role. Dyer, for example, accepts that 'many medieval peasants were compelled to hand over a high proportion of their surplus production in rent, which deprived them of their potential capital and sometimes of their food, and contributed to the crisis': in this way, 'the power of lords over peasants' undoubtedly contributed to the latter's poverty.[53] Yet he also acknowledges the other factors that brought about the crisis, including climatic instability and prolonged warfare, and so concludes that while 'social inequalities and lordly power' contributed to the crisis, they were not its 'prime cause'.[54] In a similar vein, Britnell acknowledged that rising levels of exploitation through rents and taxes during the thirteenth century were a factor in diminishing the capacity of the wealthier serfs to maintain their holdings, and of the poorer serfs to feed themselves and to reproduce, but regarded this as just one of a number of adverse developments. He concluded that the crisis requires 'a mixed bag of explanatory devices rather than a monocausal explanation'.[55]

Finally, following on from the recent work showing that serfdom was less widespread and weak than traditionally portrayed, other historians have further downplayed its role in the slowdown and crisis of the pre-plague era.[56] Campbell has been the most prominent advocate of this viewpoint, arguing that the 'agrarian problem' of the pre-plague era owed less to the demands of feudal lordship and the supposed oppressions of serfdom, and more to the structural inefficiencies generated by the awkward co-existence of customary, contractual and commercial relationships.[57] For him, the powers of lordship were so diluted that they were incapable of fully capitalising on the rising value of land, which meant that, far from exploitation increasing during the course of the thirteenth century, the seigniorial share of total rural income actually fell.[58] Hence, 'this was not a crisis born out of feudal socio-property relations, except insofar as the militaristic mindsets of the seigniorial class and their rulers underpinned the spreading stain of war and the brigandage and piracy and rising tax demands which were its ill-gotten progeny'.[59] Instead, the crisis originated in the disruption to the European system of commerce, changes in the global climate, and the underlying structural deficiencies of agrarian society – fragmented holdings, rural congestion and widespread indebtedness – which proved too inefficient and unproductive to respond to the pressures of increasingly high population.[60]

How are we to decide among these three incompatible viewpoints – prime cause, contributing factor or irrelevance – on the role of serfdom in the general crisis? The insuperable problem is the impossibility of quantifying or weighing in any meaningful fashion the effects of serfdom compared with those of, say, the deteriorating climate or escalating warfare. Some historians have attempted to overcome this obstacle by calculating the weight of seigniorial demands on a 'typical' peasant household. Apart from the obvious difficulty of defining what was typical, such calculations require the reconstruction of a peasant budget and an estimation of what proportion of the produce of a servile household was extracted each year through servile rents and dues. While this might seem a straightforward task, the calculations are beset by a multiplicity of problems, the biggest of which is that peasants themselves have left no accounts. Even if they had, the income and expenditure of a villein household with 40 acres would be very different from one with 20 acres or with 5 acres, and, even then, the exact burdens of villeinage for each category of landholder varied from one manor to another.[61]

Despite such intractable challenges, a number of historians have offered estimates of the share of peasant product extracted through servile rent and other dues around the end of the thirteenth century. Postan claimed that lords frequently took over one-half of a villein's gross output, a figure subsequently adopted by Brenner, and Martin suggested that 40 per cent of the total revenue of villeins was removed annually.[62] In a similar vein, Jedwab et al. assert that 'lords were able to extract the entire surplus beyond that required for subsistence in the form of labour dues or fines', without providing a precise proportion.[63] In reality, Postan's and Martin's figures, and Jedwab et al.'s statement, are mere guesses, and even a rudimentary reworking of these estimates confirms that they are far too high, as Rigby has shown.[64] By contrast, Dyer's much more detailed attempt to calculate the budget of a villein household with 30 acres of land in Bishop's Cleeve (Worcestershire) estimated that around 35 per cent of its cash were paid in rents and dues, rising to nearly 40 per cent when tithes were included.[65] Such high extraction rates are readily compatible with the argument that serfdom was an important factor in bringing about the economic crisis, as Dyer and Britnell argued, or even, as Kitsikopoulos and Dimmock claimed, that it was its primary cause.

The problems involved in arriving at estimates of peasant output and in calculating the weight of servile rents and fines are even evident in the work of Kitsikopoulos, who has constructed the most recent meticulous and detailed estimate of the output and expenditure of a middling villein family in the early fourteenth century. He assumed that such a family held 18 acres of land and 2 acres of meadow; kept a horse, three cattle, ten sheep, a pig and some poultry; and generated an estimated 57s. 8d. of cash earnings from sales of its surplus grain and wage labour. Kitsikopoulos calculated that the seigniorial levies on such a holding came to a total of 19s. 6½d. per annum, comprising rent of 10s. 1½d., 4s. 3d. to commute labour services, tallage of 2s., and 1s. 10d. to cover irregular obligations such as heriot and merchet. From this, he concluded that payments for servile dues absorbed 34 per cent of the household's cash earnings for the year.[66]

Although Kitsikopoulos's model provides a detailed statement of the case for a high proportion of villein earnings being extracted through servile dues, its key assumptions can be challenged on two principal grounds. First, the model presents servile dues as a percentage of the household's annual cash earnings, not of its gross output. As he shows, total output was higher, since much of the villein's produce would have been consumed by the household rather than converted into cash. When the quantities of 'consumed' grain, cheese and meat in the model are converted to a monetary value using his own price series (73s.) and added to the cash earnings of 57s. 8d., then the value of the household's gross output rises to 130s. 8d. per annum: consequently, the proportion rendered in servile dues drops from 34 per cent of cash to 20 per cent of gross output.[67] Second, the payments for servile rents and dues in the model are high, partly because they include the costs of commuting a heavy package of labour services and of regular tallage payments, which, as we have seen, were not in fact characteristic of many manors. Kitsikopoulos also adopts high estimates for the annual rent per acre due from the holding, made up of 6.75d. cash and 2.85d. for commuting labour services, and so producing the figure of 9.6d. per acre. By contrast, when Kanzaka analysed the rent from 8,581 villein-holdings averaging 20 acres across five counties in the 1270s, he found that the average total rent was only 5.9d. per acre, even when allowing for the cost of commuting labour services.[68] Kanzaka's calculations were unavailable to Kitsikopoulos, but they are more reliable because of the size, range and representativeness of the sample. When applied to Kitsikopoulos's model for the 18-acre holding, they reduce the annual rent to 8s. 11d. and the grand total of servile payments to 12s. 9d. per annum. This means that seigniorial rents and fines amounted to 22 per cent of cash earnings and just under 10 per cent of gross output, even while retaining Kitsikopoulos's pessimistic assumptions about the cost of tallage and other servile dues.

Finally, Kitsikopoulos's model includes another assumption that inflates the level of 'surplus extraction' from unfree tenants, namely his estimate of the amount of grain produced on peasant-holdings. As there are no representative figures for peasant yields, his model assumes that these were the same as on the lords' demesnes, for which we do have reliable data. Yet Hatcher has argued that higher labour inputs applied to peasant-holdings would have raised the level of peasant yields above those of demesnes, perhaps by as much as 50 per cent.[69] He models how even a 25 per cent uplift in total yields would have comfortably doubled the amount of grain available for sale in Kitsikopoulos's model.[70] If Hatcher's adjustment is factored into Kitsikopoulos's original model, and if we retain the original, high, figure for servile dues (19s. 6½d.), then servile dues represented only 21 per cent of cash earnings and 12 per cent of gross output.[71] If, however, this more optimistic estimate for grain yields is combined with the lower and more realistic estimate for the level of annual rent, the figure falls to 7 per cent of gross output. Factoring in a lower figure for servile dues such as tallage – which, as we have seen, was not charged annually on perhaps more than half of all manors – would reduce it even further to around 5 per cent.

This exercise has illuminated the difficulties of estimating what proportion of the output of a middling villein family was absorbed by servile rents and dues, given the uncertainties about the output and cash income of a peasant household and given the difficulties of establishing a representative level of expenditure on servile dues. These challenges are so great as to raise grave questions about the validity of the entire exercise. However, as some historians have attributed value to it, my approach has been to address it on its own terms and to take the most credible attempt to model the budget of a middling villein household, which estimates that 20 per cent of its total product was extracted through serfdom. This represents the upper limit of the rate of extraction. I have shown how, with some reasonable adjustments, it might have been as low as 5 per cent of its total product, which is more consistent with the evidence for the weakness of serfdom marshalled in Chapters 2–4.

Peasant surpluses were also routinely extracted through two other principal mechanisms in pre-plague England, neither of which was exclusive to serfs. All adult parishioners – servile and free – owed tithes to their local church, which in theory amounted to 10 per cent of the gross produce of their grain, eggs, lambs, wool, flax, hemp and the like. It is unlikely that this proportion was collected each year, because of the obvious challenges for the recipient of the tithes of having to monitor the output of every household and subsequently to secure full payment: the scale of these challenges persuaded some parochial rectors to lease out the right to collect tithes to a third party for an acceptable cash payment instead. The actual proportion of produce collected each year may have been as low as 5 per cent.[72] Tithe was also charged at a flat rate, irrespective of ability to pay, although we simply do not know if tithe collectors waived the liability of the poorest residents in years of dearth.

The second mechanism for extracting peasant surpluses was royal taxation and purveyance, whose frequency increased from the 1290s.[73] Both were based on an assessment of the moveable goods of households, although we cannot be certain what was included and who was exempt. In practice, households appear to have been assessed on their marketable surpluses of grain, livestock and wool rather than on their entire asset base. Until 1332 the goods of each household were reassessed anew for each taxation, although any whose value did not reach 10s. was usually exempt. From 1334 the system changed and thereafter every vill was collectively liable for an amount of tax fixed at a level slightly higher than the sum it had paid in 1332. The vill was also given responsibility for determining who paid what. The rate of taxation varied from one subsidy to another, so, for example, in 1307 residents of boroughs paid at the rate of one-fifteenth of the value of their assessed goods and rural dwellers at one-twentieth, while in 1332 the rates were higher, at one-tenth and one-fifteenth respectively.

Until 1332 this mounting burden of royal taxation fell mainly on the wealthiest servile landholders, and hardly at all on the long tail of impoverished smallholders and landless.[74] For example, almost all the thirteen half-virgaters at Cuxham paid tax in each of four subsidies assessed between 1295 and 1316 for which records have survived, whereas only one of the nine servile cottagers was ever assessed, and none of the village's landless labourers.[75] On the basis of similar evidence, most historians accept that around two-thirds of the English population were deemed too poor to pay tax. From 1334 the system changed from fresh assessments of each individual whenever a tax was granted to the imposition of a fixed charge on each vill, where the fixed charge was based loosely on the sum that had been paid by the vill in 1332. Thus, from 1334 local communities determined for themselves the contributions of each individual, including their own definition of who was too poor to pay, which probably resulted in more serfs from lower down the social scale being drawn into the fiscal net. Purveyance fell on the wealthier serfs. We can therefore be reasonably certain that royal taxation made few if any demands on the resources of the long tail of poor serfs, but its principal impact was in placing a high and sustained pressure on the resources of the wealthy elite of serfs, who had been less vulnerable during the years of dearth. In these ways, pressure was being brought to bear on serfs of all standings.

Thus, by drawing on the most reliable fragments of evidence and reworking the most informed estimates, the most we can state is that these compulsory outgoings – servile, ecclesiastical and fiscal – absorbed anything between 10 and 30 per cent of the gross product of servile households each year. We might speculate that, for the poorest sections of society, even the loss of 10 per cent of their produce to such compulsory outgoings could be the difference between coping and catastrophe, but we cannot prove the point empirically. Certainly, the impact of royal taxation was socially differentiated, falling primarily on the wealthy elite of serfs and hardly at all on the poorer tail. The range of 10–30 per cent bears a passing resemblance to the rates of modern income taxation, but any further parallels are unsustainable. Modern taxes are recycled into expenditure on infrastructure projects, health care, relief from poverty and education, all of which make some positive contribution to economic efficiency and productivity. By contrast, the serf's compulsory outgoings were not diverted into productive expenditure by the kings, lords and rectors who received them. Instead, they were frittered away on household expenditure, warfare and conspicuous consumption of various kinds. Eric Jones has written of the wider economic burden imposed on preindustrial societies 'by tying up capital in structures designed to intimidate' or to assert status, such as castles, royal palaces and enormous ecclesiastical buildings, because such extravagant and unproductive expenditure drained valuable resources from the productive sectors of the economy.[76]

Serfdom and the crisis of the early fourteenth century

As serfdom was less pervasive, and extracted a lower level of surplus from villeins, than many historians have supposed, any argument that it played *the* decisive role in the slowdown and crisis of the late thirteenth and early fourteenth centuries is unsustainable. In which case, what was its role? While it is axiomatic that servile rents and dues, annual tithes and (for the wealthier villeins) taxation reduced the resources available to families to cope with the severe challenges of this tumultuous period, we can never prove empirically *how far* each of these outgoings contributed to their immiseration without extensive data on the budgets of a range of peasant households. This insurmountable problem encourages a different approach to understanding the relationship between serfdom and systemic poverty. Hence, in this section I spell out the adverse economic consequences of the mass of impoverished and landless people, then explore other ways in which serfdom contributed to the systemic problem of poverty.

As we have seen, by the 1290s an estimated two-thirds of the landholding population held fewer than 5 acres of land, and an estimated one-third of the total population existed at a bare level of subsistence. This sprawling mass of impoverished households acted as an economic deadweight, because they were burdened by debt, lacked capital and had little purchasing power.[77] Perhaps as few as 5 per cent of rural households possessed any significant spending power.[78] The preponderance of such a high proportion of the population living around subsistence levels on tiny smallholdings meant that they were incapable of generating much in the way of marketable surpluses to take advantage of high grain prices. So instead of innovating, diversifying or investing in agricultural production, they suffered falling labour productivity and widespread underemployment, and perforce adopted risk-averse strategies. Furthermore, they were dependent on the market as consumers, whether for employment for wages or to purchase the food and goods that they could not produce for themselves. Yet this very dependency increased their economic vulnerability at a time when grain prices were high and variable, wages were low, real wages were falling, and there was insufficient work to go around.[79] Their best hope of survival was to lavish as much labour as possible on whatever slivers of land they possessed, thereby raising land productivity and ensuring they were able to feed themselves in most years.[80] Yet this was an existence at the level of bare subsistence, working all hours with worn and makeshift tools to eke more food and fodder from small plots of land. The resultant endemic poverty and congestion within rural communities heightened their susceptibility to external shocks, at just the time when the frequency and severity of those shocks were increasing. Their poverty also meant that the production and consumption of foodstuffs absorbed an increasing proportion of their time and budgets, which had the effect of dampening aggregate demand for non-agricultural goods and services, in turn generating less work in non-agricultural employment.

The extreme fragmentation of rural holdings and the predominance of smallholdings was a feature of both free and, to a lesser extent, unfree holdings, so it was a fault-line across the whole tenurial structure of rural England. Most explanations for the splintering of peasant landholdings have emphasised the combination of population pressure, partible inheritance and distress land sales.[81] Yet neither population growth, partible inheritance nor the extraordinary sequence of extreme events from the 1270s provides a complete explanation as to why landholdings became *so* splintered, and why such a high proportion of English households came to hold meagre quantities of land or even to be landless.[82] Nor do they explain adequately why unfree holdings became subdivided at all, because seigniorial controls over the servile land market could have prevented subdivision: indeed, as we have seen, some landlords did manage to preserve intact the large standardised customary holdings on their manors (Chapter 3).

These puzzles have received limited direct treatment in the scholarship, with the notable exception of the work of Campbell, who drew attention to the existence of an expanding layer of subtenants in rural society, which is usually obscured in the extant documentation.[83] The extent of subtenancies is, however, occasionally visible in the sources. For example, a close analysis of the social structure of freeholders in the Hundred Rolls of 1279 revealed that more than half their land had actually been sold to other people, the majority of whom were not peasants but urban dwellers, members of the gentry or clergy, who had acquired the land to sublet rather than to occupy themselves.[84] Campbell has argued convincingly that the peculiar combination of acute land shortages and head rents frozen below the market level incentivised land-sufficient peasants to buy small parcels of land at market rates and to sublet them to others at rack rents, thereby accelerating the downward spiral of indebtedness and poverty for those who were land-deficient.

The fact that the surviving sources reveal hardly anything about such subletting arrangements means that Campbell's argument relies largely on deducing how those tenants who sublet must have acted, and what level of rents they would logically have charged, rather than providing direct evidence for what they did actually do.[85] Given that head rents were ossified at subeconomic levels, it is logical to assume that land-sufficient tenants would have sublet small parcels of land at competitive market rates on short-term contracts, and that these rack rents would have been paid either in cash or in share-cropping: otherwise, why did they bother?[86] Incidental references in the Hundred Rolls occasionally confirm that rents per acre on sublet freeholdings were four times the average charge for head rents.[87] Similarly, the exceptional inclusion of the details of two subleases of servile land in the court rolls of Codicote confirm that the rent per acre charged was at least 50 per cent higher than the prevailing ossified head rent (see pp. 280–1). Thus, Campbell's logic is convincing, and it is supported by the fragments of evidence that do exist.

Campbell's analysis can be refined further by articulating how seigniorial policies directly contributed to the fission of villein landholdings. Freemen could sell or sublet their land without restriction from their lord and split it among their heirs (partible inheritance), self-reinforcing processes, which explains why freeholdings had splintered so far under high demographic pressure. By contrast, villeins had to obtain their lord's permission to transfer servile land and were required to pay a fee for the privilege of doing so, whether an entry fine for a sale or a licence for a sublet, and local custom often dictated that villein land was held impartibly. Hence, seigniorial policy and custom could combine powerfully to restrict or prevent entirely the fragmentation of the large, standardised holdings, as was the case on manors such as Bishopstoke (Hampshire).[88] Likewise, in other circumstances custom and policy could combine to create the opposite effect. Servile holdings tended to fragment on manors where the land was held on partible inheritance, such as Coltishall, Redgrave and Walsham, and they could also splinter on manors where the land was held impartibly if the lord adopted a permissive approach to sales and sublets, such as on the Taunton group of manors held by the bishopric of Winchester.[89]

The key point is that any lord who chose to impose sizeable fines and licences on villein land transfers would have inhibited the process of fragmentation, because such heavy fines would have acted as punitive tax on the profits of vendors and lessors in the servile land market and, by extension, would have eroded their incentive to subdivide and sublet servile land in the first place. Indeed, such a policy was within their legal powers to implement, because the charge for entry fines and licences was theoretically at the lord's discretion. Perhaps landlords did threaten prohibitively high fines on manors where large holdings remained intact, but of course this would not have been recorded in the surviving documents. We are on more secure ground when stating that, on those manors where fragmentation occurred, there is no evidence that any landlord, not even the powerful ecclesiastical landlords, did demand the high fines and fees that would have discouraged such fragmentation. Instead, they consistently charged low entry fines for land sales and for licences to sublet. Where we can quantify these, the former were around 7 per cent of the sale price of servile land and the latter around 3 per cent of the value of the lease (Chapter 3). For so long as seigniorial policy throughout England was to charge villeins a subeconomic – almost token – rate for their dealings in the servile land market, thereby allowing them to pocket most of the proceeds, it was fuelling the fragmentation of villein-holdings and the proliferation of smallholdings in those areas where a servile land market was active.[90]

These observations are subject to two important qualifications. First, on those manors where the servile land market was very active, a small elite of wealthy villeins tended to prosper from successive crises, because they were the principal buyers from distressed sellers. For instance, the acquisitive activities of the Adams brothers at Hinderclay, and the Jop family at Redgrave, are well documented, and during the famine of 1315 wealthy serfs in Cuxham were able to buy up slivers of free land in nearby villages.[91] Likewise, on those manors where large servile holdings remained intact, because either a land market was not well established or subletting was unusual, there is little evidence of distress sales in years of bad harvests during this period.[92] The wealthier villeins throughout England had enough resources in terms of land and livestock to survive years of dearth: the greatest threat to their wellbeing was not the rate of servile extraction, but the demands of royal taxation and purveyance, and the possibility of a livestock panzootic wiping out a major source of their wealth. The second qualification is that even those manors where servile holdings remained largely intact did not escape the widening poverty trap, because maintaining the integrity of the standardised holdings denied those without land the opportunity to establish a toehold on the property ladder, other than as short-term sublessees paying rack rents. This in turn generated an expanding layer of landless people, who either emigrated to towns in search of work, remained in their familial home or lived in hovels within the village seeking work as paid labourers.[93] Their plight must have been even worse than that of the smallholders, but, unfortunately, they seldom feature in the surviving documentation, so we know little about them. Where documents do provide rare insights, as on the estate of Glastonbury abbey (Somerset), the landless on these types of manors were at least as numerous as the landholding tenantry.[94]

Thus, the tenurial structure constitutes the final piece of the jigsaw in explaining why the combination of partible inheritance, risk-coping strategies, demographic pressure and the sequence of extreme events caused landholdings to splinter to an exceptional degree on some manors, and the tail of landless to lengthen on others. Where a servile land market existed, the peculiar mixture of custom (fixed head rents) and emerging market forces (tenant sales and sublets) incentivised head tenants to fragment their holdings rather than to enlarge them, causing immiseration for many. By the early fourteenth century there were perhaps twice as many smallholders and subtenants paying rack rents to other low-status landholders – not to lords – as there were substantial head tenants paying subeconomic rents to lords, and the former lived on holdings that were too small to generate even a bare-bones level of subsistence without constant toil, supplementary employment, charity (if they were lucky) and continued good fortune.[95] Where larger servile landholdings were preserved mainly intact, there existed a long tail of landless people, many living in hovels, who struggled to obtain enough employment to meet their subsistence needs.[96] This institutional framework had generated enough economic growth to support a national population that was larger in 1300 than it had been in 1200 or, for that matter, than it would become in 1600. However, it was not flexible enough to promote the more productive and efficient allocation of land over the course of the thirteenth century, and as such contributed to the slowdown in economic growth and ultimately to the vulnerability of peasants and the landless to external shocks. Large sections of society became locked into an oscillating cycle of impoverishment and deficient demand. By the end of the thirteenth century the subdivision had advanced so far in the most populous regions that only comprehensive structural change could have halted, let alone reversed, the process of subdivision.[97] Ironically, it took an unexpected and terrifying catastrophe – the Black Death – to break this gridlock.

Besides extracting surpluses from villeins and fostering the splintering of landholdings, serfdom contributed to the inefficiencies of the pre-plague economy in other ways. It generated a myriad of petty constraints, obstacles and disincentives whose cumulative effect is difficult to quantify, but it undoubtedly increased the costs and risks of certain activities to serfs, and thereby reduced the efficiency of productive resources. Even if lords did not charge a licence for migration or marriage, they could still pursue a range of options involving some cost to the serf in time or in the circumscription of other choices. Seigniorial officials sometimes targeted any remaining chattels of the flown serf for seizure, exerted pressure or occasionally imposed amercements on family members for the serf's return, and ordered the physical detention of the serf if he ever returned to the manor.[98] Hence, even unlicensed emigration carried costs, which were sufficient to generate some wastage of resources and to deter the marginal migrant.[99] As Ogilvie has argued, just because landlords did not intervene 'in *all* marriages or land transfers does not mean they lacked the power or interest to intervene in *any*', which meant that just the threat of prospect of seigniorial intervention affected serf behaviour.[100] The serf who risked not paying a merchet in anticipation of forthcoming nuptials faced the prospect of a fine for marrying without licence, which might be charged at a higher rate than the merchet.[101]

Labour services may have been relatively unimportant as a proportion of total rent, but they still carried some opportunity cost for the peasants required to perform them, or some expense if they opted not to perform them. In some ways, the institution of serfdom did not encourage lords to utilise resources in the most productive manner. Coerced labour on seigniorial demesnes was relatively inefficient, because serfs tended to work shoddily, slowly and less productively compared to paid labour.[102] The guarantee of a secure rental income from their large base of tenants each year may have been a disincentive for lords to innovate and invest in major capital improvement projects.[103] Quantifying the effects of all these structural constraints is almost impossible, let alone when trying to add to them the effects of an (in itself) uncertain rate of surplus extraction as discussed above, but they certainly existed. Some were clearly marginal, but cumulatively they resulted in serfs, and even lords, operating 'within institutional constraints that prevented land and labour from being allocated productively'.[104]

There is one other area whereby the taint or suspicion of serfdom provided unscrupulous lords with a legal hook on which to hang extortion of wealthier serfs. Serf families who had long left their home manors and made a good living, or even a fortune, elsewhere were in theory vulnerable to subsequent claims on their goods and chattels by a lord who had initially been indifferent to their departure but was now determined to lay claim to their chattels. An allegation of servility enabled a lord to bring sustained legal pressure to bear on such individuals, including selecting which court should hear the case (thus tipping the scales of justice in the lord's favour), and it also provided a pretext for harassment and the seizure of goods as distraint. For example, in the mid-1340s Richard Spynk, Norwich's wealthiest citizen and the principal sponsor of the rebuilding of the city's walls, was subject to a campaign of intimidation, threats, assaults and cattle-rustling by supporters of Thomas de Lisle, the new bishop of Ely, who was claiming the Spynks as hereditary serfs of the episcopal manor of Doddington (Cambridgeshire). This was a complex case, doubtless with various hidden strands, but the basic point is that Lisle was able to use the taint of serfdom as a legal device to bring pressure to bear on Spynk.[105]

In the pre-plague era serfs who had emigrated from their home manor permanently without any interference from their lord had obtained de facto freedom, but they were only in possession of a conditionally secure right, which was contestable if a lord so chose.[106] Serfs who had resided in certain boroughs for a year and a day could claim their freedom under the common law, as we saw in Chapter 1, and therefore possessed a stronger legal defence against such claims, but even this would not prevent a determined and unscrupulous lord from causing trouble, as Richard Spynk discovered. Herein lay the 'uncertainty' and the indignity of serfdom, ingrained in societal prejudices against serfs. Serfs who had acquired wealth still faced an element of unpredictability, most obviously in a claim for a large fee for a formal charter of manumission to formalise their legal freedom. Such cases were highly unusual, but if a lord chose to extort and intimidate, and if the lord had the sheriff in his pocket, the position of the serf was weak.

Conclusion

The population of England reached a high around 1310, with estimates varying from 4.75 million to 6.2 million people. At the same time, the welfare of the majority of that population fell to a historic low as most households came to be either landless or to occupy small landholdings. There was not enough employment to go around, and food prices were high and volatile. Levels of charity and institutionalised poor relief were inadequate. A frequent line of argument within the scholarship is that such immiseration was primarily a consequence of the onerous demands and high extraction rate of serfdom, which, when coupled with tithes and taxes, impoverished the peasantry to the benefit of landlords, who then wasted these revenue streams on non-productive expenditure. Yet these low levels of welfare can no longer be attributed primarily to serfdom, because serfdom was neither sufficiently widespread nor powerful enough to determine the wellbeing of the whole mass of ordinary people. Extreme poverty afflicted the free population and the long tail of urban dwellers as much as serfs. Serfs represented only around one-third of the total population and they occupied only one-third of the available arable land. Lords seldom enforced the full range of dues on all serfs and, when levying them, their demands were tempered by custom. Even on the large manors of the most powerful landlords, where villeinage weighed heaviest, its demands extracted, at the very most, 20 per cent of peasant output annually, and perhaps as little as 5 per cent.

Other compulsory exactions probably absorbed more of the resources of the unfree than did serfdom, and they applied equally to the free peasantry. Tithes removed up to 10 per cent of key peasant resources, and royal taxation and purveyance were demanded repeatedly from the wealthiest third of rural dwellers. The combination of these outgoings removed anything from 10 to 30 per cent of total peasant output. Whatever the exact rate, which is unknowable, it is undeniable that the diversion of such resources occurred at precisely the time when both the free and the unfree could scarcely afford to render them, and that, unlike modern taxation, the sums extracted were not invested productively into social support services or infrastructure improvements.

The most significant contribution of serfdom to economic development over the long thirteenth century was the way in which the particular structure of servile rents and seigniorial policy combined to encourage the fragmentation of servile holdings. Custom fixed head rents on villein-holdings at artificially low levels, yet tenants could, with seigniorial permission, sublet or sell land to third parties at market rates. Where lords permitted subletting and sales of villein land, they charged entry fines and licences at a mere fraction of the market value. When this structural arrangement is placed within the wider context of high demographic pressure and acute land shortages, the effect was to incentivise tenants to fragment their holdings rather than to construct larger, more efficient, agrarian units. The profound irony is that if lords had exercised their full legal rights under villeinage, or if they had behaved in the 'exploitative' or oppressive manner attributed to them by many historians, they would have charged punitive sums for entry fines and licences and thereby have minimised the process of fragmentation. On those manors where a servile land market had hardly developed, and where, consequently, large servile holdings remained intact, the principal landholding villeins were relatively well protected from the episodes of dearth, although they still faced regular demands for royal taxation and perhaps purveyance, and they would have been hit hard by outbreaks of disease among livestock. On these manors, the inability of siblings and other residents to obtain a secure toehold in the land market created an expanding layer of landless people.

Thus serfdom's impact on the wider economy was double-edged. Its relatively low extraction rate and its contribution to the splintering of holdings helped the population to rise to such a lofty peak in the first decade of the fourteenth century. The scale of this achievement is worth iteration. The lowest estimate (4.75 million) comfortably exceeds the most secure estimate for the English population in 1600 (4.1 million) and the highest (6.2 million) matches that for 1700 (6.2 million).[107] Whichever estimate one prefers, it is indisputable that the medieval economy supported a population as large as that of seventeenth-century England. Those historians who prefer the higher range of estimates in 1300 face the challenge of explaining just how the economy was capable of supporting such a large population, and they will undoubtedly point to the likelihood of high levels of land productivity on smallholdings and to the relative unimportance and low extraction rate of serfdom.

Yet the boost to demographic growth provided by smallholdings was finite, and serfdom still contributed to economic inefficiency. Evading servile dues carried hidden costs and influenced the decision-making of serfs, adding to the inefficient use of their time and resources. As Richard Spynk discovered, there remained a remote possibility that a lord might behave otherwise, which added to the uncertainty, the costs and the indignity of serfdom. A tipping point would eventually be reached when the fragmentation of holdings and the growing tail of landless had progressed so far that they generated negative feedback and countervailing economic and social forces. From the 1290s in some regions of England a critical mass of the free and unfree were struggling on landholdings that were too small at a time when employment was drying up, and were declining in purchasing power; consequently they were beset by inefficient labour and structural poverty. It is possible that, as Campbell suggests, 'many of these small- and middle holder families eventually found themselves landless' as a consequence of having to sell parcels of land to survive one crisis after another.[108] We cannot know what proportion of smallholding families were forced to sell some of their land or what proportion ended up selling all of it in response to successive crises, but it is undeniable that, once holding size and real wages had fallen to a critical level, the inefficiencies and extractions of serfdom exacerbated the predicament faced by such people. It is also undeniable that tenurial fragmentation, and liability for tithes and taxation, affected the free as much as the unfree, which reinforces the point made in Chapter 2 about locating both freedom and serfdom within the broader context of manorial lordship rather than segregating them and dwelling on their differences.

Thus, on the one hand, serfdom was neither sufficiently widespread nor sufficiently extractive to have been a major cause of the crisis of the early fourteenth century, and its weak nature had probably contributed to the extraordinary level to which the English population had grown. On the other hand, from the 1290s economic growth had stalled, and ordinary people – especially those in the most populous regions of the country – faced mounting systemic difficulties, creating a different paradigm in which the inefficiencies and costs of serfdom now exacerbated their problems. Between the 1290s and 1340s most rural dwellers, including serfs, were largely starved of credit, capital, infrastructure and equipment, and operated on pitifully small farms with high unit costs. They were therefore reliant on the application of more human labour to squeeze more food out of the same, or decreasing, quantity of land.[109] When they entered land, labour and commodity markets, they did so on increasingly unfavourable terms. Government intervention, whether to improve the commercial infrastructure, to fix market failures or to provide charitable relief, was minimal. The result was institutional sclerosis: a sickly stasis of falling output per head and bare subsistence for many. The disruption to international trade from the 1280s, the slowdown of construction and manufactures, and the stagnation in towns meant that the industrial and service sectors could not pull the primary sector out of the mire.

Together these systemic factors heightened the vulnerability of a large proportion of the population to both endogenous and exogenous shocks. By a cruel coincidence, at exactly this time rapid changes to the global climate dramatically heightened the frequency of extreme weather events, which created even greater challenges for smallholders and the landless. From the 1270s sheep and cattle, the mainstays of livestock husbandry, suffered from repeated and severe outbreaks of disease. Likewise, the scale and frequency of warfare increased, which was inextricably linked to political instability and greatly increased levels of taxation. Royal taxation weighed most heavily on the wealthier villeins who had not suffered the morcellation of their holdings, extending hardship up the social scale. It is the combination of systemic poverty and the high frequency of severe contingent shocks that explains the crisis of the fourteenth century.

There is simply insufficient evidence to establish a definitive rank order of causation among the various contributing elements to the crisis, although it is no longer credible to attribute a primary role to the high extraction rate of serfdom. The peculiar structure of serfdom did contribute to the systemic poverty that lay at the heart of the institutional sclerosis within the English economy, and which greatly amplified the socio-economic effects of the extreme weather, animal panzootics and the like. Whatever the causes, the cumulative impact of the systemic weakness and repeated contingent shocks on the English population is indisputable: inexorably and inevitably, they divested the reserves of wealth of more and more people, eroding their capacity to cope and forcing them to resort to desperate survival strategies. The economy of pre-plague England was burdened with endemic poverty and buffeted by disruptions and crises that were the product of an exceptional and complex interplay of natural and induced forces.[110] It took the even greater shock of the Black Death of 1348–49 to break the deadlock and precipitate long-term structural change.

Notes

1 A useful introduction and summary are still the essays in B. M. S. Campbell, ed., *Before the Black Death: Studies in the Crisis of the Early Fourteenth Century* (Manchester: Manchester University Press, 1991). See also Rigby, *English Society*, pp. 17–144; S. H. Rigby, 'Introduction: Social structure and economic change in late medieval England', in Horrox and Ormrod, *A Social History*, pp. 10–30; Hatcher and Bailey, *Modelling the Middle Ages*, pp. 21–173; and Dyer, *Making a Living*, pp. 228–63.

2 Recently summarised and restated in Dimmock, *The Origin of Capitalism*, pp. 65–87.

3 For recent general summaries, see Britnell, *The Commercialisation*, pp. 5–151; E. Miller and J. Hatcher, *Medieval England: Towns, Commerce and Crafts, 1086–1348* (Harlow: Longman, 1995), pp. 135–408; Britnell, *Britain and Ireland*, pp. 71–83; Dyer, *Making a Living*, pp. 101–227; J. Langdon and J. Masschaele, 'Commercial activity and population growth in medieval England', *Past & Present*, 190 (2006): 35–81; and Campbell, *The Great Transition*, pp. 30–133.

4 For a general discussion of the evidence, and an estimate of 6 million, see R. M. Smith, 'Demographic developments in rural England 1300–48', in Campbell, *Before the Black Death*, pp. 25–78. For the estimate of 6.2 million, see H. la Poutré, 'English population 1086–1377: A modelling approach' (PhD thesis, University of Groningen, 2023), p. 273. For the lower estimate, see Campbell, 'The land', p. 184.

5 Langdon and Masschaele, 'Commercial activity', p. 74.

6 Britnell, *Britain and Ireland*, pp. 83–5.

7 Langdon and Masschaele, 'Commercial activity', p. 74; S. Letters, *Gazetteer of Markets and Fairs in England and Wales to 1516*, Part I, List and Index Society, special series, 32 (Kew: List and Index Society, 2003), Fig. 5; Dyer, *Making a Living*, p. 243.

8 P. Slavin, 'Mites and merchants: The crisis of English wool and textile trade revisited, c. 1275–1330', *Economic History Review*, 73 (2020): 885–913 (Figs 5 and 7).

9 Campbell, *The Great Transition*, p. 173.

10 B. M. S. Campbell, 'The long economic recession of the late thirteenth century', in J. Peltzer and N. Vincent, eds, *Thirteenth-Century England 20: Proceedings of the Heidelberg Conference, 2023* (Woodbridge: Boydell and Brewer, [forthcoming, 2026]).

11 Campbell, *The Great Transition*, pp. 160–8; S. Horrell, J. Humphries and J. Weisdorf, 'Family standards of living in the long run, England 1280–1850', *Past & Present*, 250 (2021): 87–134 (pp. 117–19, 126, 130 and Fig. 8).

12 G. Clark, 'The macroeconomic aggregates for England, 1209–1869', *Research in Economic History*, 27 (2010): 51–140 (Appendix 5.3); S. Broadberry, B. M. S. Campbell, A. Klein, M. Overton and B. van Leeuwen, *British Economic Growth 1270–1870* (Cambridge: Cambridge University Press, 2015), pp. 227–8; Campbell, 'The long economic recession'.

13 Campbell, *The Great Transition*, pp. 134–60; Campbell, 'The long economic recession'.

14 Miller and Hatcher, *Medieval England: Towns*, pp. 409–29; Langdon and Masschaele, 'Commercial activity', p. 75.

15 Dyer, *Making a Living*, pp. 243–5; Campbell, *The Great Transition*, pp. 172–82.

16 D. J. Keene, *Cheapside before the Great Fire* (London: Economic and Social Research Council, 1985), p. 20.

17 Letters, *Gazetteer*, Part I, pp. 26–7, 35; Davis, 'Reassessment', pp. 276–7.

18 Langdon, *Mills*, Fig. 2.2, pp. 26–7.

19 Campbell and Bartley, *England on the Eve*, pp. 290, 295–8.

20 Hatcher and Bailey, *Modelling the Middle Ages*, Fig. 3; Dyer, *Making a Living*, p. 244.

21 Campbell, *The Great Transition*, pp. 198–208.

22 W. C. Jordan, *The Great Famine: Northern Europe in the Early Fourteenth Century* (Princeton: Princeton University Press, 1996), pp. 17–19; Pribyl, *Farming, Famine*, pp. 111, 118–30; P. Slavin, *Experiencing Famine in Fourteenth-Century Britain* (Turnhout: Brepols, 2019), pp. 33–43.

23 Jordan, *The Great Famine*, pp. 117–23; Slavin, *Experiencing Famine*, pp. 243–89.

24 M. Livingstone, 'A snapshot in time: The weather as seen in the record of the Nonae, 1339–41', in Kowaleski et al., *Peasants and Lords*, Fig. 13.1; D. Stone, 'The impact of drought in early fourteenth-century England', *Economic History Review*, 67 (2014): 435–62; K. Pribyl and R. C. Cornes, 'Droughts in medieval and early modern England, part 1: The evidence', *Weather*, 76:6 (2020): 169–71.

25 Ravensdale, 'Population changes', p. 207; B. M. S. Campbell, 'Nature as historical protagonist: Environment and society in pre-industrial England', *Economic History Review*, 63 (2010): 281–314 (288–93); Stone, 'The impact of drought'; Campbell, *The Great Transition*, pp. 189–92; Pribyl, *Farming, Famine*, pp. 97–101, 162, 164; Schofield, 'Peasants and food security'.

26 M. Bailey, 'Peasant welfare in England 1290–1348', *Economic History Review*, 51 (1998): 223–51 (pp. 233–8); J.-P. Chavas and D. W. Bromley, 'Modelling population and resource scarcity in

fourteenth-century England', *Journal of Agricultural Economics*, 56 (2005): 217–37 (pp. 226–8).

27 M. Bailey, '*Per impetum maris*: Natural disaster and economic decline in eastern England, 1275–1350', in Campbell, *Before the Black Death*, pp. 196–205; J. A. Galloway, 'Storm flooding, coastal defence and land use around the Thames estuary and tidal river c. 1250–1450', *Journal of Medieval History*, 35 (2009): 171–88; J. A. Galloway, 'Coastal flooding and socioeconomic change in eastern England in the later Middle Ages', *Environment and History*, 19 (2013): 173–207; Livingstone, 'A snapshot in time', pp. 332–4; M. Bailey, P. Wain and D. Sear, 'The transformation of the Suffolk coast c. 1200 to c. 1600: From Orford Ness to Goseford', *Proceedings of the Suffolk Institute of Archaeology and History*, 45 (2021): 86–114.

28 Galloway, 'Storm flooding', p. 185.

29 Slavin, 'Mites and merchants', pp. 887–913 (quotation p. 897).

30 Campbell, *The Great Transition*, pp. 209–30; P. Slavin, 'The Great Bovine Pestilence and its economic and environmental consequences in England and Wales, 1318–50', *Economic History Review*, 65 (2012): 1239–66 (Table 9); T. P. Newfield, 'A cattle panzootic in early fourteenth century Europe', *Agricultural History Review*, 57 (2009): 155–90.

31 J. Scammell, 'Robert I and the north of England', *English Historical Review*, 288 (1958): 385–403; P. Slavin, 'Warfare and ecological destruction in early fourteenth-century British Isles', *Environmental History*, 19 (2014): 528–50; C. Briggs, 'Taxation, warfare, and the early fourteenth century "crisis" in the north: Cumberland lay subsidies, 1332–1348', *Economic History Review*, 58 (2005): 639–72; C. Platt, *Medieval Southampton: The Port and Trading Community, AD 1000–1600* (London: Routledge, 1973), pp. 107–21.

32 B. Dodds, *Peasants and Production in the Medieval North-East: The Evidence from Tithes 1270–1536* (Woodbridge: Boydell Press, 2007), pp. 55–71.

33 Maddicott, *The English Peasantry*; W. M. Ormrod, 'The Crown and the English economy, 1290–1348', in Campbell, *Before the Black Death*, pp. 149–83. Broadberry et al., *British Economic Growth*, p. 205, estimates GDP in 1300 at £5.43 million.

34 Livingstone, 'A snapshot in time', pp. 344–8.

35 Hatcher and Bailey, *Modelling the Middle Ages*, pp. 45–7; J. C. Whittle, 'The food economy of lords, tenants and workers in a medieval village: Hunstanton, Norfolk, 1328–48', in Kowaleski et al., *Peasants and Lords*, pp. 27–58 (pp. 41–2).

36 As expressed in Kitsikopoulos, 'Standards of living', pp. 248–50; and Bennett, 'Married and not', p. 159. Their assessments draw on earlier

works, such as Titow, *English Rural Society*, p. 90; and C. Howell, *Land, Family and Inheritance in Transition: Kibworth Harcourt, 1280–1700* (Cambridge: Cambridge University Press, 1983), pp. 162–3, Table 15. For a recent cautionary note about this assumption, see J. Hatcher, 'Peasant productivity and welfare in the Middle Ages and beyond', *Past & Present*, 262 (2024): 281–314.

37 C. T. Bekar and C. G. Reed, 'Land markets and inequality: Evidence from medieval England', *European Review of Economic History*, 17 (2013): 294–317 (pp. 296–7); Campbell, 'The agrarian problem', p. 63.

38 Kitsikopoulos, 'Standards of living', pp. 250–1.

39 Schofield, 'The social economy'.

40 Schofield, 'Peasants and food security', p. 606; Bailey, 'Peasant welfare', pp. 224–5.

41 M. Davies and J. Kissock, 'The feet of fines, the land market and the English agricultural crisis of 1315 to 1322', *Journal of Historical Geography*, 30 (2004): 215–30; Schofield, 'The social economy', pp. 43–9.

42 Campbell, 'The agrarian problem', pp. 50–3; Bekar and Reed, 'Land markets', p. 312.

43 Dyer, *Standards of Living*, p. 119.

44 Campbell, 'Population pressure', pp. 101–20; Smith, 'Families and their land', pp. 142–85; Campbell, *The Great Transition*, pp. 193–6.

45 Schofield, 'Dearth, debt', Table 2, pp. 10–17.

46 Campbell, 'The agrarian problem', p. 68; Campbell, *The Great Transition*, Fig. 3.18.

47 S. DeWitte and P. Slavin, 'Between famine and death: England on the eve of the Black Death. Evidence from paleoepidemiology and manorial accounts', *Journal of Interdisciplinary History*, 44 (2013): 37–60.

48 B. M. S. Campbell and C. Ó Grada, 'Harvest shortfalls, grain prices, and famines in preindustrial England', *Journal of Economic History*, 71 (2011): 859–86 (pp. 870–2); Campbell, *The Great Transition*, pp. 191–8; Schofield, 'Peasants and food security', pp. 591–2; Stone, 'The impact of drought'.

49 Miller and Hatcher, *Medieval England: Towns*, pp. 420–2; Dyer, *Making a Living*, pp. 236–7.

50 Chavas and Bromley, 'Modelling population', p. 234.

51 Kitsikopoulos, 'England', pp. 40–7.

52 Dimmock, *The Origin of Capitalism*, pp. 65–72, following Brenner, 'Property and progress', pp. 70, 77, and Brenner, 'Property relations', pp. 21–8, 34.

53 Dyer, *Making a Living*, pp. 253, 255.

54 Ibid., p. 255.

55 Britnell, *Britain and Ireland*, pp. 86–7, 90.
56 See, for example, Bailey, *After the Black Death*, pp. 24–52.
57 Campbell, 'The agrarian problem', p. 9.
58 Ibid., Table 2, p. 15.
59 Campbell, 'The long economic recession', 00.
60 Campbell, 'The agrarian problem', pp. 68–9.
61 Dyer, *Standards of Living*, pp. 109–18; and, for a discussion of the challenges, Rigby, *English Society*, pp. 31–3.
62 Martin, *Feudalism to Capitalism*, 43; Postan, 'Medieval agrarian society', p. 603; Brenner, 'Agrarian class structure', p. 31; Brenner, 'The agrarian roots', pp. 247, 266.
63 Jedwab et al., 'The economic impact', p. 163.
64 Rigby, *English Society*, pp. 31–3.
65 Dyer, *Standards of Living*, pp. 114–15, estimates that 26s. were absorbed through servile rents and dues out of a cash income of around £3 12s.
66 Kitsikopoulos, 'Standards of living', p. 245.
67 The model estimates that 24 bushels of wheat, 36.56 bushels of barley and 28.61 bushels of oats were produced and expended on tithe, seed corn and food: at the prices used in the model (wheat and barley at 8.6d. per bushel, oats at 6.1d. per bushel) this produces a value of 63s. The model also has 60 lb of cheese and 185 lb of meat consumed. The cheese would be valued at 3s. 5d., based on an average price of 10.1s. per wey in the period 1250–1347, and 175 lb to the wey; Farmer, 'Prices and wages', Vol. II, p. 757. There are no reliable prices for deadstock, so I have assumed that the weight is equivalent to 5 wethers, priced at 1.3s. each in the period 1300–47, which produces a value of 6s. 6d.; Farmer, 'Prices and wages', Vol. II, Table D. The cheese and meat therefore add a further 10s. to the valuation of the output of the holding, hence 63s. + 10s. = 73s.
68 Kitsikopoulos, 'Standards of living', p. 245; Kanzaka, 'Villein rents', Table 3.
69 J. Hatcher, 'Peasant productivity and welfare in the Middle Ages and beyond', *Past & Present*, 20 (2024): 281–314 (pp. 296, 298); La Poutré, 'English population', p. 235.
70 Hatcher, 'Peasant productivity', pp. 300–1.
71 The model has 36s. 8d. for sales of grain within the total of 57s. 6d. cash earnings: doubling the sales of grain would amend the figures to 73s. 4d. for sales of grain, total cash earnings to 94s. 2d., and the value of gross output to 167s. 4d.
72 Dodds, *Peasants and Production*, pp. 23–31.
73 For what follows, see J. F. Willard, *Parliamentary Taxes on Personal Property, 1290 to 1334: A Study in Medieval Administration*

(Cambridge, MA: Harvard University Press, 1934); J. F. Hadwin, 'The medieval lay subsidy rolls and economic history', *Economic History Review*, 36 (1983): 200–17; Ormrod, 'The Crown'; and M. Bailey, 'Introduction', in J. Brooker and S. Flood, eds, *Hertfordshire Lay Subsidy Rolls, 1307 and 1334*, Hertfordshire Records Society Publications, 14 (n.p.: Hertfordshire Records Society, 1998), pp. ix–xxvii (pp. ix–xxi).

74 Schofield, 'The social economy', p. 43. There were a few exceptions from taxation, such as communities in the north devastated by Scottish raids; Willard, *Parliamentary Taxes*, pp. 120–34.

75 Harvey, *A Medieval Oxfordshire Village*, p. 134 and Appendix VI.

76 E. L. Jones, *Barriers to Growth: English Economic Development from the Norman Conquest to Industrialisation* (London: Palgrave, 2020), pp. 13–15.

77 Campbell, 'The agrarian problem', p. 64; Campbell, *The Great Transition*, pp. 182–91.

78 Campbell, *The Great Transition*, p. 171.

79 Brenner, 'Property relations', pp. 14–27; Campbell, 'The land', pp. 215–17; Brenner, 'Property and progress', pp. 72–9.

80 Hatcher, 'Peasant productivity', pp. 301–2.

81 Davies and Kissock, 'The feet of fines', pp. 215–30; Campbell, *The Great Transition*, Fig. 3.18.

82 Bekar and Reed, 'Land markets', p. 299.

83 Campbell, 'The agrarian problem', pp. 45–60; Campbell, 'The land', pp. 228–32. For rare glimpses into the existence of the layers of subtenants and the landless, see M. K. McIntosh, *Autonomy and Community: The Royal Manor of Havering 1200–1500* (Cambridge: Cambridge University Press, 1986), pp. 105–16; and Bennett, 'Married and not', pp. 157–8.

84 Barg, 'The social structure', pp. 108–15; Campbell, 'The agrarian problem', pp. 57–8.

85 McIntosh, *Autonomy and Community*, p. 110.

86 Campbell, 'The agrarian problem', pp. 54–7.

87 Kanzaka, 'Villein rents', pp. 599, 611–12; Campbell, 'The agrarian problem', pp. 28–9.

88 Mullan and Britnell, *Land and Family*, p. 48.

89 Lock, *The Court Rolls 1303–1317*, p. 14; Smith, 'Some issues', pp. 66–7; Mullan and Britnell, *Land and Family*, pp. 45–7; Schofield, 'Lordship and the peasant economy', pp. 207–10.

90 Campbell, 'The agrarian problem', pp. 59–60.

91 Smith, 'Families and their land', pp. 165–71; Schofield, 'Dearth, debt', pp. 12–17; Harvey, *A Medieval Oxfordshire Village*, p. 133; Page, 'Town and countryside', p. 192.

92 Noy, 'Winslow', pp. 140–2.
93 Page, 'Town and countryside', pp. 192–4.
94 Fox, 'Exploitation'; Bennett, 'Married and not', pp. 156–65.
95 Bailey, 'Peasant welfare'; Campbell, 'The agrarian problem', pp. 60–9; Campbell, *The Great Transition*, pp. 168–72.
96 Fox, 'Exploitation', pp. 538–68.
97 Campbell, 'The agrarian problem', pp. 59–60.
98 Raftis, *Tenure and Mobility*, pp. 131, 139–43, 151.
99 Oglivie, 'Choices and constraints', pp. 278–89; Ogilvie, 'Economics and history', pp. 334–41.
100 Oglivie, 'Choices and constraints', p. 280.
101 Raftis, *Tenure and Mobility*, p. 142; Müller, 'The function'.
102 Stone, 'The productivity'; Ogilvie, 'Economics and history', pp. 346–7.
103 Dennison, 'The institutional context', p. 266.
104 Ogilvie, 'Serfdom and the institutional system', p. 43.
105 J. Aberth, 'A medieval Norwich feud: The bitter dispute between Richard Spynk and Thomas de Lisle, bishop of Ely', *Norfolk Archaeology*, 41 (1992): 294–304.
106 For a discussion of this general point, see Jones, *Barriers to Growth*, pp. 35–6.
107 Broadberry et al., *British Economic Growth*, p. 29.
108 Campbell, 'The agrarian problem', pp. 50–3; Bekar and Reed, 'Land markets', p. 312.
109 J. Belich, *The World the Plague Made: The Black Death and the Rise of Europe* (Princeton: Princeton University Press, 2022), p. 32.
110 Campbell, *The Great Transition*, pp. 395–401; Schofield, 'Peasants and food security'.

Part III

Serfdom in England: The impact of the Black Death through three case studies

7

The Black Death and serfdom

The first two sections of this book focused primarily on the mechanics of English serfdom at its supposed peak between the 1280s and the 1340s, but in this final section we shift the focus to an exploration of changes from the middle of the fourteenth century: the age of the Black Death. The Black Death arrived in England in the late summer of 1348 and within one year had killed at least one-half of the population. It returned in 1361–62, again in 1369, and repeatedly but less frequently thereafter, thwarting demographic recovery. Did its arrival have any tangible impact on the operation of serfdom and, if so, was it immediate or delayed?

At a stroke, the loss of half the population in 1348–49 introduced an entirely different economic and demographic paradigm. The severe demographic collapse, followed by at least a century of demographic stagnation, released the acute pressure on the resource base, which in turn posed four main threats to the wealth of landlords: declining revenues from rents, shortages of tenants and workers, rising wage bills, and squeezed profits on their demesne operations.[1] Conversely, it presented new opportunities for ordinary people, such as the acquisition of land on more favourable terms, falling rent values, better pay, more job opportunities, rising earnings and therefore higher standards of welfare. By improving the lot of serfs and threatening the revenue streams of landlords, the Black Death posed a fundamental challenge to the institution of serfdom. On the one hand, it provided lords with the incentive to mobilise their theoretical legal rights under common law villeinage and thereby impose a stronger version of serfdom, in which serfs were coerced to hold land and to perform labour services, servile migration was either taxed or restricted, and variable dues were fully exploited through higher fines: all of which would counter the threat to their revenues. On the other hand, if lords failed to mobilise their full legal powers serfdom would remain as weak as it had been before the arrival of plague, leaving lords at the mercy of market forces. In this scenario, serfdom would rapidly dissolve, because lords would be incapable of preventing the out-migration of serfs and forced to grant far-reaching concessions on villein tenure to retain and attract tenants.

The conventional narrative is that serfdom did indeed make a comeback in the three decades after the arrival of plague. In this view, the Black Death triggered an immediate, intense, coordinated and widespread 'seigniorial reaction', in which serfs were compelled to occupy empty holdings and to accept restrictive work agreements, labour services were reimposed, large fines were levied for chevage to discourage movement off the manor, and entry fines were hiked up to bolster flagging lordly revenues. The coercive powers available to manorial lordship were bolstered through the introduction of the Ordinance (1349) and Statute of Labourers (1351), which sought to fix a maximum wage, to force the able-bodied to work, to restrict worker mobility at harvest-time and to impose annual (rather than daily) contracts of employment, thereby uniting all types of employers in common cause against the labouring classes.[2]

Dimmock has recently restated this classic view of the third quarter of the century: 'lords went on the offensive to maintain earlier levels of rent and serfdom dues, and restrict the market in labour; and they were provided with royal statutes to that effect. For a while they succeeded.'[3] The powerful lordly reaction is said to have triggered mounting resistance from villeins, however, until in 1381 the escalating tension between them and their lords exploded into open revolt, after which chastened lords felt compelled to abandon their harsh policies and had to bargain serfdom away in line with market forces. According to Kitsikopoulos, 'landlords used manor courts to reimpose economic control, by enforcing tenant labour service obligations, collecting fines and keeping wages low. Tenants both resented and resisted attempts by landlords to reassert control over land and labour ... this peasant discontent culminated in rural rebellion: the revolt of 1381.'[4] Hence, serfdom is held to have been revived in the immediate post-plague era before beginning to wither away in the last two decades of the fourteenth century.[5]

The main difficulty with this cogent and widely held narrative of serfdom's post-plague recovery then eventual demise from the 1380s is that it is not supported by a substantial or compelling body of evidence. There are some isolated cases in the 1350s of lords attempting to assert their authority, such as on the bishopric of Durham, where some serfs were forced to hold villein land and were subject to additional controls over mobility, but this is a rare example.[6] The new labour legislation was novel in many ways and undoubtedly introduced coercive instruments to a labour market that had scarcely been regulated hitherto, but it has to be judged on proof of its effectiveness, not on the intent of the legislators. For the most part, the case for the seigniorial reaction is largely constructed on a handful of colourful and anecdotal examples of higher fines for migration, tougher action on dilapidating tenements and aggressive challenges to the personal status of lesser freemen, all drawn from a narrow range of manors, which are implicitly presented as 'typical' of a wider pattern of behaviour.[7] For example, a powerful statement from Dyer that lords 'sought to extend their profits from serfs by resorting to more arbitrary and dictatorial methods' is supported by just two examples, one of which is the charging of a large entry fine on one servile tenant in 1370 at Halesowen.[8] Sniffing out truffles and presenting them as representative of the general fare does not constitute a robust evidentiary base for what is supposed to have been an extensive and commonplace seigniorial policy across the length and breadth of England.

So, in the absence of a substantial and quantified corpus of evidence, the case for the traditional narrative of a post-plague 'seigniorial reaction' boils down to two implicit assumptions: first, that on the eve of the Black Death lords were already operating a tight and restrictive form of serfdom and, second, that a 'reaction' would be the logical, self-interested response to the shortage of tenants and workers of a seigniorial class that controlled all the legal institutions. Yet we have shown how the first assumption is incorrect, which in turn raises serious doubts about the capacity of lords to impose a much tougher form of serfdom after the Black Death. How was it possible for lords suddenly to be capable of wielding their full theoretical powers under serfdom through their manorial courts, given that beforehand they had seldom coerced serfs to hold land, they had been indifferent to out-migration, they had few effective mechanisms for retrieving flown serfs, and custom had regulated the imposition and level of 'uncertain' fines?

Doubts about the capacity of lords to impose a 'new serfdom', coupled with concerns about the flimsiness of the evidentiary base, have resulted in the construction of a very different interpretation of serfdom's development in the post-plague era. Proponents of this view argue that manor after manor yields scant or no evidence for any kind of a 'reaction', although historians have failed to comment on or record these 'nil returns'.[9] Furthermore, when the anecdotal examples of tougher management of serfdom are properly contextualised and quantified, their rarity and scarcity are laid bare, such as in the case of Adam le Bedel cited in Chapter 4. Likewise, Dyer's example of the unusually high entry fine at Halesowen in 1370 is not located in its full context, because in general terms entry fines fell after the Black Death at Halesowen: for instance, in the 1350s half of them were waived entirely to attract tenants.[10] Whenever historians have aggregated large samples of entry fines from a given manor and expressed them as an average per decade, the evidence confirms a significant and sustained fall in values after the Black Death.[11] In the few cases where tougher policies are documented in the 1350s, such as the bishopric of Durham, they were soon abandoned in the 1360s as unsustainable: indeed, the experience of trying to do the bishop's aggressive bidding in the 1350s provoked an unwillingness among the villein tenants thereafter to hold office on the estate.[12] As yet, there is no evidence that a seigniorial reaction was sustained on any manor through the 1360s and 1370s. Similarly, after the late 1350s the government's labour legislation proved ineffective. Part of the problem was that hardly any lords disciplined workers under the labour laws in their own courts, even though they were capable of doing so, which suggests that the new laws divided opinion rather than creating common cause among all employers.[13]

The most compelling evidence for the view that from the 1350s serfdom was in rapid retreat is the significant changes to the tenurial conditions on which villein land was held immediately after plague first struck on manor after manor. The changes are not always immediately apparent in the sources, but they become clear enough through detailed reconstructions. These reveal that, far from the imposition of additional burdens on villein tenants, such as renewed labour services and raised entry fines, the key incidents of servile tenure were rapidly diluted, such as dramatically reduced mean entry fines and the disappearance of merchet and mill suit as tenurial incidents. In particular, a growing proportion of villein land was converted either to monetary tenancies, which permanently removed any liability for labour services, or to leaseholds, to which servile incidents were not attached. These tactics were widespread in the 1350s and 1360s, and they were driven by a desire either to retain existing tenants or to woo new ones with more attractive terms of tenure.[14]

Those historians who remain wedded to the existence of a seigniorial reaction after 1349 seldom mention tenurial change – a notable omission, given that serfdom was as much tenurial as personal. For example, Dyer's recent claims for the existence of a seigniorial reaction in the west Midlands largely overlook the terms and conditions on which villein land was held, although he does document the collapse of entry fines between the 1340s and 1350s on two manors without drawing the obvious conclusion that this represents a significant dilution of the rent package on villein tenures and confounds the concept of a reaction.[15] Yet a close analysis of tenurial change in the generation after the Black Death on a sample of manors in the west Midlands – including those studied by Dyer – reveals a widespread slump in entry fines from the 1350s and extensive conversions of service to monetary tenures.[16] Such information is essential to any balanced assessment of how serfdom fared in the wake of plague.

Thus, in this revisionist perspective, the Black Death suddenly and graphically exposed the pre-existing weakness of villeinage, which could not be shored up, let alone resuscitated. When the evidence is interrogated forensically and quantitatively, it is apparent that the institution of serfdom was unravelling soon after the first outbreak of plague, rather than after the revolt of 1381, throughout England.[17] Thus, while it is understandable why many historians have accepted the logic of a 'seigniorial reaction' in the third quarter of the fourteenth century, there is little evidence that it really happened. The view that lords were incapable of mounting any such reaction after the Black Death is entirely consistent with the argument that serfdom was already weak when it struck. It also strikes a chord with recent work stressing how political and legal targets featured more prominently and obviously in the Peasants' Revolt than did targets associated with reimposing serfdom.[18]

Hence, the opinions of historians on the speed and nature of the impact of the Black Death on serfdom are as divided as their opinions on its cogency in the pre-plague era. In this section of the book, I test these two contrasting viewpoints with detailed case studies of three classic manors held by a highly conservative landlord, who has been selected precisely because this was the type of lord *most* capable of imposing a pervasive form of serfdom in the pre-plague era and of tightening its operation in the third quarter of the fourteenth century. The three case studies provide in-depth examples and evidence of how serfdom actually operated in the immediate pre-plague era, which helpfully illustrate how some of the judgements in Part I were reached, but they also extend the analysis to the period after the Black Death of 1348–49 to reconstruct in detail how the institution of serfdom fared in its wake on the estate of a powerful lord.

St Albans abbey and serfdom

The selection of three manors belonging to the abbey of St Albans for the in-depth case studies can be justified on four main grounds. The first, and principal, reason is that the abbey was a high-status landlord, with an extensive and dispersed landed estate characterised by large manors with sizeable demesnes and a high proportion of villeins.[19] While it is therefore atypical of most English landlords and estates, who held small manors with modest or no unfree land, it was a powerful monastic institution with a standing bureaucracy in possession of greater authority and power than most English lords to exercise its full theoretical rights under common law villeinage. Indeed, historians have argued that it did so routinely in both the pre- and post-plague periods.[20] Its conservative attitude is depicted by the language deployed in a survey of one of the abbey's manors in 1279, which asserted that the unfree tenants 'are serfs, buying their blood at the will of the abbot and doing other things attached to servile status'.[21] The abbey's determination to uphold such rights has been portrayed as a recurrent source of tension and conflict with its tenants from the thirteenth century onwards, principally over its rights to timber, pasturage and free warren, as well as its domination of the borough of St Albans.[22] While some of these disputes embroiled the abbey's burgesses and free tenants, others involved its villeins directly.

Second, the perception of the abbey as an aggressive and manipulative landlord would seem to be supported by its prominence as a target in the Peasants' Revolt, thereby conforming to the classic narrative of the seigniorial reaction. A succession of historians has argued that the violent rebel attack on the abbey in June 1381 was a direct response to the oppressions of serfdom on its estate over previous generations.[23] André Reville's early history of the revolt asserted that the abbey had exercised its seigniorial rights with extreme vigour and punished transgressions with the utmost severity, generating constant friction with its tenants.[24] Ada Levett and Juliet Barker have both cited the abbey's insistence on its rights of mill suit, and its dogged opposition to tenants using their own hand mills, as a source of discontent and a contributory factor to the ferocity of the revolt locally.[25] Indeed, the rebels demanded that the abbot hand over court books containing evidence of the abbey's rights over servile tenants.[26] Hence, for Levett, 'the St Albans rebellion was a genuine uprising of villeins against their lord and seigniorial burdens'.[27] Similarly, R. B. Dobson has suggested that St Albans was 'perhaps the only locality in England where it is possible to set the events of 1381 within a detailed context of existing manorial relationships', and Justice has supposed that 'St Albans must hold pride of place in any discussion of rebel strategy and ideology'.[28] For Dyer, 'the revolt of the tenants of St Albans abbey is a well-documented assault on seigniorial power'.[29] Hence, if any landlord in fourteenth-century England was capable of applying the full force of common law villeinage on its estates, then it should have been St Albans abbey.

The third reason for selecting a sample of three manors with the same landlord is that it allows us to examine the even-handedness of serfdom across the estate. Was this powerful monastic lord capable of implementing a consistent and standardised policy equally across all three manors, or did other factors – such as localised variations in custom and the strength of market forces – force it to adapt and vary its approach from manor to manor? For this reason, three geographically dispersed manors have been selected for analysis: Winslow (Buckinghamshire), which is located nearly 40 miles due west of the second manor, Norton in north Hertfordshire, which in turn lay 14 miles north of the third, Codicote, also in north Hertfordshire (see Map 7.1). Finally, all three manors have left a sufficiently large archive of fourteenth-century court rolls, which enables us to reconstruct how serfdom operated at its peak, and when and why it declined thereafter.

Methodology

These three case studies will address four main issues, following the approach pioneered in a previous study of the decline of serfdom in the south Midlands and East Anglia.[30] The first is to quantify the existence, frequency and value of the core incidents of villeinage (week works, harvest works, merchet, tallage, heriot, chevage, mill suit and leyrwite) and to chart the chronology of their dilution and disappearance over time. Of particular importance here is to establish, where relevant, the *absence* of some of these incidents: historians have an understandable habit of seeking out colourful examples of the enforcement of villeinage while remaining silent when its various elements were not enforced, yet recording the latter is essential to contextualising the former.[31] The second objective is to trace the

Map 7.1 The location of the abbey of St Albans and its manors of Codicote, Norton and Winslow.

chronology of tenurial change from villein land held on a service tenancy, comprising mixed renders (labour services, rents in kind and dues such as tallage) to monetary tenancies, including fixed-term leases for cash. This is especially important given the tendency of some historians to overlook the importance of tenurial change in assessing the speed and nature of the impact of the Black Death on serfdom.

The third objective is to assess how lords managed their relationship with serfs: was their approach aggressive or pragmatic? What evidence is there for attempts to impose new forms of service, or to manipulate custom, in the second half of the fourteenth century as part of a seigniorial reaction? If so, was this a short-term or a sustained policy? The fourth objective is to compare the chronology of the decline of serfdom with evidence for the main social and economic changes that caused it. The principal economic forces are represented wherever possible by local rent data from individual manors to indicate land values. The main social trends are indicated by the scale, timing and nature of recorded peasant resistance to servile incidents, especially labour services, and by the scale and timing of emigration from the manor documented in manorial court rolls.

The methodology employed in the previous study on the decline of serfdom has been slightly adapted in the following case studies in three ways. The first is a fuller analysis of the operation of villeinage in the two generations before the Black Death on each manor. This provides a corpus of evidence to test the analysis in Chapters 2–4 of how villeinage operated when it should have been at its peak, which in turn provides a baseline against which post-plague changes can be mapped. The second is the inclusion of a section on the arrival and immediate impact of the first two outbreaks of plague in 1348–49 and 1361.

The third adaptation is a more detailed and quantitative treatment of transfers of villein land in order to track the changing importance of service tenure, monetary tenure, leasehold and tenancies at will. Most studies of the peasant land market in England have focused on the size and type of the property being exchanged, the relative importance of transfers between family members and between unrelated parties, and the balance of transfers made within the lifetime of the peasant (*inter vivos*) as against those made after their death (*post mortem*), but here we focus instead on the types of tenure and whether the transfer was between peasants or directly from the lord.

In order to understand the purpose of this approach, we need first to understand the basic mechanics of the servile land market. The record of transfers from one tenant to another followed a consistent and well-established format on this estate, as elsewhere. The existing tenant surrendered the land into the lord's hands 'for the benefit [*ad opus*]' of a new tenant, who was then formally admitted through a standard form of words (as described in Chapter 3). If the transfer was through *post mortem* inheritance, then the process was straightforward whenever the rightful heir was known and willing to acquire the land. The process was more complex and protracted if the transfer was a sale between unrelated parties, when the formal court record of the transfer was merely the final act in a long (and unrecorded) process involving the two parties, including the agreement of a private sale price in cases where they were not closely related. Sometimes, however, a tenant relinquished land without there being a new tenant who was either willing or able to be admitted, in which case it remained in the hands of the lord (*in manibus domini*). Under these circumstances, the lord's officials would seek a new tenant and, when they found one, the lord had the option to vary the terms on which the land was to be offered. The format of these direct seigniorial grants is therefore different from that used in the inter-peasant transfers: the entry begins with a phrase such as 'the lord grants to' (*dominus concessit ad …*) the new tenant.

So, whenever villein land was directly and immediately transferred from one peasant to another, whether by sale or inheritance, the type of tenure on which it was held seldom changed. When the lord granted land from his own hands, however, he could opt to change the terms of the tenure, for example from the traditional service tenure to a straight cash tenure or a leasehold. It follows from this that tenurial change occurred relatively slowly, but that the pace was likely to pick up in periods when grants from the lord were more frequent, such as in the wake of a pandemic. Hence, the focus in the case studies that follow is on the types of tenancy and the balance between inter-peasant transfers and direct seigniorial grants. The number and proportion of grants on service, monetary and fixed-term tenancies are enumerated for each decade, and these are mapped against the number and proportion of grants emanating directly from the lord. In this way, tenurial change is placed firmly within the analysis of the decline of serfdom.

Notes

1 For the classic statement of the effects, see J. Hatcher, *Plague, Population and the English Economy 1348–1530* (London: Macmillan, 1977).
2 See, for example, Bolton, *Medieval English Economy*, pp. 209–18; M. H. Keen, *English Society in the Later Middle Ages, 1348–1500* (London: Penguin, 1990), pp. 37–44; Dyer, *Making a Living*, pp. 281–93; G. L. Harriss, *Shaping the Nation: England 1360 to 1461* (Oxford: Clarendon Press, 2005), pp. 225–42; and Brenner, 'Property relations', pp. 34–5.
3 Dimmock, *The Origin of Capitalism*, p. 76.
4 H. Kitsikopoulos, 'The impact of the Black Death on peasant economy in England, 1350–1500', *The Journal of Peasant Studies*, 29:2 (2002): 71–90 (pp. 82–3).
5 The literature is summarised in Bailey, *After the Black Death*, pp. 9–12.
6 R. H. Britnell, 'Feudal reaction after the Black Death in the Palatinate of Durham', *Past & Present*, 128 (1990): 28–47.
7 Hilton, *The Decline of Serfdom*, pp. 39–44; Dyer, *Everyday Life*, pp. 202–90, 228–30; Dyer, 'Villeins, bondsmen', pp, 428–33; P. V. Hargreaves, 'Seigniorial reaction and peasant responses: Worcester Priory and its peasants after the Black Death', *Midland History*, 24 (1999): 53–78; Fryde, *Peasants and Landlords*, pp. 26, 38–41.
8 Dyer, 'Villeins, bondsmen', p. 432. See also Dyer, *Peasants Making History*, pp. 78–82; and Dyer, *From Slavery to Freedom*, pp 18–20, for additional, very recent, examples of this anecdotal and unquantified approach to asserting the existence of a reaction.
9 Bailey, 'The myth', pp. 149–67; Bailey, *After the Black Death*, pp. 12–14, 83–112; M. Raven, *The Noble State: Nobles, Nobility, and the Crown, 1330–60* (forthcoming), Chapter 8.
10 Dyer, 'Villeins, bondsmen', p. 432; Razi, *Life, Marriage*, pp. 111–13.
11 Bailey, *After the Black Death*, p. 87.
12 Larson, *Conflict and Compromise*, pp. 77–198, 217–21.
13 M. Bailey, 'The implementation of national labour legislation in England after the Black Death, 1349–1400', *Economic History Review*, 78:2 (2025): 529–52.
14 Bailey, *The Decline of Serfdom*, pp. 104–337; Bailey, 'The transformation'; Bailey, *After the Black Death*, pp. 10–15, 83–112, 297–313.

15 Dyer, *Peasants Making History*, pp. 62, 78–82; Dyer, *From Slavery to Freedom*, pp. 18–20.
16 J. Baylis, 'The decline of serfdom in the west Midlands 1300 to 1450' (PhD thesis, University of East Anglia, 2026).
17 Bailey, *After the Black Death*, pp. 14–15, 326–8.
18 See, for example, J. Chick, 'The 1381 rising in Bury St Edmunds: The role of leaders and the community in shaping the rebellion', *Pons Aelius*, 13 (2016): 35–47; Bailey, *After the Black Death*, pp. 186–220; and M. Xu, 'Analysing the actions of the rebels in the English Revolt of 1381: The case of Cambridgeshire', *Economic History Review*, 75 (2022): 881–902.
19 Levett, *Studies*, pp. 67–206; E. Miller, 'The estates of the abbey of St Alban', *St Albans and Hertfordshire Architectural and Archaeological Society* (1938): 285–303.
20 Slota, 'Law, land transfer', pp. 119–20, 132–3.
21 Noy, *The Winslow Manor Court Books, 1322–1377*, p. ix.
22 R. Faith, 'The class struggle in fourteenth century England', in R. Samuel, ed., *People's History and Socialist Theory* (London: Routledge & Kegan Paul, 1981), pp. 50–80; and R. Faith, 'The Great Rumour of 1377 and peasant ideology', in R. H. Hilton and T. H. Aston, eds, *The English Rising of 1381* (Cambridge: Cambridge University Press, 1984), pp. 43–73 (pp. 63–8).
23 For a summary of the view that St Albans abbey clamped down hard on its villeins after the Black Death, generating grievances that came to the fore in the revolt of 1381, see J. Barker, *England, Arise: The People, the King, and the Great Revolt of 1381* (London: Abacus, 2014), pp. 63–4; and Hilton, *Class Conflict*, p. 62.
24 A. Reville, *Le soulèvement des travailleurs d'Angleterre en 1381* (Paris: Picard et fils, 1898), pp. 5–6.
25 Levett, *Studies*, pp. 178–9; Barker, *England, Arise*, p. 280.
26 Poos, 'Medieval English manorial courts', p. 207 n. 27.
27 Levett, *Studies*, p. 178.
28 B. R. Dobson, ed., *The Peasants' Revolt of 1381*, 2nd edn (Basingstoke: Macmillan, 2003), p. 19; Justice, *Writing and Rebellion*, p. 159.
29 Dyer, *Everyday Life*, p. 193.
30 Bailey, *The Decline of Serfdom*, pp. 16–103.
31 For further elucidation of this point and method, see Bailey, 'The regulation', pp. 142–4, 154–5; and Bailey, 'The implementation', pp. 531, 537–40, 547.

8

The manor of Codicote

The abbey of St Albans acquired the manor of Codicote, located 9 miles north-east of the borough of St Albans, in the early eleventh century (see Map 7.1).[1] It was a large manor with a conventional structure containing a sizeable 462-acre arable demesne, some freehold land and a large area of customary land.[2] The total manorial area is impossible to know, because the acreages of many holdings are not stated in the surviving documents, even for the standardised customary holdings such as 'half-virgates', 'fertlingates' (presumably quarter-virgates) and 'cotlands', but overall it comprised around 2,000 acres of arable. In the 1320s the cellarer leased the manor to a third party for an annual rent of £100, confirming its size and high value.[3] Even when the manor was leased, however, the cellarer retained direct control of the manor court, which was usually held twice a year: once in the late spring then again in the autumn, although additional courts were occasionally convened. The records of 109 courts are extant for the years between 1327 and 1377. The original court rolls themselves have not survived, but extensive extracts from them were copied contemporaneously and preserved in a book format. The copies included the records of leet courts, which summarised the revenue received from breaches of the assize of ale and bread, while carefully recording those not in tithings, those who had hunted in the lord's warren and so on. We can therefore be confident that any activity relating to the abbey's rights over the manor in general, and serfdom in particular – anything that might be proof or a precedent – was copied into this book as a matter of record.[4]

Table 8.1 Last recorded dates of key incidents of villeinage at Codicote, 1327–77

Capitage	Chevage	Presented for absence	Leyrwite	Heriot	Merchet	Mill suit	Recognition	Tallage	Licence to educate
None	1347	1377	1354	1376	1377	1337	1350	None	1336

Source: British Library, MS Stowe 849.

Serfdom in the pre-plague era

The survival of an extent for Codicote from 1332 offers insights into the rent packages attached to villein tenure on the manor, which varied widely from one holding to another, as was the case on many manors on the abbey's estate.[5] The extent confirms that the vast majority of villein land was held on service tenancies rendering a mixture of labour services, cash and rents in kind (see pp. 84–5). Each year the servile holdings collectively owed 645 eggs and 1,425 week works, ploughed 162 acres of the lord's demesne, and reaped 106 acres of his grain.[6] The balance between services, renders and cash rents was variable: some categories of holding rendered predominantly cash rents, some mainly labour services and others a mixture of the two. For example, small 'cotlands' rendered little cash, yet were saddled with forty-two 'works' and had to reap 3 acres of the demesne land in the harvest.[7] In contrast, a typical half-virgate owed just under 4s. of money rent, two hens and thirty eggs, together with ploughing, harrowing and sowing works, including one at haymaking; forty-three week works between 29 September and 1 August each year; two boon-works at harvest-time; and reaping and binding 3 acres of the lord's corn.[8] Other holdings owed principally a fixed, but low, money rent: for example, Edward atte Hathe held 2 acres in the open fields for 5½d., and a further ¾d. in lieu of carrying services.[9] Two small cottagers owed merely suit of court and heriot.[10]

In the period 1330–48, 92 per cent of all transfers of villein land at Codicote were held on a service tenancy: of these, the overwhelming majority were held heritably and a mere handful were for life (Tables 8.2 and 8.3). Put another way, fixed-term and cash tenancies were highly unusual. The wording of the conveyance of heritable service tenures was broadly consistent, usually being expressed as 'to hold to him and his, by the owed and accustomed services' (*tenendi sibi et suis per servicia inde debita et consueta*). Occasionally the phrase 'in villeinage' was added after 'him and his'.[11] In 1340 a slightly amended phrase appeared in a succession of grants – 'to hold to him and his by the rod at the will of the lord by the owed and accustomed services' – and by the time plague struck this had evolved into 'to hold to him and his in villeinage at the will of the lord by the owed and accustomed services' (*tenendi*

Table 8.2 Number of transactions of customary land at Codicote, 1327–77

Decade	Direct inter-peasant transfers	Grants from lord	Abandoned/ seized into hands of lord	Licences to sublet	Total transactions	No. and % of transfers on life tenancies
1327–29	43	3	0	3	49	3 (6%)
1330–39	108	28	5	5	146	6 (4%)
1340–48	135	18	10	4	167	5 (3%)
1349	48	5	21	0	74	0
1350–59	51	50	26	6	133	3 (2%)
1360–69	63	50	8	3	124	0
1370–77	40	15	6	0	61	3 (5%)

Source: British Library, MS Stowe 849.

Table 8.3 Breakdown of all inter-peasant transfers of customary land at Codicote, 1327–77

Decade	No. of transfers	Hereditary for services	Hereditary for money	Life for services	Custody for services
1327–29	43	40	0	3	0
1330–39	108	95	1	5	7
1340–48	135	130	0	2	3
1349	48	38	0	1	10
1350–59	51	46	0	0	5
1360–69	63	60	1	0	2
1370–77	40	38	0	0	2

Source: British Library, MS Stowe 849.

sibi et suis in villeinagio ad voluntatem domini per servicia inde debita et consueta).[12] Husbands and wives sometimes held in joint tenure.[13] Charters containing details of transfers of villein land were already in use widely.[14]

The male age of majority was twenty-one years, although occasionally heirs were admitted at a younger age.[15] If an heir was not initially forthcoming, the custom of the manor was for a formal proclamation to be made in three separate courts, after which the heir's rights were put aside and the lord could grant the land to a non-heir.[16] Whenever this happened, the lord responded in one of two ways. Most commonly, the lord granted the holding to a willing non-heir, although the tenancy was also converted from a service-based to a cash rent in 67 per cent of all such cases in the pre-plague era (Table 8.4). For example, in 1345, when one villein died without an heir holding a cottage with a yard, the lord granted it to William and Alice atte Haye for 40d. per annum for the term of their lives: it was liable for heriot but no entry fine was paid.[17] The annual money rent was fixed, but was presumably close to the market value at the time of the grant. The majority of these monetary tenures were heritable, not fixed-term, and the form of conveyance was consistent: 'to hold to him and his in villeinage at the will of the lord by the service of rendering annually to the lord [*x*]d.'.[18]

The second, and much less common, response to a failure of heirs was to instruct the jurors to identify a suitable tenant, presumably because no volunteer had come forward to take the land. In 1332, 16 acres of land fell into the lord's hands and remained there for want of a tenant after the death of Richard Baghel, and so the court was ordered to find a replacement.[19] William de Thikkeney took on the land for three years initially, with a caveat that if an heir came forward in that time and made a just claim (*in forma iuris*) then the heir would enter the land while reimbursing William for all outlays and expenses.[20] The requirement for a community of tenants to find a tenant for vacant land has been identified on some other ecclesiastical estates in England and has been interpreted as an example of seigniorial coercion, although it is important to note how the rights of any possible heir were still protected.[21] Furthermore, the community was not always directed to find a replacement tenant. In the mid-1320s William de Shortegrave had died without a known heir while holding a messuage called Beredineslond, so the court made a series of proclamations for claimants to come forward. When none did so, in 1327 'the twelve jurors and the whole halmoot [court] decided that the lord should dispose of the said messuage according to his will'.[22] Of course, the lord did not require the permission of

Table 8.4 Breakdown of all direct grants of customary land from the lord at Codicote, 1327–77

Decade	No. of grants	Hereditary for services	Hereditary for money	Custody of heir for services	Custody heir for cash	Life for money	Term of years for money
1327–29	3	1	2	0	0	0	0
1330–39	28	7	15	0	0	1	5
1340–48	18	8	7	0	0	3	0
1349	5	3	0	2	0	0	0
1350–59	50	18	18	0	0	3	11
1360–69	50	7	17	0	0	0	26
1370–77	15	0	1	0	0	3	11

Source: British Library, MS Stowe 849.

the jurors, because in legal theory it was held at his will: the phrasing reflects the precedence of custom in the disposal of villein land.

A market in villein land existed on the manor. Over 100 transactions are recorded per decade in the pre-plague era, 80 per cent of them inter-peasant transfers (Table 8.2). Most grants were of small parcels described in vague terms, such as 'lands and tenements', or crofts and cottages, and the standardised holdings – the fertlingates and half-virgates – feature less frequently and were usually transferred *post mortem*. In the two decades before the arrival of plague, there were no assarts of new land or conversions of the demesne arable to peasant-holdings. There is some evidence of the subdivision of the larger holdings through sales of fragments of arable land from them to other tenants.[23] The cumulative effects of this process of fragmentation are sometimes captured in the court rolls when the various tenants of a subdivided standardised holding had to agree among themselves on the apportionment of the head rent and associated labour services. For example, in 1333 one original *tenementum* of 19 acres 1 rood of arable, and 3 roods of meadow, was now split among six tenants, Reginald Aleyn holding 13 acres 2 roods, and five others holding the remaining 6 acres as individual tenants.[24] Likewise, a half-virgate comprising 31 acres of arable and 3 roods of meadow was held by thirteen tenants, one of whom held 18 acres 2 roods, with the other twelve holding the remaining 12 acres 2 roods between them.[25] The servile land market at Codicote was not as active as that at Winslow but was more active than at Norton, confirming that even a landlord as powerful as St Albans abbey could not impose a uniform policy across its estate, but was itself subordinate to local custom and economic forces.

All transfers of villein land had to be recorded in the court rolls and, if this was not done, any private agreement and exchange were nullified. In 1337 Roger Chaplain showed a charter to support his claim to hold a bond *tenementum* named Bromeshale, but the lord seized the land because the transfer had not also been recorded in the court rolls.[26] Hence, the purchaser's interests were best served by ensuring the enrolment of the sale and exchange in the court rolls. Likewise, temporary subletting of parcels of servile land was permitted, subject to formal prior licensing of the arrangement in the court rolls. Sublets unlicensed by the court were prone to result in the seizure of the land until the lessor paid an amercement.[27]

The volume of licensed subletting was low, however, with a total of just a dozen licences being issued in the second quarter of the century (Table 8.2). This relatively subdued land market does not reveal signs of distress sales in years of duress. For example, increased tenant deaths in 1327–28 and 1332, presumably the consequence of prevailing drought conditions, did not prompt a hair-trigger response of sales or sublets.[28]

There is no recorded evidence for the sale price of villein land in the private transfers between tenants. The Codicote material does, however, yield some fragmentary insights into the arrangements that existed when a villein tenant chose to sublet part of the holding for a fixed term to a lessee. Manorial court rolls in general only record the seigniorial licence to sublet and provide no details about the side agreement between lessor and lessee, such as the level of rent charged or any special clauses, although very occasionally such clauses are included in the Codicote rolls. In 1350 John and Alice Lorugh included draught animals and seed corn in their sublet of land to Andrew Bundy, whilst in 1341 Roger of Raveneshathe had sublet 5 roods to Thomas le Cupper for twelve years and undertook not to sell them during that term without Thomas's prior assent.[29] Presumably all subleases were subject to oral or written agreements between the two parties, even if they are not recorded in the court rolls. This practice is hinted at in occasional oblique references in the courts, as can be seen when a debt or contract litigation referred to an arrangement *per scriptum* or to unpaid rent.[30]

The inclusion of an exceptional level of detail in two recorded subleases at Codicote presents a very rare insight into the level of rent charged by a tenant to a lessee as part of their private agreement, and an opportunity to compare it with the licensing fee charged by the lord. In 1328 William le Lord sublet 14 acres of arable plus some pasture to Alice atte Felde for twelve years, for which Alice was to pay him 4 bushels of wheat, 4 bushels of oats and a bushel of peas annually; in addition, she would pay to commute the labour services owed, and it was agreed that either Alice or William would perform the harvest boon-works.[31] The value of this agreement converts to 4.6d. per acre, excluding the services.[32] This level of rent paid by a subtenant is comfortably higher than the customary valuation in 1333 of 3d. per acre for head rents on servile holdings at Codicote.[33] The lord charged William a one-off licence fee of 2s. for this sublet, which is a good deal lower than the 5s. 4d. in annual rent that William was receiving from Alice, and the total rental value of 64s. for the whole term. In a second case in 1350 a sublet for a rent equivalent to 12s. per annum (for nine years) attracted a one-off licence of 2s.[34] Hence, in neither case did the one-off payment to the lord for licence to sublet exceed 3 per cent of the total value of the lease to the villein lessor.[35]

There is no evidence for arbitrary seigniorial action in the unfree land market at Codicote, but plenty of evidence for the binding power of custom, precedent, rules and procedures. In 1329 two brothers refused to carry the lord's grain in the harvest, because they claimed this was not a customary requirement, but the evidence of the custumal showed otherwise: likewise, in 1330 six tenants refused to attend a plough service when summoned and agreed to 'submit to the customary book' to resolve the matter.[36] The court rolls were routinely searched for precedents in disputes over villein land, and the evidence of the rolls was invariably decisive.[37] In 1329 one plaintiff – William Childemere – lost his claim to a parcel of servile land because he could not provide supporting evidence from the rolls, and in 1340 another plaintiff, Alice Lorugh, won hers because she was able to do so.[38] Sometimes villeins paid the lord to empanel an inquisition jury to determine a landed dispute.[39] Complex land disputes were sometimes referred to a special session of the court held at St Albans.[40] Villein tenants were cannily aware of arcane and technical legal points concerning land.[41] Very occasionally, jurors were reprimanded and amerced for false testimony.[42]

The lord did not seize villein land arbitrarily, but only when certain conditions of tenure had not been met, such as an illicit transfer without seigniorial permission; or cases involving serious wastage of the holding; or rebellious disobedience; or, on one occasion, because the tenant had been convicted of theft and had died 'in remote parts'.[43] When tenants fell into rent arrears, the lord's first course of action was to amerce them and seek payment of the arrears rather than evict.[44] The lord struck deals with villeins when it was mutually beneficial to do so. For example, William Terri took from the lord a tenement that needed rebuilding, and so the rent of 5s. per annum was waived until the building work had been completed, whilst in 1334 John le Mulward's entry fine for admission to various lands and tenements was waived because of their dilapidated state.[45]

Freemen held villein land in Codicote, although the lord often took the precaution of reminding them explicitly of the obligations that ran with the tenure. For example, when in 1332 Thomas the Potter entered a messuage and 4 acres of villein land, he was ordered to swear an oath of fidelity, to find pledges not to make any claim on the land other than in villeinage, and not to waste the land – a set of caveats that indicate Thomas was a freeman and perhaps also an outsider.[46] No such caveats were imposed on 'lord John atte Water of East Wyttenham, vicar of Codicote', when he entered a messuage in villeinage in 1334, although when he acquired another small plot of land the court entry stated that 'he will give heriot when it falls due, and all services and customs as belong to such bond land'.[47] John's son duly paid the heriot in 1349 following his father's death at the time of the Black Death.[48] In October 1334 John Poleyn died holding a capital messuage in free tenure, which nonetheless was liable for heriot, and he had also held various other parcels of land *per virgam* that were all liable to heriot: his son entered all these holdings, paying 40s. to cover the entry fines on the villein land; the relief on the free lands; and, in the event, just a single heriot was paid.

A weekly market was active at the heart of the village, with a market cross; various shops and stalls; and even a small shambles of leather curers and, at the east end, a fishmarket: one of the shopkeepers was a resident of St Albans.[49] The shops were held heritably on villein tenure, some for services, others for cash, and the service tenures were liable for heriot.[50] In 1332 the lord granted William atte Dane a strip of land 7 feet × 7 feet opposite an existing shop to construct a stall with a roof for 6d. per annum in villeinage.[51] One shop occupied a plot twice that size.[52] Two years later William abandoned the plot in exchange for a new one, this time opposite the blacksmith's forge, presumably because the location of the first had not generated much business. Both grants were hereditary for a modest annual cash rent, although William did hold another shop in villeinage for services.[53] All this provides unequivocal evidence for the immersion of Codicote's villeins in retail and some industrial trades. In the Lay Subsidy of 1307 substantial villein families, such as the atte Hille/Hulles, the Raveneshaches and the Carpenters, were rated among the vill's highest taxpayers.[54]

The Black Death and its immediate aftermath

Before 1348 it was rare for more than a couple of deaths of villein tenants to be recorded in a single court, but the court held on 7 November 1348 recorded the deaths of five tenants with fifty-eight recorded in the court of 19 May 1349 and a further four in the next court on 20 October 1349. Thus, the Black Death probably arrived at Codicote in late autumn 1348 and had largely passed though the manor by June 1349. Levett estimated the mortality on the manor at around 50 per cent.[55] This seems reasonable, given the identification of 121 tenants in the extent of 1332 and a grand total of sixty-seven tenant deaths in the year of the Black Death.[56]

Of those sixty-seven tenant deaths, the land was reoccupied immediately in forty-six cases, although twelve of these incoming tenants were custodians taking responsibility for the land until the heirs came of age. For example, eight-year-old Mabel atte Hulle was the underage heir to her dead father's cottage, so custody of the land was given to William Cok, who presumably also became her guardian. The most striking aspect, however, is that in nine of those twelve custody cases the mother of the child was admitted to the land as custodian. It would be imprudent to read too much into such a small sample, but the disproportionate survival of mothers hints at differential gender- and age-specific mortality.

The immediate occupation of 69 per cent of the dead tenants' holdings is impressively high in the teeth of such terrifying mass mortality. The uptake was, however, facilitated by the ability of women to inherit land as heirs, including as custodians, who in total accounted for seventeen of the forty-six cases, i.e. 37 per cent of the new occupancies. The lord also intervened to encourage the uptake of land by waiving entry fines in twelve of the forty-six occupancies (26 per cent) and, furthermore, by allowing nine of the twelve custodians to pay a flat and low entry fine of 6d. or 3d. for the holding: this grand total of twenty concessions, i.e. 45 per cent of all immediate occupancies, must have helped with the rapid uptake of the land of many of the dead tenants. Mean entry fines of grants of parcels of arable land alone, as opposed to grants of arable with buildings, were notably low between 1349 and 1351 at 3.4d. per acre (ten data points), compared to c. 13d. in the pre-plague era.[57]

The mass mortality prompted the lord to question the jurors about the local custom regarding wills in the court of October 1349. Their reply was that serfs and bond tenants were to prove their wills in front of the cellarer, a custom established 'time out of memory and all cellarers without exception made use of it'. They also confirmed that free men and free tenants who 'held their messuage by charter by common law' proved their wills in the archdeaconry court. In the October court of 1349 one of the holdings abandoned in the May 1349 court for want of an heir – a messuage and 9 acres that had beloned to Simon Mulward – was granted to a new tenant, but the remainder of the land abandoned earlier in the year was still lying in the lord's hands. In April 1350 tenants were found for five of the abandoned holdings and in the November court the remaining untenanted parcels were listed in the court: fifteen separate holdings (the acreage is not given), for which the beadle had obtained ad hoc revenues (known as payments *de exitus*) totalling 28s. 8d. from various local people willing to pay a few pennies to squeeze whatever productive use they could out of the land. All the revenue was described as 'from pasture', meaning for grazing animals on uncultivated arable land, although the 'fruit' of two gardens was also included.[58] During the early 1350s the beadle continued to obtain such occasional payments from unspecified local people for taking the crop from abandoned meadow or arable land.[59]

The villein land market stirred back to life in the November court of 1350 with fifteen grants of land abandoned since early 1349 for which the heirs had not come to claim their inheritance. These grants from the lord included a significant shift in the nature of the tenancies. Only two of the fifteen grants were on the terms of the old hereditary service tenancy, whereas the remaining thirteen were all for an annual money rent: six were fixed-term grants, leases in all but name, for terms ranging from six to twenty years; four were on a hereditary tenancy; and three were grants for life. This swing to money tenures in general, and leases in particular, proved enduring. Between 1327 and 1348, 33 per cent of grants from the lord had been on service tenure, 49 per cent on monetary tenure and 11 per cent on leases, whereas between 1350 and 1369 the figures were 25 per cent, 35 per cent and 37 per cent respectively (Table 8.4).

The lord also continued to make concessions on entry fines, from one waived entirely due to the poverty of the incoming tenant (Reginald atte Hurne) to notional renders of capons and chickens rather than sizeable cash payments. This contrasts sharply with the dominance of grants of service tenancies in the immediate pre-plague era and the abundance of cash-based entry fines. Now that the manor was saddled with villein arable land that had been untenanted for nearly eighteen months, the lord had clearly decided to offer concessions in order to secure new tenants in the uncertainty of the post-plague world. The challenges facing the lord were still starkly apparent, though, because in the same court Laurence and Margaret atte Hathe abandoned a messuage and 60 acres of land, with no heir or tenant being willing to take on the land.

The epidemic offered opportunities for those with sufficient capital and enterprise to seize them. In 1354 Thomas Blakelak, described as a freeman and incomer, and his wife Christina were admitted to a variety of villein lands – messuages, cottages, arable land and a toft next to the messuage – paying a grand total of 40s. in entry fines. These lands had been lying abandoned, and all the grants were in villeinage on hereditary money rents. The lord took the precaution of requiring Thomas to swear an oath that he and Christina would be 'obedient to the lord as other serfs and in the giving of tallage', i.e. that even as a freeman Thomas would respect the obligations of servile tenure.[60] A year later Thomas obtained a further acre of land next to his messuage, again on a hereditary money tenure, so he was clearly engrossing and extending his curtilage.[61] In May 1359, however, the Blakelaks disposed of one messuage and obtained a licence to sublet all the rest of their lands in Codicote for three years, and from the mid-1360s Thomas was routinely amerced for failing to attend the manor court: he clearly retained landed interests in Codicote, but probably no longer resided there.[62] He continued to be amerced for non-attendance every year in the 1370s, and by 1371 had allowed his tenement to become waste.[63]

Although the Black Death created opportunities for survivors, these were not always to be found on their home manor. We have already encountered Mabel atte Hull, who as an orphan of eight had been placed under the guardianship of William Cok. In 1354 Mabel, now aged fourteen, was admitted to her inherited cottage, but within eighteen months she was amerced 2d. for wasting it, and it still had not been repaired in May 1356: at this court, she was amerced 2d. for default of the court and reported as living in London. Furthermore, the jury were ordered to investigate who had led (*abduxit*) Mabel away from the manor and carried off her goods. The jury duly reported to the very next court that John Cok was the responsible agent, valuing her goods at 40d., and that she was living in London, some 30 miles away.[64] No action was taken in response to this information, and for the next three years she remained in London.[65] Mabel returned to Codicote in 1360, now aged twenty, and was admitted once again into her cottage but promptly transferred it to one Geoffrey Mortimer and paid a heriot of 12d., signifying that she no longer held any villein land from the manor: she was then recorded as having flown the manor, though her destination was not stated.[66] Mabel had clearly returned temporarily to tidy her affairs, before leaving again for good. The cottage was evidently a saleable property, and she would have received a capital sum from Geoffrey. She had thus returned to Codicote, sold her inheritance, then resumed her life in London with no obvious hindrance from the lord and no payment of chevage or merchet. In 1377 she was still recorded as living in London: if correct, she was now in her late thirties, had spent at least twenty years living in the capital, and had not yet paid a penny as chevage.[67]

Few tenant deaths were recorded annually during the 1350s, but the court held on 15 October 1361 recorded six, followed by one more in the following April. This indicates that the second major plague epidemic struck in the late summer of 1361 but had largely passed by October, having claimed a death rate of around 10 per cent among the villein tenants. The lands of one of the dead tenants were abandoned because the heir (Margery Blosome) failed to claim the inheritance. The October 1361 and April 1362 courts were characterised by a spate of leases of abandoned arable land from the lord, with a total of nine being granted for an average term of around nine years. Just one death was recorded in three courts in 1369, so the third great plague outbreak left no discernible impact on the manor.

Villein tenures

A range of indicators reveal how the Black Death reduced the buoyancy of the villein land market. The volume of inter-peasant transfers in 1350–69 was down 60 per cent on 1327–48 (Table 8.2). The proportion of transfers into the lord's hands – rather than onto another tenant – rose from under 5 per cent before 1349 to 20 per cent in the 1350s, reflecting the absence of any immediately willing new tenants (Table 8.3). The proportion of transfers emanating from the lord rose from 11 per cent in 1340–48 to almost 40 per cent in the 1350s and 1360s, because more villein land was lingering in the lord's hands before a new tenant could be found. These seigniorial grants were increasingly for money rents in general and short-term leases in particular (Table 8.4). Significantly, it was the abandoned standardised holdings – half-virgates and fertlingates – that were mainly granted on leases, indicating that new tenants were cautious about committing to the permanent acquisition of large commercial holdings in the uncertain aftermath of the pandemic, preferring instead to hold them for a fixed term of around five years.[68] Finally, the proportion of heriots rendered *inter vivos* rather than *post mortem* rose from 25 per cent in 1327–48 to 79 per cent in 1350–69, because more landholders were now opting to leave the Codicote villein land market entirely.

Hence, the Black Death had an immediate, dampening, effect on the demand for villein land. Yet this is not reflected in the mean level of entry fines per acre for arable land, which in 1350–69 recovered to 13d. per acre, the same as it had been in 1330–48 (Table 8.5). This may reflect seigniorial muscle in forcing entry fines higher than the market rate for land as part of a seigniorial reaction, although it seems unlikely, given that the level of entry fines for half-virgates collapsed across the same period: in the 1360s the mean was just one-fifth of the level of the pre-plague era (Table 8.5; there is no figure for the 1350s). The most likely explanation for this discrepancy between the rate of entry fines for virgates and for arable per acre is that the land market was volatile and perhaps two-paced. Demand for the large half-virgate holdings on permanent tenures was weak, because of a perceived uncertainty of the long-term direction of the grain market in the post-plague era, whereas demand for smaller parcels of arable land remained stronger among the landless

Table 8.5 Entry fines charged for villein arable land, and for half-virgates, at Codicote, 1327–77

Decade	No. of arable-only transactions	Mean fine per acre	No. of half-virgates transacted	Mean fine per half-virgate
1327–39	34	14.4d.	2	11s. 8d.
1340–48	45	11.4d.	5	19s. 11d.
1350–59	16	12.5d.	0	—
1360–69	39	13.6d.	4	3.s 6d.
1370–77	16	8.8d.	0	—

Source: British Library, MS Stowe 849.

or land-deficient, for whom acquiring small land parcels was less risky.[69]

The swing to hereditary monetary tenures and fixed-term leaseholds was not a temporary measure, because the movement accelerated in the early 1360s. For example, parcels of villein land were granted in four separate leases in the October 1360 court, followed by five new leases in the October 1361 court (total average length of term nine years). In April 1360 two of the hereditary grants were for a low initial rent with an explicit clause to increase it at a later date, which was manifestly a tactic designed to attract reluctant tenants. For example, John Hell was to pay 2s. in annual rent for one newly acquired messuage for the first ten years, rising to 4s. thereafter, and for another messuage he was to pay 2s. in annual rent for the first ten years, after which this monetary tenure was to revert to a service tenancy.

Thus, signals from the villein land market in the 1350s and 1360s were mixed: it showed some signs of resilience, although it was undoubtedly more subdued than it had been in the 1340s. From the late 1360s, however, there were unequivocal and widespread signs of difficulties finding tenants. Entry fines were no longer charged on new leases, they were increasingly waived on the few occasions when the lord granted a holding directly on a service tenancy, and rents began to fall.[70] For example, in the June court of 1375 two incoming tenants did not pay entry fines, and in 1376 the annual rent for a half-virgate at lease was set at 13s. 4d. for the first two years then reduced to 12s. annually for the next nine years.[71] In 1369 John atte Style died holding a toft and courtyard, but his son Thomas, who was present in court, refused to take on the holding: it was relinquished into the lord's hands, and no action was taken against Thomas.[72] In 1372 John atte Thorn had abandoned a messuage and fertlingate of land, but in 1374 the lord – by his special grace – reissued the holding to John, although this time on a nine-year lease, rendering 3s. 4d. and one boon-day harvest per annum.[73] This example provides clear proof that after the Black Death villein tenants increasingly preferred leases for cash rather than permanent tenancies where the rent was paid in mixed renders and services.

Variable incidents

The absence of any surviving manorial accounts for Codicote means that we have little knowledge of how the week works and boonworks on the service tenancies were managed over the course of the fourteenth century, although in the 1320s the manor was leased out, which is likely to have resulted in the commutation of some of the labour services for a cash sum. Some services were still rendered to the lessee, however, judging by the ongoing record in the court book of some cases of non-performance of the works, although the number of refusals was small relative to the large number of services theoretically available to the lord. Non-performance was recorded in just four years in the pre-plague era, although the frequency increased after 1350. The number of services withheld in any given year was low, usually no more than a handful. All relate to seasonal services, with no reference at all to week works, which suggests that the week works had long been commuted (Table 8.6).

Two episodes from Codicote confirm the importance of codified customs in mediating disputes between lords and villeins over the nature of services owed. In the harvest of 1329 brothers John and Robert atte Strat had refused to carry the lord's grain from the fields when summoned to do so; in their defence they asserted that they had never had to perform this service, and 'they called for the record of the customary book' to support their stance. The lord's officials directed them to the monastery at St Albans to consult the customal ... which duly confirmed that they ought to carry the grain as requested.[74] On another occasion, six tenants disputed their requirement to perform certain ploughing services and 'submitted themselves to the customary book'.[75]

Heriot was due either on the death of a tenant or when a living tenant ceased to hold any villein land from the manor. Heriots were usually the best beast, but brass pots, an axe, capons and cash were also rendered.[76] Heriot might be waived after the death of a married partner when the land had been held jointly by husband and wife.[77] A tenant dying in possession of multiple holdings was liable for multiple heriots: John de London died holding three houses, 2 acres and a cottage, so his estate rendered four heriots.[78] Heriot was occasionally due from free tenure.[79] From the 1350s heriots on *inter vivos* transactions were invariably rendered in cash, whereas *post mortem* heriots continued to be of animals or chattels.

Table 8.6 Incidence of recorded non-performance of labour services at Codicote, 1327–77

Year	Non-performance of labour services
1329	2 refuse harvest boon-works
1330	6 refuse ploughing service
1336	1 defaults on 14 boon-works
1344	1 withholds 6 harvest boon-days
1353	1 withholds ploughing service 1 withholds all works
1354	7 default on 1 boon-day each 1 defaults on 5 boon-days
1355	1 withholds haymaking
1361	4 withhold bedrip
1363	1 withholds 6 harvest boon-works
1371	3 withhold boon-days
1375	2 withhold 3 harvest boon-days
1376	1 withholds 9 boon-days

Source: British Library, MS Stowe 849.

Entry fines were routinely charged on service tenancies. The average fine in the pre-plague era was around 13d. per acre for arable-only transfers, which sits around the middle of the range nationally.[80] The rate of fine was not standardised or consistent from one case to another, and was invariably lower for heirs. For example, in the court of October 1338 John le White rendered 18d. for 3 acres inherited from his father, whereas for the same sum William Cok acquired exactly half that area of land (6 roods) from an unrelated party. Other factors determined the level of fine in specific cases. In the April 1342 court a third party acquired two parcels of land, each of 1 acre from two different and unrelated vendors, yet 1 acre paid 12d. and the other 18d., possibly reflecting the relative quality of this land.[81] The entry fine was sometimes combined with a licence to marry, when the inheritance of land enabled a young man or woman to establish a separate household.[82] Fines were sometimes waived by the lord for reasons that are now obscure.[83] As with heriot, no fine was charged following the death of a husband or a wife holding jointly when the land was transferred to the surviving partner.[84]

Slota argued that fines at Codicote rose following the election of a new abbot of St Albans as part of a deliberate policy to raise revenues for the incoming abbot, although his figures were based on fines per transaction rather than fines per unit area, which are actually a more reliable test. There are few data points for fines per acre around 1335, when Michael of Mentmore was elected abbot, but the small sample shows an increase: a mean of 17d. per acre in 1334 (two data points), 22d. in 1335 (four) and 31d. in 1336 (five). In the mid-1350s entry fines per acre also rose in the first two years of the administration of a new cellarer, John Mote (see pp. 299, 386). Very occasionally, then, seigniorial power raised the level of entry fines for a couple of years to generate revenues for a specific purpose. There is no evidence for the collection of tallage annually, although recognition was collected on the election of Thomas de la Mare in 1350 (although not in 1335 or any other documented year). It was paid by 'all neifs and neif tenants', who had to find a fixed sum of 40s., which if distributed evenly would have amounted to perhaps 6–12d. per head.[85]

A large demesne water mill was located on the manor, which in 1332 was valued at a sizeable £6 per annum.[86] Breaches of mill suit were uncommon, which is surprising given the oft-attested prominence of mill suit as a source of antagonism in the fourteenth century between the abbey of St Albans and its tenants. A grand total of thirteen cases are recorded, all in the 1330s, and the last breach occurred in 1337: the mean levy was 4d. (Table 8.7). In one case, the court attributed the motive for evading mill suit to the tenant's personal enmity towards the miller. This must have been part of a wider dispute, because at the same time the court book noted that 'it was agreed between the lord and the customary tenants' that henceforth the miller would only mill malt on Wednesdays and Saturdays.[87] While the incidence of breaches of mill suit is much lower than at Norton and Winslow, and while it disappeared much earlier, the court at Codicote did actively license the use of hand mills. A total of seven hand mills are mentioned, the last in 1361, two of which were unlicensed. The permitted use of hand mills was usually restricted to the milling of oats, and they were not to be used to grind other grains.[88]

Both males and females were liable for merchet. The mean fine for women (c. 33d. in the pre-plague era) was consistently higher than for men (c. 11d.; see Table 8.8). The highest merchet was 8s., the lowest 6d.[89] Prior to the Black Death many fines for merchet were combined with an entry fine, underlining the association between holding land and household formation. Fines for marrying without

Table 8.7 Incidence of mill suit, and mean size of levy, at Codicote, 1327–77

Period	No. of cases of mill suit	Mean amercement
1327–29	0	—
1330–39	13	3.9d.
1340–49	0	—
1350–59	0	—
1360–69	0	—
1370–79	0	—

Source: British Library, MS Stowe 849.

the lord's permission were usually lower than the fine for merchet (12d. for women, 8d. for men in the pre-plague era; Table 8.8), so there was little incentive to apply for permission proactively. The retrospective licences were probably paid by the poorer sections of society. Before 1349 around twenty-two marriages were recorded per decade, but afterwards the number collapsed to around three per decade. The mean fine for male merchets halved to 6d. (1349–79) and for women it fell to 18d. In the 1360s the court repeated an order three times for one woman to be fined for marrying without licence, but the money was never forthcoming, underlining the difficulties in enforcing this incident after 1349.[90]

Leyrwite was uncommon. Just six cases were recorded before 1350, each attracting a 6d. fine, then two in the 1350s at 2d. (Table 8.9). The last case was recorded in 1354 (Table 8.1). This is consistent with an emerging body of evidence that leyrwite rapidly disappeared as an incident of serfdom after the mid-fourteenth century across England.[91] Licences for permission to educate young male serfs were a feature of serfdom on the St Albans estate, probably indicating a policy of recruiting local talent to be trained at the abbey itself.[92] Payments were rare at Codicote, however, with just two cases (both in the 1330s), both

Table 8.8 Incidence of merchet, and mean size of levy, at Codicote, 1327–77

Period	Male merchets (mean levy)	Female merchets (mean levy)	Male married without licence	Female married without licence	Merchet/ entry fine
1327–29	2 (6d.)	1 (12d.)	9 (3.2d.)	3 (5.7d.)	0
1330–39	10 (11d.)	2 (43d.)	2 (7.5d.)	1 (12d.)	7
1340–48	3 (12.7d.)	3 (33.3d.)	4 (15d.)	2 (12d.)	10
1349	0	1 (6d.)	0	0	1
1350–59	1 (6d.)	2 (27d.)	0	1 (12d.)	0
1360–69	0	1 (12d.)	0	1 (24d.)	1
1370–77	1 (6d.)	0	3 (6d.)	0	0

Source: British Library, MS Stowe 849.

paying a fine of six capons.[93] The last licence to educate was in 1336 (Table 8.9).

Chevage payments were recorded occasionally before the Black Death (Table 8.10). In 1331 Robert Faber agreed to render two capons per annum for 'licence to serve where he will, provided he appear at the view of frankpledge', and had to find four pledges to guarantee that 'he will be obedient to the lord in everything, body and goods'; in 1335 the lord confirmed that this licence extended for the next twelve years (on the same terms).[94] In 1347 John de Childemere obtained a licence 'to serve within or without the lord's domain', on condition of payment of one capon each year but only for as long as his father lived, presumably so the lord could ensure he took up his landed inheritance.[95] No chevage is recorded after the Black Death, although presentments for absence – rare before 1349 – became a regular feature of the court rolls thereafter; from the late 1350s around six serfs are recorded as absent in each year, rising to ten in the early 1370s (Table 8.10). Prior to 1349 no destinations of migrant serfs are given and no female departures are recorded: this changed after 1349, when destinations were provided in 60 per cent of all cases, and 26 per cent of recorded migrants were women.[96]

In the early fourteenth century incomers – whether freemen or the migrant serfs of other lords – were required to pay a licence

Table 8.9 Incidence of leyrwite and licences to educate, and mean size of levy, at Codicote, 1327–77

Period	No. of leyrwite	Mean fine	No. of licences to educate	Mean fine
1327–29	1	6.0d.	0	—
1330–39	4	3.8d.	2	6 capons
1340–49	1	6.0d.	0	—
1350–59	2	2.0d.	0	—
1360–69	0	—	0	—
1370–77	0	—	0	—

Source: British Library, MS Stowe 849.

to enter villein land, usually when they had married a female serf of Codicote who already held land.[97] In 1335 Simon Rustlyng paid a licence of 6s. 8d. to marry a servile widow, which was also described as a licence for him to enter the lord's domain, and he was required to swear fealty, which also has the hallmarks of an incomer and perhaps a freeman.[98] Such requirements disappeared after the Black Death.

Attitudes to serfdom

In 1327 the violent rebellion of the townsfolk against the abbey of St Albans featured a dispute over the latter's unwillingness to allow its borough residents to use hand mills to grind their corn.[99] The background tension over hand mills is oft-cited in the scholarly literature as a major factor in the festering enmity between the abbey and its servile tenants during the fourteenth century.[100] Thomas Walsingham stated that one of the longstanding aims of the villeins involved in the revolt at St Albans in 1381 was 'to be able to erect hand mills where they pleased and as they wished'.[101]

In the pre-plague era there were just six cases relating to hand mills at Codicote. The first three occurred in the immediate aftermath of the 1327 uprising, when the cellarer licensed their use for three separate tenants, each of whom was required to pay 3d. initially to obtain the licence, then 2d. per year.[102] In 1336 Roger de Hamesho and John Bonere were attached for possessing hand mills without a licence, and both responded that in a previous court they had acquired licences for the same, but neither could produce evidence of the written entries and they were therefore amerced.[103] John was then allowed to keep the hand mill for an additional 1d. in rent per annum, and paid a 10d. amercement that also retrospectively licensed his earlier use of the hand mill, although Roger was amerced 3d. and ordered to remove his quern (i.e. a hand mill).[104] In 1347 William Terry paid 6d. per annum for a licence to use a hand mill in his house, though he was not permitted to grind wheat or barley.[105] The final reference to hand mills occurred in the early 1360s, when the court ordered the seizure of an unlicensed hand mill from John Brikynden and an account for any revenues from the seizure, but nothing further is heard.[106]

Table 8.10 Recorded flight of serfs from Codicote, 1327–77

Year	No. of presentments for absence	No. of people charged for chevage
1327	0	0
1328	0	0
1329	0	0
1330	0	0
1331	0	1
1332	0	0
1333	0	0
1334	2	0
1335	0	1
1336	0	1
1337	0	1
1338	0	1
1339	0	1
1340	1	1
1341	0	1
1342	0	1
1343	0	1
1344	0	1
1345	0	1
1346	11 (6 people)	2
1347	0	1
1348	0	0
1349	0	0
1350	0	0
1351	4	0
1352	3	0

Year	No. of presentments for absence	No. of people charged for chevage
1353	6	0
1354	0	0
1355	3	0
1356	13 (7 people)	0
1357	12 (6 people)	0
1358	11 (6 people)	0
1359	11 (6 people)	0
1360	12 (6 people)	0
1361	12 (6 people)	0
1362	12 (6 people)	0
1363	12 (6 people)	0
1364	6	0
1365	12 (6 people)	0
1366	12 (6 people)	0
1367	12 (6 people)	0
1368	6	0
1369	21 (7 people)	0
1370	7	0
1371	22 (7 people)	0
1372	7	0
1373	27 (9 people)	0
1374	18 (9 people)	0
1375	19 (10 people)	0
1376	13 (7 people)	0
1377	7	0

Source: British Library, MS Stowe 849.

The October court of 1333 contains some indication of unrest on the manor. The lord had seized the lands of one Adam le Bedel for alleged rebelliousness and disobedience, although they were immediately restored to him on payment of a 5s. entry fine. Furthermore, an exceptional clause was added to some inter-peasant transfers in this court, requiring the incoming tenant to be 'obedient in all villein services, just as other bondmen of the lord'. However, similar unrest is not evident in the autumn courts of 1333 at Norton and Winslow, and so this looks like an isolated issue at Codicote rather than an estate-wide movement.

The Black Death triggered an immediate seigniorial interest in the departure of serfs. The total number of chevage payments and presentments for absence averaged 0.43 per court before the pestilence and 4.73 per court afterwards.[107] The interest was first apparent in the court of November 1351, at which four males were presented as 'serfs of the lord dwelling outside the domain without the lord's licence. Therefore the order is to seize them and keep them in custody until the lord disposes of them at will'. The order to seize and to restrain them until the cellarer determined what to do was couched in aggressive terms, although there is no evidence that any action was taken. Thereafter around six serfs were presented for absence from the manor each year. At the same time, the court officials sought to be proactive whenever a resident serf was suspected of developing itchy feet. In 1353 John Wrenne 'declared publicly that he would dwell within the domain of Codicote', and had to find two pledges to support him.[108] Likewise, in September 1357 three men were required to provide surety that Robert atte Pirye would remain on the manor and not take his goods elsewhere, under threat of a hefty 40s. penalty.

Seigniorial concern about flown serfs continued after the second plague outbreak in 1361. During the late 1350s the names of absent serfs had been listed, but not their whereabouts, yet in the April court of 1362 the locations of all six absentees were provided: two women were included in the list, both resident in London. Thereafter, the same six were presented year after year in the 1360s, although their destinations were updated.[109] There were, however, other serf departures from Codicote that passed unrecorded, because either the jurors chose not to report them or the lord was prepared to tolerate them. In 1363 William Helder surrendered a messuage, a garden and three shops to Laurence de Barough, on condition that Laurence 'make the said William an apprentice at his own expense in the county of London in the art of fishmonger [*ad artem piscenarii*]'. Given that William also disposed of a croft to another resident of Codicote, and then obtained a licence to sublet all his other lands in Codicote to Laurence for a period of fourteen years, he did indeed intend to spend the next few years in the capital. The lord excused the fine for the sublet, and William does not appear in any subsequent list of either absent serfs or chevage payers, all of which indicates that he left with tacit seigniorial permission.[110]

The closer attention to migrant serfs in the 1350s was matched by heightened action against those tenants who allowed parts of their holdings to 'waste', which usually meant the dilapidation of housing that was surplus to requirements after the great mortality. In 1351 Adam Swayne had sold and moved a surplus house from his *tenementum*, but the lord ordered that it should be rebuilt under the threat of a massive 100s. penalty. The court of April 1354 listed seven tenants for wastage, four of whom were amerced an average of 2.5d., while the others were threatened with penalties ranging from 3s.4d. to 20s. Some tenants sought the court's formal licence to remove cottages: for example, in the courts of November 1351 and May 1352 three licences to remove houses were granted, the most expensive costing 18d.[111] This close attention was maintained until the late 1350s, after which it waned sharply. However, even during the 1350s the number of amercements and forfeited penalties were few. The hardest hit was John de London, who had been presented for waste in April 1353, was amerced 12d. in December 1354 and incurred a 6s. 8d. penalty in October 1356. In June 1357 he incurred another penalty of 6s. 8d. and was threatened with loss of the holding if he still refused to repair the house. The threats of him incurring further penalties continued until October 1360, after which either the court lost interest or he finally repaired the house.[112] De London's case illustrates a wider point: the court adopted a strong posture on wastage, but it actually took limited effective or sustained action.

The court held in December 1354 was the first of John Mote's term as cellarer, and its administration was instantly and noticeably tighter. For example, the beadle was amerced for petty administrative shortcomings, there was a crackdown on tenants who had allowed their tenements to dilapidate and the first leyrwite offences were recorded since 1340. There was also the proclamation – repeated estate-wide – that any subletting of villein land must be licensed by the court and recorded in its rolls, despite the jurors' claim that they had enjoyed an ancient customary right to sublet land for less than two years without requiring seigniorial licence. No licence fee was necessary for these short-term subleases, but the court specified that the penalty for non-compliance would be 6s. 8d. and possible seizure of the land, a much tougher stance than before the plague.[113] As Slota pointed out, here is an example of how lordly action could override custom.[114] The new regime certainly meant business, because in the second court under Mote's rule as cellarer the presiding steward made an example of Margaret Meleward for failure to report the sublet of a shop for two years, by amercing her 6s. 8d. and ordering seizure of the land. In addition, the beadle was ordered to seize a tenement held by Stephen May for failure to repair a house, and a cottage was also to be seized for rent arrears.[115] Margaret came to the next court 'and petitioned to be readmitted by the grace of the lord', which was duly allowed, and she then paid an additional and hefty fine of 40d. to license the sublet for seven years.[116] In the same court, five servile holdings transferred by charter but not recorded in the court rolls were seized into the lord's hands and the errant tenants ordered to attend the very next court to obtain formal permission.[117] Entry fines per acre rose sharply in the first two courts under Mote. During the revolt of 1381 he fled St Albans to safety elsewhere, confirming the prudence of placing discretion before valour.[118]

Hence, in the early 1350s an energetic new cellarer tightened the management of transfers of villein land and, especially, the recording of flown serfs from the manor. It is, however, important to note the narrowness of this reaction. There were no recorded disputes over personal status, no compilations of serf genealogies, no novel work agreements binding serfs and no forcible returns of flown serfs.[119] Chevage was not levied. The frequency of merchets collapsed, and the average fine was around half that of the pre-plague era. There were no recorded breaches of mill suit and no licences to educate. The fine for leyrwite fell by two-thirds and was not levied after 1354. So, the tougher action was targeted narrowly on due process in tenurial issues and in recording the flight of serfs, plus it was confined to the 1350s. By the 1360s the hard line on tenurial due process softened significantly, as the difficulties finding tenants prompted major concessions on the terms of tenure. In short, at Codicote there was no sustained seigniorial reaction across a broad front, and certainly no confrontational policies in the 1360s and 1370s that might explain the vehemence of the 1381 revolt at St Albans. It is not known whether the villeins of Codicote were well represented among the rebels. Certainly, the court book makes no mention of any local disturbances, and Walsingham's chronicle does not list Codicote as one of the manors that rose against the abbey.[120] We know from other sources, however, that in 1381 the demesne water mill at Codicote was subject to an arson attack, although serious damage was averted by the prompt, extinguishing, actions of the miller.[121]

Summary

In the pre-plague era many of the characteristics of villeinage at Codicote confirm the view that its operation was neither arbitrary or uncertain. Both the lord and presentment juries of villeins respected due process, written precedents and customary practices. Disputes over services were resolved first and foremost through reference to the custumal of the manor, the rights of heirs to inherit servile land were closely observed, there were no arbitrary seizures of land or chattels, and the land market was moderately buoyant. The cellarer regulated land transfers closely, including licences to sublease, and pushed the level of entry fines above their normal levels for a couple of years on one occasion after the election of a new abbot. Although the level of an entry fine in any individual case could vary according to specific circumstances (lower for heirs or the poor, higher for non-heirs and outsiders), in general the mean level of entry fines was around average for this region and it was broadly sensitive to market fluctuations. The seigniorial licences charged for subletting were a small fraction of the overall value of the sublease. Heriot was the most common incident of villein tenure, and custom determined both the size of the render and the occasions when it was due. Merchet charges were variable, but averaged 33d. for women and 11d. for males. There was no annual tallage, and recognition was an occasional fixed sum levied on all serfs by blood and tenants of servile land, amounting to a few pennies per head. Chevage, mill suit, leyrwite and licences to educate were very infrequent. Thus, the powerful cellarer of St Albans did not enforce all of the incidents of serfdom and did not even impose mill suit heavily at Codicote, contrary to the received wisdom.

In the second quarter of the fourteenth century over 80 per cent of servile tenancies were held heritably for services, although the exact nature of the rent package was variable. Annual cash rents, renders in kind and labour services were fixed by custom, and week works were commuted for cash. Demand for villein land was buoyant, judging by the mean level of entry fines (13d. per acre), the volume of transactions per decade and the high proportion of inter-peasant transfers, which reflected the willingness and availability of heirs or buyers to acquire land.

The situation changed rapidly after the Black Death. In the 1350s the demand for servile land fell decisively: the volume of transactions of servile land halved, the proportion abandoned into the lord's hands rose fourfold and grants of land from the lord (as opposed to transfers between peasants) rose from 11 per cent to 40 per cent. Entry fines per acre held their pre-plague level into the 1360s, so the land market showed some resilience, although at the same time the mean entry fine for the large half-virgate holdings had collapsed. The 1350s also saw a rapid shift from servile land held on the old service tenancy to either heritable money rent or fixed-term leases for cash, which strengthened in the 1360s. In the 1340s, 92 per cent of the 167 transactions of servile land had been on the traditional service tenancy and just 8 per cent on money rents or leases, but the proportion of the latter rose to 29 per cent in the 1350s and 37 per cent in the 1360s (Tables 8.2–8.4). Recognition payments disappeared after 1350. Hence, significant tenurial change occurred in the two decades after the Black Death, and it correlated with a decisive fall in the local demand for servile land.

Tighter management of the recording of villein land transfers in the 1350s coincided with some evidence for heightened peasant resistance. While the incidence of non-performance of labour services was generally low at Codicote, non-performance of the seasonal services peaked between 1353 and 1355, when a total of eleven people were amerced for each withholding a boon-work and haymaking service. Likewise, recorded migration rose sharply after 1350, from a single serf absent each year in the 1340s to six in the 1350s and ten in the early 1370s. Codicote migrants tended to head for distant and urban destinations, because two-thirds of them moved more than 10 miles away and all the females headed for towns.[122] In the 1350s another source of tension was the dilapidation of buildings on servile holdings, an example of passive resistance from the tenantry that triggered a clampdown from the lord. Yet this pattern of lordly reaction and serf resistance was conducted on a narrow front and largely fizzled out in the early 1360s. Its character is exemplified by the absence of either fines for mill suit or licences to possess hand mills after the Black Death, which is hard to reconcile with the traditional argument that tension over this aspect of serfdom was a major factor in stoking peasant discontent in the Peasants' Revolt. This discovery supports Holt's shrewd observation that hand mills were more a pretext and a symbol, rather than a major cause, of the attacks on the abbey in 1381.[123]

The incidence of both direct and passive resistance to the incidents of serfdom peaked in the 1350s, and coincided with the collapse of the servile land market. Both lordly reaction and peasant resistance dissipated soon after the early 1360s. By the 1370s a sizeable minority of villein land was now held on monetary and fixed-term tenures, mill suit and recognition had disappeared, and labour services were shrinking. Merchet was now restricted to neifs, not to tenants of villein land: just four merchets were recorded in the 1370s and the charge had halved since the 1340s. Leyrwite, licences to educate and chevage were not levied. Serfdom was in terminal decline by the 1370s, well before the Peasants' Revolt of 1381.

Notes

1 W. Page, ed., *Victoria County History, Hertfordshire*, Vol. II (London: Institute of Historical Research, 1908), p. 345; Toepfer, 'The abbey at St Albans', pp. 62–3.

2 Levett, *Studies*, pp. 338–9.

3 Page, *VCH, Hertfordshire*, Vol. II, pp. 345–6.

4 Levett, *Studies*, pp. 81–96; Noy, *The Winslow Manor Court Books, 1322–1377*, pp. xi–xii; M. Tompkins, 'The manor of Park in the fourteenth century', in anon., ed., *The Peasants' Revolt in Hertfordshire 1381* (Stevenage: Hertfordshire Local History Council, 1981), pp. 53–81 (p. 55); Müller, 'The function', p. 171.
5 Levett, *Studies*, pp. 198–202; Toepfer, 'The abbey at St Albans', pp. 65–8.
6 Levett, *Studies*, pp. 366–7.
7 Ibid., pp. 342–3.
8 Ibid., pp. 339–40.
9 Ibid., p. 356.
10 Ibid., p. 357.
11 See, for example, the acre of land granted to William le Swon 'to hold to him and his in villeinage by the owed and accustomed services'; British Library (BL), MS Stowe 849, court held May 1329.
12 Ibid., court held April 1340.
13 See, for example, ibid., court held October 1327, when a holding reverted to the husband after the death of his wife 'by the courtesy of England' (*ex curialitate Anglie*).
14 See, for example, ibid.: Roger Chapman's charter, court held October 1337; John Poleyn's charter for 3 acres of villein land, court held October 1341; Stephen Tanner's charters, court held May 1350; and charters for five parcels of land, court held November 1355.
15 Ibid. Confirmation of the age of twenty-one is provided in the court of May 1332, when Agnes de Cokruth took custody of land for her twelve-year-old son for the term of nine years. Then in October 1334 John le Lord entered his dead father's cottage and ferthlingland at fifteen years of age.
16 This device was not used before the Black Death, but was followed in the 1350s: ibid., courts held May and October 1356, and June 1357. It was explicitly described as the custom of the manor, therefore binding the lord as much as the tenants, in the court held April 1361.
17 Ibid., court held November 1345.
18 For example, ibid.: the grant to William and Alice Terri, court held April 1342; and the three grants of vacant plot in the market to Henry and Sibil Sckele, to Walter and Alicia atte Dane, and to Christina Cok in May 1344.
19 Ibid., court held January 1332. See also when Roger le Dryver was chosen to take the lands relinquished by William atte Newlond, court held October 1333.
20 Ibid., court held October 1332.

21 Page, 'The peasant land market', pp. 336–8; Bailey, *After the Black Death*, pp. 85–6.
22 BL, MS Stowe 849, court held April 1327.
23 Toepfer, 'The abbey at St Albans', pp. 70–4, 93–4.
24 BL, MS Stowe 849, court held May 1333.
25 The rest held parcels ranging in size from half a rood of meadow to 2 acres of arable; tenement and half-virgate of Thomas le Dryver, ibid., court held October 1335.
26 Ibid., court held October 1337. Robert le Swon claimed to have bought a cottage from Robert Ayleward, but it reverted to the latter when, despite a search of the rolls, no record of the transfer could be found in the court proceedings; ibid., court held April 1340.
27 Three such unlicensed sublets were discovered in the court held May 1346.
28 Stone, 'The impact of drought', Fig. 1 and pp. 445–7.
29 BL, MS Stowe 849, courts held November 1350 and October 1341.
30 Ibid., courts held May 1341, April 1353 and July 1366.
31 Ibid., court held November 1328.
32 Average grain prices in 1328–29 were 10d. per bushel of wheat, 4d. for oats, and 8d. for peas, which works out at a total rent of 64d. for the 14 acres; Farmer, 'Prices and wages', p. 791.
33 BL, MS Stowe 849, court held May 1333. In 1332 the demesne arable was valued at 2½d. per acre; Levett, *Studies*, 338–9.
34 A messuage and 30 acres were sublet for nine years for one-quarter of wheat, one-and-a-half quarters of oats, and half-a-quarter of barley. At concurrent prices this roughly equated to an annual rent of 12s., which works out at 4.8d. per acre. BL, MS Stowe 849, court held November 1350; prices from Farmer, 'Prices and wages', p. 791.
35 A twelve-year agreement at a rent of 5s. 4d. per annum (64s. total) attracted a 2s. licence (3.1 per cent), and a nine-year sublet at 12s. per annum (108s.) also happened to attract a 2s. licence (1.8 per cent).
36 BL, MS Stowe 849, courts held October 1329 and May 1330.
37 There are many examples, but see ibid., courts held in May and October 1329, and a spate of disputes in May 1331 and October 1332. In April 1334 John Lorugh asked for the rolls to be searched for proof that a licence to marry (merchet) had been obtained: it hadn't.
38 Ibid., courts held May 1329 and October 1340.
39 See, for example, ibid., courts held April 1328, May 1329, May 1330 and April 1334; and the long-running saga between William Childemere and William de Tagglemere, court held January 1331 and concluded in the court of January 1332.

40 For example, ibid., courts held 'under the ash tree at St Albans' on 13 November and 11 December 1344, and 8 January 1345.

41 For example, in May 1348 Geoffrey and Christina Skynne were keen to expedite a plea of land against John de London junior, but John disputed the need for any legal action because Christina's father, Robert, was still alive. The land appears to have been inherited by Christina's deceased mother, Margery, and Christina argued that after Margery's death Robert – a freeman – had relinquished the land, and that therefore the plea should be heard.

42 Roger le May denied occupying land belonging to Richard le Taillor, who was an outsider from Rickmansworth, and the jury of twelve men had originally upheld Roger's claim, but scrutiny of the court rolls proved Richard's case and the jury was fined 2s. for false testimony; BL, MS Stowe 849, court held May 1331.

43 For unlicensed exchanges/sales, see ibid., courts held October 1329 (William de Thikkeneye) and April 1340 (Margaret Palmer). For serious wastage, see court held May 1341 (tenement Beroldyns held by William Terri). For land seized for rebelliousness, see court held October 1333 (Adam le Bedel). For the distant thief, see court held October 1337 (Thomas Ponchardon).

44 For example, in May 1341 Roger le Dryver, Roger Chaplain and Walter le Helder were amerced 3d., 2d. and 2d. respectively for two years' rent arrears of c. 3d. each.

45 BL, MS Stowe 849, courts held January 1331 and April 1334.

46 Ibid., court held January 1332.

47 Ibid., courts held April 1334 and May 1335. John continued to accumulate land close to his own tenement; court held April 1342.

48 Ibid., court held May 1349.

49 Page, *VCH, Hertfordshire*, Vol. II, pp. 345–6.Thomas le Cupper of St Albans acquired a shop in the marketplace between the shop of John de Brikendon and the stalls of the leather curers (BL, MS Stowe 849, court held October 1329), then in May 1330 acquired another shop in the vicinity of the shambles of the 'lethercurers'. More stalls are recorded in the court held November 1346; 'the place where they sell fish towards the east end' is referred to in the court held May 1359; and the market cross is mentioned in the grant of a vacant plot to Henry and Alice Lorugh, court held November 1346.

50 In April 1340 the lord granted a shop to Reginald Faber for his lifetime for an annual rent of 12d., and in April 1342 it was noted that Robert Steward held a shop heritably in villeinage for an annual rent of 6d. For stalls held on standard villein service tenure rendering

heriot, see BL, MS Stowe 849, John Lorugh senior's surrender in court held November 1346.
51 Ibid., court held October 1332.
52 A shop on the marketplace transferred in the court held October 1336 measured 15 feet × 15 feet.
53 BL, MS Stowe 849, court held April 1334. William acquired the shop for services in October 1334. In October 1336 he was described as a butcher ('flesshmonger').
54 Compare Brooker and Flood, *Hertfordshire Lay Subsidy Rolls*, pp. 124–5, with Levett, *Studies*, pp. 341, 346, 359, 364–5.
55 Levett, *Studies*, Table II.
56 Ibid.
57 Based on nine data points, including valuing capons/chickens at 3d. each.
58 BL, MS Stowe 849, court held November 1350.
59 For example, John Helle, the miller of Codicote, paid 5s. 4d. for the hay crop of a meadow abandoned in the lord's hands; ibid., court held April 1354.
60 Ibid., court held December 1354.
61 Ibid., court held November 1355.
62 See, for example, ibid., courts held July and December 1366, June 1367 and May 1368.
63 Ibid., court held January 1371.
64 Ibid., courts held May 1349, April 1354, November 1355, and May and October 1356.
65 Ibid., courts held June 1357 and May 1358.
66 Ibid., courts held April and October 1360.
67 Ibid., court held April 1377.
68 This possibility is explored in Bailey, *After the Black Death*, pp. 149–53, 238–41.
69 Ibid., pp. 158–68.
70 See, for example, the two grants to William Symond and Simon atte Pirye; BL, MS Stowe 849, court held January 1369.
71 Ibid., court held September 1376.
72 Ibid., court held May 1369.
73 Ibid., courts held January 1373 and April 1374.
74 Ibid., court held October 1329.
75 Ibid., court held May 1330.
76 Ibid. For the brass pot, see Rosa atte Dene, court held November 1343; for the axe, valued at 2d., see Agnes Thorbern, court held May 1344; for capons, see John Lorugh senior, court held November 1346; for cash, see Christina Cok, paying heriot of 3s. on the death of her husband, court held April 1345.

77 See the case of Lucy and Stephen Bray, ibid., court held April 1340.
78 Two horses valued at 8s., a heifer at 3s. and a calf at 18d; ibid., court held May 1347.
79 William atte Felde held a messuage and 21 acres of land freely, and rendered an ox as a heriot on his death; ibid., court held May 1349. See also John Poleyn, court held December 1375.
80 Dyer, 'Seigniorial profits', pp. 225, 229, Fig. 2.
81 BL, MS Stowe 849, court held April 1342, both transfers to Robert Faber.
82 For example, in April 1342 Joanna Bray inherited 2 acres of land and paid a 10s. fine to enter and to marry; likewise Agnes atte Mere paid a 12s. fine for entry and marriage after inheriting a messuage. In October 1342 Thomas le Cupper entered a messuage and 6 acres of arable for a fine of 4s. to cover entry and a heriot.
83 The cellarer pardoned the entry fines on four transactions – all land acquired by one Robert Styward – in the court held April 1340, where no reason was given.
84 See, for example, when Christina Terry survived her husband in BL, MS Stowe 849, court held May 1348.
85 Ibid., court held May 1350.
86 Levett, *Studies*, p. 339.
87 BL, MS Stowe 849, courts held October 1336 (for the enmity and order) and May 1337 (for the last amercement).
88 Ibid., courts held January 1331 and November 1347.
89 Toepfer, 'The abbey at St Albans', pp. 75–6.
90 BL, MS Stowe 849, courts held July 1366, September 1367 and May 1368: the presentment is not included in Table 8.8, which captures payments and cases where the lord waived the fine.
91 Gibbs, *Lordship, State Formation*, pp. 133–4.
92 Levett, *Studies*, pp. 246–7.
93 See also Toepfer, 'The abbey at St Albans', pp. 77–8.
94 BL, MS Stowe 849, courts held May 1331 and May 1335.
95 Ibid., court held November 1347.
96 Bailey, 'Servile and gender migration', Table 2.
97 See, for example, the distraint of Roger Chaplain of Codicote in BL, MS Stowe 849, court held May 1337.
98 Ibid., court held October 1335.
99 Toepfer, 'The abbey at St Albans', pp. 95–100.
100 Levett, *Studies*, pp. 204–5; Bennett, *Life on the English Manor*, pp. 132–3; Holt, *The Mills*, pp. 40–1, 44–5; Toepfer, 'The abbey at St Albans', pp. 84–5.
101 Dobson, *The Peasants' Revolt*, p. 270. Walsingham's use of *villani* may be a disparaging term for the townsfolk of St Albans rather

than literally the villeins on the estate; R. H. Hilton, *Bondmen Made Free: Medieval Peasant Movements and the English Rising of 1381* (London: Methuen, 1977), p. 199.

102 The three tenants were Stephen le Bray, John Raveneshacche and John Doliter; see Levett, *Studies*, pp. 352, 359 (Le Bray and Raveneshacche); and BL, MS Stowe 849, court held January 1331 (Doliter).

103 Ibid., courts held April and October 1336.

104 Settlements are documented in ibid., courts held October 1336 (John) and May 1337 (Roger).

105 Ibid., court held November 1347.

106 Ibid., courts held October 1360 and April 1361.

107 Bailey, 'Servile and gender migration', Tables 1 and 2.

108 BL, MS Stowe 849, court held October 1353.

109 For example, Robert Bishop was reported as moving from Shenley to Hatfield during the course of 1367; ibid., courts held June and September 1367. Walter Childemere was added to the list and recorded in London; ibid., court held May 1369.

110 Ibid., court held September 1363.

111 Acquired by Thomas Smith; ibid., court held December 1354.

112 Ibid., courts held April 1353–October 1360.

113 See ibid., court held November 1343, where Robert atte Pirye's illegal sublet attracted a 3d. amercement and seizure.

114 Slota, 'Law, land transfer', p. 132.

115 BL, MS Stowe 849, court held May 1355.

116 Ibid., court held November 1355.

117 William le Bole, Robert de Eure, John Martyn, John le White and Ralph Lorugh; ibid., court held November 1355.

118 Toepfer, 'The abbey at St Albans', p. 118.

119 The only record of a manumission of a Codicote serf appears in a central abbey register in 1477; ibid., p. 132.

120 Ibid., p. 119.

121 Page, *VCH, Hertfordshire*, Vol. II, p. 346; Toepfer, 'The abbey at St Albans', p. 119.

122 Bailey, 'Servile and gender migration', Table 4.

123 Holt, *The Mills*, pp. 40–1.

9

The manor of Winslow

The vast majority of English manors were small and held by low-status gentry landlords, where serfdom was relatively unimportant. Yet the findings of Chapters 2–4 confirmed that even where serfdom was prominent – on the large, classic manors held by high-status landlords – its practice was nothing like as strict as its theory would indicate. The case study of Codicote has confirmed these findings, by illustrating how the management of serfdom on a manor of one of the most bureaucratic and eminent landlords in England – the cellarer of St Albans abbey – was neither arbitrary nor uncertain. Custom; written precedents; and, to some extent, market forces all influenced the way it was implemented. The relative weakness of serfdom in the early fourteenth century helps to explain why, in the wake of the Black Death in 1348–49, a narrowly based seigniorial reaction in the 1350s soon petered out, and why, by the 1370s, serfdom was in headlong retreat. In this chapter I consider the fortunes of a second manor on the same estate to establish the typicality of Codicote's experience.

Winslow

The manor of Winslow was part of King Offa's original endowment of St Albans abbey in 792, and was a very large manor containing over 4,000 acres extending across the settlements of Winslow, Little Horwood, Granborough and Shipton in northern Buckinghamshire.[1] By the early fourteenth century it had been assigned to the cellarer of the abbey, who maintained a manorial complex at Biggin (between Winslow and Granborough), where the manorial court was held. The manor was routinely leased in its entirety to a succession of unknown lessees throughout the fourteenth and fifteenth centuries, generating £66 per annum during the first quarter of the fourteenth century, although the cellarer continued to run its court directly through his nominated officials.[2] There are 101 extant court sessions between 1327 and 1377, and a further forty-six between 1423 and 1460, with the sessions usually being held twice a year.[3] As at Codicote, these are extracts of matters of particular interest to the lord copied into a court book.

Serfdom in the pre-plague era

The manor contained small amounts of freehold land and large tracts of servile land, although their exact acreages are unknown. Some freemen held villein land.[4] The villein land had been originally organised into virgates, half-virgates and quarter-virgates (known as 'fertlingates'), although in the absence of any surviving surveys or accounts their exact number and even their precise area is unknown. Reconstructions from miscellaneous information recorded in the court books indicate that a customary virgate at Winslow contained around 36 acres.[5] Many cottages and smallholdings were also held on villein tenure. The package of rent attached to each standardised holding cannot be ascertained, because no surveys or accounts have survived, but the court rolls confirm that customary land was routinely liable for a wide range of dues, including labour services, merchet, mill suit, heriot, recognition, a fixed annual cash rent and an entry fine (see Table 9.1). The Hundred Rolls of 1279 indicate that the cash rent and labour services due annually from a servile virgate on this manor were valued at 10s. 3d. per annum at Little Horwood, 7s. 1d. at Winslow and 4s. 7d. at Shipton;[6] put another way, the fixed head rent varied from 1.5d. per acre to 3.5d. per acre on the main villein arable holdings.[7]

On the eve of the Black Death almost all servile land at Winslow was held on a heritable service tenure, with the eldest male inheriting at twenty years of age or, in the absence of a male heir, the eldest girl at sixteen.[8] Life tenancies were rare, representing less than 1 per cent of all transfers (Tables 9.2 and 9.3). On the rare occasions when heirs were not forthcoming, manorial officials observed the custom of a formal proclamation at three successive court sessions

Table 9.1 Last recorded dates of key incidents of villeinage at Winslow manor, 1327–1460

Chevage	Presentedfor absence	Leyrwite	Heriot	Merchet	Mill suit	Recognition	Tallage	Licence to educate
1439	1455	1377	1460	1451	1373	1350	None	1431

Sources: Noy, *The Winslow Manor Court Books, 1322–1377*; Noy, *The Winslow Manor Court Books, 1423–1460.*

Table 9.2 Total number of customary land transactions at Winslow manor, 1330–1459

Decade	Direct inter-peasant transfers	Licences for tenants to sublet	Grants from lord	Total transactions	No. of all transactions on life tenancies[a]
1330–39	254	31	17	302	1
1340–48	305	63	21	389	4
1349	157	2	2	161	0
1350–59	204	39	41	284	4
1360–69	252	18	34	304	4
1370–77	165	5	17	187	1
1423–29	131	0	10	141	0
1430–39	180	0	7	187	0
1440–49	128	2	8	138	1
1450–59	169	0	9	178	1

[a] *Excluding reversionary interest of widows and licences to sublet.*

Sources: Noy, *The Winslow Manor Court Books, 1322–1377*; Noy, *The Winslow Manor Court Books, 1423–1460.*

for the heir to appear before offering the property to someone else.[9] When John Ponteys had not returned from pilgrimage as promised by October 1337, his land was granted to his nearest heir, although the court noted that John's rights would be respected if he ever returned.[10] The lord only seized villein land following specified breaches in the terms of the tenancy, such as removing servile goods out of the Liberty of St Albans or serious wastage of buildings and rent arrears. In 1347 the court noted formally that a tenant in rent arrears would initially be subject to distraint of goods rather than an immediate seizure of the holding.[11] Deathbed transfers were not utilised until the 1420s, but thereafter became common practice.[12] Outsiders marrying heiresses of villein land in Winslow rendered a small fine (usually 12d.) to do so and were required to find pledges that they would not remove chattels from villein land.[13]

The formula of conveyance was expressed in a standard format with little variation from one transfer to another. In the late 1320s a villein tenant was said to hold 'for him and his heirs through due and accustomed services [*per servicia debita et consueta*]'.[14] In 1329 the phrase 'in villeinage' was first added to one transaction, and from then on became increasingly common, so that by 1335 it was routinely used in the standard form of conveyance.[15] In the May court of 1338 the phrase 'at the will of the lord' was also added to a number of conveyances for the first time, and by the late 1340s it, too, had become a standard feature.[16] Thus, by 1348 the standard formula was 'to hold for himself and his heirs in villeinage and at the lord's will through due and accustomed services', a comprehensive phrase establishing the land's unfree status beyond any doubt. Small numbers of grants of land on hereditary money tenure are recorded in the 1330s and 1340s, mainly involving grants direct from the lord (Tables 9.3 and 9.4), and grants for the life of a tenant were also recorded very occasionally.[17]

The early-fourteenth-century court rolls show that many of the standardised customary holdings had suffered some subdivision,

Table 9.3 Breakdown of all inter-peasant transfers of customary land at Winslow manor, 1330–1459

Decade	No. of grants	Hereditary for services	Hereditary for money	Licence to sublet	Life for services
1330–39	285	254	0	31	0
1340–48	368	299	2	63	4
1350–59	243	201	0	39	3
1360–69	270	249	0	18	3
1370–77	170	165	0	5	0
1423–29	131	131	0	0	0
1430–39	180	173	7	0	0
1440–49	130	92	35	2	1
1450–59	169	101	68	0	0

Sources: Noy, *The Winslow Manor Court Books, 1322–1377*; Noy, *The Winslow Manor Court Books, 1423–1460.*

Table 9.4 Breakdown of all direct grants of customary land from the lord at Winslow manor, 1330–1459

Decade	No. of grants	Hereditary for services	Hereditary for money	Until heir comes of age for services	Until heir comes of age for cash	Life for services	Life for cash	For term of years
1330–39	17	7	5	4	0	1	0	0
1340–48	21	10	9	2	0	0	0	0
1350–59	41	30	5	5	0	1	0	0
1360–69	34	26	0	4	2	1	0	1
1370–77	17	7	0	1	0	0	1	8
1423–29	10	4	2	1	0	0	0	3
1430–39	7	5	2	0	0	0	0	0
1440–49	8	3	2	0	0	0	0	3
1450–59	9	2	5	0	0	1	0	1

Sources: Noy, *The Winslow Manor Court Books, 1322–1377*; Noy, *The Winslow Manor Court Books, 1423–1460*.

such as a half-virgate in 1343 that had been split among at least six different tenants.[18] The partial fragmentation of some of the standardised holdings was the consequence of a market in customary land, in which permanent sales of small parcels of land were relatively commonplace: on average there were over thirty transfers of villein land each year (Table 9.2) – more than Codicote and Norton, but less than the number recorded annually on smaller East Anglian manors such as Coltishall and Redgrave.[19] Likewise, the degree of subdivision was not as advanced as on many East Anglian manors, which helps to explain why episodes of dearth did not trigger hair-sensitive distress sales of small slivers of land at Winslow. For example, in 1328 drought badly affected grain production in many areas of Buckinghamshire and caused higher death rates than normal among villein tenants at Winslow, but there were few survival sales of land.[20]

Maintaining a record of these transactions and charging an entry fine for admission were a major preoccupation of the court. The price actually paid for the land is recorded on just two occasions: in 1342 one purchaser paid 4s. 5d. per acre and in 1345 another paid 37s. 4d. per acre, compared with the average entry fine of 28d. in the pre-plague era.[21] Temporary subletting added to the process of fragmentation: tenants could sublet on condition that they obtained a formal licence to do so and recorded the length of the sublease and the name of the sublessee in the court rolls.[22] The most common format was for a term of stipulated years, although occasionally a sublease was made for the term of the life of the tenant.[23] The lord granted an average of over forty licences to sublet per decade in the pre-plague era (Table 9.2), so the scale of this activity was greater than at Codicote.

Presentment juries dominated by villein tenants brought most of the business to court. The court held these jurors to account, judging by occasional fines for concealing information.[24] Inquisition juries pronounced on specific disputes, as when John le Spicer paid 12d. in 1342 to have a jury consider whether he was 'not in his right mind' when he had sold a messuage and 12 acres to another resident: the jury laconically determined that John was as much in his right mind at the time of the sale 'as at any time before or after'.[25] The presentment jury could also arbitrate or rule on disputes over rent levels and rent arrears between the head tenant and the sublessee.[26] The process of consulting the manorial court rolls to prove a claim to title, and/or to verify the exact terms on which customary land was held, was already well established, underling the importance of having a written record of such transactions.[27] In some cases, the tenant also acquired their own written copy of the court roll entry, such as when Alice, widow of John Leicester, 'showed copies of the rolls through which she was joint tenant' of a piece of land, whilst another court session established that Anabilia Harry was the heir to a cottage and a croft 'as is set out in a copy made from the rolls of the court held in the Michaelmas term of the twelfth year of the reign of Edward son of Edward' (1318–19).[28] This is consistent with Levett's view that the use of copies was already well established on the St Albans estate in the early fourteenth century, and underlines their importance in proving titles to land.[29] The lord accepted a claim to land if it was appropriately documented, as in 1341 when the record of the court rolls was used to overturn an earlier judgment of the jurors in a complex case involving a widow's right to land.[30] Villeins might also call for 'the record of the rolls' to support claims that they had, for example, paid an entry fine for land or even a marriage licence, to which the court's response was to set a date for the tenant to produce the appropriate written evidence.[31]

One other tenurial development is worthy of note. In a short burst in the 1340s the lord permanently alienated nearly 250 acres of the demesne arable in various parcels on hereditary monetary tenure, rather than following the more conventional practice of making temporary grants on leasehold terms. For example, in May 1344 the lord granted Hugh Rolf and his heirs 7 roods of demesne land to create a new dwelling, plus another 40 acres of demesne arable, to be held in villeinage for a cash rent in lieu of all servile incidents, except heriot and suit of court.[32] A stream of grants occurred in the courts of October 1345, when fifteen parcels of demesne land totalling at least 29 acres were transferred to tenants, and also in April 1347, when more than fifty grants were made totalling at least 226 acres.[33] Most grants were of arable land at around 6d. per acre per annum, compared with the 3.5d. per acre paid as the ossified rent on the traditional villein virgates.[34] The standard formula of conveyance was 'to him and his heirs in villeinage by the rod at the lord's will paying for it annually [*x*]d'.[35] These represent permanent transfers of demesne land into the customary land sector for cash rents, i.e. without labour services or renders in kind, presumably because pressure and demand for land were high and reserves of colonisable land were now exhausted.[36]

A market charter had been obtained for Winslow in 1235, and by 1279 a small borough was established, with ten burgess plots each paying 3s. in rent for their land on the east side of the High Street: the borough was unsuccessful, though the weekly market continued. Most of the land and cottages surrounding the market-place, including shops and stalls, were held on villein tenure, as also was the smithy.[37]

The Black Death and its immediate aftermath

The Black Death had not struck Winslow by the time of the court held in October 1348, judging by the absence of deaths of villein tenants, but courts held in the following April and October record a grand total of 165 tenant deaths.[38] Hence, the epidemic was already raging at Winslow in mid-April 1349 and probably petered out during the early summer: on much of the St Albans estate – located to the south nearer to London – it was most active between February and May 1349.[39] The death rate was around one-half, given a combined total of around 350 named villein tenants in the court rolls of the 1330s and 1340s. The court entries provide partial insights into the tragedies suffered by many families. The Couherd family comprised John; his wife, Agnes; their son, John, aged three; and their daughter, Alice, aged four: both males had died by the April court but mother and daughter survived.[40] Juliana Henry lost her father in April 1349 and became heir to his villein land at nine years of age. She was finally admitted to the holding when she came of age in 1356 and immediately paid a licence to marry.[41]

Later epidemics also struck Winslow hard. Between May and November 1361 another thirty tenants died, and a further twelve between July and late December 1375. By contrast, the number of deaths in 1369 was not abnormal and so it is possible that the third great national plague outbreak bypassed this manor.[42] In these later epidemics, the season of death was more closely confined to the summer and early autumn, and levels of mortality were absolutely and proportionately lower than in 1349.

Despite the large number of *post mortem* surrenders of land in the spring and summer of 1349, only a handful of villein-holdings lay vacant in the early 1350s.[43] In two cases officials attempted to compel the uptake of land. First, in October 1349 the villeins of Little Horwood were given until November to find tenants for 'the lands and holdings which are in the lord's hands', although at the next court the matter was not mentioned and there were no seigniorial grants.[44] The second case looks more like an example of community care than seigniorial imposition: when Geoffrey Terry died leaving a messuage, virgate and 4 acres of land, his heir – the two-year-old John Terry, who was presumably orphaned – and the land were entrusted to 'all the villeins of [Little] Horwood'.[45] Other than these two cases, there was no seigniorial compulsion to occupy customary land, and the overwhelming majority of vacated land was reoccupied quickly either by its heirs or by willing new tenants.[46]

What explains this rapid and full uptake? The main reason must be the pre-existing heavy fragmentation of villein-holdings and the associated ready availability of small parcels of arable, which greatly facilitated the ability of the landless and land-deficient to step onto or climb the property ladder. However, the readiness of manorial administrators to waive entry fines where necessary was also an important factor, including the tactic of combining some entry fines with marriage fines to enable survivors who were newly acquiring land to establish a marital household.[47] For example, John Haukyn died holding 6 roods of land and had been too poor even to render a heriot, but in 1349 his heir, Walter Wilkyn, paid 3s. 4d. as both an entry fine and for permission to marry.[48] The reoccupation of holdings was further aided by the reduction in the level of entry fines on those occasions when a fine was paid: the mean entry fine per acre was 44 per cent lower in 1350–69 than it had been in 1330–48 (Table 9.5). A spike in marriages in 1349–50 is also striking.[49]

The high mortalities in 1349 and 1361 also left some heirs orphaned and sbelow the age of majority. The lord's principal solution was to grant the land to a third party until the rightful heir came of age, effectively as a lease for a term of years. For example, in 1364, 21 acres lying abandoned in Shipton were granted to William Robins 'in villeinage paying the lord 6s. 8d. annually' until the heir, Margaret Watkyns, came of age.[50] In the 1350s and 1360s

Table 9.5 Entry fines per acre for customary arable land at Winslow manor, 1327–1459

Decade	No. of transactions providing data	Entry fine per acre
1327–29	24	20.2d.
1330–39	138	33.3d.
1340–48	122	23.3d.
1350–59	67	15.4d.
1360–69	98	16.2d.
1370–77	66	17.9d.
1423–29	46	13.9d.
1430–39	70	10.1d.
1440–49	40	5.2d.
1450–59	83	6.0d.

Sources: Noy, *The Winslow Manor Court Books, 1322–1377*; Noy, *The Winslow Manor Court Books, 1423–1460.*

a total of eleven such grants were made, nine for services and two for cash (Table 9.4).

In the aftermath of plague the stock of buildings in Winslow suddenly exceeded its supply, judging by a sudden rise in the early 1350s of court orders for various dilapidated buildings to be restored.[51] In 1351 the court ordered the seizure of Robert William's land as a punishment for his having levelled three houses.[52] Another spate of presentments for allowing housing to fall down followed between 1355 and 1357, and occasionally a villein paid either 12d. or 2s. to be discharged from the responsibility to repair.[53] Most were threatened with a penalty of either 3s. 4d., such as seven tenants in January 1355, or 6s. 8d., as were four tenants in 1357, if they failed to repair by the next court: and in June 1355 five of the seven tenants did indeed incur the 3s. 4d. penalty and were threatened with further penalties of 6s. 8d.[54] In the vast majority of cases, however, the court opted to collect small amercements of a few pence rather than impose the heavy penalties, such as in the case of the three tenants who were amerced a total of 15d. in January

1355.[55] Furthermore, the number and frequency of amercements soon fell: for example, in 1369–70 there were just three presentments for wasting villein-holdings, with punishments ranging from 6d. to 2s.[56]

The high frequency of the subletting of customary land at Winslow in the pre-plague era continued into the 1350s, when thirty-nine such licences were recorded. Yet a succession of court orders is suggestive of some administrative uncertainties and a seigniorial concern that some subletting by the new tenants might have passed unrecorded. In May 1353 the court made a series of orders to prohibit the illegal subletting of customary land and to reaffirm the proper procedures for transfers.[57] These were followed in May 1354 by a crackdown on unrecorded subletting, which in turn triggered a dispute over the established custom. In January 1355 the jurors in the manorial court stated that servile land could be sublet for short periods of under two years without the need for seigniorial permission 'according to their ancient custom': indeed, in 1344 this custom had been recorded in the court rolls without challenge.[58] In 1355, however, the same 'new order' imposed at Codicote was introduced to Winslow, namely that in future, sublets of less than two years had to be recorded in the rolls, though no licence was payable, and failure to record would attract a 6s. 8d. penalty and possible seizure of the land.[59] As at Codicote, this is unequivocal evidence of a lord manipulating custom, although not for any financial benefit.

Villein tenures

The servile land market absorbed the shock of the epidemics in 1349 and 1361 relatively well. In the 1350s and 1360s the aggregate volume of land transactions was only around 20 per cent lower than in the 1330s and 1340s (Table 9.2), and transfers directly from one tenant to another still dominated (88 per cent). There was a slight rise in the proportion of transfers granted from the lord (from 5 per cent in the 1340s to 14 per cent in the 1350s; Table 9.2), a consequence of more land remaining in the lord's hands until the nearest heir or a new tenant could be found in the aftermath of plague. The vast majority of customary land continued to be held on hereditary service tenure, with few conversions to leasehold, life or money tenures. In the 1350s and 1360s three-quarters of grants directly from the lord were still on hereditary service tenure (Table 9.4). Hence, fixed-term and monetarised tenures made little headway in the generation after the Black Death. Life grants scarcely featured,[60] and leases for a term were unknown before the 1360s.[61] Nor did the language of conveyance of hereditary service tenure change immediately after the Black Death.

Nevertheless, despite this appearance of continuity, four broad changes to the operation of the customary land market are observable in the immediate post-plague era. First, from the 1360s the volume of inter-peasant subletting halved from its pre-plague level and never recovered: most peasants who desired land were now able to obtain permanent grants directly without the need to enter the temporary and more expensive subletting market. The estate-wide imposition in 1355 of registering all short-term subleases was soon irrelevant.[62] Second, the value of entry fines per acre fell by 44 per cent, from an average of 28d. per acre in 1330–49 to 15.5d. in 1350–69 (Table 9.5). Both these changes are clear signs that the pre-plague conditions of land shortage had largely disappeared.

The near halving of the level of entry fine exemplifies the third area of change: the rapid dilution of many elements of the rent package of service tenure. After 1350 recognition payments lapsed (Table 9.1). The number of amercements for breach of mill suit rose in the 1350s (Table 9.6), but then dropped markedly in the 1360s and the last evasion was recorded in 1373 (Table 9.1). After 1349 merchet ceased to be an obligation of tenants of servile land (see p. 330). The relative absence of presentments for failure to perform labour services (Table 9.13) is suggestive of a high level of annual commutations, and from 1370 all boon-works were commuted through a collective agreement with the villein tenants for an initial period of twenty-one years (see pp. 326, 330). Finally, after 1349 the practice of charging a small fine to outsiders who became villein tenants through marriage, and binding them not to remove servile goods from the Liberty, disappeared entirely.

Conversions of servile land to leases for a fixed term were unknown before the 1360s (Table 9.4), although leases of demesne land for a term were common enough.[63] The number of leases of villein land peaked at eight in the 1370s (Table 9.4), and thereafter they were rare. The standard format of a lease was unusual here, too, because the words normally associated with leasehold – *dimitto* and *firma* – were not used, and instead the tenant 'holds for himself in villeinage for the term of the next [*x*] years paying to the lord for it [*y*]d. per annum for all services on the four quarter days'.[64] Entry fines were not charged on any of the Winslow leases.[65] The few leases granted at Winslow were usually deployed as a temporary measure in order to find a tenant for abandoned servile land, i.e. when no one could initially be found to hold land on service tenure.[66]

When the court roll series begins again in 1423 neither leases nor money tenures have made much headway, and hereditary service tenure continues to dominate. Of a total of 141 transfers of servile land between 1423 and 1429, 131 had been on this form of tenure (Tables 9.2 and 9.3). The language of conveyance remained

Table 9.6 Frequency of merchet, leyrwite and mill suit at Winslow manor, 1325–1459

Period	Merchet	Leyrwite	Mill suit
1320–29	18	2	2
1330–39	46	25	7
1340–49	73	15	42
1350–59	31	2	39
1360–69	33	2	7
1370–79	21	2	2
1420–29	8	0	0
1430–39	8	0	0
1440–49	0	0	0
1450–59	1	0	0
1460–69	0	0	0

Merchet and leyrwite fines only (including if waived); mill suit includes fines and presentments.

Sources: Noy, *The Winslow Manor Court Books, 1322–1377*; Noy, *The Winslow Manor Court Books, 1423–1460.*

unchanged from the 1370s. The main changes in the intervening period were the downward trend in the volume of transactions and in the mean rate of entry fine, both of which had fallen by around 20 per cent (Tables 9.2 and 9.5). Occupation of customary land remained relatively high, in the sense that tenants routinely came forward to be admitted into inheritances or to acquire land through *inter vivos* transactions.

The 1430s and 1440s were a period of volatility and change in the Winslow customary land market. On the one hand, the mean entry fine remained constant in the 1420s and 1430s at around 14d. per acre, but collapsed to 5d. per acre in the 1440s and stayed at that level in the 1450s (Table 9.5). On the other hand, the total number of land transactions jumped from 141 in the 1420s to 187 in the 1430s, then fell back to its old level in the 1440s (Table 9.2). This behaviour was a consequence of the distress caused by extreme weather conditions in the 1430s and the onset of a wider economic depression in the following decade. Entry fines and heriots were increasingly waived, both of which reflected the difficulties of finding tenants.[67] These decades also saw the first significant shift from hereditary service to hereditary money tenure. In the 1420s less than 1 per cent of 141 customary land transactions were on hereditary monetary tenure, yet by the 1450s this had risen to 41 per cent of all transactions (Tables 9.2–9.4). The money tenure was held for a straight cash rent, heriot, entry fine and suit of court, with liability for labour services, recognition, mill suit, manorial office and merchet permanently removed. The difference from the service tenure was expressed in the vocabulary of the conveyance: that for hereditary service tenure was 'to hold for him and his heirs in villeinage at the will of the lord through due and accustomed services', but for the new money tenure it was 'to hold for him and his heirs by the rod according to the custom of the manor for the service of paying to the lord annually [*x*]d. for all services except suit of court'.[68] Hence hereditary cash tenures were also associated with the introduction of the phrase 'according to the custom of the manor' into the conveyance.[69] These were effectively copyholds by inheritance.

It was the tenants rather than the lord who were driving this rapid tenurial change. During the 1430s and early 1440s a few transfers from one tenant to another involved a conversion from service to money tenure.[70] From the late 1440s, however, many tenants increasingly surrendered land held on service tenure to their lord, and the lord immediately regranted it to the same tenants as a monetary tenure. This was a deliberate and coordinated process. The court of May 1448 was exceptionally long, as a succession of virgaters and half-virgaters relinquished their land on service tenure before being readmitted to their holdings for a money rent.[71] As a consequence, when the Winslow court roll series ceases in 1460, monetary tenure was now rivalling hereditary service tenure as the dominant tenurial form. The timing of these conversions coincides closely with the collapse in the rate of entry fines and the onset of a sustained depression in the land market. Presumably, then, the tenants were levering their strengthened position to convert to a money tenure, which permanently removed any liability for labour services.

Another tenurial development of note in the depressed conditions of the 1440s was a second batch of permanent alienations of demesne land on hereditary money tenure, following the first batch in the 1340s.[72] Between 1446 and 1459 thirteen new grants of demesne land totalling at least 42 acres were made on hereditary cash rents.[73] In addition, a number of parcels of demesne land, initially leased for a term of years, were converted upon their expiry to a hereditary money tenure. For example, in April 1442 Robert Janyn had leased 6 acres of demesne for 20d. per annum for twenty years, but in 1451 he decided to relinquish the lease. The parcel was immediately granted to Robert Myller 'for him and his heirs' for the same straight cash rent and a entry fine of 4s.[74] Between 1453 and 1459 nine conversions of fixed-term leases to, or direct grants of demesne land on, hereditary tenures held 'according to the custom of the manor' are recorded. In two of these cases entry fines were not imposed, but the scribe was careful to note the potential liability of the land to fine in the future. Such changes constituted a seigniorial concession brought about by the depressed fifteenth-century customary land market.

Thus, in two short bursts in the 1340s and the 1450s a minimum of 340 acres of demesne land had been converted to hereditary money tenures and was now held in villeinage for a cash rent, a heriot, entry fine and suit of court. These were permanent alienations, and therefore only a failure of heirs would enable the lord to recover the land and reabsorb it into the demesne. Around 70 per cent of these conversions had occurred in the 1340s, when pressure for landholding at Winslow was very high, with the remainder dating to the 1440s and 1450s, when the land market was at its lowest. In other words, opposite extremes in the land market provoked the same response from the lord. Brenner once argued that English landlords responded to the depressed land market of the fifteenth century by absorbing customary land into the demesne sector, but the cellarer of St Albans did the opposite and switched demesne land into the customary sector.[75]

Variable incidents

No custumal for Winslow has survived, but the heavy burden of week and seasonal boon-works on the standardised holdings, as revealed in that for Codicote in 1338, was probably also typical of the arrangements at Winslow.[76] Similarly, in the absence of a set of manorial accounts, it is impossible to know what proportion of labour services was actually performed and how much had been commuted over time. The likelihood is that many labour services were commuted, given that the manor was routinely leased in the fourteenth century and that in the 1340s a sizeable chunk of the demesne had been converted to villein tenure. A few services were still demanded, judging by the record of failures to perform them, although these were small scale and infrequent (Table 9.13). As we have seen, in 1370 all boon-works were commuted for cash for a term of twenty-one years through a collective agreement, although thereafter a few haymaking services were still performed.[77]

Heriot was liable either on the death of a tenant or whenever a tenant ceased to hold any customary land from the manor.[78] In addition, in the pre-plague era some serfs who were personally unfree but did not hold land were required to render heriot after their death: five such heriots were paid between 1330 and 1348.[79] For example, John Clerk died landless in 1347, but his estate nonetheless rendered a brass pot worth 16d. as a heriot, whilst in the same year the family of the landless Alice Combe paid a ewe worth 8d.: her father questioned whether she was liable for heriot, given that *he* was still alive and a landholder, but the court confirmed that she was liable after her premature death.[80] The last recorded case of the estate of a landless serf rendering heriot *post mortem* occurred in 1355, so this was another practice abandoned soon after the plague.[81]

The best beast of the outgoing tenant was the usual render for heriot, although those without animals were required to hand over some other goods instead, which in practice might be a brass pot, a tunic, a chest, an axe, a goose, a box, a dish or a cash sum.[82] The practice of rendering goods declined over time, so that fifteenth-century heriots mainly took the form of beasts or, increasingly, of cash. The lord occasionally waived heriot because of poverty, or because the deceased did not have any goods within the manor, but otherwise it was routinely enforced.[83] Indeed, a tenant who died in possession of multiple holdings was liable for a heriot on each of them, as in April 1345 when Richard of Chersdale was liable for three heriots for his three unfree holdings.[84] The East Anglian custom of waiving heriot when the incoming tenant was a direct heir and paid an entry fine did not apply, although in exceptional circumstances the lord permitted a heriot payment to be wrapped up with the fine.[85]

Table 9.7 Frequency of heriot at Winslow manor, 1330–1460

Period	No. of heriots[a]	No. of heriots on *inter vivos* transfers	Proportion of *inter vivos* heriots
1330–39	45	0	0%
1340–48	68	6	9%
1349	165	14	8%
1350–59	48	16	33%
1360–69	76	34	45%
1370–79	47	23	49%
1423–29	29	15	52%
1430–39	57	35	61%
1440–49	38	20	53%
1450–59	23	17	74%

[a] *Includes heriots recorded but waived through poverty.*

Sources: Noy, *The Winslow Manor Court Books, 1322–1377*; Noy, *The Winslow Manor Court Books, 1423–1460.*

The frequency of heriots was marginally higher in the 1360s and 1370s (average of sixty-one per decade; Table 9.7) than it had been in the 1330s and 1340s (fifty-six). The rise was partly due to the deaths of tenants in the epidemics of 1361 and 1375–76, but also to a significant rise in the proportion of heriots rendered because a tenant ceased to hold customary land from the manor. Between the 1340s and the 1370s the proportion of heriots levied on *inter vivos*, rather than *post mortem*, transfers rose from 9 per cent to 49 per cent (Table 9.7). Thus, after the second plague epidemic a higher proportion of servile tenants in Winslow were now offloading all their villein land, presumably to move or work elsewhere. In this circumstance, heriot could be avoided by retaining a sliver of land. In 1352 Walter le Western surrendered a messuage and a virgate of land, but retained 2 roods of the virgate, which meant that no heriot was liable because, as the court explained, 'he still holds the said half acre, since by the custom of the manor of Winslow he need not pay heriot while he holds any [customary] land'.[86] Thereafter, other tenants also deployed this practice occasionally.[87]

In the fifteenth century, the frequency of heriot was around a third lower than it had been in the third quarter of the fourteenth century.[88] One reason was the slowing of the land market, since there were now fewer tenants and transfers, but another was the increasing willingness of the lord to waive heriot entirely, or simply to ignore non-payment following the death of a tenant even when it was due and the tenant was capable of paying.[89] Prospective tenants had to be incentivised in this slack land market.

Mill suit was keenly enforced in the 1340s and 1350s at around forty recorded transgressions per decade (Table 9.8), but enforcement then collapsed in the 1360s (seven) and the last breach was recorded in 1373 (Table 9.1). The mean amercement was 2.4d. in the 1340s, 3d. in the 1350s, then 2d. in the 1360s.

Annual tallage is not recorded in the court rolls, although recognition was due from villein tenants, and presumably from serfs by blood, on the election of a new abbot. In May 1350, £13 6s. 8d. was paid as recognition from 'all the villeins of Winslow, Shipton, Horwood and Granborough' on the election of Thomas de la Mare.[90] It is not possible to calculate a mean charge per head. De la Mare died in 1396, but there is no subsequent record of the collection of tallage.[91]

Table 9.8 Incidence of mill suit, and mean size of levy, at Winslow manor, 1327–1459

Period	No. of cases of mill suit	Mean amercement
1327–29	2	3.5d.
1330–39	7	2.0d.
1340–49	42	2.4d.
1350–59	39	3.0d.
1360–69	7	2.1d.
1370–79	2	2.0d.
1420–29	0	—
1430–39	0	—
1440–49	0	—
1450–59	0	—
1460–69	0	—

Sources: Noy, *The Winslow Manor Court Books, 1322–1377*; Noy, *The Winslow Manor Court Books, 1423–1460.*

Entry fines were payable on the transfer of servile land, although the rate was variable according to circumstances: on the one hand, transfers to non-heirs attracted higher rates whereas, on the other, new tenants might pay a lower sum on the grounds of poverty. The high volume of transfers of small parcels of arable land provides a large sample for calculating the mean rate per acre. Before the plague, the mean fine was high, being around 28d. in the 1330s and 1340s, but then nearly halved (15.4d.) in the 1350s, recovered slightly in the 1370s (17.9d.), before collapsing to 5d. per acre in the mid-fifteenth century (Table 9.5). The probable hiking of entry fines in the mid-1330s to raise funds for a newly elected abbot, which Slota identified at Codicote (see p. 291), was not evident at Winslow, where instead the rate of entry fine actually fell slightly. The number of land transfers from which to obtain data is higher than for Codicote, and the mean fine in was 32.6d. per acre in 1334 (nine data points at Winslow, 2 at Codicote), 32.3d. in 1335 (16) and 29.9d. in 1336 (34).[92] The sale price of villein land was not normally recorded in the courts, although in 1453 a 12-ascre holding exchanged hands for £9 6s. 8d. and the incoming tenant paid a 13s. 4d. entry fine, or around 7 per cent of the value.[93]

Both males and females were liable for merchet at Winslow, and in 1327–48 the average fine was 31d. (Table 9.9).[94] Before the Black Death merchet was payable not only by hereditary serfs but also by the holders of villein land, even when, as was sometimes the case, they were personally free.[95] After 1349 there are, however, no explicit cases of merchet being charged as a condition of tenure. Between 1330–49 and 1350–69 the number of merchets fell by 46 per cent, the total income they generated fell from 305s. to 149s., and their frequency fell a further 36 per cent in the 1370s.[96] The average fine held steady, at 29d. in 1350–69, then rose in the 1370s to 41d. The mean fine for merchet was lower than the mean fine for illegal marriages, which is suggestive of an incentive to obtain a licence proactively in order to marry.[97] The number of merchets

Table 9.9 Incidence of merchet, and mean size of levy, at Winslow manor, 1327–1459

Period	No. of merchets	Mean levy
1327–29	5	25d.
1330–39	46	49d.
1340–49	73	20d.
1350–59	31	37d.
1360–69	33	21d.
1370–79	21	41d.
1420–29	8	24d.
1430–39	8	30d.
1440–49	0	—
1450–59	1	12d.
1460–69	0	—

Excludes combined marriage and entry fines, and illegal marriages.

Sources: Noy, *The Winslow Manor Court Books, 1322–1377*; Noy, *The Winslow Manor Court Books, 1423–1460.*

levied in the 1420s was one-quarter that of the 1370s, when male merchets were now rare. The last female merchet was recorded in 1451 (Tables 9.1 and 9.9).

There were around ten cases of leyrwite per decade in the pre-plague era at an average fine of 6d. In the 1350s only two cases were recorded, albeit yielding a greatly increased mean fine of 23d. The last case was recorded in 1377 (Tables 9.1 and 9.8). Licences to educate servile sons were more enduring. The number each decade varied widely, peaking at thirteen in the 1340s, and the average fine rose from 16d. in the 1340s to 26d. in the 1370s, before dropping to 12d. in the 1420s (Table 9.10).[98] The last recorded licence was in 1431 (Table 9.1).

Only two cases of chevage are recorded before the Black Death and in both the serf paid an unspecified fine to be absent, plus a nominal annual payment. In 1346 John Punteys paid a fine and one capon per annum for chevage 'on condition he does not become a freeman of any community without fine from the abbot'.[99] Likewise, there was merely one presentment for absence (Table 9.11). After 1349 this changed rapidly, which indicates the cellarer's heightened concern about serf migration. This increased interest did not, however, generate a commensurate rise in chevage payments, because just three are recorded in the entire period between 1350 and 1374, although the level of the fine rose from an average of 3.5d. to 15.3d. (Table 9.11).[100] Hence, there were 0.07 cases of chevage and presentments for absence per court in 1327–48, yet 5.56 in 1350–77.[101] In the fifteenth century there was seldom more than one chevage case per annum, and the fine had fallen to c. 9d. (Tables 9.11 and 9.12). The last chevage payment was received in 1439 (Table 9.12), and the last recorded presentment for absence was in 1455 (Table 9.1).

Attitudes to serfdom

In the 1350s the cellarer diluted many of the incidents of villein tenure at Winslow, while simultaneously clamping down on the subletting of land and wasting of buildings. The estate-wide requirement in 1355 that all short-term subleases should be recorded in the court rolls was largely irrelevant, given the shrinkage in the number of licensed sublets from the 1350s. The action against dilapidated buildings (see pp. 320–1) involved a sharp increase in the number of presentments and the threat of sizeable penalties for non-compliance in the early-to-mid 1350s. In the majority of cases, however, these penalties were not imposed, and instead small amercements of a few pennies were collected. The number of presentments fell in the 1360s.

The cellarer's generally concessionary attitude to tenurial villeinage in the 1350s contrasted with a raft of aggressive policies towards hereditary serfs in that decade. Although the number of merchets halved between the 1340s and 1350s, the size of the average fine doubled (Table 9.9).[102] The number of reported evasions of marriage rose to a peak in the 1350s (twenty-two in that decade, compared with thirteen in the 1340s), although they fell markedly

Table 9.10 Incidence of leyrwite, licences to educate and mean size of levy, at Winslow manor, 1327–1459

Period	No. of leyrwite	Mean fine	No. of licences to educate	Mean fine
1327–29	2	6d.	0	—
1330–39	25	9d.	2[a]	3d.
1340–49	15	4d.	13[a]	16d.
1350–59	2	23d.	1	3d.
1360–69	1[a]	2d.	4	21d.
1370–79	2[b]	6d.	2	26d.
1420–29	0	—	1	12d.
1430–39	0	—	0	—
1440–49	0	—	0	—
1450–59	0	—	0	—
1460–69	0	—	0	—

[a] *Includes presentment.*
[b] Excludes one case where leyrwite combined with marriage fine.

Sources: Noy, *The Winslow Manor Court Books, 1322–1377*; Noy, *The Winslow Manor Court Books, 1423–1460.*

in the 1360s (ten) and 1370s (one). The fine for leyrwite increased nearly sixfold between the 1340s and the 1350s, although by the 1360s it was back below its pre-plage mean (Table 9.10). The mean fine rendered for chevage was well above its pre-plague norm, rising from a couple of pennies to 15d. (Table 9.11). Finally, in the 1360s and 1370s licences to educate servile sons were around one-half higher than they had been in the 1340s (Table 9.10). The number of reported evasions of marriage rose to a peak in the 1350s (twenty-two in that decade, compared with thirteen in the 1340s) before falling markedly in the 1360s (ten) and 1370s (one).[103]

The principal focus of this 'seigniorial reaction' in the 1350s was the tighter management of the movement of hereditary serfs. A single presentment for absence had been recorded in the period 1327–49, then a grand total of 215 cases in 1350–75 (Tables 9.11 and 9.12). The more assiduous recording of departures was, initially at least, backed by aggressive new tactics designed to enforce compliance. Two presentments for absence in the January court of 1351 were followed in June by the collective amercement of the villeins of Granborough for 40d. for their failure to prevent Richard Wattes

Table 9.11 Frequency of chevage and presentments for absence at Winslow manor, 1327–1460

Period	No. of annual presentments for absence	No. of chevage cases	Mean fine per case
1327–49	1	2	3.5d.[a]
1350–74	215	3	15.3d.
1375–77	15	0	—
1423–24	18	6	10.7d.
1425–49	126	15	8.5d.[a]
1450–60	1	0	—

[a] *One case required the render of one capon per annum, which has been allocated a monetary value of 6d.*

Sources: Noy, *The Winslow Manor Court Books, 1322–1377*; Noy, *The Winslow Manor Court Books, 1423–1460.*

Table 9.12 Recorded flight from Winslow manor, 1327–1457

Year	No. of people presented for absence	No. of people charged for chevage
1329	0	1
1346	1	1
1351	3	0
1352	8	0
1353	15[a]	0
1354	12	0
1355	20[a]	0
1356	24[a]	0
1357	19	0
1358	17	0
1359	20[a]	0
1360	20[a]	0
1361	3	1
1362	8	0
1363	10	0
1364	0	2
1365	10[a]	0
1366	6[a]	0
1367	4	0
1368	2	0
1369	2[a]	0
1370	4	0
1371	6	0
1372	0	0
1373	2	0
1374	0	0
1375	0	0

Year	No. of people presented for absence	No. of people charged for chevage
1376	7	0
1377	8	0
1423	9	3
1424	10	3
1425	10	2
1426	12	1
1427	13	1
1428	13	1
1429	9	1
1430	10	1
1431	9	1
1432	9[a]	1
1433	5	1
1434	6	1
1435	3	1
1436	6	1
1437	6	1
1438	5	0
1439	3	1
1440	3	0
1441	—	—
1442	0	0
1443	0	0
1444	2	0
1445	0	0
1446	1	0
1447	0	0
1448	0	0

(*continued*)

Table 9.12 (Cont.)

Year	No. of people presented for absence	No. of people charged for chevage
1449	1	0
1450	0	0
1451	0	0
1452	0	0
1453	0	0
1454	0	0
1455	1	0
1456	0	0
1457	0	0

[a] *In these years there were more presentments for absence than people presented for absence because some individuals were presented for absence twice within the calendar year.*

Sources: Noy, *The Winslow Manor Court Books, 1322–1377*; Noy, *The Winslow Manor Court Books, 1423–1460.*

from leaving with his chattels.[104] In May 1352 John Hausby was made to swear in full court that he would stay and serve within the manor, and the jurors of Little Horwood were amerced 2s. for concealing the names of flown serfs.[105] At the same court, all the goods and chattels of Nicholas Northburgh were ordered to be seized on account of his unlicensed absence in London.[106] Between 1352 and 1360 twelve marriage fines were coupled with an explicit instruction for the newlyweds to remain within the lordship, some being required to provide sureties of compliance.[107] In January 1355 officials made a strident order to all those attending the court to seize all fugitive serfs by body and deliver them to St Albans.[108] The attendees were unlikely to comply, of course, but the lord was making a point. The cumulative effect of all this heightened activity was to generate more information about absentees. Prior to 1349 the courts included hardly any information about either the location of migrants or flown women, but thereafter 45 per cent of all cases included the destination of the migrant serf and 15 per cent of all recorded servile migrants were women.[109]

On three occasions the abbey's officials did indeed seize and return emigrant serfs, all relating to members of the Adams family. William Adam was reported as absent in May 1352 and then, in the spring of 1353, he was seized and arrested by the abbot's servants in nearby Swanbourne and returned to Winslow. This triggered an immediate act of retaliation from one Richard le Barn, who travelled to Winslow and escorted William straight back to Swanbourne. The court noted how this audacious counterstroke contravened the 'will' of the abbey and its officials, but then sought advice from St Albans and advocated obtaining a royal writ (presumably *de native habendo*).[110] The response of the central officials is not recorded, but it was ineffective because William remained permanently absent from the manor over the next ten years, initially at nearby Swanbourne with Richard le Barn, then at Lee (Buckinghamshire), until 1365 when he was recorded as being somewhere in Kent.[111] William Adam's son, John, was also seized physically in 1353 by one Henry Boveton, who soon afterwards released John 'on his own initiative but against the will of the lord'. John never returned to Winslow, remaining at Swanbourne for at least the next decade. The third and final seizure occurred in 1355, when Walter Adam was 'attached and delivered to John Adam, who undertook to have him attend the next court'.[112] However, nothing more is recorded about him.[113]

The tighter management of serfs in the 1350s is evident in other ways. The jurors at the October court of 1349 confirmed that the wills of serfs and of villein tenants had to be 'proved before the cellarer' – i.e. registered in the manorial court of Winslow – whereas those of freemen were proved at the archdeaconry court of St Albans.[114] This proclamation of an established custom signalled a crackdown, because after 1349 servile wills are registered in the court rolls more frequently. The only recorded disputes over personal status also date from the 1350s. In the first case, in January 1352 an inquest jury confirmed Robert William and his family to be serfs.[115] In the second, John Albyn's audacious attempt to sue the abbot for damages in a royal court failed after an inquiry established that he was the abbot's serf.[116]

There is no evidence locally in the wake of the Statute of Labourers for wage capping, for forcing the able-bodied to work, or for the restriction of movement during harvest-time. There is just one example of enforced service, when in May 1352 William le Smyth was threatened with a 40s. fine if he refused to take on the forge and smithy in Winslow market in order 'to serve the community of the vill and others', and he duly arrived in late 1352 to establish his trade.[117]

Thus, there is ample evidence from the 1350s for the sudden introduction of novel and aggressive policies against hereditary serfs. However, the nature, scale and duration of this seigniorial reaction needs contextualising. First, its bark was rather worse than its bite, as is clearly illustrated by the response of the three serfs who in the early 1350s had been seized and forcibly returned to Winslow: all three quickly left the manor again, never to return or to pay chevage. The cellarer of St Albans, one of England's most powerful and ancient lords, was incapable of retaining or retrieving his own serfs, but instead was obliged to compete for them with other lords.[118] For example, in 1355 William Howes was on the estate of the abbot of Woburn (Bedfordshire) at Swanbourne.[119] The Richard le Barn who successfully retrieved William Adam in 1353 probably had claim on William's employment under the Statute of Labourers. There is no evidence that other lords or employers respected the cellarer's prior claim over his serfs. Furthermore, the surge of presentments generated just three chevage payments, amounting to less than 4s., in the whole of the third quarter of the fourteenth century (Table 9.11). So, for all the heightened attention paid to absent serfs, the cellarer was unsuccessful at either forcing reluctant migrants to return or generating more chevage payments.

A second important contextual point is that the frequency of many servile incidents was lower in the 1350s than in the 1340s, even allowing for the fall in population. For example, around twenty cases of leyrwite were recorded every decade before the Black Death, but just two per decade thereafter. Likewise, licences to study or to attend school peaked at eleven in the 1340s, but only one was issued in the 1350s (Table 9.10). Third, in many respects the tougher policy did not endure beyond the end of the decade. In the 1360s the high mean fines for merchet and leyrwite dropped sharply (Tables 9.9 and 9.10, respectively), in the latter case from

23d. in the 1350s to 2d. in the 1360s. The number of presentments for absence fell from around nineteen per annum in the late 1350s to only six in the 1360s (Table 9.12). Fourth, while mill suit presentments peaked in the 1350s, they too fell precipitously in the 1360s and 1370s (Table 9.6). Finally, after the 1350s there are no more disputes over servile status, no enforced service and no physical seizures of serfs. In sum, the seigniorial reaction was limited in scale and did not endure beyond the 1350s.

There are very few examples of overt and collective peasant resistance to seigniorial demands documented within the court records. Mill suit was unusual in the 1360s and 1370s, and there is nothing in the court rolls to indicate that it was a source of conflict at Winslow. The most significant source of tension was non-performance of labour services on two particular occasions, in 1352 and 1370 (see also Table 9.13). In the January court of 1352 eight tenants had failed to collect nuts 'as they ought to and as accustomed', but in their defence they claimed to be neither accustomed nor required to do so. The court sought clarification from the custumal of the manor and gave the dissenters eight days to answer on the point at St Albans, but at the next court they admitted that they were required to perform this service and duly paid amercements totalling 14d. for their attempted evasion.[120] In 1370 the villein tenants successfully petitioned the lord for a collective

Table 9.13 Incidence of recorded non-performance of labour services on Winslow manor, 1327–1460

Year	Non-performance of labour services
1352	8 refuse to collect nuts
1356	1 withholds two works
1359	2 default half a day in harvest
1369	3 do not attend mowing
1374	4 do not attend hay lifting
1376	2 do not attend hay lifting 6 do not attend straw gathering

Sources: Noy, *The Winslow Manor Court Books, 1322–1377*; Noy, *The Winslow Manor Court Books, 1423–1460.*

agreement to commute boon-works until Michaelmas 1391 at the annual rate of 2s. per villein tenant, which hints at some prior disquiet.[121] Although these are the only instances of collective protest documented in the court rolls, villeins of Winslow were implicated to be among those extorting charters from the abbey during the revolt of 1381.[122]

When the court series revives again in the 1420s, there is no evidence for the aggressive management of serfs. Merchet was the main surviving incident, but much diminished in frequency (Table 9.6). The repetitious naming of unlicensed migrants and calls for their return continued, but still failed to translate into actual revenues from chevage. In 1425–49 a grand total of 126 presentments for absence generated just six chevage payments at an average of 8.5d. each. The last payment of chevage in 1439 coincided with a sharp fall in presentments for absence (Tables 9.1 and 9.12), and by the 1440s the manor had largely lost interest in both. On one occasion the lessee of the Winslow demesne was ordered (along with the bailiff) to seize two serfs living elsewhere and to bring them to the abbey's court at Biggin.[123] The practice of requiring the farmer of the manor to be responsible for absent serfs was unlikely to be successful, unless the farmer had some financial or contractual incentive for so doing. A hint that such an arrangement may have been in place at Winslow is evident in 1431, when Geoffrey King claimed that a chevage payer, Richard Evresden, owed him 16s. for back payments of chevage over twelve years when Geoffrey was farmer of the manor, but his plea was thrown out.[124] The repeated recording of absent serfs in the courts did not generate any worthwhile financial benefit to the lord from chevage, merchet and leyrwite. It may have resulted in the occasional windfall payment for manumission, but these are not documented in the manor courts.

Why, then, did the cellarer maintain until the 1440s the administrative dogma of presenting absent serfs? Two reasons suggest themselves. The first is that it was the consequence of bureaucratic doggedness and momentum: the abbey possessed a formidable administrative structure, and it also possessed certain ancient privileges acquired in the good name of St Alban, so consequently the privileges were asserted irrespective of the financial benefit from them. The second is that the entries in the rolls maintained a legal record of servility, which might bestow some future benefit to the abbey. The most likely benefit was the prospect of demanding a financial payment for a manumission from a wealthy and long-flown serf.

Some flown serfs did eventually return to Winslow, but only when it suited them to do so.[125] Most settled nearby. Two-thirds of Winslow's flown serfs moved to destinations within 10 miles, and just 15 per cent went to towns. There was, however, a clear demarcation between the preferences of female and male serfs: 27 per cent of the former headed for towns compared with only 11 per cent of the latter. These figures are all low by the standards of other Midland manors, which may reflect the wide range of opportunities for obtaining land and work in the vicinity of Winslow.[126] Certainly, those serfs who did opt to live nearby cannot have feared harassment from the cellarer's officials or forcible repatriation to the home manor.

Summary

The example of Winslow illustrates once again how the operation of villeinage on the eve of the Black Death did not reflect the legal theory. The cellarer seldom acted in an arbitrary fashion. Villein tenants here enjoyed de facto security of tenure, and the rights of heirs were protected. Set procedures and written precedents were commonplace in resolving disputes over servile land, whether relating to rent payments or claims to title, and codified custom resolved the only recorded dispute between lord and tenants over labour services. A servile land market was active at over thirty transfers per annum, mainly involving the permanent alienation and subletting of small parcels of arable. Rates of entry fines per acre were highly varied, but the mean of 28d. per acre is closer to East Anglian levels than to south Midland norms and reflects the locally buoyant servile land market. The range of incidents of personal servility was wide, with the exception of chevage. Fines for these incidents were variable, and the average charges – such as 2s. 7d. for merchet and 6d. for leyrwite – were close to national norms.

In 1349 the Black Death struck Winslow severely, although in the short term the customary land market absorbed the shock relatively well. In the 1350s and 1360s customary land was quickly and fully reoccupied, and there were few conversions to leases or money rents. However, between the 1340s and the 1350s the volume of annual land transfers fell by one-fifth; subletting withered; the level of entry fines nearly halved; surplus buildings became dilapidated; and mill suit, recognition and merchet all lapsed from the rent package of service tenancies. Labour services appear to have been widely commuted. The fragmented structure of holdings, the ready availability of small parcels of land available to those seeking an initial step on the property ladder, and the immediate yet selective seigniorial granting of concessions on the rent package were the main reasons for the relative resilience of the land market.

The concessions to the rent package of servile tenures in the wake of plague contrast with the sudden tighter management of hereditary serfs in the 1350s, characterised by a spike in presentments for absence, the physical seizure of flown serfs, higher fines for servile incidents and disputes over personal status. Pre-plague court rolls had not maintained a rigorous distinction between servile tenure and status, but after 1349 it became sharper as the former was diluted and the latter became a matter of greater seigniorial focus. Yet this aggressive stance was largely posturing, because it was ineffective at either squeezing much revenue from serfs or at preventing their departure, and early in the 1360s it was dropped, never to be revived. As we have seen, just three chevage payments, amounting to less than 4s., were collected in the third quarter of the fourteenth century at Winslow, and after 1350 the income from the two other incidents chargeable on hereditary serfs – leyrwite and merchet – declined dramatically. The payment of heriot by some landless serfs ceased after 1355.

Thus, the 1350s and 1360s were the key period for the decline of serfdom at Winslow. The rent package on villein service tenure was diluted through the shedding of incidents such as merchet and recognition, and the halving of the level of entry fines. The seigniorial reaction of the 1350s mainly involved a clampdown on hereditary serfs, yet it generated little cash and it was largely abandoned in the following decade. Thomas Walsingham stated in his chronicle that in 1381 the St Albans rebels threatened arson attacks on the manors of Aston, Sandridge and Winslow if the abbot did not accede to their demands, but there is no obvious link between the management of serfdom at Winslow in the 1360s and 1370s and the possible participation of its tenants in the revolt. One of the issues for the rebels at St Albans was the persistence of service tenancies for villein land, which was certainly the case at Winslow.[127] Thereafter villeinage withered on the vine, although it was not until the mid-fifteenth century that service tenancies were finally converted to money tenures. The speed and scale of serfdom's initial decline correlate closely with the immediate impact of the Black Death and the second plague epidemic of 1361–62, and reveal the lord's inability to counter the pervasive effects of market forces. The lord's heightened sensitivity to the growth of migration of serfs in the 1350s indicates that it was demographic decline and tenant mobility, rather than organised and overt challenges, that triggered the decline of villeinage.

Notes

1 Noy, 'Winslow', p. 140.
2 Noy, *The Winslow Manor Court Books, 1322–1377*, pp. vi–xiv.
3 Levett, *Studies*, p. 136.
4 Noy, *The Winslow Manor Court Books, 1322–1377*, pp. 83–4.
5 Ibid., p. xvi. See also Seebohm, *The English Village Community*, pp. 20–32.
6 Noy, *The Winslow Manor Court Books, 1322–1377*, p. ix.
7 Noy, 'Winslow in 1341', pp. 142–3.
8 Noy, *The Winslow Manor Court Books, 1322–1377*, pp. 37, 48.
9 For example, when those of Henry Pounty failed to respond to the final call in June 1433, they were formally and perpetually excluded from entering his cottage as heirs; Noy, *The Winslow Manor Court Books, 1423–1460*, p. 550.
10 Noy, *The Winslow Manor Court Books, 1322–1377*, pp. 81–2.
11 Ibid., pp. 43, 205.
12 For deathbed surrenders attracting heriot, see, for example, Noy, *The Winslow Manor Court Books, 1423–1460*, pp. 474, 476, 509.
13 Noy, *The Winslow Manor Court Books, 1322–1377*, pp. 6–7.
14 See, for example, ibid., pp. 16–17.
15 See, for example, ibid., pp. 13, 22–3, 25, 31, 34, 36, 38–40, 45–7. Hence, from the mid-1330s the standard format was 'hold to him and his heirs in villeinage through due and accustomed services'.
16 Ibid., pp. 83ff.; hence, 'to hold to him and his heirs in villeinage at the will of the lord through due and accustomed services'.

17 For example, in 1346 John and Isabella Tonne transferred a cottage to William Chonneson, who held 'for him and his heirs according to the custom of the manor paying to the abbot and his successors for all services 18d.' per annum; ibid., p. 187. The addition of 'according to the custom of the manor' was associated explicitly with monetary, as distinct from service, tenure. John of Halden held a plot in the marketplace for the term of his life; ibid., p. 17, see also pp. 106, 120, 155, 164, 168.

18 Ibid., p. 55.

19 D. Noy, 'Leyrwite, marriage and illegitimacy: Winslow before the Black Death', *Records of Buckinghamshire*, 47:1 (2007): 133–52 (pp. 137–8).

20 Noy, 'Winslow', Fig. 1; Stone, 'The impact of drought', Fig. 1 and pp. 445–7.

21 The lower valuation related to a disputed land sale, together with the circumstances, render this a less reliable guide to contemporary sale prices than the second valuation, which is closer to the evidence presented in Chapter 3, where entry fines were around 5–10 per cent of sale prices; Noy, 'Winslow', p. 142.

22 Noy, *The Winslow Manor Court Books, 1322–1377*, p. xix.

23 Ibid., pp. 17, 59, 107.

24 Ibid., pp. 17, 22, 59, 273, 283, 547.

25 Ibid., pp. 131–2.

26 Ibid., pp. 43, 51.

27 Among the many examples, see ibid., pp. 44–5, 54–5, 59, 98–9, 106, 110, 117–18, 158, 290.

28 Ibid., pp. 290, 327; also p. 357.

29 Levett, *Studies*, pp. 139, 150.

30 Noy, *The Winslow Manor Court Books, 1322–1377*, pp. 114, 274.

31 For example, ibid., pp. 128–9, 254.

32 Ibid., pp. 154–5.

33 Ibid., pp. 173, 195–205. A number of grants do not specify the area of land.

34 For arable grants at around 6d. per acre, see ibid., pp. 168–75, and for house plots, pp. 153–5; Noy, 'Winslow', pp. 142–3.

35 The April 1347 court repeatedly states that these lands are 'granted and demised'; see Noy, *The Winslow Manor Court Books, 1322–1377*, p. 205.

36 One of the grants in the 1340s was for a life; ibid., pp. 200–1.

37 Ibid., p. viii–ix, xiv; for plots and cottages, see pp. 194, 295; for shops and stalls, see pp. 36, 53, 72; for the smithy, see p. 32.

38 Ibid., pp. 220–50. Levett, *Studies*, Table 2, has 156 deaths.

39 Levett, *Studies*, p. 250.

40 Noy, *The Winslow Manor Court Books, 1322–1377*, pp. 234–5, 333, 335.
41 Ibid., pp. 229, 312.
42 Ibid., pp. 352–3, 356–9, 410–17, 452–6.
43 Levett, *Studies*, Table 2; Noy, *The Winslow Manor Court Books, 1322–1377*, pp. 221–56; Noy, 'Winslow', p. 139.
44 Noy, *The Winslow Manor Court Books, 1322–1377*, pp. 250, 253–4.
45 Ibid., p. 248.
46 As shown by the treatment of land in the lord's hands in 1359; ibid., p. 336.
47 For the waiving of entry fines, see ibid., pp. 224–5; combining with merchets, see pp. 226–31, 233, 235, 237–9. For the same tactic at the St Albans manor of Park, see Tompkins, 'The manor of Park', p. 61.
48 Noy, *The Winslow Manor Court Books, 1322–1377*, p. 235.
49 Levett, *Studies*, Table 2.
50 In a similar arrangement in 1363 William Bate took on 3 acres of abandoned land until the rightful heir, Geoffrey Thomas, came of age, on a greatly simplified package: 'in villeinage at the lord's will for one boonwork annually with one man', with the entry fine waived; Noy, *The Winslow Manor Court Books, 1322–1377*, pp. 382–3. In both cases an entry fine was waived.
51 Ibid., pp. 274–5, 282–3, 285–6, 290.
52 Ibid., p. 260.
53 Ibid., p. 298 (June 1355), 385 (1365).
54 Ibid., pp. 293, 298–9, 315–20.
55 Ibid., p. 293.
56 Ibid., pp. 407, 425.
57 Ibid., p. 282.
58 Ibid., p. 152.
59 Ibid., pp. 291, 296.
60 In June 1355 John Mayn surrendered 1 acre of customary land to Richard Evresden 'to hold to the end of Richard's life in villeinage at the will of the lord for due and accustomed services', and in 1366 William Lombe acquired 6 roods 'for himself for life in villeinage at the lord's will through due and accustomed services'; ibid., pp. 302, 386, 393.
61 The main use for fixed-term tenures was to lease small parcels of demesne.
62 Noy, *The Winslow Manor Court Books, 1322–1377*, p. 296; Slota, 'Law, land transfer', p. 132.
63 For the lease of demesne land to tenants for years, see, for example, the list of thirteen grants in 1345, mostly for the term of twelve years; Noy, *The Winslow Manor Court Books, 1322–1377*, pp. 160–2.

64 See the grant to William Evresden in 1372; ibid., p. 435.
65 See, for example, ibid., p. 449.
66 Noy, *The Winslow Manor Court Books, 1423–1460*, pp. 480–1, 503, 611.
67 See ibid., pp. 630–1, 643–6.
68 Prior to 1448 the phrase 'according to the custom of the manor' had not featured much at all in conveyances. For the handful of examples, see one conveyance in June 1335 ('to hold for him and his heirs in villeinage and according to the custom of the manor through due and accustomed services'), but this seldom featured thereafter; Noy, *The Winslow Manor Court Books, 1322–1377*, pp. 55, 187, 233.
69 Compare the conveyances in the June 1446 court (without the phrase) with those from May 1448; Noy, *The Winslow Manor Court Books, 1423–1460*, pp. 627–35.
70 In April 1440 John and Isabella Eynesham granted 2 roods of customary land to John Cok deploying the standard conveyance, but now an annual cash rent of 1½d. replaced 'all services except suit of court'. Four similar transactions are recorded in this court; ibid., pp. 601–3, also pp. 605, 607, 613, 622, 627–8.
71 Ibid., pp. 631–45.
72 As grants of demesne rather than customary land, they are not included in the computations of transfers in Table 9.2.
73 They were all liable for an entry fine, and were all granted on cash rents; ibid., pp. 628 (a meadow), 640 (6 acres), 646 (4 acres), 663 (1 acre), 664 (unspecified area), 666 (9½ acres), 673 (7 acres), 679 (2 acres), 684 (2 acres), 686 (5 acres), 702 (5 acres).
74 Ibid., pp. 608, 650.
75 Brenner, 'Agrarian class structure', pp. 47–9; Brenner, 'The agrarian roots', pp. 293–6. Restated more recently by Dimmock, *The Origin of Capitalism*, pp. 90–104.
76 Levett, *Studies*, p. xxx.
77 Noy, *The Winslow Manor Court Books, 1322–1377*, p. 430.
78 Ibid., p. xx.
79 Ibid., pp. 22, 24, 48, 119, 206.
80 Ibid., p. 206.
81 Ibid., p. 294.
82 Ibid.: brass pot (p. 69); tunic (p. 83); chest (p. 77); axe valued 2d. (p. 235); goose valued 2d. (p. 240); a box valued 3d. (p. 225); a dish valued 1½d. (p. 248); or a cash sum, for example 12d. (p. 144).
83 Ibid., p. 265.
84 A horse valued at 20s., and two cash heriots of 4s. each; ibid., p. 163.
85 Ibid., pp. 244, 255, 292–3.

86 Ibid., p. 278.
87 Ibid., pp. xx–xxi; for an example see Noy, *The Winslow Manor Court Books, 1423–1460*, pp. 683–4.
88 1350–77 mean = 57 heriots, 1423–59 mean = 37: a fall of 35 per cent. See Table 9.7.
89 The lord had previously waived the collection of heriot in the case of tenant poverty, but these cases from the 1440s and 1450s simply stated that 'heriot is waived' without justifying the waiver on specific grounds; ibid., pp. 512–13, 517, 519, 570, 626, 635, 638, 639, 642, 643, 644, 645, 646, 658, 664.
90 Noy, *The Winslow Manor Court Books, 1322–1377*, p. 256.
91 Page, *VCH, Hertfordshire*, Vol. II, pp. 486–7.
92 Noy, *The Winslow Manor Court Books, 1322–1377*, pp. 42–73.
93 Noy, *The Winslow Manor Court Books, 1423–1460*, p. 538.
94 Levett, *Studies*, 237.
95 Noy, *The Winslow Manor Court Books, 1322–1377*, pp. 83, 241.
96 Müller, 'The function', p. 183.
97 Ibid., p. 179.
98 Levett regarded this level of fine as light and 'in no way prohibitive' for aspiring families; Levett, *Studies*, p. 246.
99 Noy, *The Winslow Manor Court Books, 1322–1377*, p. 178; see also p. 16.
100 For example, in 1363 Ralph Adam agreed to pay 3s. 4d. annually to live wherever he wished: ibid., p. 383.
101 Bailey, 'Servile and gender migration', Table 1.
102 Müller, 'The function', p. 172.
103 Ibid., p. 181.
104 Noy, *The Winslow Manor Court Books, 1322–1377*, p. 265.
105 Ibid., pp. 272–3.
106 Ibid., p. 274.
107 The first in 1352, two more in December 1353, another in May 1354, one in 1358 and seven in 1360; ibid., pp. 280, 287, 293, 323, 339–40, 342.
108 Ibid., p. 293.
109 Bailey, 'Servile and gender migration', Table 2.
110 This was a common law writ to initiate a plea concerning personal status. Noy, *The Winslow Manor Court Books, 1322–1377*, pp. 273, 280.
111 Ibid., pp. 205, 297.
112 Ibid., p. 306.
113 John was prevailed upon to make his brother attend court, but nothing happened; ibid., p. 309.

114 Ibid., pp. 243–4; Levett, *Studies*, p. 209.
115 Noy, *The Winslow Manor Court Books, 1322–1377*, p. 270.
116 Ibid., p. x, although there is no record of this event in the Winslow court.
117 Ibid., p. 278.
118 Similarly, the lack of any effective response is evident at Abbot's Langley; Levett, *Studies*, p. 255.
119 Noy, *The Winslow Manor Court Books, 1322–1377*, p. 293.
120 Ibid., pp. 268–9, 273–4.
121 Ibid., p. 430.
122 Ibid., p. x.
123 They were also directed to seize the goods and chattels of John Cok of Winslow (valued at £7) to pressurise him to persuade one of the serfs to return and take over her father's holding; Noy, *The Winslow Manor Court Books, 1423–1460*, p. 494.
124 Ibid., p. 539.
125 Bailey, 'Servile and gender migration', pp. 64–6.
126 Ibid., Table 4.
127 Personal communication, Andrew Prescott.

10

The manor of Norton

The case studies of Codicote and Winslow revealed that a powerful monastic lord possessing a classic manor dominated by villeinage imposed a heavier weight of labour services and a wider range of servile dues than the typical English manor, including licences to educate hereditary male serfs. Yet in the pre-plague period the cellarer of St Albans abbey did not manage serfdom in an arbitrary manner; instead it was regulated through a combination of custom, written precedents, set procedures and market forces. The relative weakness of serfdom in practice in the early fourteenth century was quickly exposed following the arrival of plague in 1348–49, because by the 1360s many incidents of servile tenure had disappeared or had been commuted for cash on both those manors. In this chapter I explore whether the same characteristics were evident on a third manor of the cellarer, before drawing the findings together into a general conclusion.

Norton

The manor of Norton lay 1 mile north-west of Baldock within Hertfordshire on the Bedfordshire border, just within the Liberty of the abbey of St Albans. There are no extant accounts or extents, so the exact size and composition of the manor are unknown, although it did contain sizeable quantities of customary land. The manor appears to have been directly managed during the late thirteenth and early fourteenth centuries rather than being leased out.[1] A very good sequence of court records has survived, which are contemporary copies of selected entries from the original rolls.[2] A handful of original court rolls survive from Norton, and a direct comparison confirms that the copies included all issues relating to the cellarer's rights – and therefore to serfdom – and that they are accurate.[3] Court records survive from Norton from the mid-thirteenth century, although this study only aggregates data from the second quarter of the fourteenth century for purposes of comparison with Codicote and Winslow. There were usually two courts a year, and a total of 184 court sessions have survived: 117 between 1325 and 1388, twenty-six between 1391 and 1415, thirty-nine between 1423 and 1460, and one each in 1464 and 1484.[4]

Serfdom in the pre-plague era

Most of the customary land at Norton was organised into half-virgates, each containing approximately 36 acres of land, together with some quarter-virgates of 18 acres and a variety of smaller holdings and cottages.[5] All this land was held on hereditary service tenure. The exact rent burden on each holding cannot be ascertained because of the absence of accounts and surveys, but we do know that customary tenants were liable for a cash rent, some grain renders, labour services, merchet, suit of mill, heriot, recognition, election to the offices of reeve and beadle, and an entry fine (Table 10.1).

Customary land in Norton was inherited impartibly through the eldest male. The court fastidiously upheld the right of the heir to succeed to a customary holding, and in 1332 proclaimed that any heir who resided 'within the realm and out of prison' had five court sessions following the death of a tenant in which to appear and secure the inheritance, after which the land was forfeit to the lord and could be granted to another tenant.[6] If an heir refused outright to accept a landed inheritance, then the court recorded formally their perpetual disinheritance.[7]

There were no arbitrary seizures of land, although the lord did remove tenants following specific breaches of custom or a failure to render appropriate dues.[8] For example, in 1326 a cottage held in villeinage was seized from Ivetta Aubrey, a widow who had remarried without permission, until she paid the requisite fine for merchet.[9] Rightful heirs who were deemed incapable of managing their

Table 10.1 Last recorded dates of key incidents of villeinage at Norton, 1325–1459

Capitage	Chevage	Presentment for absence	Leyrwite	Heriot	Merchet	Mill suit	Recognition	Tallage	Licence to educate
None	1448	1453	1357	1460	1453	1355	1350	None	1413

Source: Foden, *Records of the Manor of Norton.*

inherited landholding properly (two for impotence, one for foolishness) were prevented from entering it, and the land was instead allocated to other tenants.[10] A judgment about the competence of a villein to manage his holding was potentially contentious, so the lord was careful to respect custom and due process. For example, in 1325 two tenants were deemed incapable of either running their lands and tenements or performing the services due, so the lord relieved them of the holdings 'with the consent and election of all the villeins of Norton' and granted them instead temporarily on leasehold to three other local tenants. However, the court noted that, should the rightful heirs to these holdings appear during the term of the leases, they would be admitted to their lands subject to recompensing the lessees their reasonable expenses.[11]

Villein land reverted into the lord's hands in the event of an heir failing to claim an inheritance. The land was swiftly regranted to an unrelated third party if the lord's officials were able to identify a willing tenant. If not, the cellarer could instruct the community of villeins to take full responsibility for the holding and its services. For example, the lord directed the jurors to choose a suitable tenant when, in the late 1320s, three villein-holdings fell vacant without an heir. For two of these holdings, a willing tenant was identified and formally admitted.[12] For the third, a tenant was not immediately identified and so the community was made responsible for performing the services due from the holding until one was found.[13] The power to force the community to assume responsibility for vacant villein land was unusual, but is also documented on the estates of the bishops of Durham and Winchester.[14]

The formula of conveyance for heritable service tenure at Norton followed a standard format with little variation from one transfer to another. A villein tenant held land 'for him and his heirs in villeinage through due and accustomed services [*per servicia debita et consueta*]'.[15] In October 1339 the phrase 'at the will of the lord' was added to a number of conveyances for the first time, and became a permanent feature of subsequent conveyances: the same development is recorded at Winslow from 1338, so this may have been an estate-wide initiative.[16] In the 1290s and 1300s a handful of court roll entries had specified additionally that servile land was liable for merchet and tallage, clearly to emphasise its status, but by the 1320s they were no longer mentioned because the wording of the standard conveyance was deemed sufficiently robust and watertight to withstand

Table 10.2 Number of customary land transactions at Norton, 1330–1469

Decade	Direct inter-peasant transfers	Grants from lord	Abandoned into hands of lord	Total transactions
1330–39	38	7	1	46
1340–48	53	3	1	57
1349	21	0	3	24
1350–59	16	9	7	32
1360–69	13	6	7	26
1370–79	15	9	1	25
1380–89	8	9	6	23
1390–99	20	15	0	35
1400–9	7	10	8	25
1410–19	4	4	3	11
1420–29	5	9	0	14
1430–39	11	5	1	17
1440–49	6	3	0	9
1450–59	6	7	0	13
1460–69	2	1	0	3

Excludes reversionary interest of widows and licences to sublet.

Source: Foden, *Records of the Manor of Norton.*

any legal challenge over its status.[17] The issuing of copies of the court roll entry to a villein landholding as proof of title was well established by the mid-fourteenth century.[18] Very little servile land was held on life tenures, or had been converted to monetary tenures, in the pre-plague period (Tables 10.2–10.4). On the rare occasions when the latter had occurred, it was reflected in an amendment to the vocabulary of the conveyance: 'for him and his heirs in villeinage *for rent service*' instead of '*through due and accustomed services*' (my italics).[19] The phrase 'rent service' signified that the cash payment had permanently displaced the requirement to renders in kind and labour services.

Tenants could sell and exchange customary land, subject to a proper record of its transfer in the manorial court rolls, as a result of which some of the standardised half- and quarter-virgates had suffered a small degree of subdivision.[20] The court punished tenants who attempted to transfer land without following the correct procedures with amercements and threats of seizure.[21] In the pre-plague era there were relatively few transfers – around fifty per decade or five per annum – 90 per cent of which were inter-peasant transfers (Tables 10.2 and 10.3). The majority were transfers of cottages and smallholdings of various kinds of undisclosed area, whereas the standardised half- and quarter-virgates were transferred infrequently and remained largely intact. Hence, the Norton servile market was not as active as at either Codicote or Winslow. There is little evidence for distress sales following a spate of deaths in 1328, presumably as a result of the local drought conditions noted also at Winslow.[22] Nevertheless, the lord did license around ten temporary sublets of villein land per decade in the 1330s and 1340s, which were usually parcels of the standardised holdings (Table 10.3).[23] Seigniorial control over subletting is evident in directives that precedence must be given to resident villeins of Norton, after which land could be sublet to freemen, outsiders and residents of the borough of Baldock.[24] In the wake of this directive, thirteen tenants were accused in 1329 of illegally subletting parcels of the customary land to residents of Baldock, although all were immediately pardoned, subject to a 40s. penalty each for any future repetition.[25]

The court books contain occasional references to free tenants, because some free tenures owed heriot.[26] Likewise, some free tenants held unfree land.[27] Whenever serfs acquired a freehold through purchase, they were required to surrender the land in the court and pay an entry fine for re-entry to it, and thereafter the tenure was described as being held for ‘due and accustomed services’: the equivalent of what was known as ‘soiled’ land in East Anglia.[28] Outsiders who married female villein landholders in Norton were amerced for entering the lord’s villeinage and bound over not to remove any chattels from the Liberty without permission.[29] Hence, in 1336, when one Sarra le Fuller inherited half a virgate of land, her husband, Richard, was formally admitted to the holding on condition that he should render merchet, tallage, entry fine and heriot, and he had to find pledges to ensure ‘he shall be obedient in

Table 10.3 Breakdown of all inter-peasant transfers of customary land at Norton, 1330–1469

Decade	No. of grants	Grants as % of all transactions	Hereditary for services	Hereditary for money	Licence to sublet	Life for services/ money	To full age for services
1330–39	38	83%	30	0	8	0/0	0
1340–48	53	93%	42	0	11	0/0	0
1349	21	88%	20	0	0	1/0	0
1350–59	16	50%	13	0	1	0/0	2
1360–69	13	50%	13	0	0	0/0	0
1370–79	15	60%	14	0	1	0/0	0
1380–89	8	35%	7	0	1	0/0	0
1390–99	20	57%	13	5	0	1/1	0
1400–9	7	28%	7	0	0	0/0	0
1410–19	4	36%	4	0	0	0/0	0
1420–29	5	36%	5	0	0	0/0	0
1430–39	11	65%	8	2	0	1/0	0
1440–49	6	67%	6	0	0	0/0	0
1450–59	6	46%	3	3	0	0/0	0
1460–69	2	66%	2	0	0	0/0	0

Source: Foden, *Records of the Manor of Norton.*

Table 10.4 Breakdown of all direct grants of customary land from the lord at Norton, 1330–1469

Decade	No. of grants	Grants as % of all transactions	Hereditary for services	Hereditary for money	Until heir comes of age for services	Until heir comes of age for cash	Life for services	Term of years
1330–39	7	15%	3	1	1	1	0	1
1340–48	3	1%	1	2	0	0	0	0
1349	0	0%	0	0	0	0	0	0
1350–59	9	28%	7	1	1	0	0	0
1360–69	6	23%	6	0	0	0	0	0
1370–79	9	36%	9	0	0	0	0	0
1380–89	9	39%	8	1	0	0	0	0
1390–99	15	43%	12	3	0	0	0	0
1400–9	10	40%	10	0	0	0	0	0
1410–19	4	36%	4	0	0	0	0	0
1420–29	9	64%	2	0	0	0	1	6
1430–39	5	29%	2	1	0	0	0	2
1440–49	3	33%	2	1	0	0	0	0
1450–59	7	54%	1	6	0	0	0	0
1460–69	1	33%	0	1	0	0	0	0

Source: Foden, *Records of the Manor of Norton*.

all things just as other customary tenants are and shall be': clearly, Richard was either a freeman or an outsider or both.[30]

The importance of written precedents in resolving disputes over servile land is a common feature of the Norton courts. Villeins routinely requested a search of earlier court rolls in cases involving villein land transfers or inheritance. Likewise, disputes over the terms of licences to sublet might call upon the record of the court. A lordly claim that an entry fine or merchet had been evaded sometimes elicited a request to search the rolls to prove otherwise.[31] Jurors were occasionally empanelled to inquire and pronounce on disputes over servile land, which was an established procedure here from an early date: for example, as early as 1246 and 1247 two separate tenants paid the lord to hold an inquiry into their rights to servile holdings.[32]

Presentment juries routinely ran much of the business of the court and were dominated – no less than inquisition juries – by the leading villein landholders.[33] They were expected to follow established protocols and were sometimes punished for not doing so. Presentment juries were also occasionally amerced for concealing information and the court was careful to enforce a form of due process, as in 1294 when a serf was amerced 2s. for speaking to jurors on a matter where he had a direct interest after they had taken their oaths.[34]

Villein tenants were not clearly distinguished from hereditary serfs in the court rolls of this period. Servile wills had to be registered in the court rolls, a practice common to all manors on the St Albans estate.[35] The 1307 lay subsidy returns confirm that villeins were among the leading taxpayers in the vill. The lower-to-middling taxpayers included families such as the Wardes, Bates, Beneses, Sawyers and Bondes, all hereditary serfs paying dues such as leyrwite and merchet, and licences to educate.[36] John Boveton and John Prudde, both villein landholders and hereditary serfs, were among the very highest taxpayers in Norton.[37]

The Black Death and its immediate aftermath

No deaths of villein tenants were recorded in the court of April 1348, with two in the October court of 1348 and four in the next court held in April 1349, but twenty in July and three in October 1349.[38] None were recorded in the April 1350 court. This pattern indicates that the Black Death arrived in Norton in the spring of 1349 and raged into midsummer. Levett estimated a minimum death rate of villein tenants here of 35 per cent, although a recent and more thorough estimate puts the rate closer to 50 per cent.[39] Of the twenty-four recorded deaths of villein tenants in April and July 1349, the nearest heir was admitted in fourteen cases, an unrelated tenant was admitted in six, a ward was appointed in one, and in three cases the land remained untenanted in the lord's hand. This represents an impressive rate of reoccupation, although the pool of available tenants had unquestionably shrunk. Nine of the twenty-one reoccupied holdings (43 per cent) in 1349 were either taken by women (in the absence of a nearest male heir) or had their entry fine waived because of the incoming tenants's poverty. In the case of nine of the new tenants in 1349, the lord also permitted a combined entry fine with permission to marry, a special concession and inducement used here only in the plague year.[40] A surge of fourteen marriages occurred in 1349, including the nine linked with entry fines.

The court records hint at how the pandemic fractured lives. Adam Ward died leaving a single heir, an adult daughter named Alice whose 'foolish nature' prevented her from taking over the half-virgate that was her legitimate inheritance. John Loveleg therefore agreed to take on the holding and care for Alice, providing her with food and clothing for her lifetime, but the very next entry in the same court recorded her death and identified John Loveleg as her heir. John was given licence to marry, but he died in 1355.[41] In another case, Alice Swetekyn, who in 1347 had borne a child out of wedlock, died in the pandemic as a single woman, therefore leaving her house and croft to Alice, her two-year-old daughter, about whom nothing more is recorded: in 1351 the croft was granted to a third party, so little Alice probably succumbed soon after her mother.[42]

The Black Death immediately sapped the vitality of the villein land market: the volume of transactions in the period 1350–59 (thirty-two) was 42 per cent lower than the mean (fifty-two) in the years from 1330 to 1348, the proportion of inter-peasant transactions fell from 88 to 50 per cent, and the proportion of transfers abandoned into the lord's hands rose from 2 to 22 per cent (Tables 10.2 and 10.3). The average level of an entry fine for a half-virgate fell by 72 per cent over the same period (Table 10.5). In 1354 the Norton court record included the 'new order' (*novum preceptum*) across the cellarer's estate that henceforth the subletting of villein land for terms of one or two years had to be recorded in the court rolls, whereas previously only longer subleases had to be licensed.[43] Although no licence was payable for such short-term lets, failure to comply with the new requirement to register the sublease was to attract a penalty of 6s. 8d. and forfeiture of the land. This direct manipulation of manorial custom by the cellarer had little practical impact at Norton, because after 1350 the subletting of villein land virtually ceased (Table 10.3).[44] The drying up of licensed subleases of parcels of land from the standardised holdings reflects the ability of the survivors of plague to obtain land directly and permanently.[45]

During the 1350s few abandoned holdings lay untenanted for any length of time, so the land market retained some resilience. Furthermore, most grants continued to be on hereditary service

Table 10.5 Mean entry fines charged for half-virgates at Norton, 1330–1409

Decade	No. of half-virgates	Total entry fines	Mean fine
1330–39	8	68s. 4d.	8s. 7d.
1340–48	6	90s. 0d.	15s. 0d.
1350–59	4	13s. 4d.	3s. 4d.
1360–69	7, of which 2 waived	33s. 4d.	4s. 9d.
1370–79	2½, of which 1 waived	3s. 8d.	1s. 6d.
1380–89	3, of which 1 waived	3s. 0d.	1s. 0d.
1390–99	5, of which 3 waived[a]	10s. + 2 capons	2s. 2d.
1400–9	7, of which 3 waived[a]	3s. 4d. + 7 capons	0s. 12d.

[a] *Entry fine on a messuage and half-virgate:* transfers involving a fraction of half-virgate, or where entry fine includes fine for additional land, are not included; capon valued at 6d.

Source: Foden, *Records of the Manor of Norton.*

tenure, including those granted directly from the lord: in the 1350s, 78 per cent of the latter were for services (Table 10.4), so there were few conversions to fixed-term tenures or to monetary tenures in this decade. Indeed, just one parcel of land – an abandoned croft – was converted to a heritable money rent, in 1351, but even this grant involved the caveat that the holding would be returned to the rightful heir if he appeared in the future (and the new tenant duly compensated).[46]

No deaths of customary tenants are recorded in the April court of 1361, then five in October 1361 and one more in April 1362, suggesting that the second national outbreak of pestilence was confined here to the late summer and autumn of 1361.[47] No deaths are recorded in the three courts covering the period of the third great pestilence in 1369, and just two deaths in that of 1375.[48]

Villein tenures

Various indicators confirm that the pandemics of 1349 and 1361 served to dampen the customary land market significantly. The total number of servile land transactions per decade fell from an average of fifty-two in the pre-plague era to twenty-five in the two decades from 1360 (Table 10.2). The proportion of grants direct from the lord had risen from under 10 per cent to over 30 per cent (Table 10.4), reflecting the tendency for land to lie in the lord's hands for a while before tenants could be found. The mean entry fine for a half-virgate was barely one-quarter of its pre-plague mean of 11s. 10d. (Table 10.5).

Hereditary service tenancies continued to be the dominant form of tenure, with few conversions to leaseholds or money tenures. Some new tenants were enticed to take on holdings by waiving entry fines or other deals. For example, in 1364, when John Jecob succeeded his deceased father into a half-virgate, the heriot of one horse due from his father was returned to him and his own entry fine waived: a spate of such waived fines is also recorded in the mid-1360s.[49] The collapse in the number of merchets from thirty-one in the 1340s to six in the 1350s was partly due to the fact that merchet was no longer being collected from villein landholders (Table 10.6). Amercements for mill suit and payments for recognition were last recorded in the

Table 10.6 Incidence of merchet, and mean size of levy, at Norton, 1325–1469

Period	Male merchets	Mean levy	Female merchets	Mean levy	Married without licence
1325–29	2	9.0d.	4	13.5d.	4 (18.0d.)
1330–39	17	34.8d.	19	29.5d.	3 (12.0d.)
1340–49	15	13.7d.	16	27.8d.	12 (8.5d.)
1350–59	1	24.0d.	5	11.3d.	4 (16.8d.)
1360–69	1	24.0d.	4	12.0d.	0
1370–79	1	12.0d.	3	4.0d.	0
1380–89	0	0	1	12.0d.	0
1390–99	0	0	0	0	0
1400–9	1	12.0d.	0	0	0
1410–19	1	80.0d.	0	0	1 (12.0d.)
1420–29	0	0	0	0	0
1430–39	0	0	0	0	0
1440–49	0	0	2	12.0d.	0
1450–59	0	0	2	10.0d.	0
1460–69	0	0	0	0	0

Combined marriage and entry fines and illegal marriages are excluded.

Source: Foden, *Records of the Manor of Norton.*

1350s, and it is highly probable that labour services were extensively commuted (Table 10.1).[50] Hence, from the 1360s hereditary service tenancies at Norton owed a reduced package of heriot, nominal cash rent, commutation payments for labour services, entry fine, possible election to manorial office and suit of court.[51]

By the 1380s the servile land market reveals clear signs of depression. Both the aggregate number (eight) and proportion (35 per cent) of inter-peasant transfers fell to their lowest point to date (Table 10.3), while the abandonment of holdings into the lord's hands reached its highest proportion at 26 per cent (Tables 10.2 and 10.4). Entry fines on half-virgates fell to a token offering of a capon or two (Table 10.5). The market recovered slightly in the 1390s, in the sense that tenants were found for most of the holdings that had been abandoned in the 1380s and the volume of transactions did pick up temporarily, but this was only achieved through a raft of seigniorial concessions. First, tenants who were still willing to hold heritably for services had to be enticed with waived entry fines: between 1393 and 1395 they were waived on eleven of fifteen land transfers.[52] Second, in the 1390s the number of grants of land on money rents rose sharply to represent 26 per cent of all transfers during that decade (Tables 10.3 and 10.4). Finally, in 1394 all labour services were formally commuted for a fixed term of twenty years through a collective agreement between the cellarer and the villein tenants. The timing was a function of the lord negotiating a new long-term lease of the manorial demesne, whereupon the customary tenants had petitioned the lord to commute all labour services for its duration. The lord agreed, subject to the caveat that any failure on the part of an individual tenant to pay the commuted sum on the due date would result in the defaulting tenant performing all his works in full for that year.[53]

The minor recovery of the land market in the 1390s was short-lived, and in the first decade of the fifteenth century another surge of abandoned holdings followed. When, in 1402, the court called for heirs of 'vacant lands and tenements in the lord's hands' to come forward to claim their inheritances, few did so.[54] In 1410 the court noted that one half-virgate, two quarter-virgates, two tenements, two cottages and three tofts were all vacant.[55] The number of villein land transactions halved over the course of the first two decades of the century and thereafter remained at the same low level until the court records cease in the 1460s (Table 10.2). To some extent this reduction disguises the increasing tendency for individual tenants to hold multiple customary holdings and to transfer them en bloc, but mainly it indicates the low level of demand for land.

Chronic difficulties in finding tenants in the 1420s and early 1430s must explain the lord's sudden and short-lived experiment of granting abandoned land to tenants for a fixed term of years, with a total of eight such grants being made in this period (Table 10.4), each involving just an annual money rent fixed for the duration of the term, and owing suit of court. The length of such grants varied from six to forty years, so these grants constituted leases.

They were notionally liable for entry fine, although in reality just one lessee actually paid the fine, with all of the other lessees having their fines waived.[56] A grant of 27 acres in 1427 to Walter Hale included a reduced rent for the first two years, which emphasises the concessions required to attract tenants during this depressed land market.[57] The last fixed-term grant was made in 1439.[58] Its disappearance thereafter coincided with a rise in conversions of service tenancies to hereditary money tenancies. By the 1450s 70 per cent of the thirteen grants of customary land in that decade were on hereditary cash tenancies (Tables 10.2–10.4). Some grants of hereditary cash tenancies stated that only suit of court was owed with the annual fixed rent, whereas others included heriot explicitly.[59] The conveyance usually stated that the land was held 'by the service of rent'. The money tenure removed liability for all other forms of rent, such as labour services, and was effectively a copyhold by inheritance.

Variable incidents

The relative weight and importance of labour services on the 36-acre half-virgate at Norton is revealed by their fixed commutation value of 16s. 6d. per holding in 1394, comprising 9s. 4d. for 'smalewerkes' (probably week works) and ploughing works, 8d. for haymaking, and 6s. for harvest works, plus 6d. for boonworks: the smaller holdings owing proportionally fewer services.[60] The absence of manorial accounts for Norton means that we cannot know to what extent such services had been utilised on the demesne or the extent to which they had been commuted at any point in the fourteenth century. However, the complete absence of any defaults of, or refusals to perform, labour services after 1359 is highly suggestive of extensive commutation by that date (Table 10.7). Perhaps the demesne was now no longer managed directly, which would explain the reduced need for labour services, although the first explicit mention of demesne leasing occurs as late as 1383, when the lessee was nominated as being responsible for the care of two horses that had been rendered as heriots.[61] As we have seen, in 1394 all labour services were formally commuted for twenty years.

Table 10.7 Incidence of recorded non-performance of labour services on Norton manor, 1325–1469

Year	Non-performance of labour services
1325	3 default on 9½ boon-days
1326	11 refuse carrying service
1328	1 defaults on ploughing 1 defaults on harvest 1 defaults on 2 boon-days
1335	2 default on harvest
1353	1 defaults on boon-days
1354	7 default on 1 boon-day each 1 defaults on 5 boon-days
1355	1 defaults on 10 boon-days
1358	3 default on 11 days at harvest
1359	1 defaults on 2 boon-days

Source: Foden, *Records of the Manor of Norton.*

Heriot was due whenever a tenant relinquished customary land, but not from landless serfs.[62] It was due on certain categories of free land.[63] Heriots usually took the form of the tenant's best beast, although those without animals paid either in cash or with their best chattel (pots, plates and a ploughshare are recorded).[64] Heriots were occasionally waived because of poverty, or because the deceased did not have any goods within the manor, but otherwise they were routinely enforced. There is not a single example at Norton of a tenant making a deathbed surrender of customary land to avoid paying heriot. The number of heriots drifted downwards during the fifteenth century, from twelve per decade in 1380–99 to two in 1450–69 (Table 10.8). In 1437 – a year of widespread harvest failure – the 'poor tenants' of Norton had petitioned the cellarer of St Albans for some relief from heriot, and the response was to introduce cash tariffs for each size of holding – 3s. 4d. for a virgate, 20d. for a half-virgate and 12d. for a cottage – an arrangement that remained in place for the next sixty years.[65] This represented a hefty

Table 10.8 Frequency of merchet, heriot, leyrwite and mill suit at Norton, 1325–1469

Period	Merchet	Heriot	Leyrwite	Mill suit
1325–29	6	8	4	46
1330–39	36	11	9	25
1340–49	31	48	16	17
1350–59	6	11	8	6
1360–69	5	16	0	0
1370–79	4	13	0	0
1380–89	1	12	0	0
1390–99	0	11	0	0
1400–9	1	9	0	0
1410–19	1	5	0	0
1420–29	0	3	0	0
1430–39	0	10	0	0
1440–49	2	6	0	0
1450–59	2	2	0	0
1460–69	0	2	0	0

Merchet, heriot, mill suit and leyrwite fines only (including if waived).

Source: Foden, *Records of the Manor of Norton.*

remission from the customary render of a best beast, because these had been routinely valued at between 5s. and 10s., and the decision to fix this agreement for sixty years indicates that neither lord nor peasants expected the general economic position to improve in the near future: the fixing of heriot at a lower rate must have helped the latter negotiate whatever short-term challenges they were facing.

Entry fines were liable on the transfer of customary land, although the exact level varied according to individual circumstances. In the pre-plague era, the average fine for a half-virgate was 12s., which, at around 4d. per acre, was low by national standards. As we have seen, in the third quarter of the fourteenth century entry fines per half-virgate fell to around one-quarter of their pre-plague level and did not recover (Table 10.5). Indeed, from the 1390s fines were extensively waived to attract tenants.

Recognition payments were also due on the election of a new abbot of St Albans. In 1277 the court roll had listed thirty-two tenants paying specified sums ranging from 6d. to 6s., and the total owed was 56s. 6d. – i.e. a mean of 21d. per head.[66] These sums were thus clearly linked to some assessment of the tenant's ability to pay. In 1350, on the election of abbot Thomas de la Mare, the villein tenants paid a collective fine of 60s., described as 'common tallage in subsidy at the creation of the lord abbot'.[67] The villeins must have decided among themselves how much each of them was to pay. There are no other references to recognition or tallage in the Norton records.

In the second quarter of the fourteenth century, mill suit was assiduously enforced, judging by the mean of thirty amercements for breaches in each decade (Table 10.8). The average amercement was just under 3d. (Table 10.9). The number of amercements dropped to six in the 1350s, and the average fine to 2d., with the last amercement for evasion recorded in 1355. In 1369 two men were presented, but not amerced, for failing to grind at the lord's mill, then in 1372 the court stated that no tenants were grinding grain at the lord's mill and all were placed under a penalty of 20s. for any subsequent failure to grind there.[68] There is, however, no evidence that the tenants complied with this order or that the lord imposed the penalty. In 1446 the jurors affirmed that all tenants must grind at the lord's mill under threat of a 3s. 4d. penalty. A manorial mill continued to function throughout the later Middle Ages, because millers were amerced for taking excessive tolls there well into the sixteenth century.[69] It appears that after 1355 the cellarer occasionally postured over mill suit, but never again enforced it.

In 1330–49 an average of twelve cases of leyrwite were recorded in each decade, with an average fine of around 4d. In the 1350s the mean fell to eight cases, although the mean fine rose to 7d. (Table 10.10). The last case was recorded in 1357 (Table 10.1). Similarly, the number of licences to educate servile boys fell from seven in the 1330s to one in the 1350s, although the mean fine doubled from 12d. in the 1340s to 24d. in the 1350s. There were only two such fines thereafter, both at much reduced rates (6d. and 12d.), the last in 1413 (Table 10.10).

Table 10.9 Incidence of mill suit, and mean size of levy, at Norton, 1325–1469

Period	No. of cases of mill suit	Mean amercement
1325–29	46	2.4d.
1330–39	25	2.4d.
1340–49	17	3.6d.
1350–59	6	2.2d.
1360–69	0[a]	—
1370–79	0[a]	—
1380–89	0	—
1390–99	0	—
1400–9	0	—
1410–19	0	—
1420–29	0	—
1430–39	0	—
1440–49	0[a]	—
1450–59	0	—
1460–69	0	—

[a] *In this decade one order for villeins to grind at the lord's mill was made, but no presentments.*

Source: Foden, *Records of the Manor of Norton.*

Both males and females were liable for merchet and the fine varied according to individual circumstance. For example, servile women marrying freemen usually paid higher fines to do so.[70] Equal numbers of males and females were charged in the pre-plague era, around seventeen of each per decade, and the mean levy for both men and women was around 27d. Marriages without licence were much less common and attracted a much lower fine of around 12d. (Table 10.6), so this was probably imposed on some poorer serfs. Before the Black Death, merchet was due from customary landholders and hereditary serfs.[71] In 1343 a villein tenant, Ralph Boveton, paid 2s. for permission to marry his daughter, and 'lord'

Table 10.10 Incidence of leyrwite and licences to educate, and mean size of levy, at Norton, 1325–1469

Period	No. of leyrwite	Mean fine	No. of licences to educate	Mean fine
1325–29	4	6.0d.	1	6.0d.
1330–39	9	3.4d.	7	3.8d.
1340–49	16	4.6d.	1	12.0d.
1350–59	8	6.8d.	1	24.0d.
1360–69	0	—	1	6.0d.
1370–79	0	—	0	—
1380–89	0	—	0	—
1390–99	0	—	0	—
1400–9	0	—	0[a]	—
1410–19	0	—	1	12.0d.
1420–29	0	—	0	—
1430–39	0	—	0	—
1440–49	0	—	0	—
1450–59	0	—	0	—
1460–69	0	—	0	—

[a] *One presentment, no fine.*

Source: Foden, *Records of the Manor of Norton.*

Henry Bate obtained, but did not pay for, permission for his sister to marry where and to whom she pleased.[72]

The number of merchets and marriages without licence collapsed from a combined mean of thirty-three per decade in 1330–49 to five in 1350–69. From the 1350s merchet ceased to be an incident of villein tenure and was now due only from hereditary serfs, although male merchets had become rare (Table 10.6). The mean levy on the (small sample of) male merchets was 24d. in 1330–49 and 24d. in 1350–69, whereas the corresponding figures for females were 28d. and 12d. Only seven merchets were levied after 1380 (Table 10.8). The last male merchet was an isolated

Table 10.11 Frequency of chevage and presentments for absence at Norton, 1325–1474

Period	Total no. of annual presentments for absence	Total no. of annual chevage cases
1325–49	35	5
1350–74	206	0
1375–99	79	0
1400–24	204	2
1425–49	205	2
1450–74	24	0

Source: Foden, *Records of the Manor of Norton.*

and unusually expensive case in 1415. Not one female merchet was levied between 1384 and 1440, and the last occurred in 1453 (Tables 10.1 and 10.6).[73]

In the first half of the fourteenth century the management of servile migration was very lax. Between 1249 and 1348 an average of only 0.21 cases of chevage and presentments for absence were recorded per court, of which just 7 per cent included information about the whereabouts of the serf, and not a single one of these cases involved a female.[74] This cannot have reflected the real extent of the outward movement of the landless and land-deficient, male or female, in search of a livelihood in the pre-plague period. Indeed, a sudden clampdown in 1345 identified ten serfs who were 'serving [*deservit*] outside the lordship without chevage' (Table 10.12). Court officials ordered the arrest of these serfs, although nothing further is recorded.[75] Just five chevage payments were received between 1325 and 1349 (Table 10.11). The earliest payments were described not as 'chevage', but as licences for the serf, 'serve where he will'. They involved the up-front payment of a small lump sum, followed by the render of a capon for each year spent away from the manor, plus a requirement to return for the annual view of frankpledge.[76] For example, in 1340 William le Newman agreed to pay 12d. plus one capon annually for licence to marry and 'to serve and be an apprentice where he will'.[77] In 1336 the court noted

Table 10.12 Recorded flight of serfs from Norton, 1327–1454

Year	No. of people presented for absence	No. of people charged for chevage
1327	1	0
1328	2	0
1329	1	0
1332	1	0
1336	0	1
1340	0	1
1343	1	0
1345	10	0
1346	11[a]	2
1347	0	1
1349	8	0
1350	5	0
1352	11[a]	0
1354	3	0
1355	6	0
1356	14[a]	0
1357	18[a]	0
1360	12[a]	0
1361	14[a]	0
1362	7	0
1363	7	0
1364	7	0
1365	14[a]	0
1366	11[a]	0
1367	6	0
1368	13[a]	0
1369	12[a]	0

Year	No. of people presented for absence	No. of people charged for chevage
1370	12[a]	0
1371	12[a]	0
1372	12[a]	0
1373	5	0
1374	5	0
1375	4	0
1376	8[a]	0
1377	7[a]	0
1379	7	0
1380	6	0
1381	13[a]	0
1382	6	0
1383	7	0
1384	6	0
1386	10[a]	0
1388	5	0
1400	2	0
1402	5	0
1403	5	0
1404	5	0
1405	4	0
1406	9	0
1407	11	0
1408	14	0
1409	17	0
1410	17	0
1411	18	0

(*continued*)

Table 10.12 (Cont.)

Year	No. of people presented for absence	No. of people charged for chevage
1412	18	0
1413	36[a]	0
1414	19	0
1415	10	2
1423	13	0
1424	11	0
1425	11	0
1426	6	0
1427	9	0
1428	8	0
1429	11	0
1430	12	0
1431	12	0
1432	10	0
1433	10	0
1434	7	0
1435	6	0
1436	7	0
1437	4	0
1438	4	0
1439	4	0
1440	4	0
1441	8	0
1442	16[a]	0
1443	10	0
1444	10	0
1445	11	0

Year	No. of people presented for absence	No. of people charged for chevage
1447	11	1
1448	11	1
1450	6	0
1451	6	0
1452	6	0
1453	6	0
1454	0	0

[a] *In these years there were more presentments for absence than people presented for absence because some individuals were presented twice within the calendar year.*

Source: Foden, *Records of the Manor of Norton.*

that an emigrant was still liable for tallage in proportion to his goods.[78] After 1346 the payment to remain outside the manor was routinely described as chevage, with the lump sum being discarded and replaced with a fixed annual sum.[79]

In the post-plague era the reporting of absent serfs increased to an average of 5.4 cases per court, reflecting the heightened sensitivity to their departure. There followed surges of reporting activity, such as the rapid rise from the 1350s, which then waned after the early 1370s, until another surge of interest after 1406 (Table 10.12). The majority of these cases were presentments for absence, which were repeated assiduously each year until they ceased in 1453. Yet none of this heightened interest in migrant serfs resulted in an increase in the number and size of chevage payments. Only four chevage payments are recorded after 1350: two in 1415, at an average fine of 16d., and two others in 1447 and 1448, which yielded 2d. each (Table 10.11).[80] Therefore, the purpose of reporting those who were absent must have been to retain track of hereditary serfs either out of a sense of bureaucratic duty or for the prospect of pressurising a successful migrant for a sizeable manumission. Manumissions, however, are not recorded in the court rolls.

As the frequency of recorded absences increased after 1350, so did the quality of the information provided about individual migrants: 82 per cent of all entries included the location of the serf and 25 per cent now concerned women.[81] Most migration remained local, with around 60 per cent of all migrants being resident within 10 miles of Norton. A high proportion of serfs, around one-half, headed for towns, with very little difference in the gendered pattern of migration.[82]

Attitudes to serfdom

Evidence of direct conflict between the cellarer and serfs from the court rolls is very limited. The contention over mill suit in the riot of 1327 at St Albans is perhaps reflected in the highest incidence of breaches of mill suit at Norton, with forty-six cases being recorded in 1325–29 compared with only seventeen in the whole of the 1340s (Table 10.8). The only other overt contention over serfdom occurred in the late 1330s, when hereditary serfs came under unusual and specific scrutiny in successive courts for no obvious reason. In 1337 Agnes Boveton claimed to be free, but an inquisition found that she was a serf.[83] In May 1338 a series of proclamations implied some contemporary public order concerns: serfs were not allowed to wound others under threat of a 20s. penalty; they were not to waste their goods and chattels in the taverns of Baldock; brewers were reminded to sell their wares locally according to the assize of ale; villein tenants were not to sell their land, or its produce, to people in Baldock; and, finally, villeins were not to overstock Norton's pastures with the sheep of outsiders (it is clear that some had been taking money to do so).[84] The background to this flurry of ordinances is unclear and there is no record that the court subsequently enforced them.

As we have seen, many of the burdens attached to villein tenure eased immediately after the Black Death. From the 1350s merchet was no longer an incident of tenure, mill suit disappeared after 1355, and the average level of entry fines for half-virgates fell by two-thirds between 1330–48 and 1350–69 (Table 10.5). No one was forced to hold villein land. The only aggressive tactics towards villein landholders were the tighter control over the recording of subletting and an immediate seigniorial clampdown on the wastage of buildings. Presentments for the latter had been recorded occasionally before the Black Death, but in the 1350s the interest of the court heightened as some of the local housing stock became superfluous to requirements following the mass mortality of the plague. A spate of presentments was recorded between 1353 and 1361, threatening penalties of between 2s. and 10s. for non-compliance by the next court. However, in only one of these cases did the court actually enforce its threats: in 1355 John Love was warned to repair the waste on his holding, in early 1356 he was fined 3d. for not doing so and later in the year he was fined another 6s. 8d. for his continued inaction.[85] For the next five years he continued to be threatened with a 2s. penalty, as did a handful of other tenants, without ever being fined, until the presentments largely ceased in the early 1360s. Another spate of presentments for wastage of villein-holdings occurred in the 1380s and 1390s following another sharp contraction in the land market, although the court did not actually levy many amercements or penalties.[86] After the early 1360s the court's bark was much worse than its bite in relation to wastage.

In the 1350s the lord's heightened interest in hereditary serfs was apparent through the recording of migrants (Table 10.11). In April 1349 the court noted the absence of eight serfs from the manor and ordered their bodily seizure.[87] For the rest of the 1350s the annual number of presentments for absence remained high (Table 10.12) and the entries in the court rolls became more informative about the whereabouts of those who had departed. In 1357 the lord ordered that all fugitives should be seized bodily and taken directly to St Albans.[88] However, it is not at all clear how the suitors at the court, let alone the manorial officials, were supposed to implement this order, and there is no evidence that it was ever enforced. Likewise, not a single chevage payment is recorded in the third quarter of the fourteenth century, despite the sharp rise in information about migrants (Table 10.11).

Other indicators of a tighter management of serfs are evident. In 1352 John Buschel was declared a villein in full court and committed to the custody of the constable of Norton for onward transmission to the gaol at St Albans: no details are provided, but Buschel was not a flown serf and so this action may have been related to some repeated or flagrant breach of the Statute of Labourers.[89] Nothing more is heard of John and so it seems that he had not returned to the manor. There was a single dispute over personal status: in April 1352 the jury presented John le Newman for committing waste on his cottage, to which John countered that he held the land freely and therefore was not liable to be charged for wastage. When he duly produced his free charter as proof at the very next court, the lord's officials alleged instead that he was a serf by blood: John denied that this was the case and asked for a jury of inquiry to pronounce upon the matter. The cottage was ordered to be seized until the issue was resolved. In April 1353 an inquest jury declared him to be free.[90]

Other symptoms of this seigniorial clampdown are mixed. On the one hand, there is evidence for aggressive new approaches, such as the rise in the mean levy for leyrwite in the 1350s (Table 10.10) and the inclusion of males for the first time. The highest number of presentments for non-performance of labour services occurred between 1353 and 1358 (Table 10.7). On the other hand, as we have seen, merchet cases collapsed and the average fine paid by women fell by over half. No pressure was exerted upon relatives or on the community to return migrants, no physical seizures of flown serfs were made, no chevage was paid, and no novel forms of service are recorded. There is no explicit evidence of any regulation of, or intervention in, the labour market after the Black Death.[91]

Taken together, then, these examples from the 1350s are consistent with a seigniorial reaction of sorts against hereditary serfs. Yet it was not sustained into the 1360s, when leyrwite and fines for illegal marriages disappeared, and just one licence to educate was issued and at a much-reduced sum. Merchets were now infrequent and of low value. There were no more disputes over personal status, and no evidence for any form of coercion in the land or labour markets. The weakness of the lord's position is indicated by an episode in 1362 involving William Sayer, who inherited a messuage and standardised villein-holding from his father and refused outright in full court to hold them: no action was taken against him, and a year later the holding was granted to another tenant.[92] The court rolls contain no record of any dispute between the villeins of Norton and the lord over any aspect of villeinage. A court held on 2 July 1381 in the immediate aftermath of the Peasants' Revolt contains no hint of any disturbance having taken place there.[93]

There was one short surge of renewed interest in migrant serfs from the May court of 1406, which identified nine absent serfs, more than double the number of the previous court (Table 10.12), and also noted those who had progeny.[94] The lord must have directed the jurors to produce detailed and up-to-date information about migrants. By highlighting those absent serfs with children, the lord's officials were able to elicit even more information over the next few years, and consequently the number of serfs – and females in particular – recorded as absent increased markedly. Increased details about individual serfs were also acquired, such as identifying the names and occupations of the men with whom servile women were now living.[95] In 1413 this clampdown also yielded the first payment for licence to educate since 1361 – and the last ever charged on this manor – and, 1415, two isolated chevage payments (Tables 10.1 and 10.12).[96]

Summary

The general management of serfdom in the pre-plague period at Norton conforms closely to the characteristics identified in Chapters 2–4. The codification of custom had caused head rents to ossify. Custom also dictated the size of recognition payments, and the arrangements governing heriot and entry fines. Mill suit appears to have been consistently enforced. Licences to educate were routinely enforced on hereditary serfs, whereas merchet and leyrwite were common but more selectively imposed. There were few controls on, or fees for, movement off the manor. The title to villein tenure was secure if customary procedures were followed, and disputes over title were resolved by reference to written precedents. The standardised virgates remained virtually intact and were heritable by the eldest male, and the servile land market was not very active, as can be seen from the relatively low number of land transfers per annum (five) and the low mean sum paid for entry fines to half-virgates (4d. per acre). In total, there were just two disputes over personal status and the lord abided by the testimony of the court in resolving them.

In the immediate aftermath of the Black Death, when around half of the villein tenantry died, villein tenure underwent rapid and significant change. Although hereditary service tenure remained dominant, its rent package was quickly diluted: merchet, recognition and mill suit ceased to be conditions of tenure, entry fines collapsed, and after 1358 labour services appear to have been extensively commuted. The servile land market contracted significantly between the 1340s and 1350s: the volume of transfers halved, one-fifth of transfers now lingered in the lord's hands for want of an immediate replacement, and the mean entry fine for a half-virgate fell by 72 per cent. The demand for servile land dropped further in the 1380s, when entry fines became nominal or were routinely waived. Recorded migrations rose sharply in the 1350s. Refusals to perform labour services were low and infrequent, and confined to seasonal works, but their incidence was highest in the 1350s. A seigniorial reaction is evident in the 1350s, but it was narrowly targeted and rapidly fizzled out.

Villeinage was severely weakened in the decade following the Black Death and its remaining vestiges withered during the fifteenth century. This chronology correlates closely with the demographic shock of 1348–49. The latter triggered an immediate collapse in the demand for servile land, far beyond anything within the cellarer's power to control, which was partly exacerbated in the 1350s by some servile fight from the manor and, to a much lesser extent, minor outbreaks of direct resistance to labour services.

Notes

1 Foden, *Records of the Manor of Norton*, pp. xxxii–xxxiv.
2 Ibid., pp. xxv–xxvi.
3 Ibid., p. xxvi.
4 Ibid., p. xxix.
5 Ibid., pp xli, 35.
6 Ibid., p. 102.
7 Ibid., p. 157.
8 The court was clear too that free tenants who failed to perform their services were also vulnerable to seizure, so this approach was not exclusively a feature of servile tenures; ibid., p. 147.
9 Ibid., p. 89. Likewise, John Bale failed to render merchet, and his lands were ordered to be seized (p. 87).
10 Ibid., pp. 117, 139.

11 Ibid., p. 86.
12 Ibid., pp. 88, 91.
13 Ibid., p. 87.
14 Bailey, *After the Black Death*, p. 85.
15 Foden, *Records of the Manor of Norton*, p. 84.
16 Ibid., pp. 117ff. Hence, from 1339: 'to hold to him and his heirs in villeinage at the will of the lord through due and accustomed services'.
17 Ibid., pp. 35, 40–1.
18 Ibid., pp. 49, 133, 137, 146.
19 Ibid., p. 133.
20 Ibid., p. xliv. See the moiety of a half-virgate held by John Smith; ibid., p. 185.
21 For example, ibid., pp. 61–3, 97.
22 Ibid., pp. 91–2.
23 Ibid., pp. xliii–xliv.
24 Ibid., pp. xliv, 111.
25 Ibid., p. 92.
26 Ibid., pp. 125, 138.
27 Ibid., pp. 73, 111, 125.
28 Ibid., p. 62.
29 Ibid., pp. 94, 108.
30 Ibid., p. 111.
31 See, for example, ibid., pp. 49, 76, 83, 95, 101, 107, 112, 119–20, 133, 137 (land disputes); 68 (sublet dispute); 40, 61 (merchet payment).
32 Ibid., pp. xxx–xxxi, 2.
33 Such as the Bates (ibid., pp. 45–6, 49), the Bovetons (pp. 18, 41, 45, 47, 55), the Pruddes pp. (40, 45–7, 58), the Hales (pp. 40–1, 45, 47, 49, 54) and the Sayers (p. 46).
34 Ibid., pp. 43–4, 118.
35 Ibid., pp. 198–225.
36 Brooker and Flood, *Hertfordshire Lay Subsidy Rolls*, p. 134; Foden, *Records of the Manor of Norton*, pp. 38 (Warde and Bate), 39 (Benes), 40 (Sawyer), 45 (Bonde).
37 Brooker and Flood, *Hertfordshire Lay Subsidy Rolls*, p. 134; Foden, *Records of the Manor of Norton*, pp. 40–1, 42 (John Boveton son's merchet).
38 Foden, *Records of the Manor of Norton*, pp. 136–46 Cf. Levett, *Studies*, Table II, which has four deaths in October 1348, four in April, twenty in June (*sic*) and three in October.
39 Levett, *Studies*, Table II; Foden, *Records of the Manor of Norton*, p. l.

40 Foden, *Records of the Manor of Norton*, pp. 138–46.
41 Ibid., pp. 142–3, 157.
42 Ibid., pp. 139, 149.
43 Ibid., p. 156.
44 Ibid., pp. 154–6; Slota, 'Law, land transfer', p. 132.
45 See, for example, McGibbon Smith, 'Reflections', pp. 171–2, 212–13; and Faith, 'Fourteenth century: Berkshire', pp. 126–7.
46 Foden, *Records of the Manor of Norton*, p. 149.
47 Ibid., pp. 166–8.
48 Ibid., pp. 176–7, 182–3.
49 Ibid., pp. 170–3.
50 Ibid., p. 147.
51 The election of beadle on rotation from among the customary landholders continued until the 1440s; see ibid., p. xxxiii.
52 Ibid., pp. 201–4.
53 Ibid., p. 203.
54 Ibid., p. 213.
55 Ibid., p. 225.
56 Ibid., p. 239.
57 Ibid., p. 240.
58 Ibid., p. 251.
59 Ibid., pp. 261, 263.
60 Ibid., p. 203.
61 Ibid., p. 191.
62 Noy, *The Winslow Manor Court Books, 1322–1377*, p. xx.
63 Foden, *Records of the Manor of Norton*, pp. 130, 138–9, 142–3.
64 The custom is stated at ibid., p. 249. For examples of plates, pots and ploughshares, see ibid., pp. 97, 127, 157, 166; for waiving on grounds of poverty, see ibid., p. 89.
65 Ibid., p. 249.
66 Ibid., p. 22.
67 Ibid., p. 147.
68 Ibid., pp. 156, 176, 179.
69 Ibid., pp. 226, 236, 278, 297.
70 Ibid., p. 113.
71 The explicit attachment of merchet to land is recorded at ibid., p. 111.
72 Ibid., p. 124.
73 Ibid., pp. 192, 252, 264.
74 Bailey, 'Servile and gender migration', Tables 1 and 2.
75 Foden, *Records of the Manor of Norton*, p. 131.
76 Ibid., pp. 37, 112, 120.
77 Ibid., p. 120.

78 Ibid., p. 112.
79 For two isolated references to chevage in 1271 and 1336, see ibid., pp. 16, 112, then p. 132.
80 Ibid., pp. 233–4, 259.
81 Bailey, 'Servile and gender migration', Tables 1 and 2.
82 Ibid., Table 4.
83 Foden, *Records of the Manor of Norton*, p. 114.
84 Ibid., pp. 114–15.
85 Ibid., pp. 158–60.
86 Ibid., pp. 190, 192, 194–5, 197, 199, 201–2, 205–12.
87 Ibid., p. 139.
88 Ibid., p. 160.
89 Ibid., pp. 149–50.
90 Ibid., pp. 150–2.
91 For the court's activity in matters relating to common rights, see ibid., pp. 55, 71–2, 78, 115, 182, 233, 254, 265.
92 Ibid., pp. 168–70.
93 Ibid., pp. 190–1.
94 Ibid., p. 217.
95 Ibid., p. 228.
96 Ibid., p. 231.

11

Serfdom, the Black Death and three manors of St Albans abbey

St Albans abbey possessed a large estate comprising mainly classic demesne manors with a high proportion of villein land and hereditary serfs. It deployed a standing bureaucracy and its powers over the peasantry were greatly enhanced in Hertfordshire by its additional judicial rights exercised through the Liberty of St Albans. For these reasons, and because of the ferocity of the rebels' attacks in the revolt of 1381, historians have routinely cited the abbey as the epitome of vigorous and onerous seigniorial power. Our three case studies have sought to test this viewpoint on three dispersed manors of the cellarer of the abbey by reconstructing in detail the frequency and severity of servile incidents; the changing nature of villein tenures; the extent to which the lord exercised an arbitrary will; the consistency of the approach to serfdom across the estate; and, finally, the chronology of the decline of serfdom and its correlation with market forces, migration and acts of resistance.

On all three manors in the pre-plague period the range of servile burdens was wide and potentially onerous. Villein tenure involved a cash rent, a relatively heavy load of labour services, an entry fine, heriot, suit of mill, merchet, recognition, election to manorial office and suit of court, while hereditary serfs were liable for the 'uncertain' incidents – i.e. those where the size of the fine was variable – of merchet, leyrwite, chevage, recognition and licences to educate. Yet, in practice, all these incidents were regulated by customary practices and set procedures, which made them less onerous than might first seem to have been the case. Hence, proprietary rights in villein land were reasonably secure and a villein land market existed, subject to standard processes for transfers, registration of title and control over subletting. Head rents were immutable, labour services were fixed and largely commuted for cash from an early date, and the collective sum owed by tenants as recognition was fixed rather than being varied at the will of the lord. The cellarer hardly bothered with mobility restrictions on hereditary serfs, hence chevage was rare, and merchet and leyrwite were imposed selectively. The indifference to migration is especially striking.

Beyond these common features, local influences – whether the specifics of custom or the power of market forces – tended to have more impact than any centrally imposed and standardised policy of the cellarer in determining the management of villeinage. For example, while the cellarer was able to prevent the fragmentation of the standardised holdings at Norton, he was less successful at Winslow, where market forces had served to splinter the standardised virgates through permanent sales of small parcels of land to third parties. Market forces are also evident in the gradations in the rate of entry fine, from the equivalent of 4d. per acre where the land market was subdued at Norton, to 13d. at Codicote and to 28d. at Winslow, where it was most active. The influence of custom is evident in the values for the other 'uncertain' servile dues, which were not standardised across the estate but rather varied locally: the average pre-plague fine for merchet varied from 27d. to 33d., for leyrwite from 4d. to 6d., for mill suit from 2½d. to 4d. and for licences to educate from 7d. to 16d. Similarly, custom dictated the operation of heriot from manor to manor. Thus, at Winslow it was due from landless serfs, but not at Norton or Codicote; it was due whenever villein land was relinquished at Norton, but at Codicote only on the death of a tenant or when a tenant ceased holding any servile land. Thus, local forces, whether customary or market, trumped the power of the cellarer of St Albans to dictate or standardise the size of servile levies across his estate.

In the pre-plague era the operation of serfdom on all three manors conforms broadly to the processes, procedures and practices reconstructed in Chapters 2–4, and hardly at all to the exercise of the arbitrary will of the lord in the legal theory sketched in Chapter 1. There are just two examples of arbitrary seigniorial behaviour from the scores of court rolls studied. The first is the rise in the rate of entry fine at Codicote in the mid-1330s, which coincided with the election of a new abbot, although the sample is small, and the pattern is not replicated at Winslow where the average fine declined marginally in the same period based on a larger sample. The second, and more secure, example is the overturning of custom in the mid-1350s when the cellarer directed a new estate-wide policy that henceforth all subleases should be recorded in the court rolls rather than, as had previously been the case, only those for leases of more than two years. The cellarer was not requiring tenants to pay for a licence to sublet, merely requiring that these shorter leases be recorded in the court rolls, and in any event the frequency of subletting declined sharply after the Black Death.

The breach of custom on subletting in the 1350s coincided with a seigniorial crackdown on all three manors on wastage of villein buildings; on the migration of hereditary serfs; and, to a lesser extent, on the claims of individual peasants to be of free status. This evidence provides the only credible support for the existence of a post-plague seigniorial reaction across the estate, but the case is weak. Even in the 1350s the cellarer was unable to enforce a consistent policy on the management of servile dues across all three manors, as when the mean fine for merchet doubled between the 1340s and 1350s at Winslow yet halved at Norton. The rent package on villein service tenure was rapidly diluted in the 1350s on all three manors, through the collapse of the value of entry fines and the disappearance of merchet and tallage. Finally, the tougher policies on migrants and dilapidations were seemingly unsustainable, because in the early 1360s both fizzled out quickly and hardly any licences to migrate were paid. The failure to maintain even a narrowly constructed seigniorial reaction across the estate beyond the 1350s offers unequivocal confirmation that the arbitrary will of one of the most powerful and conservative lords in fourteenth-century England was circumscribed by what the local market would bear and what local custom would allow. It also testifies to the pre-existing weakness of serfdom. The sudden shortage of tenants and workers after the Black Death of 1348–49 caused the servile land market to lose much of its buoyancy. The cellarer had not controlled servile migration before the Black Death and his attempts to reassert some control in the 1350s were ineffective, however irksome they may have been to serfs. Serfdom – especially tenurial serfdom – was terminally wounded by the 1360s, principally by the shift in market forces caused by the Black Death and the failure to control out-migration. Thereafter its vestiges suffered a slow demise in the second quarter of the fifteenth century.

The experience of serfdom on these three manors is exemplified particularly well by the cellarer's management of mill suit. As we have seen, conflict over the seigniorial monopoly of mill suit and milling in the fourteenth century is oft cited as a major source of conflict between the abbey and its tenants, and was apparently a major issue for the St Albans rebels in 1381.[1] Yet mill suit was not a recurrent or significant source of contention on any of the three manors studied here. It was certainly enforced in the pre-plague era, but after 1350 its enforcement was low-key and infrequent. Recorded breaches of mill suit ceased as early as 1337 at Codicote and 1355 at Norton, while at Winslow the number of presentments collapsed in the 1360s, never to recover. It may be that mill suit enforcement was more an issue on the abbatial manors, or indeed for the residents of the borough of St Albans itself. However, Matthew Tompkins's study of the court books of the manor of Park, a vast manor on the outskirts of the borough of St Albans, would suggest that this was not the case. Here the abbot did threaten large fines for non-performance of mill suit in the run-up to the revolt, but this was largely a matter of bluff, and the size of actual amercements was low (a penny or two): in reality, enforcement of mill suit largely 'eluded [the lord's] grasp'.[2] As yet, not a single detailed study of a St Albans manor has yielded evidence that the abbey was aggressively imposing mill suit on its villeins throughout the century, let alone in the build up to 1381.

By the 1360s merchet, recognition and mill suit had decayed on service tenure, entry fines were barely one-third of their pre-plague value, and labour services were extensively commuted. There were, however, few conversions of villein land to leases and monetary tenures before the 1390s, so that there remained the remote possibility that, one day, all these old dues could be restored, and labour services and the like could once again be demanded. Consequently, during the fifteenth century tenants on all three manors began to seek a formal arrangement to close off any future prospect of their reinstatement through the transfer of land from service to monetary tenure – owing a fixed cash sum annually, suit of court, a notional entry fine and a cash heriot – on which the only variable due was now the entry fine. These were, in effect, hereditary copyhold tenures.

Evidence from the court rolls for tension between lord and serfs peaked in the 1350s and eased thereafter. Peasant resistance in that decade to the cellarer's attempts to tighten aspects of hereditary servility and the dilapidation of buildings must have convinced the lord of the futility of persisting with such a policy across the estate. As there was no sustained 'seigniorial reaction' to reimpose serfdom in the third quarter of the fourteenth century, then it manifestly cannot have been the primary cause of the 1381 uprising at St Albans. Having said that, the rebels are unlikely to have forgotten John Mote's actions as cellarer in the 1350s, which may well have made him a prime target.[3] None of this evidence undermines the ferocity of the rebels' actions or their enmity towards the abbey in June 1381, or indeed the likelihood that the residual burdens of villeinage were a strand of discontent, because the rebels did demand the abbey's copies of manorial court books.[4] It does, however, demand that we seek a more nuanced understanding of their frustrations with villeinage, and other explanations for their ire than those cited in the traditional narratives. It may well be that the principal source of tension was between the townsfolk and the abbey within the borough of St Albans itself. If rural rebels and serfs really were prominent participants in the revolt, perhaps their discontent was directed at the widespread persistence of service tenure across the estate, in contrast to other manors in this area of England, where by 1381 conversions to monetary tenures and leases had made considerable headway. Andrew Prescott has shown convincingly how a key element of the rebel demands in London – including representatives from Hertfordshire – was to replace service tenure with money tenancies capped at 4d. per acre.[5] Another possible explanation for the involvement of rural serfs might be protests against the maladministration of justice within the Liberty of St Albans, because profiteering through the leasing of privatised judicial franchises such as these had become a national concern in the third quarter of the fourteenth century.[6] Whatever the reason for the events of 1381 in St Albans, the cellarer of this great abbey hardly ever behaved arbitrarily towards his serfs; could not enforce the full legal theory of common law villeinage on his estate; was unable to reimpose serfdom after the Black Death; and, by the end of the 1360s, had greatly diluted both villein tenure and personal servility.

Notes

1 Justice, *Writing and Rebellion*, pp. 136, 168–70.
2 Tompkins, 'The manor of Park in the fourteenth century', pp. 71–2.
3 Levett, *Studies*, p. 204.
4 Poos, 'Medieval English manorial courts', p. 207 n. 27.
5 A. Prescott, 'The *Anonimalle Chronicle* narrative of the Peasants' Revolt of 1381', in Dodd and Lacey, *Fourteenth Century England*, Vol. XIII, pp. 131–60 (pp. 155–6).
6 Bailey, *After the Black Death*, pp. 94–5, 204–6, 262–3.

Conclusion

For well over a century historians have debated the nature of serfdom in medieval England, exploring its influence on social relations, its implications for economic development, its role in the crisis of the early fourteenth century, its possible reimposition in the immediate aftermath of the first pandemic and the reasons for its subsequent decline. Since the 1980s a succession of localised case studies has provided us with detailed reconstructions of how it operated, particularly in the pre-plague period. Yet the implications of these local studies remain at odds with many of the recent general assessments of the subject. Scholars such as Brenner, Kitsikopoulos, Dimmock, Hole, Peters, Jedwab et al., Carocci and Ghosh have all continued to propagate – to various degrees – the traditional stereotype of English serfdom as socially restrictive, highly extractive and deeply pervasive, even though painstaking research at the local level has actually revealed a very different picture.[1] The co-existence in the scholarship of two directly contradictory views of the nature of English serfdom in the age of the Black Death – one portraying it as strong, the other as weak – and the oscillation of historical opinion from one to the other is confusing to students and historians who are unfamiliar with the subject. Furthermore, the two viewpoints lead to two fundamentally different explanations for the trajectory of economic and social development in the pre- and post-plague eras, one emphasising the major role of serfdom in the crisis of the first half of the fourteenth century, its contribution to the Peasants' Revolt of 1381 and its decline from the later fourteenth century, whereas the other downplays its influence on both crisis and revolt, and projects a rapid decline in the third quarter of the fourteenth century.

One of the objectives of this book has been to explain how the traditional view of English serfdom as 'pervasive', 'exploitative' and 'oppressive' has remained doggedly persistent in the face of a mounting and ultimately overwhelming body of evidence demonstrating conclusively that such a position misrepresents a much more complex reality. This process has involved a reconstruction of different methodologies, and of illustrating the different ways of treating historical evidence, as much as an exploration of serfdom itself. One reason for the persistence of the original view is the tendency of some historians to view serfdom critically through a moral lens. Another is that many of the scholars who promote the traditional view are not English medieval specialists, and their work understandably exhibits a lighter-touch engagement with the evidentiary base and a limited knowledge of the raft of detailed case studies. For example, Brenner's influential and wide-ranging arguments about the different trajectories of serfdom in England, France and eastern Europe (published in 1976 and 1982) relied on the patchy evidence in the medieval scholarship published between the 1950s and 1970s. When he returned to the debate on European serfdom with powerful restatements of his original arguments (published in 1996, 1997 and 2007) he still did not mention, let alone respond to, major critiques of his work that had appeared in high-profile publications by four historians in 1990 (Hoyle), 1993 (Mate), 1995 (Rigby) and 2000 (Whittle), which drew upon major advances in the scale of the evidence base.[2]

The lack of familiarity of non-specialists with the growing library of technical and localised studies is understandable, given that such works are often hard to access and tend to be little known outside a small circle of scholars of medieval England. However, even some of the latterhave occasionally compounded the misunderstandings, thereby perpetuating the traditional view, by cherry-picking an eye-catching anecdote or two of a heavy servile due or the heavy-handed treatment of a serf. Such truffles are picked and presented with the strong implication that they are typical of arrangements on that particular manor and, by implication, everywhere else.[3] They are also selected to illustrate the social dimension of serfdom rather than its economic significance.[4] But in order to understand the lived experience of the serf, let alone to assess the economic burden of serfdom, we have to reconstruct what was normal or typical rather than dwelling on exceptions, and this requires the aggregation of large samples, averages calculated from many data points and information drawn from a wide area. As I have demonstrated, whenever a robust quantitative method is deployed, and whenever anecdotal examples are properly contextualised to establish their typicality, the individual examples of harsh treatment are exposed as isolated occurrences, and the traditional view looks unconvincing. Campbell and Bartley's monumental research into the geography and structure of manorial lordship, based on thousands of manorial extents, demonstrates unequivocally that villeinage was largely insignificant on many lay manors and relatively unimportant in some regions of England.[5]

Another reason for the persistence in the modern scholarship of the traditional view that English serfdom was powerful and peaked in the pre-plague era is the pervasive influence of theoretical presuppositions and political ideology on the subject. Serfdom's importance within the discipline of economic and social history makes it a magnet for theorists, particularly those preoccupied with the history of the inequality of wealth and status within societies. Indeed, theory was central to the work of the pioneering scholars who in the mid-twentieth century blazed a trail across the largely unchartered territory of the medieval English economy. Postan was a neo-Malthusian who sought evidence of overpopulation and demographic checks in the pre-plague period, whereas Kosminsky and Hilton were neo-Marxists seeking signs of exploitation and immiseration.[6] For them, such ideological and theoretical concepts functioned as a searchlight to identify and illuminate the research pathway through an otherwise vast and largely uncharted academic landscape. The theory also determined their selection, presentation and interpretation of supporting evidence, which explains their specific focus on the issue of rent in general and variable dues in particular. Hence, Postan and Hilton both sought local examples of the ascent of entry fines to unprecedented levels in the early fourteenth century, because they both presumed that the level of rent was the key to defining the relationship between lord and serf, even though their very different explanations for the high rates were determined by their different ideological presumptions: Postan interpreted them as proof of the primacy of extreme pressure of population on landed resources, whereas Hilton interpreted them as proof of the primacy of arbitrary seigniorial power.[7]

The foundations of the grand political ideologies most commonly applied to the study of serfdom have well-documented methodological shortcomings.[8] In part, this is due to the nature of the theoretical beast. Ideology involves presumptions about what happened and thereby predetermines the principal research pathway and its explanatory framework. It predicts where the path is leading, it knows why, and the researcher goes searching for positive proof. Consequently, evidence tends to be used selectively or fleetingly to confirm the theory rather than to test its validity robustly. On occasions, insufficient heed is paid to fresh empirical studies and a mounting body of contradictory data, whereby the theory becomes self-confirming, such as in the works of Brenner and Dimmock cited earlier.[9] In other cases, historians become so fixated on the predetermined pathway ahead, and on searching exclusively for evidence to confirm the theory, that they overlook (or are unable to see) contradictory evidence. For example, in single-mindedly searching for evidence of conflict over serfdom in fourteenth-century Brandon, Müller omits to mention that annual tallage was not collected there and that merchet was uncommon, and skates over the lord's sustained indifference to migration. The failure to record these nil returns, or to discuss their implications, creates a very skewed and partial picture, but the picture is invariably transformed when they are admitted.[10] Thus, whereas ideology is very useful in shaping the research agendas of historians and the questions they ask, its utility diminishes when it dictates their answers, predetermines their explanations for observed events and creates blind spots.

The final reason for the persistence of the traditional narrative is an assumption that the legal theory of serfdom provided lords with pervasive and arbitrary powers over servile people and land, and that this theory closely resembled practice. Yet the law of villeinage was not as powerful and clear-cut as it is often portrayed, because it was riddled with loopholes, exceptions and complications, which had the effect of diminishing its force. Medieval legal theory drew a line of sorts between freedom and unfreedom, but it exaggerated and oversimplified the differences. For example, proving the personal servility of an individual in the courts of common law was fraught with difficulties, because the presumption in law was to liberty and the tests for paternity were not watertight. Likewise, the formal exclusion of villeins from the royal courts on matters of personal status and tenure did not mean that they were rightless or abandoned to the lord's arbitrary will, because they routinely accessed the courts of other jurisdictions – and, on occasions, even the courts of common law – themselves.

The gap between theory and practice becomes even wider when we dissect the operation of serfdom on the ground, even on the manors of the greatest and most conservative lords. Liability for servile dues was very uneven. For example, leyrwite was almost unknown in southern England and less than one-half of English manors rendered tallage annually. The effects of such unevenness were exacerbated by wide variations in their enforcement and management from one manor to another and, indeed, on the same manor over time. Although all female serfs and offspring of villein tenants were theoretically liable for merchet, only an estimated one-third actually paid it. Similarly, many manors recorded migrant serfs episodically rather than consistently, and only a tiny proportion paid chevage. The infrequency of merchet and chevage conveys a powerful signal about the weakness of English serfdom, given the importance assigned to the restrictions on peasant marriage and movement in most narratives of European serfdom. Brenner himself stressed how high levels of seigniorial coercion were only possible when there also existed effective controls over serf mobility, and he is surely correct: in which case, their ineffectiveness across much of England was a major factor in explaining the weak nature and speedy decline of serfdom during the fourteenth century.[11]

Legal theorists writing between the twelfth and fourteenth centuries asserted the precarity of the proprietary rights and dues associated with unfreedom, but in reality tenants of villein land enjoyed de facto security of tenure and rights of inheritance, and so lords hardly ever removed them from their land without due cause, and respected local inheritance customs. The levels of cash, renders and labour services due as rent from land held on villein service tenure remained virtually unchanged from the mid-thirteenth century, so the stated ability of lords to vary them 'at will' was a legal fiction. In practice, therefore, a villein's right to owe fixed and predictable rent for his holding was more powerful than a landlord's legal might to vary that rent.[12] By the end of the thirteenth century, head rents on villein land were comfortably below market rates, given the inexorable rise in population and grain prices. The charges for other occasional dues varied according to circumstance, without being changeable at the whim or arbitrary will of the lord. Instead, they were either fixed by custom, as for heriot, or were variable within locally consistent parameters, as for marriage and entry fines. Servile fines were partly determined by other villeins acting as court officials. Thus, the theoretical uncertainty and variability of the servile rent package were not evident in its actual practice, and therefore the rising scarcity and value of land did not translate into a commensurate increase in seigniorial revenues from this source, as might have been expected.

Ascertaining the affordability of these rents and dues when the living standards and welfare of ordinary people plummeted between the 1290s and 1320s is highly problematic, because we do not have any direct evidence for the composition of peasant budgets and the weight of serfdom on servile households was almost infinitely varied. Yet, despite this, Postan's casual guess at an extraction rate of at least one-half the total output of a servile household in c. 1300 has proved enduring. The most sophisticated subsequent attempt to reconstruct the budget of a 'typical' villein household estimated that servile rents and dues extracted 20 per cent of annual gross output. Our reworking of this same budget, based on more reliable figures for the level of servile dues, showed how the extraction rate could have been as low as 5 per cent.

We should be sceptical of such calculations, however, because the sources are incapable of answering the questions we pose about extraction rates. Instead, the approach here has been to focus on what the sources themselves can reliably reveal about the affordability of servile rents and dues, rather than what historians have guessed. By ascertaining the mean charge levied for each servile incident from large samples and comparing them with the mean daily wage rate for unskilled labour, we can obtain the most objective available contemporary reference points for assessing their affordability. The mean charge for uncertain and variable dues on manor after manor – such as mill suit, chevage, leyrwite and licences to educate – could be covered by two to three days' wages, and those for merchet and tallage by a couple of weeks' work. As stated earlier, many serfs did not pay these charges. Very rarely, the extant sources provide an exceptional amount of contextual detail about either the sums charged for servile dues or the asset base of the serf, which present the most accurate insights into just how far the charges cut into servile resources, although their typicality cannot be ascertained. They are highly consistent in showing that heriot and tallage absorbed less than 10 per cent of the moveable asset base of the serf, licences to sublet villein land were charged at around 3 per cent of the value of the lease, and entry fines were equivalent to 5–10 per cent of the sale value of the land.

Thus, taken together, the various strands of evidence create a compelling picture of the patchiness of serfdom from manor to manor and confirm that, in contrast to both medieval legal theory and the views of many modern historians, the powers of lords under English serfdom on the eve of the Black Death were weak. The reasons for this weakness are complex. In reality, common law villeinage offered lords few effective means of enforcement, especially for recovering flown serfs. Statute law would have been a much better vehicle for creating watertight legislation to subjugate villeins, but it was never deployed in this way in England, partly because the royal courts regarded villeinage as a matter for the lord, not the state. Local custom exerted greater influence on relations between lords and villeins, and during the thirteenth century the widespread practice of codifying custom in written sources extended that influence. The codification of custom explains why head rents, labour services and tallage subsequently became ossified; why mill suit was liable on some manors but not on others; why occasional 'recognitions' were charged rather than annual tallages on other manors; and why the fine for leyrwite was 6d. on many manors, irrespective of lordship. Manorial courts were the private courts of lords, but they were also customary courts whose business and decision-making were not exclusively matters for the lord to determine: consequently the 'will of the lord' was a will subject to customary usages and precedents. The process of defining and recording such local customs involved negotiation between lord and serfs, including, on occasion, resistance and collective action from the latter to protect their position.

The codification of custom and the running of the manor courts were in turn heavily influenced by practices imported from the direct management of estates and the common law. Although the common law excluded villeins from the royal courts, during the thirteenth century its culture and procedures spread through other legal tribunals and into estate management in a manner that standardised and impersonalised lord–peasant relations, which in turn corroded the formal and coercive legal powers of lords under villeinage. The spread of royal justice and the associated legal knowledge and culture had the effect of converting servile dues and local custom from an oral and malleable tradition into a written definition of the terms of villeinage, and established the importance of written precedents in determining the behaviour of all parties. Written records of servile obligations bound villeins, but they also bound lords, and in the long run protected serfs from both arbitrary seizures of their land and the imposition of burdensome seigneurial renders. Common law culture also reinforced the underlying principle that disputes should be resolved through a consistent and due legal process, accelerating the shift away from justice determined at the personal discretion of the lord towards a system based more on standardised processes and legal principles. These developments could not guarantee fair or impartial justice for the serf, but process and precedent brought protection from seigniorial whim.

The business and decision-making of manor courts came to rely heavily on presentment and inquisition juries, mainly comprising villeins themselves, who routinely referred to custom and deferred to written precedents. Serfs serving in the office of affeerer influenced the size of financial charges imposed for licences, fines and punishments. Serfs could also plead cases in, or be called as witnesses to, other local tribunals, such as church, market and even royal courts. They served as market officials and even leased commercial franchises themselves, thereby becoming responsible for the provision and implementation of all aspects of statute, common and merchant law relating to commercial activity there. In all these ways, many English serfs had become immersed in the law and, together with the estate stewards and the small army of petty scribes and clerks resident in the countryside, had become the de facto disseminators and guardians of an emerging legal culture.

Thus, over the course of the thirteenth century the complex interplay among custom, the law, legal culture and the reformation of estate management had the effect of deterring arbitrary behaviour, reducing the likelihood of disputes arising or escalating, and weakening the coercive powers of seigneurs. The weakness and unevenness of serfdom increased serf agency. Serfs enjoyed access to a variety of local courts for formal remedies when disputes arose and, indeed, such courts were more suitable than the royal courts for resolving disputes based on the types of oral or informal contracts routinely deployed in petty commodity and labour exchange. Serfs accessed labour and commodity markets without any legal discrimination or prohibition on the basis of their status. Around one-third of all productive labour was waged in some form, and lords exercised little influence over how the rural market in wage labour functioned.[13] Lords were still able to license villeins' participation in the land market in many areas of southern and eastern England, but they neither controlled nor directed it. Villeins with large landholdings marketed their surpluses routinely and were among the wealthiest taxpayers in their communities. Access to various legal franchises reduced the risks of their participation in emerging factor markets in land, labour and capital, and the growth of a mass market for subsistence and non-subsistence goods.

The existence of land, labour and commodity markets, and even rudimentary capital markets, further increased the opportunities accessible to English serfs. The availability of a range of options for obtaining work and land away from the manor further weakened serfdom by increasing the difficulties and the costs to lords of its enforcement. The most powerful single act of resistance available to an individual serf was to leave the manor in search of land or employment elsewhere, an option greatly facilitated by the widespread seigniorial indifference to emigration in the pre-plague era. Licences to migrate were levied infrequently and, where they were, could be acquired cheaply, which meant that emigration incurred few direct costs for most serfs. One explanation for this lordly indifference to servile emigration is that their rent rolls were full and hired labour was widely and cheaply available, so the departure of underemployed and landless serfs was of little economic significance and may even have eased social pressures and poverty on the home manor. Another is that lords possessed no rigorous system for enforcing chevage and no third-party help to return flown serfs, and they depended almost entirely on either self-reporting by serfs or information supplied by villein juries. Nevertheless, the lords' indifference had some unintended but significant long-term consequences. It greatly increased the degree of rural mobility, swelled the ranks of the waged labour force and fuelled the growth of petty crafts and trades, which expanded the outside options available to serfs in both rural areas and urban centres and which, in turn, made serfdom too expensive to enforce when the competition for workers and tenants sharpened after 1349.

Thus, by the end of the thirteenth century, villeinage in England had become, in Hatcher's words, a set of 'financial burdens, rather than direct and inescapable limitations upon freedom of action'.[14] The principal vulnerability of serfs was their lack of any formal legal redress on those occasions when their lord did opt to defy custom or written precedent. In similar circumstances, the freeman could utilise the royal courts as a court of appeal, whereas the serf had no such recourse against his lord. If arbitration or negotiation failed, and the lord was intent on asserting his will, all that serfs could do was to protest and resist, individually or collectively. Such vulnerability even extended to those serfs who had long flown their home manor and whose servile roots were obscure, especially if they had made their fortune in some distant town. As Richard Spynk of Norwich discovered, anyone with a hint of servile stock faced the risk of their lord suddenly demanding a sizeable payment for manumission to confirm formally their freedom. Even those who proactively approached their lord for manumission would expect to pay one-third the value of their estate for a charter of freedom, which probably explains why manumissions were unusual.[15] Herein lay the uncertainty of villeinage, and the main source of its social stigma. The social indignity of villeinage was a greater drawback than its economic burden: serfs might be leading figures in their communities as jurors and tax assessors, and among the wealthiest, but they were subject to language and attitudes that were discriminatory and humiliating, they were made painfully aware of their stigmatised status, and they were vulnerable to the possibility of an unwelcome and uncustomary demand from their lord.[16]

The manifest and widespread weakness of serfdom forces us to reassess its role in economic development. Given its uneven geographical distribution, and given that no more than 40 per cent of the population were serfs and no more than one-third of all households (including towns) held land on villein tenure, it is impossible to sustain the traditional argument that the high extraction rates associated with serfdom were responsible for a crippling crisis of productivity in the peasant sector by the late thirteenth century and, by extension, the primary cause of the crisis of the early fourteenth century.[17] Nonetheless, it still contributed in various ways to the inefficiencies and arrested development of the English economy at this time, including its systemic vulnerability to external shocks. Even a low rate of extraction of peasant output through servile rents and dues diverted precious resources away from households that could barely cope with the exceptional sequence of extreme economic, climatic and biological stressors. In turn, lords did not recycle this revenue in the form of economically productive investment, diverting it instead through conspicuous consumption such as castles and cathedrals, and spending it on expensive military ventures. Furthermore, the restrictions of serfdom still constrained some of the choices available to villeins, such as when and whether to marry, and attached additional costs and risks to others, such as emigrating without licence.

The principal contribution of serfdom to economic development in the pre-plague era was its peculiar rental and tenurial structure. The combination of ossified head rents, a rising and high demand for land, and the ability of head tenants to sell or sublet land to others at market rates incentivised the fragmentation of holdings. In theory, landlords possessed the ability to prevent or to subdue the development of a market in villein land through the imposition of punitively high entry fines on land sales and licences to sublet but, in practice, they did not do so. As a consequence, mean landholding size plummeted in the most populous areas of the country, where a critical proportion of the population were condemned to lives of barest subsistence and high sensitivity to calamity. The plight of many freeholders was even worse, since no seigniorial controls applied to their tenures and so their holdings were even more likely to fragment, and they too were liable to tithes and taxes. The shared economic experience of many free and serf families, when combined with the considerable overlap in practice between 'free' and 'unfree' incidents, underlines the fact that freedom and unfreedom existed on the same continuum, and warns against drawing too sharply the differences between them. The tenurial structure of villeinage, backed by permissive seigniorial policies, helped sustain a national population in c. 1300 between double and triple the size it had been in c. 1100, but at the cost of low living standards after the 1280s for a critical mass of ordinary people. Serfdom was not the primary cause of England's economic malaise, but it still features in the ranks of contributory causes through its contribution to the widespread poverty within, and associated economic drag on, pre-plague England.

What was the impact of the Black Death of 1348–49 and the halving of the population on the mechanics of serfdom? The sudden then sustained shortage of tenants and labourers could have resulted in one of two, highly divergent, outcomes. One option was the rapid mobilisation of the full legal force of common law villeinage through a powerful seigniorial reaction to the plague, whereby the workforce would be coerced into labouring and holding land on terms favourable to lords in defiance of the new market situation. In this scenario, peasant resistance would eventually have to break the tightened shackles of serfdom. Alternatively, if the powers of lords were to remain as weak in the aftermath of plague as they had been on its eve, then the monumental shift of market dynamics in favour of serfs would prove irrepressible and inexorable. Serfdom would dissolve rapidly, as lords bargained away its most irksome elements in order to secure tenants for servile land and workers for their demesnes.

One obvious way of confirming the viewpoint that serfdom was strong in the 1340s and reimposed in the aftermath of the Black Death would be to target research on the classic manors of the type having a high-status landlord most capable of implementing the full legal force of common law villeinage. If the traditional view were credible, then there would be plentiful evidence of heavy and arbitrary dues in the pre-plague era and a sustained seigniorial reaction after the Black Death on such estates. Consequently, Chapters 8–10 offered detailed, quantitative and qualitative case studies of the operation of serfdom on three manors held by the cellarer of St Albans abbey, which historians have routinely cited as the exemplification of aggressive lordship and whose harsh treatment of its villeins during the fourteenth century is cited as a reason for its ransacking in the violence of June 1381.

Instead of confirming the view of strong serfdom before the Black Death and its reimposition afterwards, these three case studies confirmed its weakness and rapid decline. In the pre-plague era servile tenure dominated landholding, labour services were heavy, and the range of servile dues was wide on all three manors. Yet, even here, custom, written precedents, due processes and market forces were more powerful influences on the management of serfdom than the abbey's legal rights and policies. The Black Death of 1348–49 triggered a decade of tighter management of some aspects of personal servility, most notably the increased record of those serfs who had departed the manor, but this policy was abandoned in the 1360s. Few licences to migrate were ever paid, so the cellarer neither controlled nor profited from servile migration. Furthermore, he was helpless to counteract the dramatic and sudden fall in the demand for villein land: the volume of transfers of villein land fell by nearly one-half between the 1340s and 1350s, and the number of vacant holdings rose, forcing the abbey into implementing a raft of immediate concessions to retain and attract tenants, such as halving the rate of entry fines; abandoning merchet and recognition as incidents of tenure; and converting more land from service to monetary tenures, including short-term leases for cash. Vestiges of serfdom certainly remained after the 1360s – most notably the persistence of traditional service tenancy, which became a key issue for the rebels at St Albans – and their survival may have been all the more irksome to hereditary serfs as a consequence: however, the first plague pandemic and the lack of control over migration had inflicted a mortal wound.

If any English landlord could impose serfdom as the law decreed, or reimpose it in the wake of the Black Death, it was St Albans abbey. Yet serfdom was weak and in headlong retreat years before the Peasants' Revolt on three of its manors, but this can only be revealed through a systematic and quantified approach to computing all the incidents of serfdom on a manor over time. To date, wherever this methodology has been applied, not a single English manor has been found to have reimposed serfdom in a sustained fashion across a broad front during the third quarter of the fourteenth century. Thus, on the St Albans estate, as elsewhere, the arrival of plague and the associated sudden and severe shortages of workers and tenants exacerbated the weakness of lords under serfdom. Serfs now enjoyed a wide range of options for obtaining work and land away from the manor, whereas lords possessed no effective means of preventing or profiting greatly from servile migration, and no reciprocal system for returning the serfs of others, so consequently the social and financial costs of imposing serfdom were prohibitive.[18] Lords now had little option but to compete with one another for tenants, through offering concessions on the terms of servile tenure, and for workers, through providing perks and bonuses. Plague accelerated the swing from service to monetary tenures on villein land, because the latter emulated free tenancies and removed the tenants' liability for many of the dues attached to service tenure, such as labour services, merchet and tallage. There was no sustained or widespread seigniorial reaction, because lords were in a relatively weak position when plague struck, and the demographic collapse exacerbated their plight by exposing them to unfavourable market forces.[19] Consequently, the Black Death had dealt a immediate blow from which it could not recover.

The broader significance of the pervasive weakness of English serfdom in the early fourteenth century and of its rapid dissolution in the generation after the Black Death, even on the estate of one of England's mightiest landlords, is worth labouring. It renders the traditional view of onerous serfdom as archaic and unsustainable. It establishes a new orthodoxy that there was no post-plague seigniorial reaction. The findings also underline the importance of avoiding presumptions and generalisations about how serfdom operated across Europe and Asia, and the paramount importance of reconstructing each local or regional system on its own terms.[20] This requires careful attention to differences in the composition of their institutional framework and the complex interaction between their various components. It also requires avoiding fixed presumptions about what components resulted in strong and what in weak systems. As the comparison of the structure of English serfdom with that of parts of early modern central and eastern Europe revealed (in Chapter 5), a high proportion of demesne land and a state-based legal code do not invariably lead to a heavy weight of labour services and a powerful form of serfdom.

The new orthodoxy of English serfdom raises an obvious question: when *was* its heyday? The answer to this question requires greater consideration than is possible here, but the survey of mill suit in Chapter 2 offers a pointer. Mill suit was extended in many areas of northern England during the late eleventh and early twelfth centuries. Similarly, during the course of the twelfth century merchet was extended to new groups of tenants.[21] Hence, it appears that the period between the Norman Conquest and the emergence of the common law – broadly the 1070s to the 1180s – saw the imposition of some servile dues on new populations. Indeed, this is consistent with the other innovations in the wake of the Conquest recently identified by Rosamond Faith, such as the concept of a tenurial bond between lord and dependent landholder, legal rules to govern their relationship, and the dispensing of private justice through the personal court of the lord rather than public courts.[22] According to Campbell, 'Norman estates were the greatest bastions of serfdom.'[23] If serfdom was at the peak of its powers in the generation or so after the Norman Conquest, it would be consistent with the arguments in this book for the ameliorating effects of the codification of custom and the common law from the late twelfth century onwards.

The traditional view of a powerful and oppressive form of serfdom in England in the age of the Black Death is inextricably linked to a powerful explanatory framework that attributes to serfdom a primary role in the crisis of the early fourteenth century and in the Peasants' Revolt of 1381. This view is now exposed as long on presumption, short on evidence and superseded by a wealth of new information. Serfdom was weak in the 1340s and in rapid, irreversible, decline in the 1350s. The disassembling of the old order reveals something of the agendas and methods that underpinned much of the formative research into medieval economic and social history. It has also underlined the need for more complex and pluralist explanations of historical episodes as unique and extraordinary as the socio-economic crisis of the early fourteenth century and the Peasants' Revolt. If there is an underlying presumption in the approach taken here, it is the belief that explanations of historical phenomena are best explored after we have arrived at a clear understanding of what happened and when. This approach, which is essentially empirical, is manifest in the determination to describe as accurately as possible, and with as much disinterest as possible, the nature of serfdom and how it operated in practice between the 1270s and the fifteenth century. It also explains the determination to steer clear of the predetermined answers implicit in ideology, and of modern value judgements.

Although the species of medieval English serfdom has featured prominently in discussions of the European genus, there has been no presumption in this book that the English system is worthier of study than those systems operating in other parts of the world. There are no claims here for English exceptionalism, other than in the sense that the sources available for the study of English serfdom between the 1270s and the mid-fifteenth century are unparalleled anywhere in the world: we are fortunate to be able to reconstruct the nature and decline of serfdom in greater detail in England than is possible anywhere else on the globe. Our reconstruction of the mechanics of serfdom has drawn upon large samples, the use of averages rather than exceptional outliers and consideration of nil returns wherever possible, all of which offer a means of objectifying and quantifying medieval economic history without the need for yet another regression analysis, which has become characteristic of many recent forays into economic history. The adoption of a consciously empirical approach has not, however, meant the rejection of the use of theory and ideology per se. Indeed, there is recognition throughout this book of the importance of political ideologies in providing a package of intellectual tools and concepts, and a set of searching questions, which have greatly enhanced our understanding of serfdom and our attempts to explain its role in social and economic development. While my approach has been sceptical of the predictive claims of theory and ideology, and of their tendency to dictate the answers to the questions asked, it has also engaged with them in an eclectic and open-minded manner to understand and test complex phenomena against a robust evidentiary base.[24]

Notes

1 Brenner, 'The rises and declines', pp. 258–72; Brenner, 'Property and progress', pp. 95–9; Dimmock, *The Origin of Capitalism*, pp. 65–87; Kitsikopoulos, 'England', pp. 45–7; Hole, *Economic Ethics*, pp. 177–204; Jedwab et al., 'The economic impact', p. 163; Peters, 'Government finance', Map 1; Carocci, 'The pervasiveness of lordship', pp. 45–6; Ghosh, 'Rural economies', p. 258; Van Bavel, *Manors and Markets*, p. 87.

2 R. J. Hoyle, 'Tenure and the land market in early modern England; or, A late contribution to the Brenner Debate', *Economic History Review*, 43:1 (1990): 1–20; M. E. Mate, 'The east Sussex land market and agrarian class structure in the late Middle Ages', *Past & Present*, 139 (1993): 46–65; Rigby, *English Society*; Whittle, *The Development*.

3 For a critique of truffle-picking, see Hatcher, 'Lordship', pp. 126–38.
4 Dyer, *From Slavery to Freedom*, pp. 5, 11–18.
5 Campbell and Bartley, *England on the Eve.*
6 Hatcher and Bailey, *Modelling the Middle Ages*, pp. 7–120.
7 Postan, 'Medieval agrarian society', pp. 552–65; Hilton, *A Medieval Society*, pp. 145–8.
8 Rigby, *English Society*, pp. 1–177; Hatcher and Bailey, *Modelling the Middle Ages*, pp. 1–174; S. H. Rigby, 'Approaches to pre-industrial social structure', in J. Denton, ed., *Orders and Hierarchies in Late Medieval and Renaissance Europe* (London: Bloomsbury, 1999), pp. 6–25.
9 See n. 1; Rigby, 'Introduction', p. 30.
10 Müller, 'Conflict and revolt', pp. 1–9.
11 Brenner, 'The rises and declines', pp. 248, 263; Brenner, 'Property and progress', p. 64.
12 Campbell, 'The agrarian problem', p. 8.
13 B. M. S. Campbell, 'Factor markets in England before the Black Death', *Continuity and Change*, 24 (2009): 76–106 (pp. 84–92); Bailey, 'The regulation'.
14 Hatcher, 'English serfdom', p. 14.
15 Bailey, *The Decline of Serfdom*, pp. 62–5; Baylis, 'The decline of serfdom'.
16 Dyer, 'From slavery to freedom', pp. 12–15, 20–7.
17 Campbell, 'The agrarian problem', p. 36.
18 For another detailed case study revealing a similar chronology of decline and causation, see M. Bailey, 'Serfdom and lordship in late-medieval England: The example of Bredfield (Suffolk)', in S. Gibbs and T. Sambachs, eds, *The Economics of Lordship in Late Medieval Europe*, Jahrbuch für Wirtschaftsgeschichte/Economic History Yearbook (forthcoming, 2026).
19 Bailey, *After the Black Death*, pp. 83–112.
20 Cerman, 'Seigniorial systems', pp. 188–94.
21 See Chapter 2; Faith, *The English Peasantry*, pp. 257, 264; Hatcher, 'English serfdom', pp. 26–33; and Hatcher, 'Lordship', p. 138.
22 Faith, *The Moral Economy*, pp. 127–95; Faith, *The English Peasantry*, pp. 255–9.
23 Campbell, 'The land', pp. 211–12, 237.
24 Rigby, 'Approaches'; Hatcher and Bailey, *Modelling the Middle Ages*, pp. 174–242.

Bibliography

Primary sources

Aldous, V., ed., *Monks Eleigh Manorial Records, 1210–1683*, Suffolk Records Society, 65 (Woodbridge: Boydell Press, 2002).

Arnold, M. S., ed., *Select Cases of Trespass from the King's Courts, 1307–1399*, Vol. I, Selden Society, 100 (London: Selden Society, 1987).

Baildon, W. P., ed., *Court Rolls of the Manor of Wakefield*, Vol. I, *1274 to 1297*, Yorkshire Archaeological Society Record Series, 29 ([Leeds]: Yorkshire Archaeological Society, 1901).

Baildon, W. P., ed., *Court Rolls of the Manor of Wakefield*, Vol. II, *1297–1309*, Yorkshire Archaeological Society Record Series, 36 ([Leeds]: Yorkshire Archaeological Society, 1906).

Bailey, M., ed., *The English Manor c. 1200 to c. 1500* (Manchester: Manchester University Press, 2002).

Birrell. J., and D. Hutchinson, 'An Alrewas rental of 1341', *Collections for a History of Staffordshire*, 20 (2004): 59–81.

Britnell, R. H., C. Etty and A. King, eds, *The Black Book of Hexham: A Northern Monastic Estate in 1379* (Hexham: Hexham Local History Society, 2011).

Brooker, J., and S. Flood, eds, *Hertfordshire Lay Subsidy Rolls, 1307 and 1334*, Hertfordshire Records Society Publications, 14 (n.p.: Hertfordshire Records Society, 1998).

Brownhill, J., ed., *The Ledger-Book of Vale Royal Abbey*, Record Society for Lancashire and Cheshire, 68 ([Manchester]: Record Society of Lancashire and Cheshire, 1914).

Clough, M., ed., *Two Estate Surveys of the Fitzalan Earls of Arundel*, Sussex Record Society, 67 ([Lewes]: Sussex Record Society, 1969).

Davis, J., and J. Sear, eds, *Records of Medieval Newmarket: Manor Court Rolls 1399–1413 and Manor Account Rolls 1403–1483*, Suffolk Records Society, 66 (Woodbridge: Boydell Press, 2023).

Denney, A. H., ed., *The Sibton Abbey Estates: Select Documents 1325–1509*, Suffolk Records Society, 1 (Ipswich: Suffolk Records Society, 1960).

Farrer, W., ed., *Some Court Rolls of the Lordship, Wapentakes and Demesne Manors of Thomas, Earl of Lancaster 1323–4 in County of Lancaster* ([Manchester]: Record Society of Lancashire and Cheshire, 1901).

Field, R. K., ed., *Court Rolls of Elmley Castle, Worcestershire 1347–1564*, Worcestershire Historical Society, 20 (n.p.: Worcestershire Historical Society, 2004).

Foden, P., trans., *Records of the Manor of Norton in the Liberty of St Albans 1244–1539*, Hertfordshire Record Publications, 29 (n.p.: Hertfordshire Record Society, 2014).

Gross, C., ed., *Select Cases Concerning the Law Merchant, 1293–1633*, Vol. I, Publications of the Selden Society, 23 (London: B. Quaritch, 1908).

Habberjam, M., M. O'Regan, B. Hale and C. M. Fraser, eds, *The Court Rolls of the Manor of Wakefield from October 1350 to September 1352*, Yorkshire Archaeological Society, Wakefield Court Rolls Series, 6 (Leeds: Yorkshire Archaeological Society, 1985).

Harrop, J., P. Booth and S. Harrop, eds, *Extents of the Lordship of Longdendale, 1360*, Record Society of Lancashire and Cheshire, 140 (n.p.: Record Society of Lancashire and Cheshire, 2005).

Hervey, S. H. A., ed., *Suffolk in 1327: Being a Subsidy Return* (London: G. Booth, 1906).

Horwood, A. J., ed., *Yearbooks of the Reign of Edward III*, Vol. VI (London: Longman, 1883–1911).

Jeayes, I. H, trans., *Court Rolls of the Borough of Colchester*, Vol. I, *1310–1352* (Colchester: Colchester Town Council, 1921).

Jeayes, I. H., trans., *Court Rolls of the Borough of Colchester*, Vol. II, *1353–1367* (Colchester: Colchester Town Council, 1938).

John, T., ed., *The Warwickshire Hundred Rolls of 1279–80: Stoneleigh and Kineton Hundreds* (Oxford: British Academy, 1992).

Lister, J., ed., *Court Rolls of the Manor of Wakefield*, Vol. IV, *1315–1317*, Yorkshire Archaeological Society, 78 (Leeds: Yorkshire Archaeological Society, 1930).

Lock, R., ed., *The Court Rolls of Walsham le Willows 1303–1350*, Suffolk Records Society, 41 (Woodbridge: Boydell Press, 1998).

Lock, R., ed., *The Court Rolls of Walsham le Willows 1351–1399*, Suffolk Records Society, 45 (Woodbridge: Boydell Press, 2002).

McLaughlin, A., and M. Bailey, eds, *Manorial Account Rolls and Rentals of Walsham le Willows, 1327 to 1559*, Suffolk Records Society, 68 (Woodbridge: Boydell Press, 2025).

Maitland, F. W., ed., *Year Book of Edward II 2 and 3*, Vol. II (London: Selden Society, 1904).

Maitland, F. W., and W. P. Baildon, eds, *The Court Baron* (London: Selden Society, 1891).

Noy, D., ed., *The Winslow Manor Court Books, 1322–1377*, Buckinghamshire Record Society, 35 ([Aylesbury]: Buckinghamshire Record Society, 2011).

Noy, D., ed., *The Winslow Manor Court Books, 1423–1460*, Buckinghamshire Record Society, 36 ([Aylesbury]: Buckinghamshire Record Society, 2011).
Oschinsky, D., ed., *Walter of Henley and Other Treatises on Estate Management and Accounting* (Oxford: Clarendon Press, 1971).
Poos, L. R., ed., *Lower Ecclesiastical Jurisdiction in Late-Medieval England*, Records of Economic and Social History, new series, 32 (Oxford: British Academy, 2001).
Poos, L. R., and L. Bonfield, eds, *Select Cases in Manorial Courts 1250–1550: Property and Family Law* (London: Selden Society, 1998).
Powell, E., ed., *A Suffolk Hundred in the Year 1283* (Cambridge: Cambridge University Press, 1910).
Raban, S., ed., *The White Book of Peterborough*, Northamptonshire Record Society, 41 (Peterborough: Dean and Chapter of Peterborough, 2001).
Salter, H. E., ed., *The Cartulary of the Abbey of Eynsham*, Vol. II, Oxfordshire History Society, 51 (Oxford: Clarendon Press, 1908).
Thompson, J. S., ed., *Hundreds, Manors and Parishes*, Bedfordshire Historical Record Society, 69 (Bedford: Bedfordshire Historical Record Society, 1998).
Thomson, W. S., ed., *A Lincolnshire Assize Roll for 1298*, Lincoln Record Society, 36 (Hereford: Hereford Times, 1944).
Tringham, N. J., ed., *Three Thirteenth- and Fourteenth-Century Surveys of Burton Abbey Manors*, Collections for a History of Staffordshire, 4th series, 20 ([Stafford]: Staffordshire Record Society, 2004).
Troup, K. M., ed., *The Court Rolls of the Manor of Wakefield, October 1338 to September 1340*, Wakefield Court Rolls Series, 12 (Leeds: Yorkshire Archaeological Society, 1999).
Walker, J. W., ed., *Court Rolls of the Manor of Wakefield*, Vol. V, *1322–31*, Yorkshire Archaeological Society, 109 (Leeds: Yorkshire Archaeological Society, 1944).
Walker, S. S., ed., *The Court Rolls of the Manor of Wakefield from October 1331 to September 1333*, Yorkshire Archaeological Society, Wakefield Court Rolls Series, 3 (Leeds: Yorkshire Archaeological Society, 1983).
Watson, C. J., ed., *The Court Rolls of the Manor of Wakefield from 5 October 1360 to 28 September 1361*, Yorkshire Archaeological and Historical Society (Leeds: Yorkshire Archaeological and Historical Society, 2019).
Wilson, A. E., ed., *Custumals of the Manors of Laughton, Willingdon and Goring*, Sussex Record Society, 60 (Lewes: Sussex Record Society, 1961).
Wilson, J. M., ed., *Account Rolls of the Priory of Worcester, 1521–2*, Worcestershire Historical Society, 24 (Oxford: J. Parker, 1907).

Secondary sources

Aberth, J., 'A medieval Norwich feud: The bitter dispute between Richard Spynk and Thomas de Lisle, bishop of Ely', *Norfolk Archaeology*, 41 (1992): 294–304.

Acemoglu, D., and A. Wolitzky, 'The economics of labour coercion', *Econometrica*, 79 (2011): 555–600.

Alfonso, I., ed., *The Rural History of Medieval European Societies: Trends and Perspectives* (Turnhout: Brepols, 2007).

Andermann, K., 'Leibeigenschaft in der Markgrafschaft Baden an der Wende vom Mittelalter zur Neuzeit', in Freedman and Bourin, *Forms of Servitude*, pp. 197–212.

Arthur, P., 'The Black Death and mortality: A reassessment', in C. Given-Wilson, ed., *Fourteenth-Century England*, Vol. VI (Woodbridge: Boydell Press, 2010), pp. 49–72.

Ashley, W. J., *An Introduction to English Economic History and Theory*, Vol. I (London: Longmans Green, 1909).

Aston, T. H., and C. H. E. Philpin, eds, *The Brenner Debate: Agrarian Class Structure and Economic Development in Pre-Industrial Europe* (Cambridge: Cambridge University Press, 1985).

Bailey, M., *A Marginal Economy? East Anglian Breckland in the Later Middle Ages* (Cambridge: Cambridge University Press, 1989).

Bailey, M., '*Per impetum maris*: Natural disaster and economic decline in eastern England, 1275–1350', in Campbell, *Before the Black Death*, pp. 184–208.

Bailey, M., 'Introduction', in Brooker and Flood, *Hertfordshire Lay Subsidy Rolls*, pp. ix–xxvii.

Bailey, M., 'Historiographical essay: The commercialisation of English society 1086–1350', *Journal of Medieval History*, 24 (1998): 297–321.

Bailey, M., 'Peasant welfare in England 1290–1348', *Economic History Review*, 51 (1998): 223–51.

Bailey, M., ed., *The English Manor c. 1200 to c. 1500* (Manchester: Manchester University Press, 2002).

Bailey, M., *Medieval Suffolk: An Economic and Social History 1200 to 1500* (Woodbridge: Boydell Press, 2007).

Bailey, M., 'Villeinage in England: A regional case study c. 1250–1349', *Economic History Review*, 62 (2009): 430–57.

Bailey, M., 'The transformation of customary tenures in southern England 1350–1500', *Agricultural History Review*, 62 (2014): 210–30.

Bailey, M., *The Decline of Serfdom in Late Medieval England: From Bondage to Freedom* (Woodbridge: Boydell Press, 2014).

Bailey, M., 'The myth of the seigniorial reaction in England after the Black Death', in Kowaleski et al., *Peasants and Lords*, pp. 147–72.

Bailey, M., 'Tallage-at-will in later medieval England', *English Historical Review*, 134:566 (2019): 25–58.

Bailey, M., *After the Black Death: Economy, Society and the Law in Fourteenth Century England* (Oxford: Oxford University Press, 2021).
Bailey, M., 'Austin Crembell: A medieval Suffolk commuter', *Proceedings of the Suffolk Institute of Archaeology and History*, 45:2 (2022): 284–8.
Bailey, M., 'Servile and gender migration in late medieval England: The evidence of manorial court rolls', *Past & Present*, 261 (2023): 47–85.
Bailey, M., 'The regulation of the rural market in waged labour in fourteenth century England', *Continuity and Change*, 38 (2023): 137–62.
Bailey, M., 'The implementation of national labour legislation in England after the Black Death, 1349–1400', *Economic History Review*, 78:2 (2025): 529–52.
Bailey, M., 'Comparing serfdom in England to southern Germany in the century before the Black Death: Possibilities and pitfalls', in J. Peltzer and N. Vincent, eds, *Thirteenth-Century England 20: Proceedings of the Heidelberg Conference, 2023* (Woodbridge: Boydell and Brewer, [forthcoming, 2026]).
Bailey, M., P. Wain and D. Sear, 'The transformation of the Suffolk coast c. 1200 to c.1600: From Orford Ness to Goseford', *Proceedings of the Suffolk Institute of Archaeology and History*, 45:1 (2021): 86–114.
Bak, J. M., 'Servitude in the medieval kingdom of Hungary (a sketchy outline)', in Freedman and Bourin, *Forms of Servitude*, pp. 387–400.
Baker, J. H., 'The law merchant and the common law before 1700', *Cambridge Law Journal*, 38 (1979): 295–322.
Baker, J. H., *Collected Papers on English Legal History*, Vol. I (Cambridge: Cambridge University Press, 2013).
Barg, M. A., 'The social structure of manorial freeholders: An analysis of the Hundred Rolls of 1279', *Agricultural History Review*, 39 (1991): 108–15.
Barker, J., *England, Arise: The People, the King, and the Great Revolt of 1381* (London: Abacus, 2014).
Baugh, G. C., ed., *Victoria County History [VCH], Shropshire*, Vol. XI (London: Institute of Historical Research, 1985).
Baugh, G. C., ed., *Victoria County History [VCH], Shropshire*, Vol. IV, *Agriculture* (London: Institute of Historical Research, 1989).
Baugh, G. C., ed., *Victoria County History [VCH], Shropshire*, Vol. X (London: Institute of Historical Research, 1998).
Baylis, J., 'The decline of serfdom in the west Midlands 1300 to 1450' (PhD thesis, University of East Anglia, 2026).
Beckerman, J. S., 'Procedural innovation and institutional change in medieval English manorial courts', *Law and History Review*, 10 (1992): 197–252.
Beckerman, J. S., 'Toward a theory of medieval manorial adjudication: The nature of communal judgments in a system of customary law', *Law and History Review*, 13 (1995): 1–22.

Beckerman, J. S., 'Law writing and law teaching: Treatise evidence of the formal teaching of English law in the late thirteenth century', in Bush and Wijffels, *Learning the Law*, pp. 33–50.

Bekar, C. T., and C. G. Reed, 'Land markets and inequality: Evidence from medieval England', *European Review of Economic History*, 17 (2013): 294–317.

Belich, J., *The World the Plague Made: The Black Death and the Rise of Europe* (Princeton: Princeton University Press, 2022).

Bennett, H. S., *Life on the English Manor: A Study of Peasant Conditions 1150–1400* (Cambridge: Cambridge University Press, 1937).

Bennett, J. M., 'Medieval peasant marriage: An examination of marriage license fines in the *Liber Gersumarum*', in Raftis, *Pathways*, pp. 193–246.

Bennett, J. M., *Women in the Medieval English Countryside: Gender and Household in Brigstock before the Plague* (Oxford: Oxford University Press, 1987).

Bennett, J. M., *Ale, Beer and Brewsters in England: Women's Work in a Changing World, 1300–1600* (Oxford: Oxford University Press, 1996).

Bennett, J. M., 'Writing fornication: Medieval leyrwite and its historians', *TRHS*, 6th series, 13 (2003): 131–62.

Bennett, J. M., 'Married and not: Weston's grown children in 1268–1269', *Continuity and Change*, 34 (2019): 151–82.

Birrell, J., 'Manorial custumals reconsidered', *Past & Present*, 224 (2014): 3–37.

Bloch, M., 'Avènement et conquêtes du moulin à eau', *Annales*, 7 (1935): 538–63.

Blum, J., 'The rise of serfdom in eastern Europe', *American Historical Review*, 62:4 (1957): 807–36.

Bolton, J. L., *The Medieval English Economy, 1150–1500* (London: Dent, 1980).

Bonfield, L., 'The nature of customary law in the manor courts of medieval England', *Comparative Studies in Society and History*, 31:3 (1989): 514–34.

Bonfield, L., 'What did Edwardian villagers mean by customary law?', in Razi and Smith, *Medieval Society*, pp. 102–16.

Bonfield, L., 'The role of seigneurial jurisdiction after the Norman Conquest, and the nature of customary law, in England', in Bonfield, *Seigneurial Jurisdiction*, pp. 177–94.

Bonfield, L., ed., *Seigneurial Jurisdiction* (Berlin: Duncker & Humblot, 2000).

Bourin, M., and P. Martínez Sopena, eds, *Pour une anthropologie du prélèvement seigneurial dans les campagnes médiévales (Xie–XIVe siècles)*, Vol. II, *Les mots, les temps, les lieux* (Paris: Publications de Sorbonne, 2004).

Brakensiek, S., 'North-west Germany, 1000–1750', in Van Bavel and Hoyle, *Rural Economy and Society*, pp. 227–52.

Brand, P., 'Legal education in England before the Inns of Court', in Bush and Wijffels, *Learning the Law*, pp. 51–84.
Brand, P., *Kings, Barons and Justices: The Making and Enforcement of Legislation in Thirteenth-Century England* (Cambridge: Cambridge University Press, 2003).
Brand, P., 'Stewards, bailiffs and the emerging legal profession', in Evans, *Lordship and Learning*, pp. 138–53.
Brand, P. A., and P. R. Hyams, 'Seigneurial control of women's marriage', *Past & Present*, 99 (1983): 123–32.
Brenner, R., 'Agrarian class structure and economic development in pre-industrial Europe', in Aston and Philpin, *The Brenner Debate*, pp. 10–63.
Brenner, R., 'The agrarian roots of European capitalism', in Aston and Philpin, *The Brenner Debate*, pp. 213–320.
Brenner, R., 'The rises and declines of serfdom in medieval and early modern Europe', in Bush, *Serfdom and Slavery*, pp. 247–76.
Brenner, R., 'Property relations and the growth of agrarian productivity in late medieval and early modern Europe', in A. Bhaduri and R. Skarstein, eds, *Economic Development and Agricultural Productivity* (Cheltenham: Edward Elgar, 1997), pp. 9–42.
Brenner, R., 'Property and progress: Where Adam Smith went wrong', in C. Wickham, ed., *Marxist History-writing for the Twenty-first Century* (Oxford: Oxford University Press, 2007), pp. 49–111.
Briggs, C., 'Taxation, warfare, and the early fourteenth century "crisis" in the north: Cumberland lay subsidies, 1332–1348', *Economic History Review*, 58 (2005): 639–72.
Briggs, C., 'Manor court procedures, debt litigation levels, and rural credit provision in England, c. 1290–c. 1380', *Law and History Review*, 24 (2006): 519–58.
Briggs, C., 'Seigniorial control of villagers' litigation beyond the manor in later medieval England', *Historical Research*, 81:213 (2008): 399–422.
Briggs, C., *Credit and Village Society in Fourteenth-Century England* (Oxford: Oxford University Press, 2009).
Briggs, C., 'English serfdom, c. 1200–c. 1350: Towards an institutionalist analysis', in Cavaciocchi, *Serfdom and Slavery*, pp. 13–32.
Briggs, C., 'Peasants, lords and commerce: Market regulation at Balsham, Cambridgeshire, in the early fourteenth century', in Kowaleski et al., *Peasants and Lords*, pp. 247–72.
Briggs, C., and P. R. Schofield, 'Understanding Edwardian villagers' use of law: Some manor court litigation evidence', *Reading Medieval Studies*, 40 (2014): 117–39.
Briggs, C., and P. R. Schofield, 'The evolution of manor courts in medieval England, c. 1250–1350: The evidence of the personal actions', *The Journal of Legal History*, 41 (2020): 1–28.
Briggs, C., P. M. Kitson and S. J. Thompson, eds, *Population, Welfare and Economic Change in Britain 1290–1834* (Woodbridge: Economic History Society, 2014).

Britnell, R. H., 'Production for the market on a small fourteenth-century estate', *Economic History Review*, 19 (1966): 380–7.
Britnell, R. H., 'Minor landlords in England and medieval agrarian capitalism', in T. H. Aston, ed., *Landlords, Peasants and Politics in Medieval England* (Cambridge: Cambridge University Press, 1987), pp. 227–46.
Britnell, R. H., 'Feudal reaction after the Black Death in the Palatinate of Durham', *Past & Present*, 128 (1990): 28–47.
Britnell, R. H., *The Commercialisation of English Society, 1000–1500* (Manchester: Manchester University Press, 1996).
Britnell, R. H., ed., *Pragmatic Literacy, East and West 1200–1330* (Woodbridge: Boydell and Brewer, 1997).
Britnell, R. H., *Britain and Ireland 1050–1530: Economy and Society* (Oxford: Oxford University Press, 2004).
Britton, E., *The Community of the vill: A Study in the History of the Family and Village Life in Fourteenth-Century England* (Toronto: Macmillan, 1977).
Broadberry, S., B. M. S. Campbell, A. Klein, M. Overton and B. van Leeuwen, *British Economic Growth 1270–1870* (Cambridge: Cambridge University Press, 2015).
Buhler, T., 'Seigniorial jurisdictions in the territories of the diocese of Basle according to sources of the thirteenth to fifteenth centuries', in Bonfield, *Seigneurial Jurisdiction*, pp. 77–102.
Bush, J. A., and A. Wijffels, eds, *Learning the Law: Teaching and the Transmission of Law in England 1150–1900* (London: Hambledon Press, 1999).
Bush, M. L., 'Introduction', in Bush, *Serfdom and Slavery*, pp. 1–17.
Bush, M. L., 'Serfdom in medieval and modern Europe', in Bush, *Serfdom and Slavery*, pp. 199–224.
Bush, M. L., ed., *Serfdom and Slavery: Studies in Legal Bondage* (London: Routledge, 1996).
Cam, H. M., ed., *Selected Historical Essays of F. W. Maitland* (Cambridge: Cambridge University Press, 1957).
Campbell, B. M. S., 'Population pressure, inheritance and the land market in a fourteenth-century peasant community', in Smith, *Land, Kinship*, pp. 87–134.
Campbell, B. M. S., 'The complexity of manorial structure in medieval Norfolk: A case study', *Norfolk Archaeology*, 39 (1986): 225–61.
Campbell, B. M. S., ed., *Before the Black Death: Studies in the Crisis of the Early Fourteenth Century* (Manchester: Manchester University Press, 1991).
Campbell, B. M. S., *English Seigniorial Agriculture, 1250–1450* (Cambridge: Cambridge University Press, 2000).
Campbell, B. M. S., 'The agrarian problem in the early fourteenth century', *Past & Present*, 188 (2005): 3–70.
Campbell, B. M. S., 'The land', in Horrox and Ormrod, *A Social History of England*, pp. 179–237.

Campbell, B. M. S., 'Factor markets in England before the Black Death', *Continuity and Change*, 24 (2009): 76–106.
Campbell, B. M. S., 'Nature as historical protagonist: Environment and society in pre-industrial England', *Economic History Review*, 63 (2010): 281–314.
Campbell, B. M. S., *The Great Transition: Climate, Disease and Society in the Late Medieval World* (Cambridge: Cambridge University Press, 2016).
Campbell, B. M. S., and K. Bartley, *England on the Eve of the Black Death: An Atlas of Lay Lordship, Land and Wealth, 1300–49* (Manchester: Manchester University Press, 2006).
Campbell, B. M. S., and C. Ó Grada, 'Harvest shortfalls, grain prices, and famines in preindustrial England', *Journal of Economic History*, 71 (2011): 859–86.
Carocci, S., 'The pervasiveness of lordship (Italy, 1050–1500)', *Past & Present*, 296 (2022): 3–47.
Carpenter, D. A., 'English peasants in politics 1258–1267', *Past & Present*, 126 (1992): 3–42.
Cavaciocchi, S., ed., *Serfdom and Slavery in the European Economy, 11th–18th Centuries* (Florence: Firenze University Press, 2014).
Cerman, M., 'Social structure and land markets in late medieval central and east-central Europe', *Continuity and Change*, 23 (2008): 55–100.
Cerman, M., 'Demesne lordship and rural society in early modern East Central and Eastern Europe: Comparative perspectives', *Agricultural History Review*, 59:2 (2011): 239–58.
Cerman, M., *Villagers and Lords in Eastern Europe, 1300–1800* (London: Bloomsbury, 2012).
Cerman, M., 'Seigniorial systems in east-central and eastern Europe 1300–1800: Regional realities', in Cavaciocchi, *Serfdom and Slavery*, pp. 188–211.
Chavas, J.-P., and D. W. Bromley, 'Modelling population and resource scarcity in fourteenth-century England', *Journal of Agricultural Economics*, 56 (2005): 217–37.
Cheyney, E. P., 'The disappearance of English serfdom', *English Historical Review*, 15 (1900): 20–37.
Chick, J., 'The 1381 rising in Bury St Edmunds: The role of leaders and the community in shaping the rebellion', *Pons Aelius*, 13 (2016): 35–47.
Clanchy, M. T., *From Memory to Written Record: England 1066–1307*, 3rd edn (London: Wiley Blackwell, 2012).
Claridge, J., and S. Gibbs, 'Waifs and strays: Property rights in late medieval England', *Journal of British Studies*, 61 (2022): 50–82.
Clark, E., 'Debt litigation in a late medieval English vill', in Raftis, *Pathways*, pp. 247–79.
Clark, E., 'Medieval labor law and English local courts', *American Journal of Legal History*, 27 (1983): 330–48.

Clark, G., *A Farewell to Alms: A Brief Economic History of the World* (Princeton: Princeton University Press, 2007).

Clark, G., 'The macroeconomic aggregates for England, 1209–1869', *Research in Economic History*, 27 (2010): 51–140.

Coss, P., *The Foundations of Gentry Life: The Multons of Frampton and Their World, 1270–1370* (Oxford: Oxford University Press, 2010).

Coulton, G. C., *The Medieval Village* (Cambridge: Cambridge University Press, 1925).

Crook, D., 'Freedom, villeinage and legal process: The dispute between the abbot of Burton and his tenants of Mickleover, 1280', *Nottingham Medieval Studies*, 44 (2000): 123–40.

Davies, M., and J. Kissock, 'The feet of fines, the land market and the English agricultural crisis of 1315 to 1322', *Journal of Historical Geography*, 30 (2004): 215–30.

Davis, J., *Medieval Market Morality: Life, Law and Ethics in the English Marketplace, 1200–1500* (Cambridge: Cambridge University Press, 2011).

Davis, J., 'Reassessment of village markets in late medieval England', in Kowaleski et al., *Peasants and Lords*, pp. 272–96.

Davis, J., 'Market courts and *lex mercatoria* in late medieval England', in M. Allen and M. Davies, eds, *Medieval Merchants and Money: Essays in Honour of James L. Bolton* (London: Institute of Historical Research, 2017), pp. 271–90.

Dennison, T. K., 'The institutional context of serfdom in England and Russia', in Briggs et al., *Population, Welfare*, pp. 249–68.

Dennison, T. K., *The Institutional Framework of Russian Serfdom* (Cambridge: Cambridge University Press, 2011).

Dennison, T. K., 'Contract enforcement in Russian serf society', *Economic History Review*, 66 (2013): 715–32.

Dennison, T. K., and S. Ogilvie, 'Serfdom and social capital in Bohemia and Russia', *Economic History Review*, 60:3 (2007): 513–44.

DeWindt, E. B., *Land and People in Holywell-cum-Needingworth: Structures of Tenure and Patterns of Social Organization in an East Midlands Village, 1252–1457* (Toronto: Pontifical Institute of Medieval Studies).

DeWitte. S., and P. Slavin, 'Between famine and death: England on the eve of the Black Death. Evidence from paleoepidemiology and manorial accounts', *Journal of Interdisciplinary History*, 44 (2013): 37–60.

Dimmock, S., *The Origin of Capitalism in England, 1400–1600* (London: Brill, 2014).

Dobb, M., *Studies in the Development of Capitalism*, 2nd edn (London: Routledge, 1976).

Dobson, B. R., ed., *The Peasants' Revolt of 1381*, 2nd edn (Basingstoke: Macmillan, 2003).

Dodd, G., and H. Lacey, eds, *Fourteenth Century England*, Vol. XIII (Woodbridge: Boydell Press, 2025).

Dodds, B., *Peasants and Production in the Medieval North-East: The Evidence from Tithes 1270–1536* (Woodbridge: Boydell Press, 2007).

Domar, E. D., 'The causes of slavery or serfdom: A hypothesis', *Journal of Economic History*, 30 (1970): 18–32.

Dopsch, H., 'Neue Leibeigenschaft oder alte Hörigkeit? Zu den Beschwerden und Forderungen aufständischer Bauern im Ostalpenraum an der Wende zur Neuzeit', in Freedman and Bourin, *Forms of Servitude*, pp. 313–42.

Dyer, C., *Lords and Peasants in a Changing Society: The Estates of the Bishopric of Worcester, 680–1540* (Cambridge: Past & Present Publications, 1980).

Dyer, C., *Standards of Living in the Later Middle Ages: Social Change in England c. 1200–1520* (Cambridge: Cambridge University Press, 1989).

Dyer, C., 'The English medieval village community and its decline', *Journal of British Studies*, 33 (1994): 407–29.

Dyer, C., *Everyday Life in Medieval England* (London: Hambledon Press, 1994).

Dyer, C., 'Memories of freedom: Attitudes towards serfdom in England 1200 to 1350', in Bush, *Serfdom and Slavery*, pp. 277–95.

Dyer, C., *Making a Living in the Middle Ages: The People of Britain 850–1520* (London: Yale University Press, 2002).

Dyer, C., 'The language of oppression: The vocabulary of rents and services in England, 1000–1300', in Bourin and Martínez Sopena, *Pour une anthropologie*, Vol. II, pp. 71–86.

Dyer, C., *An Age of Transition? Economy and Society in England in the Later Middle Ages* (Oxford: Oxford University Press, 2005).

Dyer, C., 'Seigniorial profits on the land market in late medieval England', in Feller and Whickham, *Le marché de la terre*, pp. 219–36.

Dyer, C., 'Villeins, bondsmen, neifs, and serfs: New serfdom in England c. 1200–1600', in Freedman and Bourin, *Forms of Servitude*, pp. 419–36.

Dyer, C., 'The ineffectiveness of lordship in England, 1200–1400', in C. Dyer et al., *Rodney Hilton's Middle Ages*, pp. 69–86.

Dyer, C., *Peasants Making History: Living in an English Region 1200–1540* (Oxford: Oxford University Press, 2022).

Dyer, C., *From Slavery to Freedom: How Worcestershire People Gained Their Liberty 1000 to 1600*, Worcestershire Historical Society, Occasional Publications, 15 (Worcester: Worcestershire Historical Society, 2024).

Dyer, C., and P. R. Schofield, 'Recent work on the agrarian history of medieval Britain', in Alfonso, *The Rural History*, pp. 21–56.

Dyer, C., P. Coss and C. Whickham, eds, *Rodney Hilton's Middle Ages: An Exploration of Historical Themes*, *Past & Present* Supplements, 195, suppl. 2 (Oxford: Oxford University Press, 2007).

Dygo, M., 'Zur Genese der sog. "zweiten Leibeigenschaft" in Polen 15–16 Jahrhundert', in Freedman and Bourin, *Forms of Servitude*, pp. 401–18.

Eldridge, L., *Law and the Medieval Village Community: Reinvigorating Historical Jurisprudence* (Abingdon: Routledge, 2023).

Ertl, T., T. Frank and S. Nussbaum, 'Introduction', in T. Ertl, T. Frank and S. Nussbaum, eds, *Busy Tenants: Peasant Land Markets in Central Europe (15th to 16th Centuries)* (Stuttgart: Franz Steiner Verlag, 2021), pp. 7–13.

Evans, R., 'Merton College's control of its tenants at Thorncroft, 1270–1349', in Razi and Smith, *Medieval Society*, pp. 199–259.

Evans, R., ed., *Lordship and Learning: Studies in Memory of Trevor Aston* (Woodbridge: Boydell Press, 2004).

Evans, R., 'Whose was the manorial court?', in Evans, *Lordship and Learning*, pp. 154–68.

Faith, R., 'The class struggle in fourteenth century England', in R. Samuel, ed., *People's History and Socialist Theory* (London: Routledge & Kegan Paul, 1981), pp. 50–80.

Faith, R., 'Seigneurial control of women's marriage', *Past & Present*, 99 (1983): 123–33.

Faith, R., 'Fourteenth century: Berkshire', in Harvey, *The Peasant Land Market*, pp. 106–77.

Faith, R., 'The Great Rumour of 1377 and peasant ideology', in R. H. Hilton and T. H. Aston, eds, *The English Rising of 1381* (Cambridge: Cambridge University Press, 1984), pp. 43–73.

Faith, R., *The English Peasantry and the Growth of Lordship* (Leicester: Leicester University Press, 1997).

Faith, R., *The Moral Economy of the Countryside* (Cambridge: Cambridge University Press, 2020).

Farmer, D. L., 'Prices and wages', in H. E. Hallam, ed., *The Agrarian History of England and Wales*, Vol. II, *1042–1350* (Cambridge: Cambridge University Press, 1988), pp. 716–817.

Farmer, D. L., 'Marketing the produce of the countryside', in E. Miller, ed., *The Agrarian History of England and Wales*, Vol. III, *1348–1550* (Cambridge: Cambridge University Press, 1991), pp. 324–430.

Feller, L., and Wickham, C., eds, *Le marché de la terre au Moyen Age* (Rome: Ecole française de Rome, 2005).

Finberg, H. P. R., *Tavistock Abbey: A study in the Social and Economic History of Devon* (Newton Abbot: David and Charles, 1969).

Forrest, I., *Trustworthy Men: How Inequality and Faith Made the Medieval Church* (Princeton: Princeton University Press, 2018).

Fox, H. S. A., 'Exploitation of the landless by lords and tenants in early medieval England', in Razi and Smith, *Medieval Society*, pp. 518–68.

Franklin, P., 'Politics in manorial court rolls: The tactics, social composition, and aims of a pre-1381 peasant movement', in Razi and Smith, *Medieval Society*, pp. 162–98.

Freedman, P., *The Origins of Peasant Servitude in Medieval Catalonia* (Cambridge: Cambridge University Press, 1991).

Freedman, P., *Images of the Medieval Peasant* (Stanford: Stanford University Press, 1999).

Freedman, P., and M. Bourin, 'Introduction', in Freedman and Bourin, *Forms of Servitude*, pp. 1–18.
Freedman, P., and M. Bourin, eds, *Forms of Servitude in Northern and Central Europe: Decline, Resistance and Expansion* (Turnhout: Brepols, 2005).
Fryde, E. B., *Peasants and Landlords in Later Medieval England* (Stroud: Alan Sutton, 1996).
Galloway, J. A., 'Storm flooding, coastal defence and land use around the Thames estuary and tidal river c. 1250–1450', *Journal of Medieval History*, 35 (2009): 171–88.
Galloway, J. A., 'Coastal flooding and socioeconomic change in eastern England in the later Middle Ages', *Environment and History*, 19 (2013): 173–207.
Gatrell, P., 'Historians and peasants: Studies of medieval English society in a Russian context', *Past & Present*, 96 (1982): 22–50.
Ghosh, S., 'Rural economies and transitions to capitalism: Germany and England compared (c. 1200–c. 1800), *Journal of Agrarian Change*, 16:2 (2016): 255–90.
Ghosh, S., 'Rural commercialisation in southern Germany, c. 1200–c. 1500: Sources, problems, and potential', *Mediaeval Studies*, 82 (2020): 207–74.
Gibbs, J., 'Restraints on landlords in the moral literature of late-medieval England' (BA dissertation, University of Cambridge, 2008).
Gibbs, S., 'Lords, tenants and attitudes to manorial office holding, c. 1300–c. 1600', *Agricultural History Review*, 62 (2019): 155–74.
Gibbs, S., '"Open" or "closed"? Participation in English manorial presentment juries, c. 1310–c. 1600: A quantitative approach', *English Historical Review*, 137:587 (2022): 1003–51.
Gibbs, S., *Lordship, State Formation and Local Authority in Late Medieval and Early Modern England* (Cambridge: Cambridge University Press, 2023).
Gingerich, D. W., and J. P. Vogler, 'Pandemics and political development: The electoral legacy of the Black Death in Germany', *World Politics*, 73:3 (2021): 393–440.
Goldberg, P. J. P., *Medieval England: A Social History 1250–1550* (London: Hodder Arnold, 2004).
Hadwin, J. F., 'The medieval lay subsidy rolls and economic history', *Economic History Review*, 36 (1983): 200–17.
Hagan, W., 'Subject farmers in Brandenburg-Prussia and Poland: Village life and fortunes under manorialism in early modern central Europe', in Bush, *Serfdom and Slavery*, pp. 296–310.
Haren, M., *Sin and Society in Fourteenth-Century England: A Study of the 'Memoriale presbiterorum'* (Oxford: Oxford University Press, 2000).
Hargreaves, P. V., 'Seigniorial reaction and peasant responses: Worcester Priory and its peasants after the Black Death', *Midland History*, 24 (1999): 53–78.

Harriss, G. L., *Shaping the Nation: England 1360–1461* (Oxford: Clarendon Press, 2005).
Harvey, B., *Westminster Abbey and Its Estates in the Middle Ages* (Oxford: Oxford University Press, 1977).
Harvey, P. D. A., *A Medieval Oxfordshire Village: Cuxham, 1240 to 1400* (Oxford: Oxford University Press, 1965).
Harvey, P. D. A., ed., *The Peasant Land Market in Medieval England* (Oxford: Oxford University Press, 1984).
Harvey, P. D. A., 'Introduction', in Harvey, *The Peasant Land Market*, pp. 1–28.
Harvey, P. D. A., 'English estate records', in Britnell, *Pragmatic Literacy*, pp. 107–18.
Hatcher, J., *Rural Economy and Society in the Duchy of Cornwall 1300–1500* (Cambridge: Cambridge University Press, 1970).
Hatcher, J., *Plague, Population and the English Economy 1348–1530* (London: Macmillan, 1977).
Hatcher, J., 'English serfdom and villeinage: Towards a reassessment', *Past & Present*, 90 (1981): 3–39.
Hatcher, J., 'Lordship and villeinage before the Black Death: From Karl Marx to the Marxists and back again', in Kowaleski et al., *Peasants and Lords*, pp. 113–46.
Hatcher, J., 'Peasant productivity and welfare in the Middle Ages and beyond', *Past & Present*, 262 (2024): 281–314.
Hatcher, J., and M. Bailey, *Modelling the Middle Ages: The Theory and Practice of England's Economic Development* (Oxford: Oxford University Press, 2000).
Heidecker, K., ed., *Charters and the Use of the Written Word in Medieval Society* (Turnhout: Brepols, 2000).
Helmholz, R. H., 'Crime, compurgation and the courts of the medieval church', *Law and History Review*, 1 (1983): 1–26.
Helmholz, R. H., *Canon Law and the Law of England* (London: Hambledon Press, 1987).
Helmholz, R. H., 'Independence and uniformity in England's manorial courts', in L. Bonfield, *Seigneurial Jurisdiction*, pp. 215–36.
Henry, R. L., *Contracts in the Local Courts of Medieval England* (London: Longmans, 1926).
Hilton, R. H., *A Medieval Society: The West Midlands at the End of the Thirteenth Century* (Cambridge: Cambridge University Press, 1966).
Hilton, R. H., *The Decline of Serfdom in Late Medieval England*, 2nd edn (London: Macmillan, 1969).
Hilton, R. H., *Bondmen Made Free: Medieval Peasant Movements and the English Rising of 1381* (London: Methuen, 1977).
Hilton, R. H., 'Introduction', in Aston and Philpin, *The Brenner Debate*, pp. 1–9.
Hilton, R. H., *Class Conflict and the Crisis of Feudalism*, 2nd edn (London: Verso, 1990).

Hole, J., *Economic Ethics in Late Medieval England, 1300–1500* (Basingstoke: Palgrave Macmillan, 2016).

Holt, R., *The Mills of Medieval England* (Oxford: Basil Blackwell, 1988).

Homans, G. C., *English Villagers of the Thirteenth Century* (Cambridge, MA: Harvard University Press, 1941).

Horrell, S., J. Humphries and J. Weisdorf, 'Family standards of living in the long run, England 1280–1850', *Past & Present*, 250 (2021): 87–134.

Horrox, R. E., and W. M. Ormrod, eds, *A Social History of England, 1200–1500* (Cambridge: Cambridge University Press, 2006).

Howell, C., *Land, Family and Inheritance in Transition: Kibworth Harcourt, 1280–1700* (Cambridge: Cambridge University Press, 1983).

Hoyle, R. J., 'Tenure and the land market in early modern England; or, A late contribution to the Brenner Debate', *Economic History Review*, 43 (1990): 1–20.

Hoyt, R. S., *The Royal Demesne in English Constitutional History, 1066–1272* (New York: Greenwood Press, 1968).

Hudson, J., *The Formation of the English Common Law: Law and Society in England from the Norman Conquest to Magna Carta* (London: Longman, 1996).

Hyams, P. R., 'The proof of villein status in the common law', *English Historical Review*, 89 (1974): 721–49.

Hyams, P. R., *King, Lords and Peasants in Medieval England* (Oxford: Clarendon Press, 1980).

Hyams, P. R., 'What did Edwardian villagers mean by law?', in Razi and Smith, *Medieval Society*, pp. 69–102.

Hybel, N., *Crisis or Change: The Concept of Crisis in the Light of Agrarian Structural Reorganisation in Late Medieval England* (Aarhus: Aarhus University Press, 1989).

Ibbetson, D. J., *A Historical Introduction to the Law of Obligations* (Oxford: Oxford University Press, 1999).

Jedwab, R., N. D. Johnson and M. Koyama, 'The economic impact of the Black Death', *Journal of Economic Literature*, 60:1 (2022): 132–78.

Johanek, P., 'Seigneurial power and the development of towns in the Holy Roman Empire', in A. Simms and H. B. Clarke, eds, *Lords and Towns in Medieval Europe: The European Historic Towns Atlas Project* (London: Routledge, 2015), pp. 117–54.

Jones, A., 'Bedfordshire: Fifteenth century', in Harvey, *The Peasant Land Market*, pp. 178–251.

Jones, E. D., 'The medieval leyrwite: A historical note upon fornication', *English Historical Review*, 107:425 (1992): 945–53.

Jones, E. D., 'Medieval merchets as demographic data: Some evidence from the Spalding priory estates, Lincolnshire', *Continuity and Change*, 11:3 (1996): 459–70.

Jones, E. D., 'The Spalding priory merchet evidence from the 1250s to the 1470s', *Journal of Medieval History*, 24:2 (1998): 155–75.

Jones, E. L., *Barriers to Growth: English Economic Development from the Norman Conquest to Industrialisation* (London: Palgrave, 2020).

Jordan, W. C., *The Great Famine: Northern Europe in the Early Fourteenth Century* (Princeton: Princeton University Press, 1996).

Justice, S., *Writing and Rebellion: England in 1381* (Berkeley: University of California Press, 1984).

Kanzaka, J., 'Villein rents in thirteenth-century England: An analysis of the Hundred Rolls of 1279–1280', *Economic History Review*, 55 (2000): 593–618.

Kanzaka, J., 'Manorialisation and demographic pressure in medieval England: An analysis of the Hundred Rolls of 1279–1280', *Journal of Historical Geography*, 60 (2018): 11–23.

Keen, M. H., *English Society in the Later Middle Ages, 1348–1500* (London: Penguin, 1990).

Keene, D. J., *Cheapside before the Great Fire* (London: Economic and Social Research Council, 1985).

King, E., *Peterborough Abbey 1086–1310: A Study in the Land Market* (Cambridge: Cambridge University Press, 1973).

Kitsikopoulos, H., 'Standards of living and capital formation in pre-plague England: A peasant budget model', *Economic History Review*, 53 (2000): 237–61.

Kitsikopoulos, H., 'The impact of the Black Death on peasant economy in England, 1350–1500', *The Journal of Peasant Studies*, 29:2 (2002): 71–90.

Kitsikopoulos, H., 'England', in Kitsikopoulos, *Agrarian Change*, pp. 23–56.

Kitsikopoulos, H., ed., *Agrarian Change and Crisis in Europe, 1200–1500* (Abingdon: Routledge, 2012).

Klein, A., and S. Ogilvie, 'Occupational structure in the Czech lands under the second serfdom', *Economic History Review*, 69 (2016): 493–521.

Klima, A., 'Agrarian class structure and economic development in pre-industrial Bohemia', in Aston and Philpin, *The Brenner Debate*, pp. 192–212.

Kosminsky, E. A., *Studies in the Agrarian History of England in the Thirteenth Century* (Oxford: Basil Blackwell, 1956).

Kowaleski, K., J. Langdon and P. R. Schofield, eds, *Peasants and Lords in the Medieval English Economy: Essays in Honour of B. M. S. Campbell* (Turnhout: Brepols, 2015).

Kula, W., *An Economic Theory of the Feudal System* (London: Humanities Press, 1976).

La Poutré, H., 'English population 1086–1377: A modelling approach' (PhD thesis, University of Groningen, 2023).

Langdon, J., 'Lord and peasant consumerism in the milling industry of early fourteenth-century England', *Past & Present*, 145 (1994): 3–46.

Langdon, J., *Mills in the Medieval Economy: England 1300–1540* (Oxford: Oxford University Press, 2004).

Langdon, J., and J. Masschaele, 'Commercial activity and population growth in medieval England', *Past & Present*, 190 (2006): 35–81.
Larson, P., *Conflict and Compromise in the Late Medieval Countryside: Lords and Peasants in Durham 1349–1400* (London: Routledge, 2006).
Letters, S., *Gazetteer of Markets and Fairs in England and Wales to 1516*, Part I, List and Index Society, special series, 32 (Kew: List and Index Society, 2003).
Levett, A. E., *Studies in Manorial History* (Oxford: Oxford University Press, 1938).
Livingstone, M., 'A snapshot in time: The weather as seen in the record of the Nonae, 1339–41', in Kowaleski et al., *Peasants and Lords*, pp. 325–52.
Lomas, T., 'Fifteenth century: Durham', in Harvey, *The Peasant Land Market*, pp. 252–327.
Lucas, A., *Ecclesiastical Lordship, Seigneurial Power and the Commercialization of Milling in Medieval England* (London: Routledge, 2014).
McGibbon Smith, E., 'Reflections of reality in the manor court: Sutton-in-the-Isle, 1308–1391' (PhD thesis, University of Cambridge, 2005).
McIntosh, M. K., 'The privileged villeins of the English Ancient Demesne', *Viator*, 7 (1976): 295–328.
McIntosh, M. K., *Autonomy and Community The Royal Manor of Havering 1200–1500* (Cambridge: Cambridge University Press, 1986).
McIntosh, M. K., *Controlling Misbehavior in England, 1370–1600* (Cambridge: Cambridge University Press, 1998).
McLoughlin, V., 'Medieval Rothley: Leicestershire manor, soke and parish' (PhD thesis, University of Leicester, 2006).
Maddicott, J. R., *The English Peasantry and the Demands of the Crown 1294–1341*, *Past & Present* Supplements, 1 (Oxford: Past & Present Society, 1975).
Maitland, F. W., *The Court Baron*, Publications of the Selden Society, 4 (London: B. Quaritch, 1889).
Malanima, P., 'Serfdom in eastern Europe after the revisions', in Cavaciocchi, *Serfdom and Slavery*, pp. 677–88.
Martin, J., 'Russia', in Kitsikopoulos, *Agrarian Change*, pp. 292–329.
Martin, J. E., *Feudalism to Capitalism: Peasant and Landlord in English Agrarian Development* (Basingstoke: Macmillan, 1983).
Masschaele, J., *Peasants, Merchants and Markets: Inland Trade in Medieval England, 1150–1350* (Basingstoke: Palgrave Macmillan, 1997).
Masschaele, J., *Jury, State and Society in Medieval England* (Basingstoke: Macmillan, 2008).
Masschaele, J. 'The public life of the private charter in thirteenth-century England', in B. Dodds and C. D. Liddy, eds, *Commercial Activity, Markets and Entrepreneurs in the Middle Ages: Essays in Honour of Richard Britnell* (Woodbridge: Boydell and Brewer, 2011), pp. 199–216.

Mate, M. E., 'The east Sussex land market and agrarian class structure in the late Middle Ages', *Past & Present*, 139 (1993): 46–65.

Melton, E., 'The agrarian East', in H. Scott, ed., *The Oxford Handbook of Early Modern European History, 1350–1750*, Vol. I, *Peoples and Place* (Oxford: Oxford University Press, 2015), pp. 428–54.

Miller, E., 'The estates of the abbey of St Alban', *St Albans and Hertfordshire Architectural and Archaeological Society* (1938): 285–303.

Miller, E., *The Abbey and Bishopric of Ely* (Cambridge: Cambridge University Press, 1951).

Miller, E., and J. Hatcher, *Medieval England: Rural Society and Economic Change 1086–1348* (London: Longman, 1978).

Miller, E., and J. Hatcher, *Medieval England: Towns, Commerce and Crafts, 1086–1348* (Harlow: Longman, 1995).

Milsom, S. F. C., *Historical Foundations of the Common Law*, 2nd edn (Oxford: Oxford University Press, 1981).

Mitchell, W., *An Essay in the Early History of the Law Merchant* (Cambridge: Cambridge University Press, 1904).

Mullan, J., and R. H. Britnell, *Land and Family: Trends and Local Variations in the Peasant Land Market on the Winchester Bishopric Estates, 1263–1415* (Hatfield: University of Hertfordshire Press, 2010).

Müller, M., 'The function and evasion of marriage fines on a fourteenth-century English manor', *Continuity and Change*, 14 (1999): 169–90.

Müller, M., 'Seigniorial control and the peasant land market in the 14th century', in Feller and Wickham, *Le marché de la terre*, pp. 297–313.

Müller, M., 'Conflict and revolt: The Bishop of Ely and his peasants at the manor of Brandon in Suffolk c. 1300–81', *Rural History*, 23 (2012): 1–23.

Musson, A. J., *Medieval Law in Context: The Growth of Legal Consciousness from Magna Carta to the Peasants' Revolt* (Manchester: Manchester University Press, 2001).

Myking, J. R., and C. P. Rasmussen, 'Scandinavia 1000–1750', in Van Bavel and Hoyle, *Rural Economy and Society*, pp. 287–314.

Mysliwski, J., 'Central Europe', in Kitsikopoulos, *Agrarian Change*, pp. 250–91.

Neilson, N., 'Customary rents', in P. Vinogradoff, ed., *Oxford Studies in Social and Legal History*, Vol. II (Oxford: Clarendon Press, 1910).

Newfield, T. P., 'A cattle panzootic in early fourteenth century Europe', *Agricultural History Review*, 57 (2009): 155–90.

North, D. C., and R. P. Thomas, 'The rise and fall of the manorial system: A theoretical model', *Journal of Economic History*, 31 (1971): 777–803.

North, M., *The Expansion of Europe, 1250–1500* (Manchester: Manchester University Press, 2012).

North, M., 'Serfdom and corvée labour in the Baltic area, sixteenth to eighteenth centuries', in Cavaciocchi, *Serfdom and Slavery*, pp. 139–54.

North, T., 'Legerwite in the thirteenth and fourteenth centuries', *Past & Present*, 111 (1986): 3–16.

Noy, D., 'Leyrwite, marriage and illegitimacy: Winslow before the Black Death', *Records of Buckinghamshire*, 47:1 (2007): 133–52.
Noy, D., 'Winslow in 1341: The *Nonarum Inquisitiones* and the reliability of medieval tax self-assessment', *Records of Buckinghamshire*, 55 (2015): 137–45.
Ogilvie, S., 'Choices and constraints in the pre-industrial countryside', in Briggs et al., *Population, Welfare*, pp. 269–305.
Ogilvie, S., 'Serfdom and the institutional system in early modern Germany', in Cavaciocchi, *Serfdom and Slavery*, pp. 33–58.
Ogilvie, S., 'Economics and history: Analyzing serfdom', in R. Bourke and Q. Skinner, eds, *History in the Humanities and Social Sciences* (Cambridge: Cambridge University Press, 2022), pp. 329–53.
Ogilvie, S., and A. W. Carus, 'Institutions and economic growth in historical perspective', in P. Aghion and S. Durlauf, eds, *Handbook of Economic Growth* (Amsterdam: Elsevier, 2014), pp. 403–513.
Olson, S., 'Jurors of the village court: Local leadership before and after the plague in Ellington, Huntingdonshire', *Journal of British Studies*, 30 (1991): 237–56.
Olson, S., *A Chronicle of All that Happens: Voices from the Village Court in Medieval England* (Toronto: Pontifical Institute of Medieval Studies, 1996).
Olson, S., *A Mute Gospel: The People and Culture of the Medieval English Common Fields* (Toronto: Pontifical Institute of Medieval Studies, 2009).
Ormrod, W. M., 'The Crown and the English economy, 1290–1348', in Campbell, *Before the Black Death*, pp. 149–83.
Page, F. M., *The Estates of Crowland Abbey* (Cambridge: Cambridge University Press, 1934).
Page, M., 'The peasant land market on the estates of the bishop of Winchester before the Black Death', in R. H. Britnell, ed., *The Winchester Pipe Rolls and Medieval English Society* (Woodbridge: Boydell Press, 2003), pp. 61–80.
Page, M., 'The peasant land market in Southern England: The estate of the bishops of Winchester, 1260–1350', in Feller and Wickham, *Le marché de la terre*, pp. 315–40.
Page, M., 'Town and countryside in medieval Ivinghoe', *Records of Buckinghamshire*, 51 (2011): 189–203.
Page, M., 'The smallholders of Southampton Water: The peasant land market on a Hampshire manor before the Black Death', in S. Turner and B. Silvester, eds, *Life in Medieval Landscapes: People and Places in the Middle Ages. Papers in Memory of H. S. A. Fox* (Oxford: Oxford University Press, 2012), pp. 181–97.
Page, T. W., *The End of Villeinage in England* (New York: Macmillan, 1900).
Page, W., ed., *Victoria County History* [*VCH*], *Hertfordshire*, Vol. II (London: Institute of Historical Research, 1908).

Palmer, R. C., 'The origins of property in England', *Law and History Review*, 3:1 (1985): 1–50.
Palmer, R. C., 'The economic and cultural impact of the origins of property: 1180–1220', *Law and History Review*, 3 (1985): 375–96.
Palmer, R. C., 'England: Law, society and the state', in Rigby, *A Companion to Britain*, pp. 242–60.
Parkin, K., 'Courts and the community: Reconstructing the fourteenth-century peasant society of Wisbech Hundred, Cambridgeshire, from manor court rolls' (PhD thesis, University of Leicester, 1998).
Peters, M. E., 'Government finance and imposition of serfdom after the Black Death', *European Review of Economic History*, 27 (2023): 149–73.
Phillips, J., 'Collaboration and litigation in two Suffolk manor courts 1289 to 1364' (PhD thesis, University of Cambridge, 2005).
Platt, C., *Medieval Southampton: The Port and Trading Community, AD 1000–1600* (London: Routledge, 1973).
Pollock, F., and F. W. Maitland, *The History of English Law before the Time of Edward I*, Vol. I (Cambridge: Cambridge University Press, 1895).
Poos, L. R., *A Rural Society after the Black Death: Essex 1350–1525* (Cambridge: Cambridge University Press, 1990).
Poos, L. R., 'Medieval English manorial courts: Their records and their jurisdiction', in Bonfield, *Seigneurial Jurisdiction*, pp. 195–214.
Poos, L. R., Z. Razi and R. M. Smith, 'The population history of medieval English villages: A debate on the use of manor court rolls', in Razi and Smith, *Medieval Society*, pp. 298–368.
Postan, M., 'The chronology of labour services', *Transactions of the Royal Historical Society*, 4th series, 20 (1937): 169–93.
Postan, M. M., 'Medieval agrarian society in its prime: England', in M. M. Postan, ed., *The Cambridge Economic History of Europe*, Vol. I, *The Agrarian Life of the Middle Ages*, 2nd edn (Cambridge: Cambridge University Press, 1966), pp. 549–659.
Powell, E., *The Rising in East Anglia in 1381* (Cambridge: Cambridge University Press, 1896).
Power, E., *The Wool Trade in English Medieval History* (Oxford: Oxford University Press, 1941).
Prescott, A., 'The *Anonimalle Chronicle* narrative of the Peasants' Revolt of 1381', in Dodd and Lacey, *Fourteenth Century England*, Vol. XIII, pp. 131–60.
Pribyl, K., *Farming, Famine and Plague: The Impact of Climate in Late Medieval England* (Berlin: Springer, 2017).
Pribyl, K., and R. C. Cornes, 'Droughts in medieval and early modern England, part 1: The evidence', *Weather*, 76:6 (2020): 169–71.
Raban, S., 'Landlord returns on villein rents in north Huntingdonshire in the thirteenth century', *Historical Research*, 66 (1993): 21–34.
Raban, S., *A Second Domesday? The Hundred Rolls of 1279–80* (Oxford: Oxford University Press, 2004).

Raftis, J. A., *The Estates of Ramsey Abbey: A Study in Economic Growth and Organisation* (Toronto: Pontifical Institute of Medieval Studies, 1957).
Raftis, J. A., *Tenure and Mobility: Studies in the Social History of the Mediaeval English Village* (Toronto: Pontifical Institute of Medieval Studies, 1964).
Raftis, J. A., *Warboys: Two Hundred Years in the Life of an English Medieval Village* (Toronto: Pontifical Institute of Mediaeval Studies, 1974).
Raftis, J. A., ed., *Pathways to Medieval Peasants* (Toronto: Pontifical Institute of Medieval Studies, 1981).
Raftis, J. A., *Peasant Economic Development within the English Manorial System* (Stroud: Alan Sutton, 1996).
Ravensdale, J., 'Population changes and the transfer of customary land on a Cambridgeshire manor in the fourteenth century', in Smith, *Land, Kinship*, pp. 197–226.
Raw, A., 'Life after leyrwite: Sexual subjectivity on the medieval manor, c. 1270–c. 1330', in Dodd and Lacey, *Fourteenth Century England*, Vol. XIII (Woodbridge: Boydell and Brewer, 2025), pp. 1–18.
Razi, Z., *Life, Marriage and Death in a Medieval Parish: Economy, Society and Demography in Halesowen 1270–1400* (Cambridge: Past & Present Publications, 1980).
Razi, Z., 'Manorial court rolls and local population: An East Anglian case study', *Economic History Review*, 49 (1996): 758–63.
Razi, Z., and R. M. Smith, 'The origins of the English manor courts as a written record', in Razi and Smith, *Medieval Society*, pp. 36–68.
Razi, Z., and R. M. Smith, eds, *Medieval Society and the Manor Court* (Oxford: Clarendon Press, 1996).
Rees, U., 'The leases of Haughmond abbey, Shropshire', *Midland History*, 8 (1983): 14–28.
Reville, A., *Le soulèvement des travailleurs d'Angleterre en 1381* (Paris: Picard et fils, 1898).
Richardson, H. G., and G. O. Sayles, *Law and Legislation: From Aethelberht to Magna Carta* (Edinburgh: Edinburgh University Press, 1966).
Rigby, S. H., *Medieval Grimsby: Growth and Decline* (Hull: Hull University Press, 1993).
Rigby, S. H., *English Society in the Later Middle Ages: Class, Status and Gender* (Palgrave: London, 1995).
Rigby, S. H., *Marxism and History: A Critical Introduction* (Manchester: Manchester University Press, 1998).
Rigby, S. H., 'Approaches to pre-industrial social structure', in J. Denton, ed., *Orders and Hierarchies in Late Medieval and Renaissance Europe* (London: Bloomsbury, 1999), pp. 6–25.
Rigby, S. H., 'Serfdom', in J. Mokyr, ed., *The Oxford Encyclopaedia of Economic History*, Vol. IV (Oxford: Oxford University Press, 2003), pp. 463–7.

Rigby, S. H., 'England: Literature and society', in Rigby, *A Companion to Britain*, pp. 497–520.
Rigby, S. H., ed., *A Companion to Britain in the Late Middle Ages* (Oxford: Basil Blackwell, 2003).
Rigby, S. H., 'Introduction: Social structure and economic change in late medieval England', in Horrox and Ormrod, *A Social History*, pp. 10–30.
Rigby, S. H., 'Justifying inequality: Peasants in medieval ideology', in Kowaleski et al., *Peasants and Lords*, pp. 173–200.
Rio, A., *Slavery after Rome 500–1100* (Oxford: Oxford University Press, 2017).
Rosener, W., *Peasants in the Middle Ages* (Cambridge: Cambridge University Press, 1992).
Rosener, W., *The Peasantry of Europe* (Oxford: Basil Blackwell, 1994).
Salzman, L. F., ed., *Victoria County History [VCH], Cambridgeshire and Isle of Ely*, Vol. II (London: Institute of Historical Research, 1948).
Scammell, J., 'Robert I and the north of England', *English Historical Review*, 288 (1958): 385–403.
Scammell, J., 'Freedom and marriage in medieval England', *Economic History Review*, 27 (1974): 523–37.
Scase, W., *Literature and Complaint in England 1272–1553* (Oxford: Oxford University Press, 2007).
Schafer, R., 'Inheritance disputes from Ingelheim court records on the threshold of the early modern period (fourteenth to fifteenth Centuries)', in M. Lanzinger, J. Maegraith, S. Clementi, E. Forster, and C. Hagen, eds, *Negotiations of Gender and Property through Legal Regimes (14th–19th Century): Stipulating, Litigating, Mediating* (Leiden: Brill, 2021), pp. 52–83.
Schmitt, S., 'Wildfange, Ausleute und rechte Untertanen: Die Herausbildung der Territorialleibherrschaft im Mittelrheingebiet (15.–16. Jahrhundert)', in Freedman and Bourin, *Forms of Servitude*, pp. 213–27.
Schofield, P. R., 'The late medieval view of frankpledge and the tithing system: An Essex case study', in Razi and Smith, *Medieval Society*, pp. 408–49.
Schofield, P. R., 'Dearth, debt and the local land market in a late thirteenth-century village community', *Agricultural History Review*, 45 (1997): 1–17.
Schofield, P. R., 'Peasants and the manor court: Gossip and litigation in a Suffolk village at the close of the thirteenth century', *Past & Present*, 159 (1998): 3–42.
Schofield, P. R., 'Seigneurial exactions in eastern England, c. 1050–1300', in Bourin and Martínez Sopena, *Pour une anthropologie*, pp. 383–409.
Schofield, P. R., 'The market in free land on the estates of Bury St Edmunds, c. 1086–c. 1300', in Feller and Wickham, *Le marché de la terre*, pp. 273–95.
Schofield, P. R., 'Lordship and the peasant economy, c. 1250 c. 1400: Robert Kyng and the abbot of Bury St Edmunds', in Dyer et al., *Rodney Hilton's Middle Ages*, pp. 57–8.

Schofield, P. R., 'The social economy of the medieval village in the early fourteenth century', *Economic History Review*, 61 (2008): 38–63.
Schofield, P. R., *Peasants and Historians: Debating the Medieval English Peasantry* (Manchester: Manchester University Press, 2014).
Schofield, P. R., 'Lordship and the early history of peasant land transfer', in Kowaleski et al., *Peasants and Lords*, pp. 201–24.
Schofield, P. R., 'Peasants and food security in England and Wales c. 1300', *Journal of Medieval History*, 49:5 (2023): 588–606.
Scott, J. C., *Weapons of the Weak: Everyday Forms of Peasant Resistance* (New Haven: Yale University Press, 2008).
Scott, T., *Society and Economy in Germany 1300 to 1600* (Basingstoke: Macmillan, 2002).
Searle, E., *Lordship and Community: Battle Abbey and Its Banlieu, 1066–1538* (Toronto: Pontifical Institute of Medieval Studies, 1974).
Searle, E., 'Freedom and marriage in medieval England: An alternative hypothesis', *Economic History Review*, 29 (1976): 482–6.
Searle, E., 'Seigniorial control of women's marriage: The antecedents and function of merchet in England', *Past & Present*, 82 (1979): 3–43.
Searle, E., 'A rejoinder', *Past & Present*, 99 (1983): 148–60.
Seebohm, F., *The English Village Community*, 4th edn (Cambridge: Cambridge University Press, 1890).
Simpson, A. W. B., *A History of the Land Law*, 2nd edn (Oxford: Oxford University Press, 1986).
Simpson, A. W. B., *A History of the Common Law of Contract: The Rise of the Action of Assumpsit* (Oxford: Oxford University Press, 1987).
Slavin, P., 'The Great Bovine Pestilence and its economic and environmental consequences in England and Wales, 1318–50', *Economic History Review*, 65 (2012): 1239–66.
Slavin, P., 'Peasant livestock husbandry in late-thirteenth-century Suffolk: Economy, environment and society', in Kowaleski et al., *Peasants and Lords*, pp. 3–26.
Slavin, P., 'Warfare and ecological destruction in early fourteenth-century British Isles', *Environmental History*, 19 (2014): 528–50.
Slavin, P., *Experiencing Famine in Fourteenth-Century Britain* (Turnhout: Brepols, 2019).
Slavin, P., 'Mites and merchants: The crisis of English wool and textile trade revisited, c. 1275–1330', *Economic History Review*, 73 (2020): 885–913.
Slota, L. A., 'Law, land transfer, and lordship on the estates of St Albans abbey in the thirteenth and fourteenth centuries', *Law and History Review*, 6 (1988): 119–38.
Smith, A., *An Inquiry into the Nature and Causes of the Wealth of Nations* (New York: The Modern Library, 1937).
Smith, R. M., 'Some thoughts on "hereditary" and "proprietary" rights in land under customary law in thirteenth and early fourteenth century England', *Law and History Review*, 1 (1983): 95–128.

Smith, R. M., 'Some issues concerning families and their property in rural England 1250–1800', in Smith, *Land, Kinship*, pp. 1–86.

Smith, R. M., 'Families and their land in an area of partible inheritance: Redgrave, Suffolk 1260–1320', in Smith, *Land, Kinship*, pp. 135–96.

Smith, R. M., ed., *Land, Kinship and Life-Cycle* (Cambridge: Cambridge University Press, 1984).

Smith, R. M., 'Demographic developments in rural England 1300–48', in Campbell, ed., *Before the Black Death*, pp. 25–78.

Smith, R. M., 'Further models of medieval marriage: Landlords, serfs and priests in rural England, c. 1290–1370', in C. Duhamel-Amado and G. Lobrichon, eds, *Georges Duby: L'écriture de l'histoire* (Brussels: De Boeck Université, 1992), pp. 161–74.

Smith, R. M., 'The English peasantry 1250–1650', in T. Scott, ed., *The Peasantries of Europe from the Fourteenth Century to the Eighteenth Century* (London: Longman, 1998), pp. 339–71.

Smith, R. M., 'Moving to marry among the customary tenants of late thirteenth-century and early fourteenth-century England', in P. Horden, ed., *Freedom of Movement in the Middle Ages: Proceedings of the 2003 Harlaxton Symposium* (Donington: Shaun Tyas, 2007), pp. 169–85.

Stock, M., 'The exercise of manorial lordship on the manor of Chedzoy, Somerset, 1327–1377' (MSt thesis, University of Cambridge, 2023).

Stone, D., 'The productivity of hired and customary labour: Evidence from Wisbech Barton in the fourteenth century', *Economic History Review*, 50 (1997): 640–56.

Stone, D., 'The impact of drought in early fourteenth-century England', *Economic History Review*, 67 (2014): 435–62.

Swanson, R. N., *Church and Society in Late-Medieval England* (Oxford: Basil Blackwell, 1989).

Thompson, M. G., 'The Polden Hill manors of Glastonbury Abbey: Land and people c. 1260–1351 (PhD thesis, University of Leicester, 1996).

Thornton, M. J., 'Rural society in the manor courts of Northamptonshire, 1350–1500' (PhD thesis, University of Leicester, 2004).

Titow, J. Z., *English Rural Society 1200–1350* (London: George Allen and Unwin, 1969).

Toepfer, R., 'The abbey at St Albans and its relationship with its lordship in the late Middle Ages' (PhD thesis, University of Southampton, 2017).

Tompkins, M., 'The manor of Park in the fourteenth century', in anon., ed., *The Peasants' Revolt in Hertfordshire 1381* (Stevenage: Hertfordshire Local History Council, 1981), pp. 53–81.

Van Bavel, B. J. P., *Manors and Markets* (Oxford: Oxford University Press, 2010).

Van Bavel, B. J. P., *The Invisible Hand* (Oxford: Oxford University Press, 2016).

Van Bavel, B. J. P., and R. W. Hoyle, eds, *Rural Economy and Society in North-Western Europe, 500–2000: Social Relations, Property and Power* (Turnhout: Brepols, 2010).

Vinogradoff, P., *Villeinage in England: Essays in English Medieval History* (Oxford: Clarendon Press, 1892).

Walker, S., 'Order and law', in Horrox and Ormrod, *Social History of England*, pp. 91–112.

Wells-Furby, B., *The Berkeley Estate 1281–1417: Its Economy and Development*, Bristol and Gloucestershire Monographs, 1 (n.p.: Bristol and Gloucestershire Archaeological Society, 2012).

Whittle, J., 'Individualism and the land–family bond: A reassessment of land transfer patterns among the English peasantry, 1270–1580', *Past & Present*, 160 (1998): 25–67.

Whittle, J., *The Development of Agrarian Capitalism: Land and Labour in Norfolk 1440–1580* (Oxford: Oxford University Press, 2000).

Whittle, J. C., 'The food economy of lords, tenants and workers in a medieval village: Hunstanton, Norfolk, 1328–48', in Kowaleski et al., *Peasants and Lords*, pp. 27–58.

Willard, J. F., *Parliamentary Taxes on Personal Property, 1290 to 1334: A Study in Medieval Administration* (Cambridge, MA: Harvard University Press, 1934).

Williamson, J., 'Norfolk: Thirteenth century' in Harvey, *The Peasant Land Market*, pp. 30–105.

Williamson, J., 'Dispute in the manorial court: Lakenheath in the early fourteenth century', *Reading Medieval Studies*, 11 (1985): 133–41.

Wood, D., *Medieval Economic Thought* (Cambridge: Cambridge University Press, 2012).

Woods, M., *Medieval Hadleigh: The Chief Manor and the Town* (Hadleigh: published privately, 2018).

Xu, M., 'Analysing the actions of the rebels in the English Revolt of 1381: The case of Cambridgeshire', *Economic History Review*, 75 (2022): 881–902.

Yates, M., *Town and Countryside in Western Berkshire, c. 1327–c. 1600: Social and Economic Change* (Woodbridge: Boydell and Brewer, 2007).

Index

EU authorised representative for GPSR:
Easy Access System Europe, Mustamäe tee 50,
10621 Tallinn, Estonia
gpsr.requests@easproject.com

www.ingramcontent.com/pod-product-compliance
Ingram Content Group UK Ltd.
Pitfield, Milton Keynes, MK11 3LW, UK
UKHW021834100926
8556IPUK00004B/340
* 9 7 8 1 5 2 6 1 7 2 9 7 6 *